The Ultimate
FILM
FESTIVAL
Survival Guide

Chris Gore

THE ULTIMATE FILM FESTIVAL SURVIVAL GUIDE
The Essential Companion for Filmmakers and Festival-Goers

Copyright © 1999 by Chris Gore

LONE EAGLE PUBLISHING COMPANY, LLC™
2337 Roscomare Road, Suite Nine
Los Angeles, CA 90077-1851
Tel: 800-FILMBKS • Toll Free Fax: 888-FILMBKS
www.loneeagle.com & www.eaglei.com

Printed in the United States of America

Cover design by Lindsay Albert
Book design by Carla Green
Edited by Lauren Rossini
Photo of author by Ilona Lieberman

Library of Congress Cataloging-in-Publication Data

Gore, Chris, 1965-
    The ultimate film festival survival guide / by Chris Gore.
        p. cm.
    ISBN 1-58065-009-0
    1. Film festivals--Directories. I. Title.
PN1993.4.G67 1999
791.43'079--dc21   98-32407
                                                    CIP

Lone Eagle books may be purchased in bulk at special discounts for promotional or educational purposes. Special editions can be created to specifications. Inquiries for sales and distribution, textbook adoption, foreign language translation, editorial, and rights and permissions inquiries should be addressed to: Jeff Black, Lone Eagle Publishing, 2337 Roscomare Road, Suite Nine, Los Angeles, CA 90077 or send e-mail to: info@loneeagle.com

Distributed to the trade by National Book Network, 800-462-6420

Lone Eagle Publishing Company is a registered trademark.

For Marion,
Haley and
Zachary

CONTENTS

Special Thanks 9

Introduction—Catching the Film Festival Bug 11

A Brief History of Film Festivals 14

Politics 17

Celebrity Etiquette 19

What Makes a Great Festival 21

Staying Alive: Tips for the Festival Traveller 23

Essential Film Festival Terms 25

SECTION 1—WINNING THE FILM FESTIVAL GAME

Apply Yourself 30
   Getting Into the Best Festivals for You 30
   10 Important Factors to Consider
   When Applying to Festivals 30

Forming a Festival Strategy 33

Seeking Acceptance 35
   Avoiding Mistakes on the All-Important
   Festival Application 35

Getting a "Thumbs Up" From the Gatekeeper:
   Behind the Scenes With Geoff Gilmore,
   Director of the Sundance Film Festival 38

SECTION 2—CREATING HYPE: EVERYTHING YOU NEED TO KNOW ABOUT MARKETING

Introduction to Guerrilla Marketing 52
   "Out of the Box" Quick Marketing Ideas 53

Poster the Town 54
   10 Elements of Great Movie Poster Design 56
   10 Most Common Mistakes of Poster Design 57

Publicity: What You Need to Know 59
    On the Publicity Trail with PR Pro Linda Brown 59
    Journalist David E. Williams on Getting Press 63
    Publicity Terms You Should Know 64
    Margot Gerber on Publicity and Press Kits 64

The Parties 67
    Get Invited, Make an Impression, Crash,
    Avoid Spilling Something 67
    The Party Dos 68
    The Party Don'ts 69

Crashing Film Festival Parties 70
    10 Lines to Use When Crashing a Party 71

Putting on a Successful Party 73
    Create Buzz and Leave Them Talking 73

SECTION 3—STORIES FROM THE FRONT LINES

The Voices of Experience 76
    Questions & Answers 77

The Filmmakers 79
    Arthur Borman 79
        Borman's Advice and Lessons 84
    Joe Carnahan 86
    Mark Edgington 95
        Short-Sighted: How Some Festivals
        Treat Their Short Filmmakers 99
    Brian Flemming 101
    Sarah Jacobson 106
    Dan Mirvish 115
    Lance Mungia 121
    Joal Ryan 133
        Joal Ryan's Advice on How to Win the
        Film Festival Game (Or At Least Not Be
        Reduced to Tears While Playing): 143

The Decision Makers 144
    Peter Broderick, Acquisitions Executive 144
    Stephen Gates, Agent 147
    Patrick Lynn, Producer's Rep 150

SECTION 4—FILM FESTIVAL LISTINGS

The Top Ten Film Festivals 156
    1. Sundance Film Festival 157
    2. Toronto International Film Festival 160
    3. Telluride Film Festival 161
    4. Cannes Film Festival 163
    5. Los Angeles Independent Film Festival (LAIFF) 164
    6. New York Film Festival 165
    7. Slamdance International Film Festival 167
    8. Seattle International Film Festival (SIFF) 171
    9. South by Southwest Film Festival (SXSW) 172
    10. Taos Talking Pictures Festival 175
Domestic Film Festivals (U.S. and Canada) 177
Foreign Film Festivals (Alphabetical by Country) 233

APPENDICES

Index of Festivals by Name 284
Listing of Festivals by Month 291
Listing of Festivals by Genre 297
Best Bars 302
Best Places for Breakfast 304
Power Invitation List for Festival Screenings and Parties 306
Filmmaker Resources 310

About the Author 312

SPECIAL THANKS

There are so many people to thank, here is a list, in no particular order, of the people and organizations without whom this book would not have been possible: the unbelievably cool Jeff Black, the ever-hip Joan Singleton, my always supportive agent Laurie Fox; my editor, Lauren Rossini, who laughs at all my jokes; Arthur Borman, Leon Corcos, Victor Minjares, Peter Broderick, Lance Mungia, Stephen Gates, Mark Altman, David E. Williams, Anthony Miele, Jeffrey Wells, Martin Jedlika, Dan Mirvish, Margot Gerber, Linda Brown, Peter Baxter, John Pierson, Rich Raddon, Joal Ryan, Eugene Hernandez, Ilona Lieberman, R.J. Millard, Saundra Saperstein, Sarah Jacobson, Geoff Gilmore, Joe Carnahan, the readers of *Film Threat* magazine, Mom (can't forget her) and especially my wife, Marion. Thanks to all of my interview subjects for their cooperation and candor. I'd also like to thank all the various members of the film festival staffs for their assistance in this project—you really made this book possible. I thank you all sincerely. And the biggest thanks goes out to all the filmmakers themselves—without their daily battle to make uncompromising films, there wouldn't be any film festivals. Thanks a lot gang.

iNTRODUCTiON

Catching the Film Festival Bug

My very first film festival experience was as a filmmaker. At the age of twelve, I entered the Michigan Student Film Festival and won a certificate of merit for some particularly bizarre clay animated films. Although my mockumentary *Cafeteria Food: The Untold Story* failed to win first prize, I enjoyed watching my Super 8 epic unspool in front of an audience of disgusted adults. The top prize at the festival went to sixteen-year-old Doug Chiang for his brilliant short, *A Private Little War.* I remember how excited I was to see a movie that I knew could never see in any other setting—not in the theater, on television or on video. I never forgot that short film or Doug Chiang. I only recently learned that the talented filmmaker is now working as a production designer on the new trilogy of *Star Wars* films.

After starting the *Film Threat* fanzine in college, I attended my first real film festival as a journalist in 1987. I arrived at the Toronto Film Festival in Canada where I became the toast of the festival. Well, not really. Basically, I ignored festival protocol and covered not just the movies, but everything about the festival—including the inner workings of the fest, the parties and the exploits of the celebrities. In graphic detail. Which turned out to be a big mistake. I was rewarded by being banned from the festival. But that didn't stop me. The very next year I posed as a completely different person sent by a fake magazine called *Film Form: The Art of the Cinema.* Sounded pretentious enough. The phony press kit I sent was enough to fool the festival staff into granting me a coveted press pass. When the article about "Crashing the Toronto Film Festival" appeared within the pages of *Film Threat,* a truce was called and I've been invited back, officially, ever since.

From that very first screening of films when I was twelve, I caught the festival bug. It's exciting to arrive at a festival in anticipation of discovering some new filmmaker. I especially enjoy seeing a film without having the movie ruined by hype or trailers that reveal everything. That is perhaps the best thing about film festivals—seeing a film in its most pure form, as a film first without having been marketed as a product.

There certainly is a need for a useful guide for festival-goers because there are just way too many film festivals. Festival-goers will quickly discover they do not need to travel over hill and dale to find a great film festival. Many are within driving distance or in their own backyards. Festivals are a lot of fun and shouldn't be seen as being only for filmmakers. To combat this, I've included tips to help festival-goers navigate through the film festival maze. (Many of these tips are just as useful for filmmakers.)

While I have been lucky enough to see the festival debuts of filmmakers like Michael Moore, Tom DiCillo and Lance Mungia, among others, something has always troubled me—what happens to the losers. I wrote this book because I was frustrated witnessing the failure of first-time filmmakers. So many filmmakers attend a festival for their very first time and have no idea what they are about to experience. It is worse than a baptism by fire—it's more like being drawn and quartered in front of an audience.

> "Text books attempt to teach us how things are supposed to be done and then real life experience teaches us how things are really done."

It is my belief that film schools do not adequately prepare filmmakers for a career in the industry. Sure they tell students how films are *made*, but not how the movie industry *really works*. One need only note the emergence and success of so many filmmaking seminars and how-to books to conclude that film schools fall short when providing students with real world information. For example, film students are not told that they will spend three times as much energy, time and effort raising money for their movie, as they will making it. Most film schools do not touch on the financial realities of filmmaking. Textbooks attempt to teach us how things are supposed to be done, then real life experience teaches us how things actually are done. It is my philosophy that the textbook way of doing things generally does not apply when confronted with the real life situation. This is true for movies, writing or anything else creative. My intention is to present real information for filmmakers and hopefully entertain you along the way.

This edition is merely the first in an ongoing series that will cover the expanding film festival market. As film festivals grow, and as new ones are created, the landscape of festivals will change. Through the Ultimate Film Festival Survival Guide, I will be there to document the industry every step of the way.

I intend to teach, offer tips, give sound advice, fill you in on secrets, give you the inside dope and, with any luck, entertain the hell out of you. I hope you enjoy it.

—Chris Gore

P.S. If you see me at a film festival and my eyes seem a little glazed over, that's because I've generally seen way too many films. Please be kind, and buy me a drink.

A BRiEF HiSTORY OF FiLM FESTiVALS

Film, being only about 100 years old, is a young medium. The film festival, a medium for exhibiting and celebrating film, is likewise still in its youth.

While the date of the very first film festival may be lost to antiquity, the oldest still in business is the Venice Film Festival founded in the 1930s by Italian dictator Benito Mussolini. It was originally an adjunct to a larger, pre-existing arts festival but proved so popular that within a few years it had become a free-standing festival of its own. Unfortunately, in the days leading up to World War II, the Venice festival leaned heavily toward German and Italian films and Americans ultimately boycotted the gathering, which was subsequently suspended for the remainder of the war. While the fascist Italian state did not survive the global conflict, the Venice Film Festival was revived in the late forties and remains an important international exposition today.

The Cannes Film Festival was also conceived in the 1930s and materially affected by the war. Set to debut on September 1, 1939, such Hollywood luminaries as Mae West, Gary Cooper and Tyrone Powers travelled to the French seaside community for the festivities. Establishing a Cannes tradition of excess, a replica of the Notre Dame cathedral was built on the beach to promote the then-current *Hunchback of Notre Dame*. As it happened, *Hunchback* was the only film presented at the fledgling festival because that same day, Adolph Hitler invaded Poland and began his own festival of destruction: the Second World War. The first Cannes Film Festival was cancelled and Hitler went on to invade France. Thankfully, the good guys ultimately won, Hitler was defeated and the Cannes festival made its real debut in 1946.

The third of the old-line European festivals, the Berlin Film Festival, was established in 1951 as an outpost of post-war culture sanctioned by the occupying Allied forces in West Berlin. Initially slighted by the comission that tried to oversee and coordinate the European festivals, Berlin eventually rose to its current position as one of the top ranking European film festivals.

And so it went during the early years. Organizations like the Society for Cinephiles established festivals that were quietly run by afficionados and favored older films. Film festivals were not a rarity, but you didn't find them everywhere you turned. Ironically, rather than one of the big international festivals, it was the Society for Cinephiles' Cinecon, which travelled to different cities each Labor Day to view rare silents, that was the forerunner of the festival that ushered in the modern era.

Like Cinecon, The Telluride Film Festival was created as a film buff's festival. It even involved some of the same fans, such as the late William K. Everson. But unlike the humble Cinecon, Telluride was a pricey and exclusive affair held (also during the Labor Day holiday) in the privacy of a remote area of Colorado. When the Sundance Film Festival was founded, it used Telluride as a model.

The Sundance Festival, devoted to independent films, was founded in 1978 as the United States Film Festival. The first two sessions were in Salt Lake City; in January 1981, the festival moved to its current home in Park City, Utah. Robert Redford's Sundance Institute (founded in 1983) took over festival operations in 1984. The name was formally changed to the Sundance Film Festival in 1989, the year *sex, lies and videotape* put the festival on the map as the place where iconoclastic young directors could achieve a commercial breakthrough. Bloated and weighted by success, Sundance eventually became its own kind of establishment film festival and a concurrent festival of Sundance rejects, the Slamdance festival, debuted in 1995, also in Park City. The Sundance organizers reportedly admired their pluck.

With the success of Sundance, the floodgates had been well and truly opened. Aspiring filmmakers who couldn't make the cut at Sundance might instead opt for Cleveland, Ohio's film festival. In the realm of tourist-bait, there was the late Sonny Bono's Palm Springs Film Festival. Over the years, significant film festivals have established themselves in Chicago, Denver and Portland (Oregon); Edinburgh, Krakow and Hong Kong.

Today, if you are a professional or a lover of film, you can go to Santa Barbara. If you want to see naked starlets, you can go to Cannes. If you're into animation, you can go to Annecy or Ottawa. If you like edgy and inexpensive, there is the New York Underground Film Festival. There are also the film buyers markets such as those held in Milan and Los Angeles.

Film festivals have both proliferated and changed. Once upon a time, festivals were mostly creatures of the arts, which are powerfully connected to politics. In 1968, the Cannes festival was shut down as a result of French student riots. Similarly, in 1970, the Berlin festival was cancelled as a result of controversy over a German film titled *O.K.*, about an American rape and murder in Vietnam. This kind of excitement is lacking at the more modern film festivals, which seem built around the entertainment/business model rather than the art/politics combination. But the current era features a different kind of excitement. As entertainment has become the central element of our culture, film festivals have become a veritable market of celluloid, wherein dreams are bought and sold; lives made and destroyed. On that very human level, they are exciting as hell.

POLiTiCS

In the film industry, politics means meeting the right people, rallying them to your cause (the film) and enlisting them in your mission to get your movie made and seen by as many people as possible.

Unfortunately, it's not always about "Who is the best filmmaker." More often, it comes down to a question of who excels at the political game of the film industry. You must learn to become astute in politics if you intend to be a successful (i.e. working and solvent) filmmaker. Let me let you in on a little secret—you already know how to do this. You may not be aware of it, and you might not have done it on purpose, but you have used politics to your advantage every moment that you have been working on your film.

- You raised the money you needed for your film from somewhere.
- You secured the perfect location—for free!
- You begged the lab to go the extra mile—and they did.
- You fought to have that scene kept and shot your way.
- You convinced the rental house to give you a break on your equipment.
- You kept spirits up when disaster struck and rain ruined a day of shooting.
- You inspired the cinematographer to come up with a solution for that troublesome set-up—and it turned out beautifully.
- You talked the entire crew into working through the night.
- Your sense of humor saved the first A.D.'s life when the entire crew wanted to kill him.
- You even persuaded your actor to do that embarrassing nude scene. (Full frontal. You rock!)
- You assembled a group of people to create a film and see your vision through to completion and you smiled through it all even though you know you could have made a better film under more ideal circumstances.

So you see, you are a political animal, you just never thought of it that way before. Now, you must take these Svengali-like abilities and translate them into the selling of your movie. (Pay attention and write the next sentence down. It's a run-on, and completely grammatically incorrect. I already know that, and I've beaten my editor over the head to keep it just the way it is; basically, it is the crux of the entire book.) All you have to do is use these very same skills to apply to festivals, lobby the festival staff, convince them your film must be seen, get into the festival, hire a publicist, a lawyer, a producer's rep, travel to the festival; don't forget to make a killer poster, get some press, create great buzz for your movie, pack the screening with press, friends, celebrities, acquisitions executives; be humble, engaging and funny at the post-screening Q&A session, get some good reviews, create more good buzz, get an agent, get "the call," make the distribution deal, negotiate tough to get the best deal, read the trades to look for your name and the announcement, travel the world showing your film at other festivals, support the release of the film by doing interview after interview—and during this whole process get into as many parties to have fun and exhibit your ability to remain witty after too many drinks. That's all you have to do.

The rest of this book explains how the above can be achieved. I would like to point out that no two filmmakers realize success by following the same path. Each one "makes it" differently and your experience will be completely different and completely your own.

CELEBRiTY ETiQUETTE

You're...You're...You're...That Guy in the Movies!

Celebrities are a necessary evil. They help film festivals get much needed local and national press. They donate their time to worthwhile causes. They bring a sense of glamour and excitement to a party. They take cuts to get to the front of the line at screenings. They get into parties first. They get seated immediately in restaurants—in front of you! They steal your date. Okay, so celebrities may not be that great in person and sometimes they can be downright annoying. But the last thing you want to do is annoy America's royalty.

First, don't be shocked. That *is* exactly the person you're thinking of and they *are* standing right in front of you. Most actors bear very little resemblance to the beautiful characters they portray on the screen. They're short. In many cases, their heads are bigger. Yes, physically bigger! Just like a Peanuts comic strip. For some reason, people with big heads just seem to photograph better on film. Don't ask me why, I'm just a guy with a normal-sized noggin, but I've seen it again and again. Up close, they are human and you can see all their wrinkles and imperfections; it can be kind of disappointing. So, don't be shocked when you see a celebrity in an everyday situation. You'll be seeing them everywhere. The best reaction is none at all.

Second, do not ask them for anything like an autograph or a picture. Celebrities are at festivals to enjoy themselves, just like you. How would you like to be badgered into signing autographs, getting your picture taken with strangers or getting sexually propositioned by strangers? (Okay, maybe the last part isn't so bad.) Try not to be bothersome. If you must do something, the best thing to do is to hold up your camera and say, "Would you mind?" Then hand the camera to the celebrity to take a photo of you. That gets a different reaction.

Third, if you do attempt to make conversation with a celebrity, try to say something intelligent. Reminding them about their latest bomb is like someone walking up to you and announcing your most embarrassing moment. Pointing isn't good either, avoid pointing.

Pitching them your script idea is bound to get a "call my agent" reaction at best. The best reaction is to be respectful and, if you say anything, compliment their work. Actors tend to be more insecure than the rest of us and they'll never turn down a compliment.

Finally, if you're really anxious to make that personal connection, speak to them as a colleague, not as a star. Have a real conversation from one actor to another. I mean, who's to say that you're not an actor yourself? I have introduced myself as that guy on that Wednesday night CBS sitcom since I know that no one watches television on Wednesday, much less CBS. "You know me?! I'm the funny guy, the one on that show, you know? The one on Wednesdays?" I've had celebrities politely claiming to have seen the show and enjoyed my performance. While this is not a recommended way to meet a celebrity(you know, lying and all), it will result in a deeper conversation and not a brush off. (Uh, on second thought, completely disregard that last part, don't impersonate an actor. While good for laughs, it's probably a bad idea for some legal reason that I haven't thought of yet.)

WHAT MAKES A GREAT FESTiVAL

I have been attending film festivals for over ten years now and had my share of good and bad experiences. I rate a film festival as "great" based on a very specific set of criteria. I try not to judge a festival by a few technical mistakes because those can plague even the largest, and most respected festivals. As a festival-goer, there are three main things that make an enjoyable festival for me and they are: great films, good organization, and fun parties. These are three very simple things, but too many festivals get bogged down in other details—seminars, panels, charging exorbitant amounts—and neglect the three things that matter most.

I want to see great films. I look for a festival, first and foremost, showing films that I am interested in seeing. Sure, that's pretty obvious, but you'd be surprised at the hype that can be generated for certain films that no one, if they were at home, would ever go to a theater to see, much less watch on television or rent on video. Quality films are key to the success of a great festival and a great festival experience. I attend a festival to discover films I'd never have the chance to see anywhere else and to see uncommercial movies that seem available only on the independent circuit.

If a film festival is well organized, you probably won't even notice because things are running so well. Badly organized festivals call attention to their shortcomings and can be miserable for everyone involved. But, even the best festivals can have organizational difficulties—that is the price of success and high attendance. However, there are no excuses for keeping audiences waiting, creating nonsense rules or projectors chewing up prints. Good organization is key. You only seem to notice it when things go wrong, but when things run smoothly, it's pure joy.

And fun parties are always key. I think that's obvious. Having a good time at a party is due in large part to the guest list and this varies greatly from festival to festival. For me, a pretension-free party devoid of snobs is generally the first ingredient of a successful party.

Great conversation and partygoers interested in doing something totally ridiculous like jumping into a swimming pool fully clothed is the second. Add an open bar that doesn't close, and you've got a good party.

For filmmakers, the criteria for a great festival are slightly different, since it is all about how the festival can advance their film or career. But a festival with those three elements sure doesn't hurt.

STAYiNG ALiVE: TiPS FOR THE FESTiVAL TRAVELLER

Simple Suggestions for Survival

While a travel guide to your festival destination will contain the best specific information to enhance your travel experience, there are some tried and true travel tips that I've learned along the way. Sometimes, the hard way.

- **Make reservations.** For hotel, car, plane, the works. You cannot overdo it when it comes to reservations and that includes dinner reservations. Be sure to check the restrictions on any reservation— you may even consider making multiple reservations to cover your butt if there are no penalties for late cancellations. Remember, the further in advance you make the reservations for flights, the more money you will save. Flights fill up fast, so reserve your ticket early. Do not wait until the last minute as so many do. Making advance dinner reservations is key as well. You don't want to wait an hour for a table.
- **Planning.** Get the festival schedule in advance—either by mail or on the festival web site—and make a plan. Don't be afraid to deviate from the plan; you can always pawn off a few tickets to a movie you discover you want to avoid. I type up a schedule before I leave so I know what films I'm seeing when, what parties I'm going to (or crashing) and who I'm meeting with and when. I rarely follow my plan exactly, but at least I made one.
- **Address book.** On my schedule, I also print a mini-address book. Basically, this is just a collection of local phone numbers and pals I plan to meet. This is all printed in very tiny type and I make multiple copies so I never lose it. The info is printed small enough so it fits right in my wallet. (Is it just me, or do I sound like a compulsive geek?)
- **Backpack.** You have to have one. It's the guy's version of a purse and totally essential to navigating a festival. I'm prepared for anything with my pack in tow. Mine always contains: the all-

important address book, festival schedule, Chapstick, water bottle, cell phone, pens, flyers, a folder of party invitations, something to read, granola bar (emergency meal), camera, map, tape recorder, notepad, batteries, gum, business cards, matches, headache pills, Visine, eyeglass cleaner, Kleenex, comb, sunglasses, mini flashlight and a hat (used for early morning screenings. When bedhead is at its worst, a hat can be a lifesaver).

Use basic common sense when travelling. Don't hesitate to ask a festival staffer or a local for advice or help when lost. You'll almost always find them ready to give you the information you need.

ESSENTiAL FiLM FESTiVAL TERMS

Here are some terms you should know if you're going to play the film festival game:

Archivist A man (or woman) involved with the scheduling and maintenance of the older movies being shown at the festival. You don't have to know them.

Festival Organizers 1) Either near-bankrupt shysters with fearful looks on their faces, unshaven men or women close to collapse and constantly distracted by their need to hold things together OR 2) politically connected front-persons reaping the benefits of years of ass-kissing. Depends on the festival.

Festival Sponsors Businesses that have been prevailed upon to provide financing for the event in exchange for a visible presence. Sometimes they give out free stuff. Sometimes it's even something you want.

Jury A selection of luminaries whose job it is to choose the prize winners at competitive festivals. Not to be confused with an assemblage of your peers.

Judges Here's where we learn that a film festival is not a court of law. In a courtroom, the judge presides over the proceedings while the decision-makers compose the jury. At a film festival, judges are exactly the same as members of the jury—they decide who wins.

Volunteers People who didn't manage to get into the festival through money or talent. They wear identical T-shirts and get closer to celebrities than you ever will. This can actually be a prime position (though for some unfortunates, it turns out to be a career). Volunteers generally have the best parties and know all the gossip. Get to know them and they can help you. Volunteers are generally underappreciated and they do all the horrible jobs even the lowliest fast food employee wouldn't stoop to—all for the love of film. They deserve our respect.

Crashers Scrappy types and psychos who manage to show up but lack the credentials and/or wherewithal to officially attend the festival. If they were more noble and/or stable, they could have been volunteers. Regardless, they get into better parties than volunteers (though—like volunteering—this sometimes turns out to be a life's work).

Press Crafty crashers. Weasels. Be careful. All press people talk and share information. Be nice to press as you never know who even the lowest press weasel may end up writing for in the future. The *Filmmaker* writer of today could be the *Entertainment Weekly* writer of tomorrow.

Admission Fee Self-explanatory (though crashers and volunteers don't need to know about it).

Entrance Fee Money that must be paid in order to enter your film in the competition.

Festival Badge Coveted pass to everything.

Bidding War Competition between film distributors to purchase the rights to the films made by the people who have paid the entrance fee. (This doesn't happen much anymore. At the primo "independent" film festivals, many of the films have already acquired pre-festival distribution deals. Nowadays, bidding wars at the festival are more likely to happen over films whose makers did not pay the entrance fee and presented their films on the sly.)

Projectionist Dedicated loner who may be able to help you show your film on the sly.

Acquisition A film (yours?) "acquired" by a film distributor...for money! This is the pot of gold at the end of the rainbow.

Points Percentage of the money a film takes in. There are gross points, which are based on the overall amount of money a film takes in at the box office. There are also net points, which are based on how much money a film earns after deductions relating to costs and expenses. Despite their name, you want "gross" points. Despite what you want, even most experienced filmmakers get only net—or nothing. This is because careful accounting can assure that there never are any net points. You will want to talk this over with your lawyer if a distributor shows any interest in your film. Then you can forget about it because you will probably not receive gross points or net points. Just make sure you get enough cash to cover the cost of your film. Comprendé?

Lawyer Individual who will tell you he can get you gross points and will barely negotiate enough to cover the cost of your film. (This can also be handled by an "agent.")

Agent Similar to a lawyer but with less education. Never around when you need one.

Friends Festival attendees who want the same things you do and think you might be able to help them get it. Generally, after casually meeting someone at a festival it is acceptable to refer to them as a "friend." Be sure you know the difference between "industry" friends and real ones.

Good Friend Same as above but you've had lunch together. Once is fine and with a group is acceptable.

Best Friend Same as above but you've had dinner.

Townies People who actually live in town despite having no connection to the festival. (As with college townies, festival townies are most useful for making fun of and sleeping with.)

Parties The life's blood of a film festival. You're not likely to be invited to the better ones by a townie.

Galas (Attended mostly by stars and the press.) Similar to parties, they are official festival events. Usually held on opening and closing nights, they are large and expensive and perhaps your only chance to meet the most venerable luminaries in a semi-social environment. After the galas, most of the fun people move on to parties.

Honored Guests Film festivals are often a sort of Miami for older film professionals—a last stop before death. If historic figures are your interest, catch them while you can. (They are most often found at galas or polite and carefully controlled question and answer sessions.)

Executives Modern film industry-types who sometimes attend the festivals. (Most often found at parties.) Also referred to as "Suits."

Weinstein Surname of two brothers who run the Miramax film company. Though the company is owned by Disney, it is perceived to be the leader in the world of "independent" film. If Harvey Weinstein sweats on you, there is a good chance that someone will acquire your film.

Circuit The series of film festivals held annually. If you are a young filmmaker and you become a "fixture" on the festival circuit, you have not succeeded. On the other hand, the circuit is an excellent place to renew the acquaintance of volunteers and crashers whose P.O. Box or voice mail number you've misplaced.

Nutty Ladies in Crazy Hats A staple of all festivals. These loons sometimes make great conversation while waiting in a movie line. Careful. Always have an excuse to get out of particularly long discussions.

Festival Program The actual films and events scheduled at the festival (essentially irrelevant).

SECTION 1
WiNNiNG THE FiLM FESTiVAL GAME

"Like the lottery, you can't win if you
don't play. Sundance is the mother of
all film festivals—you MUST apply."

—Joal Ryan, filmmaker, *Former Child Star*

APPLY YOURSELF

Getting into the Best Festivals for You

So, you've worked hard, had the wrap party, you're close to finishing your film and it's now time to begin to send in that festival application and travel the world showing your masterpiece. Having finished a film you certainly have the right to be on a creative high, but don't let that sway you from reality; it's time to get serious.

Aimlessly filling out applications and writing checks is generally how most filmmakers go about submitting to festivals. That method usually results in paying a cool $40 bucks for each rejection letter—a total waste of cash. You can do better than that. You need a submission plan.

First, you need to get to know the festivals. (Which is why we included the handy festival appendix in the back of the book.) Choose a group of festivals that best fit the profile of your film. There are many factors to consider when choosing festivals that are right for you.

10 Important Factors to Consider When Applying to Festivals

As the filmmaker (writer, director, producer, or combination of the three), your job is to act as the ambassador of your film. When you travel to a festival, you represent everyone who worked on the movie and the movie itself. Make no mistake, selecting the festivals to submit your film to is an important decision. You will be throwing away vast amounts of time and money if you do not consider these ten important factors before submitting to any festival. In approximate order of importance, they are:

1. **Prestige.** Submitting your film to a prestige festival will give your movie its best chance to be sold to a distributor, receive loads of press coverage, get your next film deal and (cross your fingers) launch a brilliant career as a filmmaker. Also, even something as simple as being *accepted* into a prestige festival can make a great

quote on a video box—something as simple as "Official Selection Sundance Film Festival." I'll bet you've noticed that on more than a few video sleeves. Prestige counts for a lot. To just be accepted into one of the top ten festivals is an honor, so keep that in mind.

2. **Distributors.** Is this a film festival that distributors attend? If the ultimate goal is to sell the film, this must be of paramount concern to you. Make sure to ask the festival staff which acquisitions executives will be attending.

3. **Reviews and press coverage.** Getting covered in publications like the *Los Angeles Times,* the *New York Times, Entertainment Weekly, Premiere* and the trades is another important factor to consider. Your chances of being reviewed by these publications, and others, increase when they send representatives. (Duh!) But it's also your job to be sure that they attend a screening of your film. Ask the festival office to provide a list of the journalists attending the festival. If the festival has only attracted local press, it may not be worth your time. Unless, of course, that local press is in one of the top ten markets in the U.S.

4. **Prizes and awards.** From sizable cash awards to film equipment to lab deals, prizes should play a role in your decision to submit. Winners of the 1998 Slamdance award for Best Editing received $20,000 in Avid editing equipment—that's a damn good prize! Cash awards are always a nice dividend. Be sure to research the prizes awarded and consider this when submitting. Inquire about audience awards, judges awards, etc.... Any type of award that your film receives only serves to increase its overall value.

5. **Location.** Could this film festival be a well-earned holiday as well as a chance to schmooze with the bigshots of the movie world? If it's a choice between the Hawaii Film Festival and a festival in Ohio; the choice is clear. Surf's up! Hawaii!

6. **Perks.** How does the festival treat you? Is the flight paid for? Are you put up for free? The Florida Film Festival treats filmmakers like royalty, even offering passes to Disneyland and Universal Studios Theme Park while the filmmakers are in town. Be sure to inquire about paid expenses and other perks.

7. **Application fee.** Festival application fees can be really steep. Upwards of $50 for some. At that price, enter twenty fests and you've spent a $1,000 bucks. With over 1,000 festivals worldwide and new ones being announced on a weekly basis (or so it seems)

those application fees can add up. You could end up spending enough in application fees to finance your next film!

Be sure to ask if a festival is willing to waive the fee. Some of them will actually be willing to waive the fee when asked. If your film has no chance of being accepted anyway, why bother writing the check and submitting the film? Do your homework. Don't submit your twenty-something talky drama to the Transgender Documentary Film Festival, since you obviously don't have a chance.

8. **Recommendations.** There are recommendations contained in the appendix at the end of this book, but you should consider contacting others who have either attended or had their films shown at that particular festival, if at all possible.

9. **Contacts.** It's vitally important to make contacts for investors in future films, distributors, acquisitions executives, agents, lawyers and especially other filmmakers who often turn out to be very helpful. Or simply to make friends in the industry. You never know how these contacts can pay off later. For many, a festival can be an opportunity to meet their heroes in a social setting. I know a filmmaker that attended a small film festival for one reason only— the Coen brothers were going to be there and he wanted to meet them. Nothing is more fun than slugging down beers and talking film until all hours of the night with a longtime film hero. You'd be shocked at what John Waters will tell you when he's feelin' loose at a party. (God, I love that guy.)

If you decide to go the route of self-distribution, making contacts will be a major factor in your submission plan. You'll need to find others in the industry willing to champion your film.

10. **Fun.** Yes, fun. If it's going to be miserable, why bother? Working the festival circuit, plugging a film day in and day out can be grueling after the fiftieth post-screening question and answer session. Select festivals in places you'd like to visit so if the festival is a bore, at least you'll have the opportunity to explore the nightlife in a new city. Ohio may not have the beach, but there are some great bars and even better people.

Basically, you need to think of your film as an investment. The value of your film (and yourself as a filmmaker) increases as you receive good press, awards of any kind and acceptance into prestige film festivals.

FORMiNG A FESTiVAL STRATEGY

In order to successfully break your film into the festival circuit, you must have a strategy. First, this involves getting to know your film. Be aware of festivals that may be more friendly to a film that fits a particular genre—whether it be gay, lesbian, documentary, student, underground, animated, ethnic—there are festivals specializing in these types and your film may best fit into one of these. It's better to be the toast of a smaller festival than be overlooked at a larger festival.

When it comes to entering festivals, there are three that you absolutely must enter: Sundance, Berlin and Toronto. These are the "A" festivals and are also markets for indie films, heavily attended by acquisitions executives. Enter these three and lobby the staff to get in.

Next, you must plan a fallback strategy in case you do not get into any of the top three. This is the category most filmmakers will fall into. There are just not enough slots no matter how many American Spectrums or Midnight Shows Sundance schedules. Compile a list of "B" festivals and these are the ones you will submit to simultaneously. These include festivals like Slamdance, Montreal, SXSW, Florida, Atlanta and the Los Angeles Independent Film Festival, among others. (See the list for good "B" festivals.) These are all great festivals, don't get me wrong, but when it comes to getting a distribution deal, statistically speaking, the top three have had more films walk away with distribution than all the "B" festivals combined. They are great for creating buzz, getting the word out and even getting a deal. Apply to ten of these festivals and lobby just as hard for admittance.

Then, and this is optional, take some chances; apply to some wild card festivals. The weird ones and the strange sounding ones located overseas. Foreign festivals can be a blast. You never know, you may end up with a free trip to Spain for your film's European debut, all because you took a chance on a smaller festival. Apply to twenty-five carefully selected, wild card festivals.

All told, you should have applied to close to forty festivals. Sure, you could apply to hundreds, but why bother? Once your film gets circulated, it WILL make it to other festivals because directors of festivals talk to each other. And while one fest may view your film and conclude that it is not right for them, they may call their buddy in Austin and pass along a recommendation to the Austin Film Festival. Once your film is in the pipeline, it is IN the pipeline. It's better to focus on lobbying these forty film festivals than to use a scattershot strategy and apply to the more than 500 festivals in this book. Remember, lobbying festival staff (politely, correctly, in a way that gets their attention and does not annoy) is time better spent than applying randomly. Work smarter, not harder.

Once your film plays one festival, other festivals will extend invites. Some invites will be very direct and others will simply imply that IF you send in your tape, it will most likely make it in, and oh, by the way, you don't have to send in the application fee. Anything to get around paying another forty bucks.

SEEKiNG ACCEPTANCE

Avoiding Mistakes on the All-important Festival Application

All you have to do is fill out the application, write a check, enclose a video, mail it off and you're in, right? WRONG! Any filmmaker that follows this path is fooling themselves. There are some very simple things you can do to make the lives of the people running the festival a little easier and increase your chances of acceptance. Follow this advice and avoid the mistakes that turn many festival entries into recycled videotapes.

1. **Follow instructions.** The first thing that can have a film teetering on the fence of rejection, is not following the directions on the application. This only serves to upset busy festival workers. If you have any questions or extenuating circumstances regarding your film, be sure to call the festival.

2. **Label correctly.** A package sent to a festival generally includes the check, application, the film on video, the sleeve and press kit, press materials, photos, etc. Be sure to label every single one of these things and include your contact information. If you send a video, the contact info should be on the video box *and* the video itself.

3. **Inquire about a festival's pre-screening process.** Most festivals won't admit this, but many submissions are viewed on video, generally by subordinates, and only the first five to ten minutes are actually viewed. It's an unfortunate reality. However, when you consider that some festivals receive over 800 films, resulting in close to 1,500 hours of viewing time (that's about two straight months with no sleep in front of a VCR—hey, you try that!), you can't blame them for rushing through the screening process. If you pay the application fee, make sure someone is going to watch the entire film.

4. **Research the number of submissions accepted.** Your chances may be better at a smaller festival with fewer submissions.

5. **Write a competent synopsis that truly describes the film.** If you must, get a publicist or friend to write the synopsis for you. Remember, the synopsis is made to *sell* the film, it may have nothing to do with the film itself. Let the sales material do its job.

   If the synopsis is poorly written, it will reflect on the film itself. Also, avoid being esoteric. Courtesy of the Atlanta Film & Video Festival, here are a couple of examples of what to avoid. If you are making an experimental film, don't write something like, "This film is a cinematic meditation…this film transforms the viewers sense of possibility for inner and world peace." That film quickly transformed into a reject.

   Avoid being pretentious like this synopsis from a rejected submission: "Put simply, this film is a romantic fable. However, as a film, it is a composition of auditory and visual components. Please keep in mind, the same person both photographed and scored this film thereby creating a structure of audio-visual counterpoint. Using an original, yet light archetypal story, the filmmaker has sought to compose a film that 'works' not only as an intensive audio-visual approach, but also as a carefree ride right into a big fat smile!" Uh, yeah.

6. *Do not* **include a long apologetic letter pointing out your film's faults.** "The sound is a pre-mix…this is our first rough cut…we plan to take out another 20 minutes…we're still doing some re-shoots…." Dailies are for you to examine, not the film festival. Send as close to a finished film as possible.

   A brief cover letter of no more than one page including basic details is fine. If the film is an answer print, certainly point that out, but don't dwell on it or go into exhausting detail.

7. **Make a personal connection.** Any kind of connection you can make in your cover letter or follow-up phone call to the festival is good, assumably.

8. *Do not* **include promotional junk.** T-shirts, stickers, pens, and other promotional give-aways will often make their way into the garbage. You'll need this stuff later to promote your film—*after* your film has been accepted.

9. **Have a story.** I mean your own personal story. There is a reason that you made your film and your struggle to get it on screen can be as compelling as the film itself. It makes a great story in a festival program and will set you apart from the pack. Is the film

biographical? Why is your film so important that people would pay to see it? What hardships were endured to tell your tale? The viewers of your film will look differently at it if they know you had to sell blood to get it made.

If you really have no story, be creative. The Slamdance Film Festival program book includes information about each film-maker including a short bio. I still remember reading: "Eric Kripke is a millionaire playboy director who solves baffling crimes in his spare time." His short film, *Truly Committed*, was hilarious and went on to win the audience award at Slamdance.

10. **Submit on time.** Submitting late will only give the festival staff another excuse to reject your film. It also means that most screening slots have already been filled and that your film will most likely not be viewed in its entirety. By now, the bloodshot eyes of the screening committee in the festival are highly trained at spotting films they don't like. If they are not hooked in the first five to ten minutes, your film becomes a reject.

GETTING A "THUMBS UP" FROM THE GATEKEEPER

Behind the Scenes with Geoff Gilmore, Director of the Sundance Film Festival

Sundance gatekeeper Geoff Gilmore

The Sundance Film Festival is the leading festival in the United States, if not the world. It is where indie films are picked up for distribution, where new talent is discovered and where people from all over the world travel to make deals. All festivals have gatekeepers, screening committees that often make group decisions about what films to accept. For Sundance there is only one. Geoff Gilmore: gatekeeper for Sundance. While the festival has a trusted group of screeners, he alone is responsible for the final decision to accept or reject a film for Sundance. This makes Gilmore one of the most powerful people in the independent film industry today.

Gilmore came to Sundance in 1989 when it was still called the United States Film Festival. He has been instrumental in the festival's emergence as the number one market for independent films in the United States. He teaches film classes at UCLA and has an unbridled passion for cinema that I have not seen in any other festival director. Gilmore truly cares about supporting independent films and has used Sundance to forward this admirable agenda.

In order to get into Sundance, you've got to get into the mind of Geoff Gilmore. He alone must embrace your film. In this extended interview, Gilmore reveals how he selects films and his philosophies about what makes a successful independent film.

As Director of the Sundance Film Festival, what does your job entail?

Generally speaking, I am where the buck stops in terms of what gets into the Festival. I help shape the vision of Sundance—what it is and what it will become in the long term. I also manage many of the day-to-day things that we have to deal with as an institution.

There seems to have been an explosion of film festivals, due in large part to the success of Sundance.

There has been an explosion of film festivals, in part because there are a lot of articles being written about them. Yet some of the festivals don't seem particularly concerned about film, or about supporting the film-makers they profess to support. Some seem to exist only to fill a niche in the community's calendar. They think, "Wow, this would be a great thing. We can reach out to the film industry and pull them in."

I am a little cynical about the development of some of that. There are certainly a lot of well deserved efforts and there has been such a geometric explosion in the number of films produced over the last ten years that there is certainly enough product out there to support those festivals. Yet, despite the fact that all those films are out there, the theatrical marketplace is probably in the most confused state I have seen in the last ten years. It's very difficult to understand what will succeed from the independent world in the broader commercial market and therefore what gets theatrical distribution. That is the reason for the emergence of festivals, because so few independent films ever get to anyone's community for a decent run. If you live outside of one of the twelve major markets, you have almost no chance to see them.

So, in part, festivals serve as a distribution outlet for independent films?

If they are programmed well, but sometimes it doesn't even seem as if that's the impetus. It seems that the issue is, "We have a celebrity who lives in this town, so we'll program their work," and the goal becomes building a festival around various different pockets of an industry community, rather than focusing on filmmakers and film-making. I'm a little cynical about that because I don't think it serves people well and too often it ends up being somewhat exploitative of filmmakers.

Do you feel that filmmakers are being taken advantage of, in some way?

Well, the filmmakers have to pay the application fees and then the festivals get to show the films to paying audiences.

Sundance sets the tone for a lot of these smaller film festivals. Many of those festival directors attend Sundance to see what's hot and then try their best to program those films at their festivals.

That's partially true, although in the past few years, we've really gone out of our way to put forth another thirty or forty films to those festival directors to say, "Hey, guys, you didn't see this at Sundance but look! This wasn't ready for us when we had to make our decision, or, we just couldn't include this one. Why don't you take a look at this?"

You are essentially choosing forty features out of eight hundred—an impossible task. Both my staff and I will really try to offer up some options, we go out of our way not to just say, "Hey, program the stuff that's come out of Sundance." So, for a number of different festivals (South by Southwest, Los Angeles International Festival and a number of others), we make recommendations about work we think they might be interested in.

This also gives the filmmaker another chance. There's a real need to support a range of different independent filmmakers. Theatrical distribution is very hard to get right now, and many independent filmmakers tend to see Sundance as an all or nothing goal. If they attain it, they've achieved victory and if they don't, then they've lost. I very strongly want to make the point that this is not true and that good films do surface. Good films will find a way out and they'll find a way out through a number of different paths.

A film that plays Sundance is like an endorsement that goes a long way toward helping a filmmaker secure distribution.

I am not going to argue that Sundance has a place in putting work into the marketplace or helping get work viewed, and not just for acquisition but for a lot of things. I don't think Sundance should be seen as only a market; that's too narrow. Often there are a lot of films at Sundance that people *don't* get to see, that *don't* become the buzz films and therefore people don't understand that those are also very much part of the independent world. But one of the things we're really interested in trying to do is continue to expand the sense of what the aesthetic possibilities are. Ten years ago, festivals were aesthetic enterprises for critics who went and talked about the movies and talked about the nature of the film and they talked about whether it was exciting or not. It was amazing, you could go to the Berlin Festival and not hear any talk about business whatsoever. Business was just not a big part of the film festival culture.

Now you go to these festivals and the topic of conversation is acquisition deals, or whether or not new films could have been found. That's unfortunate, because it really overloads and categorizes only one aspect of a festival's function. I think there are a range of functions. That said, I never apologize for the fact that Sundance has become a market. I think probably the nicest thing you can do for young filmmakers is to get them out of debt and get their films sold.

It's actually refreshing to hear another person in the film industry say that they are tired of hearing about the business side of film talked about and being written about more often than the art of film. Who cares whether a film was successful at the box office—I want to know whether it was successful creatively speaking.

It becomes a horse race; number one is the only position that matters. They report whether or not something is the number one grosser of the weekend; that's ridiculous because independent release distribution patterns are now similar to studio patterns. It's so much harder to keep a film in a marketplace and watch it actually find an audience.

It's amazingly difficult, the way that sets up what films the acquisitions executives are looking for—because they don't know anymore. They're finding it difficult to try to figure out what can stay out there and what can't. You can argue that it's a hit driven marketplace. But what does that mean? Was *The Full Monty* something that someone tried to hit as a home run? You bet it wasn't! It was given away by the people who produced it because they already had a working-class drama. So it becomes a question of what one thinks is the overall function of a festival. Clearly, you want to try to broaden those possibilities. I am not so naïve that I think people should come there and debate Fellini anymore. Yet I would hope that at least some of the discussions would be aesthetic and ideological discussions.

The generation of filmmakers currently very much involved in

> "I never apologize for the fact that Sundance has become a market, because I think probably the best thing you can do for young filmmakers is to get them out of debt and get their films sold."

producing independent films strikes me as being similar to the 90s professional athlete—very interested in what's in it for them, in making money, having their own position, their own status but not necessarily winning championships. A lot of guys have huge contracts without ever winning a playoff game. And in some ways that seems to be what's going on with independent filmmakers. They don't really care about making films that will be memorable, films that people will talk about ten years from now. They care desperately about making a film that can get them into the industry so they can recoup some of the investment they've put into the film; but more than that, they want to go onto a career that's lucrative and glamorous. I meet more and more filmmakers who are extremely knowledgeable about the business side of the industry and don't really know anything about film. They have a better understanding of who's who and who is influential in the business of film than they do an appreciation for the craft.

I don't hear anybody justifying themselves as a festival by saying, "The films we showed at our festival were great." They justify themselves by saying, "We had as many films picked up as they did!" Or, "We have as many acquisitions coming out of it as they do." That should not be the justification for a festival. You have to look at your program and say, "I like this program. This is a strong program. This is what we should be showing. These are the choices we made because these are the films that have value on a number of different levels."

Even so far as Sundance goes, I am not sure that we are in an era of great filmmaking at all. In fact, there are very few American independent films that we are going to be talking about as being memorable in the coming decades. But maybe the great independent films have yet to be made. Maybe a few of them have been and maybe a few in the past, yet not enough that we can really argue about it. When people talk about the twenty-somethings taking over the business the way the 70s generation did in Hollywood twenty-five years ago, I say, "Well it may appear that there's a lot of interest in that, but look at the films. Tell me, which are the key works that we are going to compare to, say, *Nashville* or *Raging Bull?*" Where are those films that signify aesthetic achievement?

The younger filmmakers are clearly savvier about the industry than they are about cinematic achievement.

I think the Rick Linklaters and the Kevin Smiths have made more interesting films as they've gotten older, which is part of the maturation process. It's a hell of a burden to place on a twenty-something filmmaker and say, "Not only do you have to produce films that are successful in the marketplace, but you have to produce great films."

Too often the critique made is "Oh, there were no wonderful things at Sundance this year." When the critique should really be, "They're flawed, but probably no more flawed than a number of the Hollywood films being made, and they indicate talent." Those are the filmmakers to be embraced, instead of those whose films were sold to the highest bidder.

Hasn't Sundance become a part of this emphasis on the business side of the film industry?

One of the odd complaints of Sundance is that the agenda we've set for everyone is the business agenda, yet I don't think that's the crisis. You really have to have a degree of balance. I would hope that to some degree that balance comes from the filmmaker: that they have not chosen filmmaking as a career because they like the accoutrements that go with being a movie director, but because they actually have some passion and a kind of creative vision and a voice they need to express. I don't know if I see that as much. You can ask a lot of filmmakers questions about any of those filmmakers in their fifties, or about guys who are dead—and they don't know them; they haven't seen them. When they do, it really shows. It comes out in their work, which doesn't always make it the most commercial, but makes it interesting. And this fails to be lauded enough by critics and by journalists, who used to be part of that mechanism that helped support the aesthetic dimensions of independent film.

Too often, that's dismissed; we are almost moving to a kind of a dismisiveness toward independent work by older critics. They just say, "This doesn't have power, it's not great." I think sometimes they are throwing out the baby with the bath water. There is a lot of talent there, but it's not yet something that deserves to be spoken in the same voice as the guys who changed Hollywood.

Your job comes with a lot of pressure, I'm sure at times, you have found yourself having to play diplomat.

Sure I do, because there are a lot of different agendas, a lot of communities. You are trying to speak to a lot of different issues and constituencies and that's something that can create a lot of pressure. You carry it around as part of the job.

How does Sundance actually select the films?

When you look at about eight hundred independent fictional features and another couple of hundred documentaries and another three or four hundred films in other categories, you really just don't have time to go through them all yourself. So the primary staff, myself, John Cooper, Rebecca Yeldham, Lisa Viola have been responsible for viewing that work. We have a support staff, and we make sure that no film is seen by at least a couple of people. I screen a lot of films cold, off the shelf. Recently, that percentage has dropped a bit. Instead of picking up fifty percent of those old films and taking them home, maybe the number is down to twenty-five percent or so. That means that there are a number of other major staff members that see material cold. We have screeners as well, and they are there to make sure the films get dealt with in a very professional way.

People think that we just throw in a tape for two minutes and that's it, and that's not what happens at all. My wife yells at me, "Haven't you seen enough of this? This is terrible," and I've watched thirty-five minutes of it; I try to give it a chance. I think that all the staff members here do the same.

The one thing I have always given my staff credit for is that they are very thoughtful. They really take a lot of time to consider work. They argue it passionately and persuasively—often fighting over different films. You are not looking for five of six people to sit there and agree. You are looking for people to support the work, and you are trying to think about what they are saying. You are trying to be a professional programmer who is able to pick a film out and say "This film should be shown." It's not necessarily my taste or a film I would buy if I were an acquisitions person, but it is a film that should be shown. You make that decision as a professional because you have reasons for this film to be shown as part of what's out there in the independent world. That's the goal for your staff and for yourself. That's what you strive for.

Unfortunately, too many people take for granted the kind of pressures that are put on you. They figure, "Well, there is a lot of political pressure coming from individuals or companies, therefore they have to respond that way." We are not about that pressure. We are certainly in a situation were some of the films we show will be distributed, but if we show six or seven films from Miramax one year, people will say, "God, Harvey [Weinstein] put in whatever he wanted this year." What people don't realize is that we looked at twenty films from Miramax and we didn't take fourteen others. The films we choose are those we think make up the best festival and represent what the independent universe is all about.

What can filmmakers do to increase their chances of getting into Sundance?
I have said time and time again that people have to realize the standard has been raised: the increase in the number of productions hasn't lowered the standard of quality—it has increased it. Filmmaking is so hard; people make films and they feel they have achieved something by just getting the film in the can, and they have. But that it isn't good enough and then you have to look at work that isn't good enough. It's good, but it isn't great. As a filmmaker you really have to look at your work and say, "Is this as great a film as I can make it?" More often than not, flaws surface because they rushed through production. They've had very limited resources or they make unfortunate casting decisions. They don't think through the fact that it's better to go off and make a better film than to rush it through because they are determined to make this year's festival. They have to understand that they have to make a *great* film, not a good film. I think that means a lot of different things, but it really means bringing quality to the film. And it's not just the standard required to get into Sundance. It's the standard required to get your money back. It's the standard required to be able to find any kind of distribution deal whatsoever.

The competition is fierce now, and it continues to grow.
Promotion and advertising (P&A) costs have tripled in the last two years. Any film you buy has to gross theatrically at a certain level to make it profitable. You can't release a film with less than $2 million of P&A. You are going to be in that situation regardless of what the film cost to make in the first place. So, you have these acquisitions

executives looking around and asking themselves, which are the films worth investing the huge amount of P&A required to make them profitable? Those are the questions that I don't think people think through clearly enough.

You need to know who your audience is. Think through what the film is about. Thinking for an audience doesn't mean that you've somehow gone commercial, or that you have to put elements in the film to make it commercial or to sell it to your audience. No, it's the opposite. It's actually thinking through what you, as a voice are trying to say, and knowing who is listening. I don't think that anybody who isn't a wonderful filmmaker doesn't think about the audience. I have talked to a lot of the major filmmakers, who talk very much about how they have the audience in mind when they are writing. I think it's kind of a myth that the true artist doesn't pay any attention to that.

Are there common mistakes that you see filmmakers make over and over again?

Rushing. I keep saying don't rush. Don't create a situation where everything is dependent on a schedule only to get into X or Y festival. You know, you spend an awful lot of time putting this project together. Make it good; take the extra time to not only shoot that extra take, but to really think about quality. Try to take a step back. Have naysayers around you. Don't just let people say, "Great, great, great!" Have someone that really gives you a critical eye. You don't want a whole bunch of people arguing with you; what you really want is someone you can trust to help support your vision and not rush it.

We look for a lot of different things, but I've always said our strength is that we respond to a lot of different things. We have a very diverse and eclectic level of response that allows us to look at a work from one kind of experimental point of view to something much more casually mainstream. People really need to look at the range. You are not trying to do something as narrowly defined as "a Sundance film."

For many years, we have attacked the industry as making formulaic work and pushed the independent film as the realm in which creative vision flourished. Yet, we have now moved into an era in which the independent world has become a derivative mess. Some of the initial perspective that motivated the independent world has been lost: the capital "Q" quirky comedy that reflects only a series of quirky comedies that have come before; the generic "Tarantino wanna-be gangster" work; the coming-of-age angst story that really isn't fresh or doesn't have the depth to make it profound, but is simply another version of the same tale.

Without being too harsh, you want to say those films aren't gonna make it anymore. You really need to find something or think about something that runs with freshness and originality. People hear these words and then go and do something straight out of TV sitcoms.

When it comes to films that are rejected, do they make many of the same mistakes?

Casting and story are the simple answers to that. Story is the most obvious one; casting is the second. People realize they can't get major actors, so they make poor decisions. Even films that have a lot to offer lose any dramatic impact because you can't squeeze a performance out of an actor who just isn't able to give it. This is something that really takes more experience and it's certainly something that filmmakers should pay more attention to.

My belief is that most films fail at the stage of the script—it always goes back to the script. The script is often underdeveloped. The thing that irks me even more is when I hear a filmmaker brag that they wrote the film in a week.

Isn't it amazing that they do that? They say things like, "This film was done on first draft." You want to tell them—*it shows.*

What is the future—the unexplored territories in independent film?

I think digital is going to open up a lot of different possibilities when it becomes cost-effective for independent film, and it's getting there very quickly. So far, almost everyone has left the realm of special effects to the industry and they haven't realized that computers have brought those costs down dramatically. You can now do special effects on a computer that could of never been done optically. So the question is, are you going to be able to create a digital on-screen persona? That's a little bit different and would cost a fair amount of money but it's definitely interesting. It's very much part of a new world.

Many times filmmakers get so wrapped up in everything film that they tend to lose a sense of real life experience; I think that some of the better films come from filmmakers with actual life experience.

I think you need life experience outside of the film world because you aren't going to find creative inspiration just by watching movies. You can learn a lot, you can find a great deal to think about in terms of your craft and you can find creative inspiration, but in terms of your stories, you really need to find those elsewhere. I think that is one of the reasons that people of different experiences, filmmakers of color, gay and lesbian filmmakers, people who come from different perspectives, have became so important over the last decade. Because they were bringing different experiences that helped fuel their own creativity. Each filmmaker's own personal history is unique, and that range is what makes them interesting. Sundance has always been very supportive of alternative voices.

What makes a good professional in this field is a real eclecticism. Being narrow or critical in your taste is a real deficit. We have tried to support a lot of different things and have managed to avoid a narrow agenda. We understand mainstream filmmaking and filmmakers and traditional aesthetics; we are supportive of those but we see try to see the world more inclusively. Filmmakers of color, gay and lesbian film-makers, different points of view and different voices, all became part of the definition of the Sundance festival.

We try to be responsive to the perspectives and the voices of both the U.S. and other continents, but we don't try to be inclusive of it in a broad way. That isn't what the festival is about. What Sundance helped do was to expand the field. When those films became not only successful at Sundance but then achieved a certain success in the marketplace, people began to say things like, "There was no gay or lesbian film up to that point." Or that there were very few African-American films that people were embracing and had a certain kind of commercial definition. So what we were doing was breaking through some of those old generalizations and saying, "Hey, look at this work."

Diversity has always been a key definition of what Sundance is about. Though to me that diversity isn't simply a position of the color of the skin. It's a diversity of aesthetics, a diversity of points of view and that sometimes has to do with the creator's experience but it also comes from a creative mind.

If you could sit down with some of these independent filmmakers before they started writing their screenplays and give them some advice, what would you tell them?

Don't just go out and make a film, make a great film. It's so hard to make films and I have so much respect for people that do it. A lot of people are very often angry at us for having to make choices, for being in a position where we have to say: these are the films we have chosen and these we have decided not to take. So often, we have people filled with righteous indignation at being rejected. We have people who think, because it is so hard to make films, that just having made a film is a significant enough accomplishment in itself. It's just not enough to spend a couple of years of your life making a movie, finally finishing it, and thinking, "Oh my goodness, I've made a movie," and pat yourself on the back. You really

"Don't just go out and make a film, make a great film."

have to look at what you made and say, "Is this successful? Does this convey the kind of energy and inspiration and storytelling and excitement? Does it work the way I want it to work?"

They read these stories in the paper about this guy making a film or that guy making a film. They feel they have to get their film made and they go out and make it—and too often it is just not good enough. It's a phrase we use around here all the time. It's "not good enough." That doesn't mean that it's bad and it's not that it doesn't have certain elements. But it's not cast well or it doesn't have any visual style, or it doesn't necessarily have the kind of creativity to it that really makes it stand apart. So you have to say to yourself, if you are a filmmaker and you have to spend all these resources and all this time, why not shoot for the top? Not enough people do.

Filmmakers need to be encouraged to really take their time. Sometimes that means you won't make it this year and that you need to work on your script. People don't like hearing that their third draft wasn't good enough, that they need to go into a fourth draft. They don't want to do that, they want to say, "Let's make it!" That sort of thinking will ultimately create something without any kind of effect and people won't care about it.

I don't believe that this generation doesn't work hard. I feel that the twenty-something generation right now is almost Protestant in its work ethic. Film students feel they should have no other life outside of their film schools. They don't even see movies because they're working so hard in school. When I was in film school, we used to say, "Are you going to go to the Nuart and watch this film?" Because it was presumed that was what you were going to do. Now, though, people are saying, "No, I've got to finish my project or I've got to work on my script or do my essay." The goal should be to go see those films. My advice is, seek that inspiration, seek that knowledge, broaden yourself, and take the time for your project to really get it right. Or else I fear we are not going to have a generation of filmmakers that will be considered memorable.

What so many of these young filmmakers forget is that you find a lot of major filmmakers doing great work in their late thirties, their forties and their fifties rather than in their twenties. You need life experience and you just don't get it when you are twenty.

It's interesting how many of the filmmakers that have made really low-budget films have become the filmmakers of note for this generation. Maybe the creative ingenuity you need when you are working with a low budget really marks them. I wonder if there isn't something to be said for that sort of initiation. I wonder if really struggling and making those really small $100,000 budget films forces them to overcome obstacles and marks them as filmmakers with ingenuity and promise for the future.

SECTION 2
CREATING HYPE: EVERYTHING YOU NEED TO KNOW ABOUT MARKETING

"Filmmakers can do their own publicity as easily as publicists can make their own films and do it well…it just isn't smart."

—Linda Brown, Indie PR

iNTRODUCTiON TO GUERRiLLA MARKETiNG

What do I mean by guerrilla marketing? Anyone in marketing could tell you what it means, but to a filmmaker, the term may seem alien. Basically, it means, "Be different." You must think beyond simply slapping the logo for your movie onto a T-shirt. You have to think, "out of the box." Get creative when it comes to getting your film the attention it deserves from festival attendees, press and especially distributors.

Take Sarah Jacobson, whose film *Mary Jane's Not A Virgin Anymore* played the 1997 Sundance Film Festival. She made cheap stickers that said "Not A Virgin." Jacobson, her mom and a posse of pals stuck them onto the festival badges of Sundance attendees. Within a few days, everyone was wearing them. One well-attended Sundance party found Geoffrey Gilmore himself wearing the "Virgin" sticker. It was hip because it was mysterious and it wasn't a T-shirt.

Jacobson took the concept further as she began passing out cigars with the logo of her film emblazoned on the wrapper. She printed these up quickly at Kinko's and put them onto some cheap, no-brand cigars. (This was, of course, when that horribly trendy cigar-smoking thing was cool. I personally never took part. I have also never grown a goatee, worn parachute pants, Flashdance shirts or engaged in any other lame trend that has made its way into the mainstream.)

Sarah Jacobson's film had great buzz because she was able to think "out of the box." She didn't spend a lot of money and she produced unexpected attention-getters and she presented her film in a creative and unexpected way. And she did this all with almost no marketing budget! This doesn't mean that you should be passing out cigars yourself, but it certainly means you should consider something other than T-shirts, which are really standard, boring and uncreative. (Uh, that doesn't mean that you shouldn't give me a free T-shirt if you see me at a festival, you see, because I always keep the cool ones.)

Following is a list of ideas that should get your creative juices flowing so you can come up with your own ideas. The ideas below are really clever, and I think they're great—but they've been done, so use them to inspire your own wacky concepts.

"Out of the Box" Quick Marketing Ideas

Get your film known with these simple and cheap ideas.

- Create a flyer for your film and make it look like a parking ticket. Put it on all the cars at the festival and in the festival parking lots.
- Make a flyer that looks like a $20 bill. On the other side is info about your screening. Spread them all over town. NOTE: Feds don't like this one. So be careful.
- T-shirts are easy, but depending on the local environment, you can come up with better items of clothing like ear muffs (cold weather), boxer shorts or panties. (Hey, that'll get attention!)
- A cereal box (the tiny kind) with the poster of your film on the front and back. Screening info is printed on the sides where the ingredients should be.
- Give Viewmaster viewers to the press with still images of your film printed on the still frames in the viewer. The frames on a Viewmaster are made from 16mm film and custom viewmaster sleeves could be made cheaply. This one would be really cool, but likely expensive.
- A comic book. This worked well for the film *Six String Samurai* which premiered at the Slamdance Film Festival in 1998.

There are plenty of ideas to come up with on your own; the point is to try and do something unique so people talk will about it and ultimately attend your screening.

POSTER THE TOWN

Most film festival movie posters just plain suck. But don't worry, plenty of successful films have had bad posters as well. Weak tag lines are commonplace even in mainstream movies. Consider Orson Welles' *Citizen Kane* whose memorable tag line was: "It's Terrific!" Wow. Or George Lucas' *Star Wars* whose original tag line read: "It's about a boy, a girl and a galaxy." Yikes. Now, *that's* a major crapola tag line.

Most posters seen at film festivals have an amateur look that, well, represents the film in a bad light. The festival is like a job interview and here you are in jeans and a dirty T-shirt. You need a poster that feels like a smooth Armani suit, not a stinky T-shirt.

The first piece of advice for any filmmaker wishing to create an impactful poster is to acknowledge that you are a filmmaker—not a poster designer. Filmmakers, especially on small productions, have a tendency to want to make the poster themselves. You made the film, now back off and allow others to do their jobs. If you tell a designer exactly what you want them to do, they will do exactly as you tell them. If you allow your designer some creative freedom, you are more likely to get some cool ideas you might not have thought of. However, if your budget does not allow for a poster designer and you are forced to create your own poster, there are some basic things you should know.

Jon C. Allen designs movie posters for a living. Allen began collecting one-sheets when he was young and knew he wanted to create them for a living. He has a degree in Visual Design and has worked at various Hollywood advertising agencies. These days, Allen freelances and has designed movie posters for Sony, Castle Rock, Miramax, New Line, HBO and many others. Allen's poster credits include films like *Palmetto, Air Force One, National Lampoon's Senior Trip, Jackie Chan's First Strike* and *The Glass Shield*, along with countless video box designs for films like *The Brothers McMullen*. Now, don't blame him for some of these bad movies, the posters are all cool. However, a designer's job is also about pleasing the client and Allen is ultimately a gun for hire.

Wildposting is key to getting attention for your film. Michael Moore's The Big One *got it with some cheap posters and an overused staple gun.*

Allen suggests asking the right questions before embarking on a design. "Is the poster positioning this film in the best possible way? Does it invoke a good reaction? Can you tell what it is as you drive by it at 40 miles an hour, looking at it in a bus shelter? Really, a designer has to be aware of the issues beyond the obvious aesthetics and layout. For me, a great poster is one that manages to straddle all of the fences just mentioned: sell the film, offer the slightest hint of something new, be well balanced in layout and design—and look cool."

In order for an indie to create a poster that stands out at a film festival, it's important to know your market. "There are a lot of factors—film markets, for example. Some foreign markets would lean towards more action oriented posters (and movies)." says Allen "But as far as the US film market goes, I would take advantage of the fact that you aren't in the studio system and avoid some of the clichés that tend to creep into those type of projects. You don't have to do *Two-Big-Heads-Floating-in-the-Sky* (an inside joke term we use for that ever popular one-sheet look). The best piece of advice I can give you for your poster look (whether on your own, or hiring a designer to do it for you) is to *KEEP IT SIMPLE*."

"Whenever we work on a smaller film, we always make it simple to make the movie feel *bigger*. Less really is more, in this case." Allen recommends a simple approach. "So often smaller indie projects with low advertising budgets fall into the kitchen sink design trap—let's show everything this movie offers so they know how hard we worked on it. Granted, in some cases, a distributor wants you to show all kinds of action, explosions, sex, etc., ...in your poster. But sometimes to get noticed, it might be better to show less. Especially if you have no stars, no photography, ... Often in those cases, we go with a simple icon, or a concept idea that captures the viewers attention."

Allen offers a few final thoughts: Often people ask, "Why do the majority of movie posters suck?" Well, it's all subjective, but those same people should ask "Why do the majority of movies suck?" Film advertising mirrors many of the same traits (good and bad) as the rest of the film industry. Whenever you have to please a significant number of people, compromises will be made. Sometimes this will improve something—often it will not. "Design by committee" just like "Filmmaking by committee" doesn't always work. I encourage someone working on their own one sheet to make the film poster their own vision. Please yourself first, everyone else second. Hopefully, those same rules applied to the movie you made that you are trying to find a distributor for.

Poster designer Jon C. Allen can be reached via his web site: http:// onesheetdesign.com

10 Elements of Great Movie Poster Design

Follow these simple rules and you are on your way to a memorable one-sheet.

1. Create some sort of emotion. This can be done through color, image, etc. A great poster sparks interest, makes people stop on the street or in a theater lobby. For example, a poster for a comedy should make you laugh.
2. Well thought out typography. Type should compliment the image, yet not attract undue attention to itself, and works with the imagery as a unit.
3. Second read. In other words, something you don't notice the first time you look at it. For example, take a look at the FEDEX logo. Have you ever noticed the hidden arrow inside the type?

4. Good photography. Head strips of stars' heads on double's bodies sometimes work, but it's always nice to have an idea for a photo shoot, have that star shot the way you envisioned, and the resulting photography to make your design work.

5. Great copy. Always important, especially for comedies. "Four Score and Seven Beers Ago…" made my *Senior Trip* poster work.

6. A logo that stands on its own. A great logo compliments the poster and works well in its own context, because it will often be used on its own in other mediums, such as trailers. The logo should actually compliment the poster, instead of "floating" out in front of the poster, and not acting as part of the artwork.

7. Translates well to other formats. Some things may look great at 27" x 41" on a one sheet, but how will it look on billboards, bus sides, web sites, or in black and white in a newspaper?

8. Relevant to the film's story/plot. Sometimes a poster has nothing to do with anything that happens in a film—for example, an idea that services the marketing, but is completely removed from the film itself.

9. Show something new. This is always a tricky issue. Movie posters mirror the movies themselves—it's rare that something new is tried as opposed to giving them what they've seen before.

10. It should please the intended audience. Know the demographic and be sure the poster appeals to this group. Studios not only hold focus groups for movies, but for the poster ideas themselves.

10 Most Common Mistakes Of Poster Design

These mistakes result in amateurish posters and poor design.

1. Kitchen sink design.
2. Not thinking conceptually.
3. "It looks cool" being a design's only redeeming quality.
4. Thinking of it as art, instead of *commercial* art…it's about marketing, not just what looks good.
5. Not positioning the film well.
6. Not designing everything to work together. Say, typography not working with the imagery.
7. Unwillingness to compromise for the best overall design. Sure, there are compromises left and right, some of which will drive

the designer crazy. Every movie poster designer has had the client change/alter their "vision" and felt that it was a fatal mistake. "How dare they compromise my art." But that's the nature of the business, you're trying to market a movie. Being able to play within those limits/boundaries and produce something worthwhile is part of the challenge.

8. Not using all the available elements to produce good work. Typography, layout, color, imagery, concept.

9. Bad finishing skills. Sure, you have a brilliant idea that will make you the next Saul Bass, but the fact that it looks like shit because you aren't comfortable in Adobe Photoshop will hinder your idea.

10. Again, not pleasing the client. Sure, it's easy to dismiss them if you don't agree with their views/opinions, but since they are PAYING YOU to market THEIR MOVIE, you should work with them, not against them.

PUBLiCiTY: WHAT YOU NEED TO KNOW

Filmmakers entering the festival game for the first time quickly learn the value of good PR. Great public relations can take an average movie and increase its value by creating hype. An average film with heat behind it is much more likely to be sold to a distributor than a great film with no heat: an unfortunate reality at film festivals. Really good films get lost in the shuffle. However, with a great press kit, some well-timed articles in the trades, a few positive reviews and some friends in the media, you'll much better positioned to achieve a sale and begin your filmmaking career.

On the Publicity Trail with PR Pro LiNDA BROWN

Linda Brown began her career at PMK Public Relations where she worked for five years on publicity campaigns with actors such as Winona Ryder, Andie MacDowell, Gregory Hines; producers such as James L. Brooks; films such as Luc Besson's *La Femme Nikita* and *My Left Foot* and television shows such as Fox's *The Simpsons*. After leaving PMK in search of some kind of life, she stopped briefly at Bragman Nyman Cafarelli, then went on as Director of Motion Pictures Los Angeles for Rogers & Cowan where she headed up campaigns and promotions for a countless number of films including *The Mask* with Jim Carrey. Currently Brown heads one of the premiere public relations firms for independent filmmakers, the Los Angeles-based Indie PR. Getting press is not just a job for Brown; she passionately believes in her clients and their films. Indie PR has been in existence since 1996 and has been successful in providing promotion, marketing campaigns, parties, festival debuts and more for indie filmmakers.

What does a publicist do?

A publicist does different things at different stages of a campaign for a film. For a festival, a publicist prepares the press to receive your film (in the intellectual and emotional sense). Presentation means a lot; a publicist advises you on the look of your poster, chooses the stills you will use in representing your film, your clips for electronic interviews and will prepare that all-important press kit which serves as a bible to the press when they write about your film.

But equally important, a publicist comes up with a strategy as to how to present your film to the public. A filmmaker's idea for how a film should be presented could be entirely different from what is going to sell. That doesn't mean the filmmaker is wrong, it just means that it's only one opinion and it sometimes helps to go at it from other angles as well.

I worked on a film at the Santa Barbara Film Festival called *Confessions of a Sexist Pig* by director Sandy Tung. Sandy came to me and said he thought the film was essentially about the love story between his two leads. Now, with a title like *Confessions of a Sexist Pig*, I knew that the love story was certainly part of the campaign…but was it the part that would bring someone into the theater? Would the love story make a distributor, when having to choose between four films playing at the same time at a festival, choose ours? The title was just too brilliant to not play up.

So I made a suggestion. In our target audience for the film, who makes the decision as to what movie a couple would see? Women. Okay, what is it about this film that women would want to see? I just knew that what women want more than anything else is to get *inside of a man's head* and find out what they are *really thinking!!!* (which is what this film does) I knew that men would be okay with seeing this film simply because of the title. It was *women* whom we needed to attract. And we did with that very campaign…we put it in our press kit, on our poster, on our promo cards…it commanded attention. We were on every radio station, newspaper and magazine that covered the festival.

Why does a filmmaker need a publicist?

The smartest filmmaker takes on a publicist at the very onset of a project and keeps one throughout the entire process. (That can get costly, but deals can be made…)

There is so much for the press to cover during a festival, from reviewing films to covering parties to eavesdropping during breakfast for items. Unless you have someone out there vying for ink and creating a buzz about you or your movie, you run the risk of getting lost in the noise pollution. My campaigns start a month prior to the festival when I start making calls to the magazines and columnists who can put a little "pre-festival buzz" on my movie. I get the press excited about your film by letting them in on it early and in a personal way. At this point, a lot of the press are friends of mine, so it is very much like my calling a friend to let them in on something they just shouldn't miss.

What do filmmakers need to know when it comes to publicity?

Publicity is less effective when it is a "one-shot-deal." It is so much better to have continuity and a steady flow of information going out to the press throughout all of the stages of your film. That way, when it comes time to do the festival thing, it's a matter of instant recognition for both the press and distributors. It is also essential in getting all of the materials you will need to help sell the film—whether it be a press kit complete with clippings (to show a studio that your film can get press), or photos and an electronic press kit complete with interviews and behind-the-scenes footage.

Can filmmakers do their own publicity? Is that method recommended? What are the advantages and disadvantages of a filmmaker going about their own publicity?

Filmmakers can do their own publicity as easily as publicists can make their own films and do it well…it just isn't smart. First of all, it takes up a lot of the filmmaker's time that should be spent other ways, but mostly because it's smarter to have those who do what they do best— DO what they do best. The ONLY advantage a filmmaker has in doing his/her own publicity is that it will save a few thousand dollars. That's it. Without the advice and careful planning of someone who lives this kind of work, an uninformed filmmaker could miss the opportunity of coming up with the perfect spin to catapult his campaign and film into the arms of a dream distributor. Without the forethought and careful planning that went into the PR campaign for *The Full Monty,* most ticket buyers would have passed it up for another film. Think of the distributor as being an audience member with a checkbook. You still have to stand out and grab their attention to be noticed.

What is a publicity campaign that you were not involved in that you admired?

The most recent and perhaps most obvious is *The Full Monty;* you just can't deny the brilliance of the Fox Searchlight team on that one! I think that campaign worked so well because it was very little about "hype" and "glitz" which the public is so aware of at this point. There was no "slick spin" put on that film. Instead, they played on the humanity and the "realness" of their cast; they presented this almost voyeuristic look into the down-and-out lives of people just like you and me, but they made it fun. How many of us can relate to the unemployment line scene? It was such a real moment and these were such real people with which everyone could identify. *and* it was strong enough on which to rest a good portion of their campaign.

What kind of advantages do filmmakers who have publicists have, over ones that don't?

For all of the reasons I mentioned before and because, ultimately, the more people you have talking about your film at a festival, the better position you are in. And who has bigger mouths and talks to more press, distributors and festival-goers than publicists? We're with the press at breakfast, between screenings, AT the screenings, in the bathroom, in their rooms...we never stop! We get 'em while they're drunk and make them commit...we're relentless and you need that kind of energy going out on your film at a festival.

What sort of questions should a filmmaker ask when hiring a publicist?

When hiring a publicist, the most important question to ask is, "How many other films are you working on at the festival?" I see it all the time: Bigger agencies pile on the clients telling them that they are at an advantage in being "in the company" of other big films. This is simply *not* true unless you are working with a publicist who can't get Sheila Benson on the phone *without* a bunch of big films.

There is no way you can *effectively* work with an exorbitant number of films—effectively being the key word. I don't like to work with more than four films per festival. I just don't find it effective and everyone leaves with a bad taste in their mouth. Part of a campaign is spending time with the filmmaker at the social function (it's where most of the interviews are set up) and if you're chained to a desk in a hotel room working on 15 films, you just can't do that. Film festival PR is not like publicity at time of release, where you *can* chain yourself to a desk and pump out the calls. The press is out and about...they're at the parties, they're at the panels. You've got to have the freedom to pound the pavement or you'll *never* get them on the phone.

What can a filmmaker expect to pay for a publicist?

Most agencies charge anywhere between $3,000-$5,000 for a film at a festival. You should allow for expense monies as well, which should cost you another couple of hundred depending upon the festival.

What was the best deal you were involved with and why?

One of my most successful festival campaigns (and certainly the most fun campaign) was with the indie film *20 Dates,* by director Myles Berkowitz at the Slamdance Film Festival in 1998. Myles came to me late in the game...we were two weeks away from opening night of Slamdance. Myles had no photos, no poster and no press kit...but what Myles did have a lot of was enthusiasm to do whatever it took to get up and running so that *20 Dates* would be "the" talked-about film of the festival.

By the end of festival, *20 Dates* had won the audience award at Slamdance and was picked up for distribution by Fox Searchlight. It was all about getting the decision-makers in the room and that was all me, baby!

What are the important things for a filmmaker to remember when working with a publicist?

A publicist is not a miracle worker...the ultimate sale of your film depends upon how good it is. But a publicist can be an essential part of your team in creating awareness and the infamous "buzz" that everyone listens for at a festival.

JOURNALIST DAVID E. WILLIAMS ON GETTING PRESS

How can a filmmaker without a publicist compete to get your attention?

If you want press, first you have to know the press and understand what each particular magazine wants. When I worked for *Film Threat,* I specifically looked for films that were in some way rebellious—either through the story, filmmaking style, or simply the maker's guts for doing what they did. For *American Cinematographer,* I look for visual accomplishment, whether the picture was shot on Super 8, 16mm, 35mm or video.

So the filmmaker has to research the target publication and devise a pitch based on that magazine or newspaper's field of interest. If someone asked if I wanted to interview the star of their picture, I'd immediately know that they had not done their research. If they had, they'd know that I'd only need to talk to the director, cinematographer, gaffer and other key production people.

Blindly pitching stories is not the way to go.

Publicity Terms You Should Know

Break, Piece, Hit These are all terms used to describe some kind of coverage on your film in the press.

Feature Term used to describe an in-depth story on your film and your film alone

Item Term used to describe a mention on your film in either a bigger story on several films or as part of a column.

Roundup Story Story on the entire festival in which you and your film should be mentioned or highlighted.

Photo Op (Photo Opportunity) Pulling specific people from the film together for a photo or putting a member of the filmmaking team together with someone who makes sense: e.g.., a photo with John Travolta and President Clinton at the *Primary Colors* premiere would be a "Photo Op." A filmmaker with the festival director would be a "photo op."

EPK or **Electronic Press Kit** A compilation of behind-the-scenes footage shot during production coupled with interviews with the filmmakers and main actors. This may include some footage from the finished movie (in :30 sec and :45 sec spots) of scenes that help tell the story of what the film is about or poignant moments from the finished film.

Clip Selected footage from the film that best represents the tone of the film and/or a poignant moment from the film. Clips are recommended and requested for inclusion in feature stories done for television and/or radio.

One-Sheet Another term for poster and sometimes used when referring to an 8x10 "mini-poster" used as handouts at festivals.

Wildposting Hanging posters of your film anywhere you can...on telephone poles, construction walls, in lobbies of hotels...anywhere!

Walk-Out The term we all dread...one who walks out of your screening. We hate them!

MARGOT GERBER, Director of Publicity and Marketing, American Cinematheque, on Publicity and Press Kits

Remember, you know your film better than anyone, but a publicist's perspective may take you down an additional path that you may not have thought of. Ask a lot of questions. Get a proposal or list of the various avenues the publicist says he/she will pursue. Check back to that list and mark each one off as they are done. Remember, publicity is not an exact science and no publicist can guarantee you an interview on *The Tonight Show*. They will query various media outlets, but they cannot promise you anything. The main advantage of having a publicist is the publicist's relationships with media people. Sometimes the relationship is the reason a journalist will agree to do an interview with an unknown person—a favor to the publicist or a gesture acknowledging that they have confidence in the types of clients that the publicist takes on.

At a big festival, publicists often take on many films. This can be advantageous because that publicist may have clients who are higher profile than you, so they are in constant communication with the press and are able to lobby for your film at the same time. The publicist, who is familiar to the press person, is more likely to get a call back than a random filmmaker who cold calls at a festival in the midst of chaos. If you have a producer's rep or a well-known producer or attorney behind your film, they are generally familiar to the press and the press may take their recommendations as to which films to see seriously. If you don't hire a publicist, you should get to know the film festival publicist for the festival you are in.

Clever is good. Humor is okay, but factual and unpretentious are the best ways to go when writing your press kit. Don't brag about how many credit cards financed your picture. It's old news. Do tell interesting stories about locations you used or research compiled for the film.

A press kit should include the following:

1) Synopsis. A description of the basic plot of the film.
2) About the Production. A narrative detailing the making of the film.
3) Bios of the key players in the production: i.e., director, writer, producer, actors and other key crew members if they are significant.

4) Film credits. If available.

5) Press Clips. Other articles or reviews of your film. All positive, of course.

6) Photos. Include captions along with photo credits and copyright information.

There are any number of methods that could be used to write the "About the Production" section of a press kit. I record an interview with the filmmaker on a cassette recorder, then play it back and take notes, and then write about the film using info I get from the interview and some of my own interpretations. The bios are written from interviews and should include all the key cast and crew. Put in any recognizable names of actors your cast has worked with and the names of the film and television projects. Do the same with your key crew members. Include a complete list of credits. Include a long synopsis that gives a blow by blow description of the film and a short one that gives an overview of the plot and ideas in the film. Include any positive press clippings you have. Include black and white photo stills— at least one really great photo and a maximum of six. You can also include slides (35mm transparencies). The press will want actual photos. Not color copies or laser outputs. Put photos on your website if you have one so people can grab them for online publications. Be sure to include a photo credit, if there is one, and carefully label all of your photos with the name of the film and a caption including the actors' names. Captions should read like this: Keith Brunsmann as Joseph Compana, a photojournalist turned shut-in in *Blue Skies Are A Lie* an independent feature film written and directed by Gregory Ruzzin.

THE PARTiES

Get Invited, Make an Impression, Crash, Avoid Spilling Something

The single most important event at a festival (besides your own screening) is the party. You may be as talented as Orson Welles when it comes to filmmaking, but your talent is truly judged by how comfortable you are with idle cocktail chit-chat. Yes, yet another unfortunate entertainment industry reality.

At the parties you'll be schmoozing with agents, entertainment lawyers, acquisitions executives, distributors, development executives, producers, actors, festival staff, and other filmmakers—basically, the masses of the movie industry. It's important that you make a good impression.

So get social. Grab a drink, grab a table, grab some food and scan the room. (Hey, you'll probably be too busy to grab dinner, so you'll save a little money on meals by eating party appetizers for days, keeping the cost of your trip very low. Living on chicken fingers and wing dings for a week won't kill you. At least, not right away.)

Now, you've got that person in your sights. The one you need to talk to. The actor for your next film. The agent you want to rep you.

The Atlanta Film and Video Festival brings out the stars. From left are Genevieve McGillicuddy, festival director Anne Hubbell, Peter Fonda, Wendy Conrad and Charity Ellis.

The festival director you want to accept your film. The executive you want to pitch for your next film. The bartender you want to pour your next drink. (Okay, I'm getting carried away, but it can be just as hard to get the bartender's attention as is to spark an agent's interest at these overcrowded events.) There are a few important things to remember at a party when you are there for business. Here is my version of the inevitable list of "Dos and Don'ts."

The Party Dos

- *Do* introduce yourself to people. Most will have festival badges with their names and companies on them. At any given party you'll find at least a few people you should meet to further your personal agenda. Remember, as annoying as it sounds, you are attending these parties to further your personal goals. If you think otherwise, you are only lying to yourself.
- *Do* try to find some common ground to begin a conversation. For example, films you each enjoy, a common city, a favorite drink, a popular actor, a filmmaker, anything at all to establish the conversation on a positive note.
- *Do* make friends with other filmmakers and get invited to their screenings.
- *Do* tell inoffensive and clever jokes.
- *Do* talk passionately (yet unpretentiously) about your love of film and how your life was changed by the defining moment of one important film. People at film festivals get all mushy when this subject comes up.
- *Do* talk business—that's what these parties are really about anyway.
- *Do* be bold and walk up to Harvey Weinstein of Miramax and invite him to your screening.
- *Do* take every person you speak with seriously, even if they do not initially seem important to your immediate agenda. The assistant of today is the festival director, agent or studio head of tomorrow. They'll remember that you showed them respect when no one else would. That's important.
- *Do* hand out business cards.
- *Do* make it a point to follow up and send letters to people you have met when appropriate. Again, you never know how those relationships will pay off.

The Party Don'ts

A party can be a great opportunity to make new friends, make an impression and, most importantly, make deals. If some studio executive likes to hang out and party with you, certainly, he'll want to work with you. That's the secret of the business—people hire other people they like. It's very simple. So keep some things in mind.

- *Do not,* as I have done, make inappropriate jokes in mixed company.
- *Do not,* as I have done, charge room service to your pals at 3 a.m.
- *Do not,* as I have done, put drinks on the tab of the table in the corner.
- *Do not,* as I have done, drink way too much alcohol.
- *Do not,* as I have done, try to dance after drinking that alcohol.
- *Do not,* as I have done, schedule 5 a.m. wake up calls for your colleagues.
- *Do not,* as I have done, mercilessly criticize the award-winning festival film as a total piece of crap when the director can hear you.
- *Do not,* as I have done, stand on a chair and thank everyone in the room for coming and for their support for your film, when you haven't made the film that the party is for.
- *Do not,* as I have done, avoid the festival party scene to see local bands, find the strip clubs and visit the after-hours bars.
- *Do not,* as I have done, yell "Fire!" at a crowded party.

I really mean it. Don't do any of these things. I've made every possible mistake anyone could possibly make at a party. Sometimes I just can't resist putting some pretentious moron in his place, or making a point through humor. Sure, I have a great time, but generally I'm attending a festival to have fun; I like to leave the business at the office. If your goal is to have fun, a few "don'ts" are fine. But more likely, you have a goal in mind—you're trying to sell a film or get another one made. Leave the hard partying for the final festival party.

CRASHiNG FiLM FESTiVAL PARTiES

In order to get the opportunity to do some schmoozing, you have to *get into* the party. Do whatever it takes to get into the party legitimately first, but when all else fails, it's time to crash!

It's always best to get on the list before arriving at a party but that's not always possible. Because if you're like me, you're probably not invited. But that little reality has never stopped me. I am the party crashing king and I'll crown you a prince (or princess) if you simply follow my lead.

The first piece of advice I can offer is put on your poker face. Security is generally loose at many film festival parties and it's up to you to take advantage of it. Remember: you were invited to this shindig and there must have been some mix-up. Make sure to deliver lines like an actor.

Also, never get upset. The publicists or people at the door are constantly bombarded with Hollywood egos, why add to their grief? Act understanding. Do something different—be nice. Be cool. Don't be a jackass. Knowingly shake your head as the jerk in front of you mouths off to the publicist. They'll appreciate it. They'll especially appreciate your patience as they frantically flip through the list, then just give up and wave you in.

You can always use someone else's business card. In fact, some fancy computer work with a handy laser printer can now produce convincing business cards with the click of the print button. In fact, I'm amazed how many times my own business card has been used as my golden ticket into a party.

One tried and true trick is to execute the bum's rush. Just walk in with a large group as if you know exactly what you are doing. If caught, just simply point way up into the crowd, too far to see and declare, "I'm with them." Wave and act convincing. Never fails.

And heck, if all else fails, there's always, the back door. Yes, the back door—this is not a movie cliché, I have actually used it to gain entry. Sure, you'll be stumbling through the kitchen, but *you're in baby!* Sometimes restrooms will have windows and those can be easily accessed from the outside. If you know of a great party that you must attend, it's best to do a little reconnaissance and check out the place first. Heck, you may even make a few new friends in the kitchen.

10 Lines to Use When Crashing a Party

No invite, not on the list, no problem! These lines, if delivered correctly, will guarantee you entry into any party.

1. "I left my invite at the hotel, but here's my card." If you're not on the list, say: "But I DID RSVP. Is it okay if I just wait over here?" They won't make you wait. You're already taking up room in the lobby. There's a good chance that they may have made a mistake and since you might be someone really important, they'll flag you in. It happens to me all the time.

2. "Karen put me on the list." There's always a Karen in every crowd. Try other common names like Mike, Bob, Harvey, John, Geoff or Cassian.

3. "I left my cellular phone in there." You can also say that you left your coat, purse, address book, whatever.

4. "I was the one that got stuck parking the car. I have to tell my ride I can't get in."

5. "I need to use the phone."

6. "I'm scouting the venue for a possible event location for a party we want to put on, I'm just observing. Is that okay?"

7. "I need to use the bathroom. Really baaaaaad." Rarely works for guys, never fails for women.

8. "I am with the press." Guaranteed to work even better when you feign a French accent. People dig a French accent. Or a British accent, if you are so inclined. Publicists can't risk offending the press. Be sure to invent some phony magazine or overseas newspaper to represent. And remember, if you go for the French accent thing, your English must be really bad. The less they understand you, the better your chances are at walking in the entrance.

9. WARNING, ADVANCED SKILLS ONLY: Casually lean over, without letting the person see you, glance at the list and pick out a name. Try to select one that is not checked off. Then say: "I'm the plus one with _____. I have to meet him/her here."

10. WARNING, VERY ADVANCED SKILLS ONLY: "Hi, I'm Jesse Damon. Matt Damon's brother? I'm supposed to meet him here."

The famous always get into parties, but you're not famous. So, who's to say that Matt Damon doesn't have some less attractive brother named Jesse? He might, maybe they're step-brothers, who knows. This line has actually worked for me. Celebrities are like royalty and publicists never want to offend a celebrity. Just be sure the celebrity you intend to impersonate as a distant relative is not actually going to attend. If they were there, it would be bad. To say the least. You may find yourself escorted to the VIP lounge being introduced to other celebrity folk.

So go ahead, pose as Parker Posey's cousin or Steve Buscemi's step-brother, why not? This is also only recommended as a last ditch effort to get into a really exclusive party since there could very well be repercussions when using this method. Remember, I warned you about this one.

I have many other lines that I use, but I can't give away all my secrets. And remember, I'm a master, so for me it's easy—but practice makes perfect. In fact, this time next year, these lines will be useless, so be creative and come up with your own. Generally, any plausible excuse delivered with a straight face, in a polite manner, should get you in.

PUTTiNG ON A SUCCESSFUL PARTY

Create Buzz and Leave Them Talking

Nothing helps create buzz for a film better than a party. (Nothing except, well, maybe a really good film.) The most successful parties are the ones that are impossible to get into. Even as you hand your party passes to friends or associates, make sure to let them know, "This is my last pass, it's going to be really tough to get in so show up early. I can't guarantee you'll make it in, but you can try."

Of course, this statement is repeated to every single person you hand the pass to which will guarantee that your party becomes a "must attend event." It's as if you are giving each person a challenge and they will rise to the occasion. The harder it is to get in, the more they will want to go.

There are certainly different opinions about what makes a great party. If you really want them to leave happy, your party must live up to the following:

1. **Make everyone RSVP.** This gives you an idea of how many will attend. The harsh reality is that 50 percent or more of those who do RSVP will NOT show up. However, those people who choose to skip your party will be offset by the party crashers, friends and press who decide to just "show up."
2. **Hold the party at a venue that you know is too small for the number of people showing up.** If you leave at least some people at the door, it's considered a party worth getting into. If it doesn't present some challenge, if it's not at least somewhat overbooked, then it's not considered a hot party.
3. **Open bar, free food.** Another unfortunate reality is that if you charge for drinks and food or use some annoying "ticket" system, you'll only piss people off. Keep the free drinks flowing and let people know when it's last call.
4. **Avoid loud music or bands.** It's hard to have conversations with any type or distraction; music set to the max is the worst.

5. **Keep any speeches really short and funny.** Most "speeches" or "announcements" given at party gatherings only serve to stop the party cold. In most cases, this is when the walk-outs begin. Start any speech about a half-hour before the scheduled end of the party, keep it less than three minutes, give thank yous, tell a joke and then encourage people to attend your screening. That's it. Otherwise, you can kill your own party.

6. **Send 'em home with something for free.** A goodie bag is always great. The bag should contain some type of useful freebie that advertises your film. A T-shirt, soundtrack CD, poster or some useful item like lip balm in cold climates or suntan lotion in warm climates works wonders.

7. **Invite famous people.** Yeah, they can be a distraction, but the fact that they showed up means something. I know, I think it's lame too, but that's reality. (See Appendix for a list of people you must invite to your party.)

8. **Do something different.** The party for the film *20 Dates* required that each male and female wear a badge with a number. The number corresponded with a male or female partner that partygoers were "required" to meet up with and ask a series of questions. The questions were typical of what one might ask on a date. It may sound stupid but it was a load of fun and people talked about this party afterwards. I have always wanted to go to a film festival party with a carnival dunking booth. You know, one of those ones that people throw baseballs at so that the person is "dunked" in a vat of cold water. It would be cool to see world-famous critics or movie actors in that dunk tank. Well, that's just my idea, but anything you do that is unique will get attention. Having your friend's band play will not help and is really not recommended.

SECTION 3
STORIES FROM THE FRONT LINES

"You have to be confident to the point
of arrogance to even think that you
can make a movie that people are
going to want to see."

—Lance Mungia, filmmaker, *Six String Samurai*

THE VOICES OF EXPERIENCE

I've interviewed countless filmmakers at festivals and most of the interviews turn out badly—they're just incredibly lame and boring to read. In fact, I don't think I've ever gotten a good interview at a film festival. I suspect it's because the subject is painfully aware that they are being interviewed for a magazine, newspaper, television, whatever, so they immediately launch into "spin mode." They talk nice about the producer, nice about the director, nice about the actors, nice about the festival, heck, everyone is nice. You'd think that these interview subjects had just consumed some type of happy drug! (In some cases, they actually have.) The truth is that they are merely doing the right thing and being political. They don't want to say anything that might offend or piss someone off and hurt their chances of getting a deal, winning the prize or launching their career.

The subjects that I've gathered for this section were NOT interviewed at film festivals. They each take a truthful, and sometimes painful, look at their experience. What you are about to read are less interviews and more like confessionals—each person offering a detailed account of their triumphs and their failures.

I have carefully selected interview subjects who would avoid politics and offer useful information to filmmakers and festival-goers. These interviewees comprise the best and the brightest in independent film. Each person delivers the real deal—hard information, free of polite spin.

The filmmakers interviewed here have created a diverse range of films; to a bloody flick about fast-talking used car salesmen, to a Gen-X drama about losing one's virginity, to a twentysomething drama, to a short film about obsessive love, to a mockumentary about the making of a film to a narrative feature about a washed-up child star. The movies are clearly diverse and the experiences of each filmmaker are even more so. Each of these filmmakers represents the numerous paths a filmmaker can take when seeking success through a film festival. These myriad paths include:

- Submit to Sundance, make it into Sundance, screen at Sundance, sell film for theatrical distribution.
- Submit to Sundance, make it into Sundance, screen at Sundance, film DOES NOT sell to distributor, filmmaker chooses to self-distribute movie.
- Rejected from Sundance, make it into Slamdance, sell film for theatrical distribution.
- Rejected from Sundance, rejected from Slamdance, start rival underground film festival to screen film in Park City.
- Rejected from Sundance, rejected from Slamdance, become a hit on the international film festival circuit.
- Rejected from Sundance, rejected from Slamdance, rejected from almost every festival, go home empty, but filled with hard lessons.

There are certainly more roads than those previously mentioned and new ones that filmmakers will invent for themselves out of necessity. Read these interviews for inspiration, entertainment and enlightenment, but most of all, learn from their experiences.

QUESTIONS AND ANSWERS

After the screening of your film, you are expected to do a quick dog and pony show and answer some questions from the audience. This is your opportunity to show some personality and potentially win some points. This is also, much like an important speech delivered by a politician, a way to win people over to your cause. There's not much to say about the "Q&A" as it is called, except the best advice is to be prepared, be genuine, be honest, tell some funny stories and anecdotes and keep your ego in check. Be gracious. Have a little humility. You may be the "filmmaker" up front doing the Q&A, but the reality is that there are at least a hundred or more people behind you that helped make the movie possible. Giving some type of acknowledgment on stage, goes a long way toward earning the respect of the audience.

As for any feelings about being nervous when speaking in front of a group, that old trick about picturing the audience naked really works, just don't let it distract you. There are some typical questions you can expect to hear at almost every Q&A, so be prepared to answer any of these:

- How much was the budget?
- How long did it take to shoot?
- Is the film autobiographical?
- Where did you find that actor?
- How did you get the money?
- Where did you get the idea for your film?
- What does the title mean?
- What kind of film did you use?
- How did you shoot that one scene?
- Who are your influences?
- Where did you shoot your film?
- What's the film about?
- What's the film *really* about?
- Do you have another film in mind?

The answers to these questions should be easy as you have struggled to make your film and you know all of this. Keep the answers short, don't meander and don't play politics—answer the question asked.

Don't fret about money questions, most audiences just don't know any better. The last thing you want to do is reveal the actual budget for your picture. Even if you do give a specific number, people will think you are either naïve or lying—so either way, they won't believe you. Just be vague and say, "Just below $10 million."

THE FiLMMAKERS

ARTHUR BORMAN, Filmmaker

Arthur Borman, the most eligible bachelor on the indie film scene.

Arthur Borman moved to Los Angeles from Michigan in 1985 to study film at UCLA. As a student, he was a production assistant for Peter Guber, Roger Corman, Ed Pressman, and Cannon Films. Borman was also a P.A. (with screen credit) on some of Hollywood's biggest bombs: *He-Man: Masters of the Universe, Problem Child 2* and *Leaving Normal*.

While at UCLA, Borman directed a short film entitled *The Udderbuddies,* which won the UCLA Spotlight Award (an award to the best student films of the year), as well as was nominated regionally for a student Academy Award. Following school, he did a Public Service Announcement campaign for women with AIDS, as well as some music videos for some pretty lame bands.

Borman's first feature, ...*And God Spoke,* was a hit at the Sundance Film Festival where it played to packed audiences at midnight showings. The mockumentary about a group of filmmakers attempts to make a movie about the Bible went on to a successful run on the festival circuit. Borman then landed a deal for his film at LIVE Entertainment which distributed it theatrically and on video. Borman candidly explains how he did it.

How did the idea for ...And God Spoke *emerge?*

I got so sick and tired of working on crap that I moved to Chicago where my brother, Mark, was living. It was there that I met Richard Raddon (he was a PA for John Hughes) and it was also there that I got the idea for ...*And God Spoke.*

Based on a lot of the miserable experiences I had as a PA on big budget flops, I decided to make a film about making a big budget flop. ...*And God Spoke* was the result.

However, the motivation to actually make the movie, instead of just talking about it, came from a visit to the Sundance Film Festival in January '93. For some reason, that was the year of the twentysomething filmmaker. There was Rob Weiss with *Amongst Friends*, Jennifer Lynch with *Boxing Helena*, Robert Rodriguez with *El Mariachi*, and my friend Bryan Singer with *Public Access*. I stayed on Rich Raddon's floor (he was a volunteer for the festival shuttling the film prints). That whole week, we watched as filmmakers our age got a lot of attention for these "under a million" dollar movies. Bryan also won the grand prize with his film. It was there that Rich Raddon and I vowed that we would be at Sundance the following year with a movie of our own.

How did you raise the money?

With my struggling writer buddy Greg Malins (who is now a Co-Executive Producer of TV's *Friends*), we wrote a draft that ultimately served as a blue print for a lot of improv comedy.

My brother and I put together a business plan and went to Miami, Florida to raise money. Eventually we found two "investors;" a couple of early retiree Wall Street playboys who drove Ferraris, owned yachts, and practically lived at strip clubs. They gave us about one weekend of sports gambling winnings and with that, we had our entire $250,000 budget.

How did the production begin?

We set up office at Raleigh Studios and shot the movie over three weeks in May. The biggest names we had at the time were Soupy Sales, Eve Plumb, and Lou Ferrigno; today our other actors, like Andy Dick and Chris Kattan, are considered more famous.

At one point, we wanted to get a famous celebrity director to be in a scene. My casting director Maryclaire Sweeters suggested Quentin Tarantino. I refused. I said I wanted someone famous. (All Quentin had done at the time was *Reservoir Dogs*, and he wasn't a household name yet). I said, "Find me someone who's face we'll recognize immediately, like John Landis." I wound up cutting the scene all together.

How did you go about getting your film into festivals?

Cameraman Lee Daniel *(Slacker, Dazed and Confused)* shot the film. Editor Wendey Stanzler *(Roger and Me)* cut it. At some point, we sent a rough cut off to the Toronto International Film Festival. A few weeks later, we got a fax from Toronto saying we were in. I wasn't even that excited, because I didn't know what it meant. Our goal was to get it into Sundance, so we didn't take Toronto too seriously at first. Really, we had no idea that Toronto was a major film festival and should be taken seriously. We also hadn't finished the film yet, and put most of our energies toward getting it done.

So, like most filmmakers, you went into this fairly naïve.

When we got accepted into the Toronto Film Festival, we knew almost nothing. The only thing we did know was that we shouldn't go alone; we knew a name...John Pierson. We called him, introduced ourselves, and sent our film. He called about a week later to say he couldn't take our film on because he already had a similar "film about filmmaking" called *My Life's in Turnaround*. He did, however, recommend a lawyer named John Sloss. Eventually John became our lawyer/sales rep.

How did you prepare for your festival debut?

When we got accepted into the Toronto Festival, we didn't understand that we needed a publicist. Instead, we spent our money on a poster, and making buttons to pin on people's shirts. We didn't understand that we needed press screenings to get critics to review the film. In fact, we never had a press screening.

My brother and Rich Raddon went to Toronto a few days early, while I worked with the film lab to get the print finished in time. I guess the Toronto press office took pity on us for not having a publicist, because they personally started spreading the word about our film.

They did a hell of a job, because by the time I arrived in Toronto with the print, we had interviews lined up.

So, you were really naïve!

If I had any idea of the position I was in or what was about to happen to me, I would have been better prepared!! I would have had a script that I wanted to make as a follow up. I would have had a publicist to market me as a "flavor of the month." I would have had all my snappy answers for the Q&A ready. Instead, I just went in blind. Big mistake. Let me repeat that. BIG MISTAKE!!

How did that first screening go?

We had our screening to a sold out room of 800. The film played huge. If you've ever been to a film festival and seen an audience have a love affair with the movie screen, you know what I mean.

During the Q&A I brought up the two lead actors, Michael Riley and Stephen Rappaport, and the audience went nuts. People asked how I got Soupy Sales in the film. I said, "Soupy wasn't that hard to get." (That quote later made the *New York Daily News,* and Soupy read it. *Ouch!*)

Did you work the festival scene?

What happened in the three days following my first screening was my fifteen minutes of fame. I went to parties, I met celebrities, I met critics, I met distributors, I met agents, I met studio executives. I was swarmed by filmgoers, filmmakers, and film fans. People even got my autograph and took pictures with me.

Within hours, I had ICM demanding we meet for coffee. I had Harvey Weinstein demanding a private showing. I had *TIME* Magazine looking to do a story. I had Alliance International in Canada throwing out numbers for an advance in the hundreds of thousands. I had drinks with Richard Linklater and Michael Moore. I had hot women hitting on me, and grabbing my leg under the dinner table. I was being touted as a shoo-in for Sundance.

How did you handle the attention?

Was I thinking about how to capitalize on this excitement? No. I was thinking about some tiny glitch on the film print that I had to fix. I was thinking about some line of dialogue that I mixed too softly—I was thinking the wrong things.

By the second screening, we had a massive overflow. The buzz was happening. John Sloss showed me every distributor in the room and said if they hadn't seen the film yet, they weren't gonna miss it now. The film played well again, and the Q&A had the exact same questions. I gave the exact same answers.

When we left the film festival, a lot of the distributors decided to take a "wait-and-see" attitude. The reviews were pretty good. Most magazines and newspapers included us in their summary articles, calling our film one of the big discoveries, but we never got an official offer on the sale of the film.

It was also soon after that we were told we could screen as at Sundance. To me, that was the crowning achievement. Rich Raddon and I said we'd be back in a year with a film, and we were. If we could make the same magic happen in Sundance that we had in Toronto, we were sure to sell our film there.

How did you get ready for Sundance?

Again, I went to the film festival unprepared. I had no new script ready to shoot, and no publicist. We did, however, have a six foot stand up cut out (a "standee") of *God* which we displayed in theater lobbies.

We expected the same excitement we got in Toronto. What we didn't anticipate was that we were considered yesterday's news. You see, once you've been to another film festival, you're considered old news. Even distributors who hadn't seen our film were no longer interested because if we weren't bought by now, they assumed we must not be worthwhile.

Also, we were now competing with a whole new crop of fresh discoveries, and there were so many. Bought at Sundance that year was *Go Fish* and *Clerks* (both sold by John Pierson), *Hoop Dreams* (sold by John Sloss), and *Spanking the Monkey.*

> "Within hours, I had ICM demanding we meet for coffee. I had Harvey Weinstein demanding a private showing. I had *TIME Magazine* looking to do a story. I had hot women hitting on me, and grabbing my leg under the dinner table."

Though we had good screenings at Sundance, we didn't have anyone important in the room. They were off watching *Hoop Dreams* and *Go Fish*. We left Sundance a little depressed, especially when none of the summary articles included us.

Tell me about the post-Sundance whirlwind festival tour?

A few things did come out of Sundance, though. We were invited to almost two dozen other film festivals. Over the next few months, I went to Dallas, Houston, Austin (which we won), Baltimore, St. Louis, Detroit, Orlando, Chicago, New York, etc.

Also, we went international. Prior to *…And God Spoke,* I had never left North America. Thanks to *…And God Spoke,* I was in France, Brazil and Australia within a two month span, and all expenses paid. We were also invited to Singapore, Italy, South Africa, and Russia.

How did the film get picked up for distribution?

We also picked up a foreign sales agent, Stranger Than Fiction, who took our film to the Cannes Market. My producers and I decided to go with them and help drum up interest in our film. It was also in Cannes that we would finally sell our film to North America.

It had been months since the Sundance Festival, and we were starting to see the writing on the wall. Our film wasn't going to sell for big bucks. We started getting interest from smaller distributors who said they could take on our film, but for no advance. We decided to turn our attention to foreign sales as a way to off set the "no advance" offers we were getting from North American distributors. In the end, we decided that if we were gonna take a loss, than at least let's get a distributor to get us maximum exposure.

That year at Cannes, Quentin Tarantino won the grand prize with *Pulp Fiction*. Though we were in the market and not the festival, we did see him hanging around one late night in a hotel bar. I still didn't recognize him.

While in France, we got a call from LIVE Entertainment. LIVE was mostly known for home video, but recently was getting back into theatrical distribution. We sent LIVE a video tape, assuming they were interested in picking up home video rights. What followed was an act of God. When we finally sat down at the meeting in the hotel bar, LIVE Entertainment made an offer to buy our film for theatrical distribution, and even made an advance offer! We closed the deal before our drinks arrived. Perhaps LIVE didn't know

BORMAN'S ADVICE AND LESSONS

1. Have a publicist.
2. Have a second project.
3. Make a good film, something that people want to see after sitting through three other films.
4. Have a sales rep and/or lawyer who knows what they're doing.
5. Remember the name and face of every person you meet.
6. Pray for good luck, good screening times and good weather.
7. Ask yourself how your personality fits your film and sell yourself as the extension of that film. Examples:
   - Kevin Smith worked in a convenience store and made a film about convenience store life.
   - Ed Burns basically plays himself in all of his films.
   - After meeting Todd Solondz, you know how he understood the pain of being a teenage nerd.
8. Filmmaking is an art, but film festivals are a business.
9. Be nice to everyone because you will see them again and again.
10. Flirt with everyone at a film festival (male or female, single or married). You don't have to act on it, but flirting is like a secret password for getting ahead at festivals.

we were yesterday's news, or perhaps they really believed in the film. Either way, we were LIVE's first theatrical release under their new regime. As we flew home back to Los Angeles, we marveled at how we had gone from accepting a loss to turning a profit in five minutes.

What happened when the film was released?
It tanked.

Arthur Borman maintains a web site about his films at www.directorscut.com.

Writer/director Joe Carnahan (left) and actor/producer Dan Leis at the IFFM where they made a remarkable impression, which helped get them into Sundance.

JOE CARNAHAN, Filmmaker

Joe Carnahan's debut feature film, *Blood, Guts, Bullets & Octane (BGB&O),* tells a gruesome tale of fast-talking used car salesmen who stumble upon a car wanted by every hit man in the country. Carnahan cast himself as one of the motor-mouthed car salesmen, and upon meeting him you have to agree with his decision. He's more than "high-energy," this guy spits words out like bullets from a machine gun. *BGB&O* played the midnight slot at the 1998 Sundance Film Festival and later sealed a distribution deal with Lion's Gate. Currently, Carnahan's film is being developed into a television series for NBC.

Carnahan was working at a tiny local television station, struggling at a nowhere job, shooting his film on weekends. The movie was shot for less than $8,000. He did all of that while balancing the responsibilities of family life with a wife and two kids! The gutsy filmmaker just woke up and decided to do it and the result is a fast-paced debut oozing with creativity.

How does a filmmaker successfully apply to Sundance and gain acceptance?
Network like a sonofabitch. Anybody who believes that simply
mailing in a VHS tape and a check for forty bucks will guarantee
democratic privilege in the judging process is completely deluded.
Don't be afraid to approach people like Geoff Gilmore or John Cooper or any of the programming staff if you see them at a festival or
some other indie gathering. We have a tendency to deify these people
and put them on a pedestal. Keep in mind a very basic precept—
without the films to make the festivals, these people would be out
of work. So strap on the same set of balls you used when you broke
your ass for months on end to make your film in the first place;
walk up to them and introduce yourself. If you fancy yourself the
shy, inhibited, introspective type, let me tell you, that will get you
about as far as the front door.

If you want to GETYOURFILMINFESTIVALS, get proactive
about it. Now. Case in point, Sarah Jacobson—she's a one-woman
marketing machine. Her film (*Mary Jane's Not A Virgin Anymore*)
might not have been picked up, but you'd be hard-pressed to find
somebody on the festival circuit that doesn't know who she is. And
that's it right there, kids, that's what it's all about. Sarah, through her
own force of will and undaunted hustle, is in a position to go out and
make more films and find people to make those films with her. It all
boils down to bare bones, dogged determination.

How did you find out you were in Sundance?
I was in the trenches, pulling an all night edit since we were still
doing our AVID cut for the lab. My wife called in a frenzy, saying
John Cooper had just called. I called, and Cooper confirmed that
BGB&O was in.

It sounds flippant as all hell, but I had a pretty good idea we were
already in. Don't get me wrong; there was a tremendous sense of re-
lief, because after month upon month of aimless speculation and second guessing, our wish came true. Even though almost nine months
earlier, our producer's rep, the dazzling, debonair, Patrick Lynn, had
a fleeting confab with Geoff Gilmore in Toronto, and Geoff basically
told Patrick that he intended to program the film. Even knowing that,
we couldn't relax until we got "real" confirmation. Usually the festival programmers, particularly in Sundance, are notoriously tight-
lipped about their line-up. Nothing short of the rack and razor blades
around the ear can pry that priceless inside skinny from the staff.

What other festivals did you apply to?

Toronto tossed us very early on, and that was tough to swallow, but after Sundance, we were carpet-bombed with fest invites. My favorite was Berlin, hands down. It is the most structurally sound festival on the face of the planet. You could drop D-Day on that festival and it will still run as smooth as a tuned engine. Next Wave films, run by the esteemed prince of indie print, Peter Broderick, was our partner in crime since they kicked in, along with IFC/BRAVO, the necessary monies to finish the film in 35mm. They were really instrumental in landing a lot of festival attention.

Were you concerned about applying to other festivals before you got word from Sundance?

No. Primarily because I believe that it is fundamentally inane to put that much into a single film festival, even the great and almighty Sundance. Everybody says how Sundance frowns on playing other festivals before you play theirs. While there is no arguing a preference for North American premieres and debuts in the festival, there were plenty of films that had played previously in Toronto and other big festivals prior to their Sundance dates. If your film is good enough, it's not going to get ignored.

How did you prepare for your first Sundance screening?

I didn't have a lot of time considering that the sound mix was still being done five days prior to our screening. I just sat around contemplating the disaster that would ensue if the print didn't arrive on time. When it did, I thought it was only about seventy percent of what the film was in my original straight-to-video cut. Basically, I just stuck with my family and played it very low key in Park City. The showing didn't end up starting until almost one in the morning, which I felt hurt us even more than the poor print quality. In the end, I just bit the bullet and trusted in the fact that key people (Lion's Gate and more importantly, Mark Urman) had viewed my original version of the film and were already big fans.

What did you do to hype your film at Sundance?

The same way we hyped it everywhere else. We gathered en masse and marched through the streets of Park City like a Fascist color parade—wearing parkas emblazoned with the film's logo, shoving it in everybody's face, creating a maelstrom of hype—getting that critical "buzz" going early and all the rest of that requisite catchphrase stuff.

I openly despise and deplore ham-handed marketing techniques; the notion of jamming something down people's throats ad nauseum. Unfortunately, the film business doesn't give you the option of subtlety. Sometimes you have to forsake your better judgment and basic common decency and just get it done…hawking your wares come hell or high water. Now, I'm not saying run up, jump on Harvey Weinstein's back and blast your film's synopsis in his ear with a bullhorn; I *am* saying stop just short of that.

Did you hire a publicist?

The PR firm of Dennis Davidson & Associates and the wonderful Nancy Willen and Melinda Hovee cut us an incredible rate after repping the film gratis for almost five months. The fee they ended up collecting from us was a pretty pitiful per diem considering the tremendous effort they put behind publicizing it.

"So strap on the same set of balls you used when you broke your ass for months on end to make your film in the first place; walk up to them and introduce yourself."

We publicized it until we were pretty sure everyone was so sick and tired of us that they'd watch the film, just to have a reason to ridicule us. Fortunately, it worked out for the best and people really dug the flick. In the end, when your film hits the street it had better deliver; particularly if you've been bragging that it cost less than eight grand to put in the can. When the lights go down, it's gutcheck time. I can't stress that enough: you can come down on people with the trumpet of God, if the film can't back your claim, scuttle the ship, the ride's over.

What would you have done differently in preparing for your film's debut?

I would've gotten a much earlier jump on the extensive post-production work that had to be done. This is the kind of thing you don't want to delay. Unfortunately, my lawyer and other lawyers were off doing their "lawyering." A process requiring you to sit on your hands for weeks at a time, waiting for contractual crap to clear and a bunch of other fascinating bits of tedium that have miraculously little to do with filmmaking. I really can't say I would have changed a thing, because the PR machine we were able to put together at that point, as well as Amy Taubin's glowing review in *The Village Voice,* really put everything on track.

How can other filmmakers create the much-needed hype for their own films?
Number one, get your film into a forum where it can be shown on a
screen. This means a place like the Independent Feature Film Market
(IFFM), held annually in New York. This is the single best place to
develop a platform for your film. They have a marvelous staff of people
who will really go the distance for you if they believe in your work. I
missed the deadline for the '97 IFFM by more than a month, but
because they really believed in the film, they found me a slot. This
was primarily the work of two fabulous souls, Milton Tabbot and
Sharon Sklar. Once you get there, adopt a style that suits your personal preference and acts in the movie's best interest. You can be obnoxious, overbearing and pushy in a very subtle, effective way if you
tailor your marketing plan to your strengths as well as your shortcomings. If you don't do well speaking to other people, or you stumble
or stutter or stammer or whatever, find someone in your group who
DOESNOTDOTHESETHINGS! Make them the point person for
public relations. Understand that this is a temporary arrangement
since at some point, you will be required, nay, *obligated*, to speak on
behalf of your work because you are the filmmaker. So beat back the
bashfuls and get verbal.

Get as many press people on board as possible. If you have some
outside connection or some way of getting a tape to a local critic or
movie reviewer or features editor, get it to them. For me, two people
were absolutely instrumental early on: Mark Ebner, formally of *Spy*
Magazine and Lisa Derrick from *New Times LA*. I met them both online and they agreed to view the tape; both were jazzed about the
film's prospects. They provided gutsy praise and some stellar copy
for the one sheet. I owe them both a tremendous debt since it was
their initial reviews that paved the way for Amy Taubin's and others.
So far, I have yet to meet Lisa in person, and it just goes to show you,
you don't have to live next door to these people to get them your film.

Understand that there are tremendously creative people out there
with a lot riding on a movie. This is not a normally cheap endeavor
and I know people that have gone several hundred thousand dollars
in debt and have seen bupkes on their return. These are the relentless,
competitive types you will encounter and are forced to compete
against. At IFFM in '97, I put my most menacing actor, Hugh
McChord, in the lobby of the Angelika and taped a huge poster-sized
standee for our film to the table. This was something that was frowned

upon by the theater's management, but since Hugh stands about 6'3"
and goes upwards of 240 lbs., nobody was willing to say anything and
with good reason; this guy never smiled once and when you walked
in, your eye immediately went to him. It worked, and two days after
our screening, we were the talk of the market. I'm not condoning an-
tisocial behavior or implied physical violence as viable marketing tools,
but if you've got the bulk, use it. I had six guys, averaging six feet in
height, walking around NY with matching T-shirts and hats promoting the film. We may have looked like idiot tourists, but the message
got across. Since no one wanted to risk a public beating by what appeared to be a goon squad, snide comments were minimal.

Just don't be afraid. Don't shy away from contact and do what
you need to do to make your point. There are thousands of filmmakers out there willing to do the necessary things to sell their film. Set
yourself apart as much as possible, do the unusual and the extreme
and ignore the whispers.

Were you nervous at the first screening?

I was more agitated than nervous because I knew the audience was
not going to be seeing the film the way I intended. I sat out in the hall
outside the Park City library looking at my six-month-old son and
hoping the fucking roof wouldn't fall in on me and my career. I dealt
with it by staying as loose as I could and joking with my brother Matt
who, like the best of the bomb squad, can always take the tension off
and clip the right wires. Bob Hawk, my hero, introduced the film and
that helped, too. Bob was a huge fan and his high praise for the film
went miles toward calming me down and helping me focus.

What did you learn from that first screening?

That I had homicidal impulses where sound designers are concerned.
That the library is just that, a library, and therefore not acoustically
kind. And that what I did in two months I should have stretched over
six months. And finally, that films should never start after midnight
unless they have "Rocky," "Horror" or "Picture Show" in the title.

What did you do to get acquisition executives into your screenings?

That was more Patrick Lynn's doing. He, in concert with my wonderful agent Neil Friedman, drummed up early support for the film,
months before the festival. We already had an idea that Lion's Gate
was going to come on strong—which was great since most in the
business believe that Lion's Gate will surpass October Films as the

legitimate heir to the Miramax throne. Lion's Gate also has a history of brilliantly handling small films like *The Daytrippers* and *The Pillow Book,* so this was a thrilling proposition for me.

Who negotiated the deal?

Neil Friedman primarily, who is truly a brilliant man. He and Patrick worked the seams to get me the best possible deal. Lion's Gate put the offer on the table one week after Sundance.

What did you look for in the deal?

A company that I knew could put the film in play, which Lion's Gate can so clearly do. Also, I wanted to work with guys like Mark Urman and Tom Ortenberg at a young company that is clearly going places. This was as exciting as anything else since we knew how much Mark loved the film and how doggedly he would push it. They gave us a great back end deal and a pretty substantial advance, so I was ecstatic.

The deal went for a modest six figure sum with great ancillary perks. Like $50,000 bumps as the film surpassed certain gross revenues. Remember, when a company, particularly one as upstart as Lion's Gate, takes a flyer on a $7,300 film, there ain't much they can do wrong as it pertains to a relationship with their filmmakers. They even assumed the costly "Errors & Omissions" insurance and agreed to pay for the MPAA rating because they knew how little money we had. Those expenses alone more than doubled the film's original budget.

Any advice on getting the distribution deal?

Yeah—don't show the film to ANYBODY who has anything to do with acquisitions. It's best that if distributors are going to see your film, they all see it at the same time. It's what is known as an "Acquisitions Screening" and it's done all the time in LA. Press is one thing— you need that. That's a risk you have to assume, try and preface all conversations with potential reviewers with the request that they not show the tape around. They're going to do it anyway, but you still want to try to contain it. When you send your film in to an agency, they will almost immediately make a copies of the film if they like it. They do this almost as a reflex, so at some point it's really out of your hands as to who is seeing your film. But, do your best to contain it early. In my own experience, it came to light that a rather powerful, prominent indie agent, one who reps some pretty big names, got a hold of my tape, liked it, then without permission, passed it on to some distribution companies. He may have thought he was doing me a favor, but he wasn't and he should have known better. Guard your film. I sent mine out to only three people at the outset. One of them, Patrick Lynn, went on to rep my film. I sent my fourth out to DDA, which gave the copy to Neil Friedman, and he instantly became my agent. From that standpoint, I was fortunate.

Any advice on handling press?

Yeah, watch your ass…and keep that switchblade taped to your ankle. Understand that the people interviewing you can put whatever spin on whatever word of yours they choose. I got interviewed by this punk kid from *Variety* and thought I was coming off humble, gregarious and generally happy to be there. What he wrote down and more importantly, put in print, made me look like a colossal asshole and consequently blew my whole notion of "objective" journalism sky high. Press people want three things: funny shit or semi-scandalous shit or shit that makes you look like you were eating Top Ramen noodles and living in a shoe box prior to making your debut film. That's it. Look at most print media about festivals and its participants and you'll find those tenets are absolutely true. You can be all bright eyed and bushy tailed so long as your answers aren't.

How were you, as the filmmaker, expected to handle supporting the release of the film?

I think, with the incredible proliferation of independent films, anything you can do to support your film is going to help. I will do print interviews, TV, radio, everything. In the last four months, a slew of Sundance films have opened theatrically and thoroughly tanked. Movies like *Hurricane Streets* and *TwentyFourSeven* and fell right off the radar…why? I think a certain amount of the blame falls on the companies releasing them—they don't aggressively go after the indie filmgoer. As advertising goes, what makes these filmgoers any less susceptible to the same kind of sharp, catchy, go-for-broke ballistics utilized by big studio marketing mavens?

Can you describe the whirlwind film festival tour?

I'm going to Edinburgh, Scotland, I took the film out of Seattle because it still wasn't ready to screen. I think once you've played Sundance, it's a two-way street. Some people immediately want the film, others rebel against it because it's seen some success elsewhere. It helps to know which ones are the biggies and that's a very simple trio of festivals. Sundance, Toronto and Telluride are probably the highest profile. New York, The Hamptons and Seattle are definitely coming into their own.

Initially the '97 IFFM was mind-blowing, because that's where everything took flight. But festival-wise, in the purest sense of the word, I would say, hands down, Berlin. The rest of the festival world should take a page from their book, because those people run a film festival like nobody's business. The Berlin people are top drawer and their festival has to be one of the most taut, finely tuned events in the world.

MARK EDGINGTON, Short Filmmaker

The unfortunate reality about short films is that most of them are just not very good. Often short filmmakers try to follow an abbreviated three act feature film structure and that doesn't always work. In general, the most common problem short films suffer from is that they are simply not short enough. The audience watching your short probably did not show up expecting to see it and if it runs just a tad too long, it can be death. However, a great short film that entertains, tells a quick, compelling story and conveys some personality and style, can work wonders for a filmmaker starting out. One such filmmaker is Mark Edgington.

Edgington attended Yale and is a graduate of NYU Film School, where his thesis film, *The Death of Mr. Frick & Other Hardships* (1992), won numerous prizes and was featured at over 30 film festivals around the world.

Edgington's most recent short film, *Anna in the Sky,* premiered at the 1997 Sundance Film Festival in Park City, Utah. *Anna In The Sky* is a witty, visually lush story about a young man's obsession with his former lover, set against a background of gritty cityscapes and voodoo incantations. It's also damn funny. The 10 minute short has screened at more than 60 film festivals worldwide. While most short filmmakers end up with little more than a pat on the back, Edgington's shorts have actually won prize money and gotten distribution deals.

Did you lobby heavily to get into Sundance?

Like many, many other filmmakers, Sundance was the first festival I applied to. Sundance is a bit unique in that many of their submissions are, in fact, unfinished. I sent them an AVID dump of the fine cut, without any sound editing. Still, the sound I did include was in decent shape, and the tape gave a pretty good indication of what the final film would be. I would guess that at least half of the films they accept are submitted in unfinished form. I thinks it's probably unwise to submit an unfinished film to any festival other than Sundance.

I think it's essential to have a good image to sell your film. The still photograph that you use in your press kit is how the world will know your film. It will be plastered in every festival catalogue that you are in, on every website, etc. I am much more likely to see a movie when I see a great still in a catalogue, than by reading the synopsis. I know that synopses are difficult to write and often don't give a good impression of what the film is really like, whereas the still is really a moment from the film. People will forget your title. But if they see that image enough, they'll begin to make the connection; at least, I do.

So, even though I did not have a sound man, or an assistant director, or wardrobe, or makeup, I did have a still photographer, and I knew in advance the probable images that I would want him to capture. And don't think you can always get a still made from your film negative; it's a nightmare you don't need.

How did you find out you were in?

I had a message on my answering machine saying, "This is Trevor Groth from Sundance; please give me a call." This was actually the day after everyone was supposed to have been notified by, so I had already given up hope.

I pogo-ed in my apartment for about an hour. Then I wondered around on the streets with huge, stupid smile on my face.

What other festivals did you apply to?

Lots. For a short film, festivals are really your main distribution outlet. (This *should not* be the case if you have a feature film.) I basically applied to any festival that had either a) prestige, b) press coverage, c) cash awards, or d) no submission fee. Also any festival that actually approached me, even if I'd never heard of it.

How are short filmmakers treated differently than feature filmmakers?

You have to realize that as a short filmmaker, your status is slightly above that of a festival intern. On very rare occasions, a festival will accord you the same status as that of the feature filmmakers. I had a fabulous experience at the Henri Langlois Festival International de Tours, where the feature, documentary, and short filmmakers were all treated the same: like royalty. Unfortunately, I don't think this festival exists anymore. It's likely that the taxpayers of Tours rebelled.

How did you hype your short film?

I may be wrong, but I think the only way you're going to get people coming to specifically see your short film is by word-of-mouth, or by having been in enough festivals that people recognize your title.

Did you go into the festival with a goal in mind?

Yes—to raise money for a feature. But I made the short mainly because I wanted to make another film; I did not have any illusions that it would lead to a feature. I think I have done about as well as you can hope to do with a short, and it has stirred up almost no interest from feature producers. Except for the film that won the best short prize at Sundance, most of the other filmmakers I know had the same experience in this respect. Still, making a short gives you confidence (hopefully) and it can't hurt when you're trying to strong-arm someone into giving you enough money to make a feature.

> "You have to realize that as a short filmmaker, your status is slightly above that of a festival intern."

How did you prepare for your first screening?

I made a feeble attempt to invite two industry people who were friends-of-friends that I knew would be at Sundance. One of them came to the first screening, which was terminated after the projector chewed up the first three shorts and before my film had screened. With the other person, I traded messages all through Sundance until I finally got him a ticket, and then he got sick that day (along with almost everyone else in Park City) and never saw it. In retrospect, I probably should have saved my energy for the slopes where I would have had a much higher probability of meeting a producer anyway.

What did you do to hype your film?

I made a website that was essentially an internet press kit for my film. I was approached by the Flickerfest International Short Film Festival in Australia as well as the Naples Film Festival on the basis of the website.

I also wrote a Sundance Diary that was published on the web (http://homearts.com/depts/pl/movie/17sundf1.htm). This actually paid for my trip to Sundance ($800 for seven days' reports). Every day at Sundance, I had to go to the press center and file my report over the internet. But once I'd done it, then I could also use this in my press kit.

Did you hire a publicist?

No. Is that even legal for a short film?

What would you have done differently in preparing for your film's debut?

I have to kick myself for dating the end credits on the film "1997." I guess I felt sheepish about dating it 1998 when I was shooting the credits in August 1997, but that's what I should have done. In the end, the film really wasn't done until March 1998.

A short film's life cycle with festivals is directly related to its completion date, so it's important to be recent.

How does a short filmmaker create any hype without getting lost in the maze?

It kind of annoys me when I see a short filmmaker relentlessly and aggressively hyping his/her short. Hyping is probably a necessary evil for features, but for a short it really seems pointless.

What did you learn from that first screening?

There was a stupid John Tesh gag in the film which I almost took out about a dozen times in the editing. When I wrote it, it seemed kind of funny, but every time I saw it after that, it just seemed really stupid. At the first screening, that moment in the film got a huge laugh, and ever since then I've been glad I didn't cut it out.

I also was conscious of how dependent short films are on the other films in the package and was thankful to the Sundance programmers. My film was a melancholy comedy, and following after two serious films and then a very funny short the audience was primed just right for my film.

I cringe when I think of another screening I once had of my previous film—a languorous, meandering film—which followed Alison MacLean's *Kitchen Sink,* a brilliant, sharp, concise masterpiece. I would not wish that slot on anyone.

Were you prepared for the questions from the audience?

At Sundance, there's no Q&A for the short films. At other festivals, it was pretty easy. People are much less likely to attack a short film-maker than a feature filmmaker. Also, your questions are more likely to come from other filmmakers.

I had a nice session at the New York Film Buffs. As far as I can tell, this is an Upper Eastside singles film society, but it was a good setup for a Q&A. Unlike a festival setting, there were no other films going on elsewhere that the audience would be running out to see, and the audience wasn't bleary-eyed from a dayful of screenings. Plus, there was a wine and cheese reception afterwards, so people were happy to spend time at the Q&A.

Can you describe the whirlwind film festival tour?

As a short filmmaker, not many festivals will pay for your plane ticket. However, keep an eye out for any festival with American Airlines as a sponsor; they provided tickets for the British Short Film Festival in London and for the Bermuda International Film Festival.

That said, you have to be judicious about which festivals you decide to attend. I had saved up my vacations in the previous 18 months so that I could attend some festivals in the guise of vacations. Mostly, I would only consider going to a festival that is at least willing to put me up for the time I'm there. If they're not willing to do that, it's a pretty good tip-off that they're not serious about welcoming you.

Could a filmmaker with a really good short film actually make money?

When it comes to prize money: your best bets are the small festivals that are off the radar. I won $1250 dollars from a festival that I'm sure almost no one has ever heard of.

Like most short filmmakers, Mark Edgington hopes to attend his next festival with a feature. Both of his short films are distributed by Jane Balfour Films of London.

SHORT-SIGHTED: HOW SOME FESTIVALS TREAT THEIR SHORT FILMMAKERS
by Mark Edgington

The Sundance Film Festival
It's difficult to have a good time here; you have to really work at it. The industry is the killjoy. As a filmmaker, you're considered a transient (the industry is there year after year). But it was great screening in front of those huge audiences. My advice: hit the slopes when you can, and keep your industry expectations low. I enjoyed slumming it at Slumdance, but unfortunately that noble experiment was not repeated last year.

The Seattle International Film Festival
This is a huge festival, a real smorgasbord if you like world cinema. As a short filmmaker you might feel lonely and unattended to. I went because my parents happened to be in town, and they hadn't seen my film. You get access and guest passes for all the films, and there are lots of parties and dinners if you happen to be in the right place at the right time.

Nantucket Film Festival

This is a serious party festival. Unfortunately, it's also an expensive island, and they don't put you up. I was only there for a day and a half, just long enough to become infatuated with the girl who served me my ice cream cone and who later turned up as a festival volunteer.

The Florida Film Festival

Florida is serious about welcoming its filmmakers. Matthew Curtis was a pro-active festival director, seeking out films from other festivals and encouraging the filmmakers to attend. They put us up for the time we were there. Florida in June is perhaps not the ideal season, but I had a lovely time hanging out, lounging in the Jacuzzi and pool of the local alternative newspaper's film critic.

Woods Hole

One of the best things that came out of Sundance for me was a solid friendship with Matt Ross *(Language of Love)*. We decided it would be fun to go up to Woods Hole, which is on Cape Cod, for our screenings there. Judy Lassiter, the festival director, offered to put us up in her house. Is that accommodating or what? Unfortunately, Matt got pulled into a dubbing session for a feature he was acting in and had to abandon his plans. But I went and enjoyed some quality beach time at the tiny (sold-out) festival. In fact, I think the shorts program I screened there had the highest caliber of films I ever screened with.

British Short Film Festival (London)

This was a lot of fun. I knew many of the American filmmakers who went and was assigned a room with my Sundance buddies Matt Ross and Kris Isaacson *(Man About Town,* which won the prize at Sundance). They also paid for many of the American filmmakers' plane tickets. There were lots of films from all over the world; the festival itself seemed to lack structure, but because there was a solid cadre of American filmmakers, we would always go out en masse anyway (with the Canadians). Strangely, I never really saw any European filmmakers there.

BRiAN FLEMMiNG, Filmmaker and Festival Organizer
(The Slumdance Film Festival)

Brian Flemming is the writer and director of *Hang Your Dog in the Wind*, a feature film comedy which won a Special Jury Prize at the 1997 Florida Film Festival and was an official selection of the 1997 Gen Art, Chicago Underground and Oldenburg (Germany) film festivals. The film has been called "an undiscovered gem" by independent film "guru" John Pierson.

After finishing *Hang Your Dog in the Wind*, Brian introduced himself to the independent film scene with the Slumdance Experience (the offbeat alternative to the Sundance and Slamdance Film Festivals), which he co-founded in the basement of a Park City cookie factory in January of 1997. The festival was designed as a promotional vehicle for the debut of *Hang Your Dog in the Wind* but quickly became a mecca for filmmakers and a significant media event. The festival was covered by *Good Morning America, the Los Angeles Times, Variety, Entertainment Weekly, Wired* and a host of other media outlets.

Brian makes his living in several other creative areas. He works as a story analyst for New Line Cinema, produces satiric segments for John Pierson's Independent Film Channel show *Split Screen* and has written for such magazines as *Spy, Filmmaker* and *Movieline.* In his spare time, Brian plays the trumpet.

Why did you decide to make a feature film?

I reached a point in my life where it was either go to film school or make a film. I chose to make a film. I took a very loosely structured story, cast mostly friends and worked up a script through a rehearsal process. The result is not astounding—it's a smart, amusing film that is nonetheless not terribly commercial or innovative, and it suffers from beginner's mistakes. It did prove to me, however, that I could make a film.

Did you lobby heavily to get into Sundance?

I had no personal contact at Sundance, no "in." Most filmmakers I know who did get into Sundance had a personal contact of some sort, so I suppose it helps. But you still have to have something Sundance will consider a good film.

From applying to other film festivals, I've found that it's best to find some excuse to call—forget to include a press kit, for example, and send it later. That way you can call up just after your package arrives, and chat up someone at the fest: "Hey, did you get my press kit?" Now you have actual contact with a person at the fest, and you have an opportunity to be witty and interesting and make this person think you might have a good film. This person might even be a programmer, especially at a small fest. Even if you have to manufacture it, it definitely helps to have that kind of personal contact—unless you're a pushy asshole, in which case it won't help you at all.

How did you find out you that you were not accepted?

Form letter. It's like being at the track, and the sixty to one shot you bet on doesn't win. You're not surprised, but you're still disappointed. I still have it on my bulletin board. It makes me feel good to look at it, because it was so essential to the birth of Slumdance.

What other festivals did you apply to?

Slamdance—now *that* was a surprising rejection. The film got into Florida, Gen Art, Oldenburg, Chicago Underground and some others, though.

Why did you create Slumdance?

Slumdance was originally created as a promotional vehicle for my feature, *Hang Your Dog in the Wind.* The other founders (most of whom were associated with my film in some way) and I looked at what Slamdance had done and figured we could probably do it, too.

Starting a film festival is similar to making a first feature—it's harder and more expensive than you ever thought it would be. One unexpected twist we encountered, however, is that the people from Sundance actually liked us. I'm sure Robert Redford considered us "parasites" (that's what he called Slamdance in *Interview* magazine), but several high-ranking programmers and others from Sundance came to our closing night party. The volunteers from Sundance were particularly supportive. So, if you're going to start a Park City festival—and why wouldn't you?—I'd advise staying away from the "fuck Sundance" attitude.

How do you select films to show in the festival?

There's a running joke among us that I still haven't seen most of the films that were "accepted" to Slumdance, let alone submitted—and the joke is actually pretty accurate. Via the internet, Slumdance announced a call for entries about two weeks before its opening night, so we did all of our selecting at the same time we were trying to slap the thing together. I was busy with the website, the logistics of leasing the site and putting the thing together, the Park City Chamber of Commerce and talking to the press—there was no way I could watch a single film, let alone fifty or a hundred. So early on I called up Doug Glazer and asked him to be a programmer. He and Keythe Farley then watched the submissions and made the selections. From what I've seen, they did a pretty good job.

In Slumdance, politics was a huge factor in certain cases. If you're Brian Flemming, for example, and you're a co-founder, your film is in. But most of the films in Slumdance were submitted by complete strangers to us and selected based on the taste of the programmers.

"Starting a film festival is similar to making a first feature—it's harder and more expensive than you ever thought it would be."

We put up a "Guide to Slumdance Material" and a detailed entry form on the Slumdance website, which was the entry point for most filmmakers. The goal of the Guide and the entry form was to weed out crappy films and filmmakers who lacked the humor or attitude we wanted.

How do you feel it was successful? Or unsuccessful?

It's hard to judge how "successful" Slumdance was. I can't remember any of us stating a set of goals we wished to achieve. We just thought it would be incredibly fun to go to Park City and set up a film festival in the basement of a cookie factory on Main Street. And simply by doing that, we pretty much did what we set out to do. I wasn't so deluded that I thought I'd end up with distribution for my film or anything.

There were many unexpected perks and goodies, however. First was the press attention. *L.A. Times, Chicago Tribune, Good Morning America, Channel 4* from England, reporters from France, Italy,

Korea—it turned into a press circus, and I have to admit we loved it. At times, everywhere you went in the Slum, you could clown around in front of a TV camera, and most of us did. If Slumdance was anything, it was a publicity stunt, and it was nice that the press played its role so perfectly.

For me, other perks included meeting several people who are important in the indie scene. I think the contacts I made at Slumdance and the reputation I gained for being involved helped enormously when I went on a festival tour in 1997. I'm not sure I would have gotten into the festivals I did without mentioning I co-founded Slumdance on my cover letter to the fests. It helps to have something to make you stand out from the hundreds of other submissions.

A final, and most important, way we were "successful" was in getting audiences to see Slumdance films. Certainly more people came to our parties than to our screenings, but we still had impressive houses, I think, for a film festival with no infrastructure and largely obscure films.

Were you nervous at the screening and if so, how did you deal with it?
I smoked something very powerful, got really paranoid, curled up on a sofa and tried to get this pair of Korean reporters at Slumdance to stop trying to interview me. But they couldn't understand English, and still they were trying interview me. They would ask, "How...you...to...make...movie...here?" And I would say, "Go away, please." They would just smile and nod and jot in their notebooks.

What did you learn from that first screening?
I learned to stop watching my film with audiences. I just can't stand it. When they don't laugh in the right places, I just want to kill myself or them. I don't usually watch my film at screenings anymore.

How did you hype your film?
There's nothing like a splashy underground fest to hype a film. People love a good party, especially with an element of the avant-garde about it. For my film, Slumdance was the "hook" that the press is always looking for in a story—my film alone would have made a boring story: "Twentysomething filmmaker makes black-and-white low-budget film about his twentysomething friends." But add Slumdance to that: "Disgruntled filmmaker creates own Park City fest to compete with Sundance." It's a natural.

So my advice would be, do something like that. If your film lacks a delicious hook, create one.

In addition to co-founding the Slumdance film festival, Brian Flemming authored the event's popular and oft-quoted satiric website, still available at www.slumdance.com.

SARAH JACOBSON, Filmmaker

Sarah Jacobson has been called "San Francisco's bad girl film-maker." Jacobson grew up in Minneapolis and was the only student at Edina High School to be suspended five times *and* graduate with honors. She spent years picking up vagrants and dopers in her 1978 Buick station wagon and working at a slacker-infested art house cinema. Jacobson spent two years at Bard College, where she attended the school's the film program. She moved to San Francisco in 1991 to study with George Kuchar at the San Francisco Art Institute, where she made raunchy feminist comedies.

Sarah Jacobson is the hardest working woman in independent film today. Just ask her mom.

In 1992, she produced and directed the 27-minute black-and-white short *I Was a Teenage Serial Killer,* which became a notorious underground hit. *Serial Killer* won a Certificate of Merit at the Chicago International Film Festival, was named one of the "Top 25 Underground Films You Must See" by *Film Threat Video Guide.*

Sarah founded Station Wagon Productions in 1993 to distribute *Serial Killer* on video. Through Station Wagon, Sarah also publishes *Hardcorn Comic Book,* an internationally-distributed comic compilation featuring some of the brightest talent in San Francisco's underground comic scene.

Mary Jane's Not a Virgin Anymore is Sarah Jacobson's first feature film. The film revolves around high-school senior, Jane, who works at an arthouse movie theater in a midwestern town. Jane is unceremoniously deflowered in a cemetery in the outrageous opening scene. Disenchanted with sex and dating, Jane turns to her co-workers for advice.

The film played the Sundance Film Festival and *did not* receive a coveted distribution deal. However, that didn't stop Jacobson, who has gone about theatrically distributing the film herself using her web site, film festival contacts, e-mail newsletter and pure adrenaline. Jacobson turned her "failure to get a deal" into a success by doing it herself.

How did you get your film into Sundance?

I called Sundance early and scheduled delivery of the film print so they would have to watch it on film. Allison Anders, Bob Hawk, and a some other people who had seen *Mary Jane* at the Independent Feature Film Market (IFFM) called the Sundance office to tell them they thought the film was an important viewpoint on sexuality from a girl's point of view. I never asked them to, though, they told me about it afterwards.

If you're not sure about the rules and regulations of applying, especially when it comes to their rules about premieres, you can actually call their offices and ask them. Be sure to have your questions organized and prepared; write down their answers. This sounds really basic, but based on the number of nimrod phone calls I get from people, I imagine it's a hundred times worse for Sundance. If too many people call they might stop being so accessible, which would be a shame. You can do that for a lot of other things, too, not just film festivals. If I'm not sure about something, I call the office and ask the receptionist who would be the best person to talk to, then ask questions. Usually if you have a decent phone manner, you can get help for everything from applying to grants, dealing with labs, organizing your film shoot, help at festivals to…just anything.

Does a particular type of film have a better chance of getting into a film festival?

People are always asking me what kind of films they should make to get into festivals. I honestly believe that the best way to succeed is to just make films you believe in, films you are passionate about. Success will follow on your terms; usually the route your film takes you on is more interesting and challenging than just going along with the pack. When I made *I Was a Teenage Serial Killer,* I didn't make it to "get into Sundance," or into any festival. I was just pissed off and wanted to vent it. I didn't get into very many film festivals, but I did end up selling 800 video copies to date. For a half hour, black and white film that's pretty damn good. With *Mary Jane,* I had no idea if anyone would ever see this film when I first started. But it was important to me to show what girls go through when they're first discovering sex. I've had a lot of success with *Mary Jane,* but definitely not the traditional "three picture deal with Miramax" type. Yet I've had so much fun and felt so fulfilled by the paths my films have taken me, I wouldn't trade it in for anything in the world.

How did you react to the news that you made it into Sundance?

I jumped up and down, I called everyone I knew. I called one of my actresses, who is a very close friend, Beth Allen. She plays the punk rock chick, Ericka, in the movie. When I told her we got into Sundance she said, "What's Sundance?"

What other festivals did you apply to?

As many as we could find. We got into about a third of festivals we applied for. I've talked to filmmakers who have gotten distribution and their films have made a ton of money—they still remember vividly the festivals they didn't get into. That's always a nice reality check.

Were you concerned about applying to other festivals before you found out if you were accepted into Sundance?

I did my homework. I knew that I could show *Mary Jane* at one festival before Sundance and still be eligible for the American Spectrum section, but not the competition, that had to be a world premiere. I actually didn't think *Mary Jane* was going to get into Sundance, I felt it was too small. So I decided to open *Mary Jane* at the Chicago Underground Film Festival (CUFF), who have always been incredibly supportive of my work, they've always believed in me 100%. I figured it would be better to premiere *Mary Jane* at a festival where they would really stand behind me rather than get lost in the shuffle at a big festival. Also, I knew the chances of getting into Sundance were really slim and I didn't want to wait half a year for just one festival. I didn't think we were headed for any A-list festivals.

Because we were opening at CUFF, we were the focus of a lot of attention from the press in Chicago. Since I only had a rough cut on video, I didn't want that tape to reflect the film and I wasn't sending out any copies for review. But for some weird reason, Roger Ebert was reviewing CUFF that year and he actually called me on the phone and asked to see my film. I freaked out. I decided it was worth the risk to send it to him, even though he told me he wasn't going to lie if he didn't like it. I sent him the rough cut and he liked it and gave it a good mini-review, which was an amazing thing to get out of any festival. All these people had told me that it was a mistake to "give away" my world premiere to such a small festival. High off our success there (two shows were totally sold out and the response was fantastic), we went to the IFFM in New York. My mom (who is producer on the film) and I went nuts promoting our screening. It was actually her idea to make the now infamous "NOT A VIRGIN" sticker right before the Sundance party. We ran to Kinko's and printed them up on sticker paper. Mom stole a pink highlighter pen (she'll never admit that) and while we were in line to get into the party we were cutting up and coloring stickers.

How did the first IFFM screening go?

Even though our screening was at 11a.m. on a Saturday, it was totally packed and the response was wildly enthusiastic. From the reaction to that screening I started to get an idea that we might have a slim chance at Sundance and decided to hold off on other festivals until I heard back. I figured if the other festivals really liked my film, they would understand and wait for the next year. One festival got really mad but screw them. Still, you don't want to put all your eggs in one basket. I've seen a lot of people who thought they were going to be so hot and when things didn't turn out the way they wanted, they had already alienated everyone who had supported them before and didn't have anywhere to turn. *Don't do that.* The people who supported *Serial Killer* were behind *Mary Jane* all the way and it really made a difference down the road.

How did you prepare for your first Sundance screening?

We made a wish list of people we wanted to see the film and faxed them with the screening info. I made personal calls to the ones I really wanted to be there and my mom and I went down to Los Angeles to meet with the distributors who were calling us. Once we met with distributors we decided that we pretty much hated them. All they said was, "Girls don't see movies without their boyfriends and guys don't see movies about girls." The best thing about our DIY (Do It Yourself) distribution is that we've proven that wrong.

Our first and third screening at Sundance were pretty much disasters. The technical director of the festival had a heart attack four days earlier. Technical problems—on their end—delayed our screening for an hour and a half. It was totally painful to see all these people walking out, a lot of them apologized, explaining that they had to get to other screenings. If you ever have to leave a screening in advance and you know the filmmaker, it makes all the difference in the world when you tell them why you have to go.

Some dumb volunteer made me go up and answer questions beforehand to "entertain" the audience while they were waiting. That was horrible. It was even written up in the trades how some poor filmmaker girl totally humiliated herself in front of an audience while Sundance was dealing with technical problems. John Anderson from *Newsday* told me later that he actually talked to Robert Redford about how appalling the technical problems were and used me specifically as an example.

"Once we met with distributors we decided that we pretty much hated them. All they said was, "Girls don't see movies without their boyfriends and guys don't see movies about girls." The best thing about our DIY (Do It Yourself) distribution is that we've proven that wrong."

The third screening was delayed an hour because the projector bulb blew out so ferociously that they had to get another projector. That was in the world's most horrible screening room, The Yarrow II. By that point I just went off and got as drunk as I could with Frank Grow from *Love God* and the rest of my cast. Sundance gave us a last minute screening to make up for it, but they had so many problems that the only slot left was at midnight on the last night of the festival during the after-awards party. We took it and the screening was well received by the fifty people there but, obviously, no big shot industry types were there. It was our best Sundance screening.

What did you do to hype your film at Sundance?

The whole cast came, except for one 'zinester guy who was saving to go to Japan. Also, my co-producer, Sunny Andersen, my sister, my mom and my mom's friend so she'd have someone her own age to get in trouble with. We put up tons of flyers every day, stuck everyone's badge with a "NOT A VIRGIN" sticker and went on countless interviews set up by the publicist we hired. I don't know if the publicist was worth it, though. The best stuff we got ourselves, like when we talked to the crew from MTV News and mom started talking about how she's met Mark Mothersbaugh and Kim Gordon. To her it's not bragging because she doesn't really know that these people are famous, it's not her generation. But the girl from MTV flipped out and turned on the cameras and started filming. My approach is to try and meet as many people as possible on a one-to-one basis and just be a nice person. It's always done really well for me at the IFFM, but people were more stuck up at Sundance than any other film event I've been to and I didn't meet as many filmmakers as I would have liked. I guess the competitiveness of it ruins any community feeling. Thank God we were there the same year as Slumdance, that was a great place to retreat and have fun in the midst of all the industry frenzy. I think my mom put it best when she said, "It feels like everyone else is a senior in high school and we're in third grade."

What would you have done differently in preparing for your Sundance debut?

I don't know, for all the technical hassles and industry intimidation, I have to say I was really happy to be at Sundance, if only for the recognition that your film is special and the innate understanding that you're someone who is going to make another film. It's great when I'm dealing with snotty film guys who are really condescending to me—and then I get to tell them that my narrative feature film was in Sundance. The condescension stops at that point, which might sound really petty but when you deal with that attitude all the time, it's a nice thing to be able to cut it off. I also like that being in Sundance makes people give the film a chance in a way that they might normally not, it's totally helped us with press on our DIY distribution. The actual staff of Sundance was really great, especially Rebecca Yeldham, who told me that *Mary Jane* reminded her of herself when she was a teenager. And the volunteers there were totally cool and supportive. All the technical stuff that happened, it's like, what can you do? All the distributors who tell you girl films won't work unless they're lesbian movies because they have a built in audience, what can you say? I decided I would just go ahead and try to work around that and prove them wrong. Maybe next time we should consider hiring a producer's rep to navigate that "industry" scene since I don't think I'm very good at getting results out of those types of people, but that could have been a big waste of money as well when we couldn't even afford our publicist.

I'd like to think that *Mary Jane* would have done well regardless of whether or not we got into Sundance. It did make things easier along the way, but it wasn't the end all be all that everyone makes it out to be. When I think of how *I Was A Teenage Serial Killer* found its audience, my approach has been pretty much the same with *Mary Jane*— except this time my mom is helping me and we're getting into bigger theaters. We get *Mary Jane* out by getting local press and reaching out to the underground arts community in each town, same thing I did with *Serial Killer*. Since *Serial Killer*, though, the internet has really exploded and we've definitely been able to use that to our advantage.

How do you create hype for your film?

The best tools that a filmmaker has are enthusiasm and passion. If you're too cool to show any kind of emotion, either you need to hire someone who can be enthusiastic for you or you're screwed. I think it's easy to be enthusiastic if you have confidence in your film and in yourself as a filmmaker. I also tend to have a really good rapport with writers; my friends who did zines always wanted to interview me because I had a lot to say and was pretty accessible about talking about my work. The zine interviews led to bigger press because if you can show people that other people are writing about your films, they take you more seriously. Zines also gave *Mary Jane* a cool grassroots following so that when I took my film on tour there was already an awareness of it. When I was on the road, zine people came to shows in every town we played in. I post a lot of stuff on the internet about *Mary Jane* and I've gotten a lot of feedback from that as well. Getting a website is one of the best things we ever did, thanks to Lenny DiFranza who built it and runs it. It was voted one of the Top 10 Indie Film Websites by *Variety*. When he was on a panel at Cannes, Roger Ebert cited us specifically as an example of using the web to promote your film! That was pretty cool. It's easy to be intimidated by the technology but it's really no big deal; once you sit down with someone to show you the ropes, it's really simple. If anything, at least get email. I keep in touch with people I've met all over the world now and it's a lot cheaper than phone calls or faxing.

Any advice on handling the press?

Press has really helped me a lot, although it's weird when people think you're rich because they read about you in a magazine. When I do interviews, I pretend like I'm speaking to a large crowd of people because…well, you are. And don't answer any questions you don't want to. If you write your own press releases, or oversee the PR, that's going to be the main gist of the article, so only include stuff you want to see reprinted later.

Were you disappointed when you finally came to realize that your film would not come out of Sundance with a distribution deal? How did you deal with that?

Yes, I was depressed for two months. There is so much pressure at Sundance to "get distribution," that's all anyone seems to care about. That was really hard. I turned to other filmmakers for advice to try and snap myself out of it. Later on, when I met a lot filmmakers who had gotten distribution at Sundance the year I was there, they were really upset at the lame way their films were handled. So it's not like getting distribution is this magic thing that's going to make your life so much better. What with doing festivals for a year, I was hoping that distributors would notice how well our film was doing with audiences, but they never did. We got some interest from minor distributors and came close with signing a deal twice, but ultimately those companies seemed too disorganized and unfocused. I figured I could do it better myself.

Since you were not able to get a distribution at Sundance, did you formulate a fallback plan?

I figured that I had done guerrilla film shows before with *Serial Killer* and I could do that again with *Mary Jane*. I also had been watching my friends from the underground film scene who would book tours around the country like punk rock bands—like Danny Plotnick (*I'm Not Fascinating*), James Schneider (*B Is For Blue*), Russ Forster (*So Wrong They're Right*) and Miranda July (*Big Miss Moviola*). I asked my friends in bands questions about setting up shows. A lot of it is shit work—sending stuff out, making follow up phone calls. I knew from the festival circuit that people liked our film. I was excited about the challenge of getting people who normally don't go to independent films to come to see *Mary Jane,* even though I knew it would postpone making another film for at least a year. I think that's why it took so long to finally decide to go ahead and self-distribute *Mary Jane,* but it's worked out so much better this way.

How did you go about self-distributing your film?

Since *Mary Jane* sold out all three screenings at South by Southwest in Austin in 1997, I called the Dobie Theater and the owner gave me a ten-day run right after the 1998 festival. I was going to be there as a panelist and judge anyway, so I could promote in person. Based on how well we did in Austin, we were able to get other bookings around the country. Pretty soon, we played seven cities and never lost money. I interspersed theatrical shows with college shows, which pay a flat fee no matter what, that paid for the transportation. From our success at those towns (Cleveland, OH. Pittsburgh, PA, Austin, TX, Portland, OR, Minneapolis, MN, Madison WI) we were able to slowly branch out to bigger cities. My favorite example is my hometown of San Francisco, where we hadn't played at all, not even a festival. None of the theaters would take a chance on *Mary Jane*, so we got five days at Artist Television Access, a small gallery in the Mission. That run did so well that we switched over to Landmark's Opera Plaza Cinema and played for a month.

Sarah Jacobson maintains a web site with information about all of her films: www.sirius.com/~lenny/maryj2.html

DAN MiRViSH, Filmmaker and Festival Organizer/Founder of The Slamdance International Film Festival

A co-founder of the upstart Slamdance Film Festival, Dan Mirvish is also an active filmmaker and screenwriter. He wrote, directed and produced the $38,000 feature *Omaha (the movie)* and on the heels of Slamdance, the film went on to play at over thirty other film festivals. Mirvish then self-distributed the film to thirty two cities in the U.S.—in both traditional urban art houses as well as mainstream multiplexes—including an eleven-week run at Laemmle's Theaters in Los Angeles. Ironically, the film went on to play on the Sundance Channel and is currently available on home video.

The mad-hatter Dan Mirvish is a filmmaker first and a festival organizer second. Guess which pays better?

Prior to getting an M.A. from USC's graduate program in film production, Mirvish was a Washington-based speechwriter for U.S. Senator Tom Harkin and a freelance journalist for such publications as *The Washington Monthly* and *The New York Times.* He's continued freelancing for such film magazines as *The Independent Film & Video Monthly, British Savvy,* and the *AIVF Guide to Film Festivals.*

Mirvish remains actively involved with Slamdance as a key programmer and master of ceremonies for the annual Park City event.

Why do you believe your film was initially rejected from Sundance?
I've heard a number of different answers to this question, some or even all of which are probably true. First of all, I know there were some Sundance programmers who really liked my film. But I also know for a fact (they told me) that some didn't—fair enough. One version I heard was that they didn't want to program two twenty-something midwestern comedies, and they had already programmed *Four Corners of Nowhere.* I finally saw Steve Chboski's film and I really liked it, but it frankly is nothing at all like *Omaha (the movie).* I also heard through the grapevine that Geoff Gilmore complained that

my film had already screened too many times: which is to say once at the IFFM, and again a few weeks later at the Mill Valley Film Festival as our official premiere. There was also a suggestion from someone on the programming committee that there was some resentment about the substantial buzz we had gotten on the film at the IFFM because Robert Altman showed up at our screening (his grandson Dana was my producing partner on the movie).

Can you talk about the politics of applying to Sundance?

Well, if I fully understood the politics of getting into Sundance, I would have gotten into it myself. Shortly after my screening at the IFFM, I signed with UTA, whose agents told me they could help me get into Sundance. I know they made a couple of calls. My sense of how things work at Sundance is that a lot of the films they select are essentially chosen early in the Fall, if not earlier—many culled from the ranks of those picked for the Toronto Film Festival. For the last few years, it clearly has also made a difference if the director or producer had a prior history of having films at Sundance.

How did Slamdance begin?

It all really started at the IFFM in September 1994. My partner, Dana, who lives and works in Omaha, had the idea that filmmakers from all over the country should communicate in some way on a more grassroots level than the IFP (Independent Feature Project) could provide. We had a couple of impromptu meetings at the IFFM, but nothing concrete really came of it. I do think that it helped plant the idea that filmmakers should work together to help each other and not just rely on the existing institutions. As the next couple of months dragged on, some of us who had met in New York stayed in touch and started to compare notes on what we might do if we didn't get into Sundance. We'd heard of a couple of films from the year before that had been rejected from Sundance had gone to Park City to do their own renegade screenings in back alleys and hotel rooms. They actually managed to get a little press attention (it turns out the two films were James Marandino's *The Upstairs Neighbor* and Trey Parker's *Cannibal: The Musical*). Shane Kuhn (who had directed *Rednecks*— also coincidentally shot in Nebraska) and I specifically talked about such renegade screenings as "Plan B." At one point in October, I had a party with eight directors who had all been at IFFM. We figured at least some of us would get into Sundance. Nope.

In fact, out of the ninety or so completed fiction features that had screened at the IFFM that year, not a single one got into Sundance. That was really pretty pathetic (considering the IFFM touted itself as the place where Sundance would come and find your film—just as it had done with *Clerks* the year before).

Back to Plan B: We'd go individually to Park City and do what we could with our own films. But early in the morning the day after Sundance made their announcements, Shane called me up with a brain-storm: If a couple individual films could have renegade screenings, why not show a whole slate of films and brand ourselves with a name. My idea to call it "Loserfest '95" was swiftly rejected when Shane's partner, Brendan Coles, came up with "Slamdance 95: The First Annual Guer-rilla International Film Festival." If nothing else, we figured the anar-chy symbol would look good on a T-shirt. One of the first filmmakers to come on board was Jon Fitzgerald *(Self Portrait)*, whom Shane and I figured was far more organized than either of us.

How did Slamdance go that first year?

Things were not easy for us that December. Shane's initial idea was to hold our screenings at the University of Utah in Salt Lake City (where he knew some people in the film department). The film department initially liked the idea, but then mentioned it to the Sundance people who said they hated the idea. The film department considered all the perks they get from Sundance over the course of the year, and called us back to tell us it wasn't going to happen. Though disap-pointed, we were quite eager to boast about the festival that had got-ten squashed by Sundance—we figured it'd be great press and we wouldn't actually have to go to the trouble of putting on a festival.

> "If a couple individual films could have renegade screenings, why not show a whole slate of films and brand ourselves with a name. My idea to call it Loserfest '95 was swiftly rejected..."

Meanwhile, Sundance had apparently consulted its lawyers, and called the school back to say that they SHOULD let us put on Slamdance. So back we were at the University—but with not much enthusiasm on their part.

We got a lucky break on December 20 when John Brodie of *Daily Variety* did a front page story about us and it got picked up by AOL. Thank God for slow news weeks. All of a sudden we were legit. Unfortunately, Brodie didn't give people a way to contact us, but he did mention that I was spending my Christmas vacation working at the Good Guys electronics store in Westwood. People started coming in and dropping off tapes, and Jon and Shane would come in while I was on shift and we'd look at tapes on the big-screen televisions. I got fired shortly thereafter.

It was still hard recruiting films. Several of our friends whom we'd known since the IFFM loved the idea but balked at the last minute because they were afraid of getting blacklisted. In the end we wound up with a dozen features, and a dozen more shorts. Most of us stayed in one condo in Salt Lake City, and by the second day of the festival, we had figured out how to do screenings in Park City itself. The rest, more or less, is history.

How do you start your own festival?

It ain't rocket science, and in many regards it's easier than making a film. But you can certainly apply some of the same lessons of making low-budget filmmaking to a low-budget festival. There's festivals cropping up all over the place—some are created by film commissions, some by filmmakers, some by rich benefactors. All of which are valid, but the most important thing is to figure out WHY you want to do it. For Slamdance it was really clear: Sundance had become the be-all and end-all for getting distribution and getting into other festivals. If you didn't get in, then it was the end of the line. It's also one of the few film events that draws industry professionals from both coasts as well as internationally—including the press. So for us, it started out as little more than a publicity stunt: even if the industry pros didn't see our films, they would have at least heard of Slamdance, and that would give us a chance later on.

What have you learned and what advice could you give to others wishing to start their own festival?

Once you figure out why you're starting a festival, that will steer every decision you make. If you're doing it to boost your community for tourists, then you'll make certain decisions about when and where to have it, and where to get sponsorship. If you're doing it to bring independent films to an otherwise underserved community, you should be making completely different decisions. If it's a group of filmmakers wanting to promote their own work, then you need to be really clear about who you think your audience will be. If you're doing it to raise money, good luck.

Now that Slamdance is established and respected, what distinguishes your festival from Sundance?

We like to think of Slamdance as more of a festival to discover new talent than Sundance. Our main competition is strictly limited to features by first-time directors, with no domestic distribution and with a relatively low budget (vaguely under $1 million, but most are far less than that). Beyond that criteria, I think one thing we've succeeded in doing is being a lot more filmmaker-friendly than Sundance. By being smaller, we literally hold the filmmakers' hands before, during and after the festival. They don't get lost in Park City, like some Sundance filmmakers have told us. Audiences also really respond to the more casual environment at Slamdance: between the cushions in the screening room, the bagels in our filmmakers' lounge and our parties, audiences just seem happier at Slamdance.

Do you believe that the sucess of Slamdance is due to the fact that there are just so many independent films being made and Sundance is in the awkward position of being forced to reject otherwise good films?

I think that Sundance has turned into a world-class film festival rivaling the best festivals in Europe. Their problem is that they've been slow to admit their own success to themselves. As long as they keep pretending to be a quaint little independent film festival, they will disappoint people. And that's exactly what's happened in the last five years or so. In contrast, Slamdance has succeeded by staying true to our initial goals (of promoting first-time filmmakers with no distribution), and maintaining a small, but potent, presence in Park City.

What films that screened at Slamdance have received distribution deals?

It seems to be getting better every year. As seemingly more films each year show up at Sundance that already have distribution in place, the distributors are realizing that the real finds are at Slamdance. In terms of percentages, Slamdance films probably do about as well as Sundance in getting distribution deals. For our 1998 festival, our Audience Award winning feature *20 Dates* was picked up by Fox Searchlight, and our cinematography and editing award winner *Six String Samurai* was picked up for reportedly a million dollars by Chris Blackwell's new Palm Pictures.

Your mantra is "by filmmakers, for filmmakers"—how do you live up to that?

Our unofficial mantra is "by unemployed filmmakers, for unemployed filmmakers." The main people running the festival all consider ourselves filmmakers first, festival organizers second. This is particularly true with the programming committee which is mostly comprised of Slamdance alumni who have nothing better to do while they're waiting for their next films.

Actor Jeff Falcon (left) and director Lance Mungia on the set of Six String Samurai, *which took top honors at the Slamdance International Film Festival. Mungia is set to do a cameo in this post-apocalyptic indie action flick.*

LANCE MUNGIA, Filmmaker

Lance Mungia is a new breed of indie film-maker. When I saw the debut screening of *Six String Samurai* at the Slamdance Film Festival, I knew that the landscape of indie film had shifted. And it's about time. No longer will independent films be relegated to subject matter involving simply two-guys-in-a-room, false-feeling "gritty crime" dramas, Lesbian wheat farmers, incest, drug use, suicide or depression. *Six String Samurai* is set in a post-apocalyptic 1950s and follows the story of a Buddy Holly look-a-like making his way to "Lost Vegas." The simple description would border on B-movie fodder if the film were not so elegantly directed. The action is simply beautiful and choreographed like a ballet thanks to actor Jeffrey Falcon.

When I saw the film in Park City, I was relieved to think indie film's reliance on depressing subject matter was about to finally change. It was refreshing to see an indie film achieve something purely cinematic. (You know? Shot A + Shot B + Shot C forms a cinematic sentence that tells a story.) It seemed the typical film contained a series of long takes after long takes, shot in a room with a couple of Gen-Xers babbling on about Pop Tarts or pop culture or some crap.

Lance Mungia is the real deal. A filmmaker to the core. The guy must have emulsion caked under his fingernails to know so much about the medium at such a young age.

Here he shares entire his festival experience with us.

So who the hell are you?

My name is Lance Mungia and I'm twenty-six years old. I grew up in agricultural Central California, knowing that I loved movies and didn't want to spend the rest of my life pulling weeds in somebody else's cotton field. I saw film school in L.A. as an escape and an excuse to make a feature film. I graduated from Loyola Marymount film school last year, in the midst of shooting *Six String*. I also did a short film called *A Garden For Rio* while at Loyola, which played the festival circuit. *Rio* played venues like Sundance, The Hamptons, Chicago and many others.

What can you do to make sure your film gets into festivals?

See what the competition is doing, then be different.

Travelling the festivals with my short was an invaluable experience. I recommend that anybody who wants to make an indie film attend as many festivals as possible first. I was able to meet other filmmakers and see what they were up to. Right away I noticed that there was a glut of similar films playing the festivals. If you've seen one "I'm Gen-X, dealing with my drug habit, and I'm gonna kill myself," film, you've seen them all.

I know it's cheap to shoot a "two guys in a room" film or something, but if you want to get noticed and really do well at festivals, you have to think in unique terms. "The spin" is what it's about. How can you take something like "two guys in a room," and futz it so it's fresh and exciting? Figure that out and you've got a festival winner. There are no rules, even a "two guys in a room" film can be unique, using enough imagination to put your own personal, cinematic "fingerprint" on it.

Why do some films get into festivals that aren't original, or are outright bad?
Why do you believe there's a glut of the same films?

Presentation is one valid reason. Some films are more reliant on presentation than others. Some dialogue films can suffer through bad sound and still play. A visual film like *Six String* will drop like a rock with bad sound or crappy visuals.

One of the best things you can do to make sure you'll get into a festival is to have a polished product to show the selection committee. These programmers see thousands of films with bad visuals and bad sound—even bad stories—you don't want to give them a reason to trash your film. After you've seen a thousand films with bad picture or sound, they all start to look the same. If there are thirteen slots in a festival, the bad presentation of your film can drop you from slot eleven to slot fourteen. There is no prize for slot fourteen.

You initially sent your film to Sundance. What happened?

I got an extension on Sundance's deadline, to try and finish our sound work and cut our negative. Sometimes festivals will give you an extension if you ask nicely and can show them something that shows that your project has promise.

We asked, and got an extension. It still wasn't enough time and I wound up having to show Sundance an AVID video output of my film with dialogue that I'd mostly ADR'd myself for a temporary mix. It was grainy, hard to hear, and generally sucked.

"Oh, we can look beyond that to see a film's potential. We see a lot of AVID cuts," the programmers told me.

"If you've seen one 'I'm Gen-X, dealing with my drug habit, and I'm gonna kill myself,' film, you've seen them all."

Right. Yeah. Finish your film, then submit it; you'll be better off. Show a print whenever possible. Every single leg up you can get is another percentage point in favor of getting into the festival. As I said, there are some "two guys in a room" films where I guess sound and picture don't matter as much, but even then...you've got a "two guys in a room film," and you need all the help you can get to compete against the billion other "two guys in a room" films being submitted.

After we finished *Six String Samurai*, I figured we'd be a shoo-in for Sundance. Our film was original enough, it wasn't about suicidal Gen-Xers, and I'd met all the Sundance guys the year before when my short was at the fest.

I was completely bummed when I found out we didn't get into Sundance. Maybe I was overconfident, but I really, really thought we'd get in, even despite our bad video and sound. It was original, dammit!

What was your fallback plan?

Weeks later, we showed Slamdance a projected print of the film, with the final sound mix. They dug the film, and we found out we got into the festival a few days later.

When I first found out we got in, it was like, "Whew, my film has a chance after all." Dan Mirvish woke me up on a Monday morning to tell me. He told me he hadn't slept and the Slamdance guys duked it out all weekend over who would get in.

It's really tough. What happened to the guy who was that four-teenth slot? People tell you that there's plenty of venues to show your film, but in reality, you need the support of a festival to create buzz for you and get your name out there. Even out of the films that get into festivals like Sundance, only a handful actually get distributed.

So, you avoided killing yourself during this difficult time?

Yeah. [Laugh] Now that I've burst your bubble, let me say your film doesn't have to get into festivals or distribution to make you a suc-cessful filmmaker, however. If you don't get in, then I guess you just suck it up and keep pushing. I say that knowing I'm a total hypocrite for saying it, because, after all, I got in. I'm not a hypocrite when I say, however, there were a lot of times I'd have liked to give up, but didn't, and that's a major reason I got the film finished and seen.

You have to be confident to the point of arrogance to even think that you can make a movie that people are going to want to see. But you also have to be objective.

Face facts, if you want to get rich, go into real estate, it ain't gonna happen in film anytime soon. But, if you're passionate about making something, if you truly love what you're doing, then go for it, because it's your passion for your work that's going to keep you going when everything screws up, and it'll be your passion that will show up on film, and it'll be your passion that, as a side-effect, actually might make you rich and famous someday.

How did your Slamdance screening go?

In the end, we got way more buzz at Slamdance than we could have gotten from something like a midnight screening at Sundance. Slamdance only showed thirteen films, and everybody likes to root for the underdog. People that made their way up Main Street to Slamdance liked to think they found some undiscovered gems, and I'd like to think they did too.

I'd hate to think there are a lot of decent indie films out there that are never seen at major festivals, but there probably are. Any aspiring filmmaker should think of that as a reality to be aware of. Most of the time a film probably won't be seen because it doesn't play for an audience. Film is a business and even though it's an art too, every project has to be commercial to a certain extent. Too many "artists" forget about that. Cinema is the last truly vibrant and evolving "art form," but it's also the most expensive "art form" ever invented. I'm not just talking about making it, I'm talking about getting it shown and marketed to audiences. Have an audience in mind when you write your script. Ask yourself, "What's the story?" "Who's this story for?" I honestly don't think a lot of people do that. They just roll the dice and wait to see who shows up.

What other post-Sundance festivals did Six String Samurai *have?*
We've been invited to some other festivals since Slamdance and South by Southwest, the other fest we played, but our distributor, Palm, decided to pull the film from other festivals in order to play the Toronto Film Festival.

Sometimes, if you play too many festivals, it's hard to get into major festivals like Toronto. It's a tricky game that I don't fully understand. The film's been sold, so I can't complain.

I guess they feel that we can use the press when we get closer to our release date. We'd much rather have a flurry of press and hype right before the release than now. If the press runs stories now, they may not run them again in the fall.

How do you manipulate the press to get good ink?
As I've said, to actually get good press at a festival, get it sold, and have it do well in the theaters, you've got to have the ability to put your fingerprints on something, to make it stand out from the crowd and you've also got to be really lucky. Most of all, artsy-fartsy filmmaker crap aside, you have to have one other, super important thing...*HYPE*. Your film might be good, but hype will make it great... at least temporarily.

How do you get hype? Personality, for starters. I've had executives tell me that there are filmmakers out there that consistently work, even though they make mediocre films, because they know how to work a room when they come in for a meeting.

Personality, is the key to success in any kind of business. Who does the boss at the carpet factory hire? The introvert genius who can't put three sentences together, or the moderately talented Joe who can hold his own in a room full of suits?

Sad but true, the shy genius is still working at McDonald's.

How did you get the film made?

When we were trying to put together the financing for *Six String Samurai,* we started out with nothing but a phone book full of numbers to call and a five minute trailer that we'd cut together. By the time we'd found an investor, we'd gotten over forty companies interested in the film, by sheer force of personality, and quality material to back up that personality once we got our feet in the door.

Personality and material...one without the other is a trip to the unemployment office.

If you don't like dealing with people, do something else. Deal with people. Too much personality and people think you're a schmuck. Too little, and they can't remember your name.

Many times we'd call a company and talk to an assistant. These people get a lot of rude phone calls. Don't be one of them. Make them think that you have something they want to see. Take advantage of what I call "The Fear Factor." Make them believe that everybody else is already seeing your glorious work and they're about to miss the proverbial boat. Be nice about it, though, and most of all: *don't lie.*

Grab onto the truth, and use it. If you can get just one company interested in producing your film, don't wait for them to call you back. Unless you have something totally solid, call ten other companies and tell them how hot you are. Tell them you've got somebody interested and ask why they haven't looked at your material yet.

Hollywood is a tiny, gossip filled community. If you tell somebody that the head of production at Fox is watching your movie trailer, it better be true, because they're gonna check.

So, how did you build hype in the industry?

Before we signed with William Morris, I got them to watch our tape by telling them specific people at Fox, Orion, and Paramount were watching our dailies and were interested in the film. The next day we went to our meeting at William Morris, and they'd checked on every count.

This made us look great to Orion, Fox, and Paramount, because even if they weren't that interested in the film, they weren't going to tell a snoopy agent at William Morris that. Because if William Morris was calling, that meant we had buzz. The studio execs would probably be vague with their answers, of course, and they'd also be even more interested in us, because now somebody else was too. That's how hype works. It's the secret that makes Hollywood go round.

What specifically did you do to build hype in Park City when you arrived for your Slamdance debut?

When we got to Slamdance with *Six String Samurai,* the first few days, we ran around like crazy handing out fliers, talking to people in the streets, going to parties and telling people about the film.

After we'd had a couple of packed screenings, the buzz was out there about the film. It would have looked bad for us to keep tooting our own horn too much. We'd just walk around wearing our *S3* hats—now, people would come up to us! At parties, in the streets, in the lobby of the Treasure Mountain Inn. It was cool.

I always thought that a publicist or agent could do great things to create hype. I thought that if I only could sign with a big agency like William Morris that my career would be made. Monkeys might fly out of my butt too, but not likely.

So, you achieved all of this without a publicist or agent or "people?"

Rule #1—You are your own best agent, publicist, and manager.

Agents and publicists can take existing buzz and make it work more for your benefit, but they can't create it from scratch. These guys won't even look at your material unless you've already got buzz. They just can't. Cassian Elwes, one of my agents at William Morris, gets roughly 200 videotapes a month. Even his assistants can't watch them all. Like I said, I had to call and tell them Orion and Fox were watching my tape before they would look at it. Before then, they'd had the tape a month and I'd called every few days with no replies.

At the American Film Market in Santa Monica last year, (where films are financed, bought and sold) my partner, Jeffrey Falcon, and I spent the whole week in the lobby cold-calling companies. Every time somebody would talk to us, and we'd get a meeting, we'd call a bunch more companies listed in the AFM catalog and tell them we just had a meeting with so and so at so and so. I'd even get Jeff to call me on my cell phone during meetings to make us look busier than we really were. It worked—and pretty soon, I didn't have to get Jeff to call, I was getting calls for real.

Okay, enough about hype. All the hype B.S. in the world is nothing compared to the first time I saw *Six String Samurai* with an audience during its first Slamdance screening. People laughed, cheered, and clapped. I wasn't so much excited as I was relieved. I was like, "Whew, people like it! Maybe I can do this for a living after all...I knew it was good!"

How did you handle that first Question and Answer session?

I always try to shy away from answering specific questions about the artistic interpretation of the film during Q&As; if you have to explain the meaning of your film, it's my feeling that you've failed as the creator of that film. Why force your viewpoint on an audience? Better to let them get whatever they want out of your work, and let them draw their own conclusions. If they don't get it or they think it sucks, nothing you can say will change that.

The most frequently asked question I get by far is "What was your budget?" It's a little frustrating, but I still take this as a big compliment. The first Q & A we had at Slamdance went really well, because we really were genuinely moved by the audience response, and I'm sure we were all wide-eyed and goofy. The audience liked the sincerity. Or at least, I liked theirs, that's for damned sure.

Sometimes I wish that somebody else could come in and pretend to be me for awhile, answering all the same questions again and again. Telling people about your work, taking all these Hollywood meetings and getting caught in this big cycle of gab; it's easy to see how people become so phony and jaded. You see these people around town, talking to hear themselves talk, with painted-on smiles and the appropriate pauses for emphasis; it makes you want to run and hide someplace far away. It makes me want to go back and pull weeds in a cottonfield sometimes.

How do you avoid sounding like a robot answering the same questions over and over?

It just makes me feel uncreative now and then. What makes me able to keep doing it, what makes me able to stay fresh, is other people's enthusiasm, and the fact that I've had so much fun making this damn thing; in the end, I still enjoy talking about it.

The best is when I'll be talking and think of something, some detail I've forgotten about the film's making until that very moment.

Most of all, I'll continue to stay fresh because I mean what I'm saying. I like talking about *Six String*. I like sharing my experiences, because, I liked it when other filmmakers shared their experiences with me as a student and I remember what that was like.

The best thing we've done since Slamdance is go to Montana and speak at the film school up there. I love sharing little gems with people who are in the same boat I was in a couple of years ago. The memories of how far away L.A. can seem are still really fresh in my mind. These kids had no clue about how to make it in the indie film scene. I think I was able to tell them it's not as scary as they think, or as simple as they might think either. I don't know if I inspired them, but they inspired me.

How was your film acquired for distribution?

William Morris sent acquisition execs to our screenings, but for whatever reason the execs didn't buy it at the Festival. They all wanted to show it to their superiors when they got back to L.A. I guess *Six String Samurai* is a little risky for conservative types.

Closed-minded execs had me really worried for awhile. Most guys who get into Sundance think they're gonna go home with a six million dollar deal. The reality is that maybe a dozen or so films got picked up from Slamdance and Sundance during and right after the festival. With the exception of a few huge Miramax buys, most of those films got picked up for low to mid-six figures.

When we got back to L.A., the second distributor screening we had was for Palm Pictures. I was there, and so was the head of Palm, Chris Blackwell. At the time, I had no idea who this guy was. Later, I found out he's a huge player. He recently sold Polygram for something like 300 million dollars. He personally discovered some big music acts (like Bob Marley and U2), and also is quite a prolific producer.

As the lights came up in the screening room, Chris said, "Wow. That was unique." To me, at the time, he was just a casual older-guy with a pony-tail, wearing beach sandals, who had a slightly annoying habit of talking on his cell phone a lot. (although he turned it off during the screening.) I didn't exactly blow him off, but I'm sure he thought me aloof. In true buzz style, that probably helped our distribution situation.

He wanted to buy the film on the spot. He asked us to cancel all other screenings and enter exclusive negotiations with Palm. Canceling our other screenings was risky, 'cause we had a screening for Michael DeLuca at New Line the next day, and a screening for some top execs at TriStar later in the week. Chris said he'd pick the film's U.S. rights up for $1million. It was a cool deal. I've since come to know him as a very sincere, dedicated guy who in the past has stuck up for the filmmakers he works with. It's a very cool deal.

Are you satisfied with the deal?

Thinking about it now, we're probably in a much better situation with Chris's company. A major studio or mini-major might have swept us to the back burner, and let us sink or swim without much effort on their part. Palm is making the film their new company's major priority. Our fortunes and theirs are tied together, for better or worse.

What about that three picture deal everybody wants to get coming out of a festival?

A major company may promise you the world, but if your film is not a hit, you're still sunk. Think about it. How many filmmakers has a company like Miramax signed to multi-picture deals in the last few years? A lot. They in-house produce maybe a dozen or so films a year, I'd guesstimate. If you want to get your material produced, you have to get in line behind Quentin and Kevin Smith. Whose film do you think's gonna get made? Yours or theirs?

The best advice I can give coming off the festival thing is to have another script ready to go. Unfortunately, if you're like me, you've just spent the last few years pouring every creative cell in your body into your last film. I ain't got jack, let me tell you. Okay, well, I've got some scripts that need work. So why don't I just get to work on fixing them up and sending them out there? Meetings. A *lot* of meetings.

It's so easy to get caught up in that whole Hollywood talking game. People pitch me things, I pitch them their things back, but better. It's not that I've seen a lot of unproduceably bad stuff. I've seen bad material, sure. But actually, I could, no doubt, take a lot of things I see and make them good. That takes time. The danger is getting caught up in development and then *BANG!* A year goes by and I still don't have jack.

How do you keep the momentum?

The thing about hype is that it goes away. Something gets put into development at some studio, you make some money, but you don't make another film; then your last film comes out. Maybe you have a hit and you can write your own ticket. Maybe it's marketed badly and it bombs. Will everybody meeting me now return my calls then? They might. But their bosses who greenlight pictures won't, that's for sure.

After a festival success, if you have your own script and some hype, you can take that combination around wherever you want and do the whole hype thing all over again with the new project. This is topical stuff for me as I'm writing this. Just a couple of days ago I told William Morris to stop getting us meetings except for maybe one day a week, so my writing partner and I can concentrate on writing our own stuff.

What was your best festival experience?

Probably the best festival experience we've had was at South by Southwest in Austin. The crowds out there are amazingly animated. During our first, packed screening there, the audience was really eating the film up. They were laughing at some stuff that was making me scratch my head. Was that funny? I guess. (The coolest thing about Austin, is that you can drink beer in the theaters, and *Six String* is surely a beer drinkin' kinda movie.)

One frustrating thing about Slamdance audiences had been how, after the screenings, the credits would roll and everybody would immediately jump up and run to another screening or go have a latte or something. Their heads would get in the way of the projector and you couldn't see the names on the screen. Sometimes some of those names were actually sitting in the audience and it was the first time they'd seen the film. That was frustrating.

In Austin, it was a different story. The credits rolled, and nobody moved. The lights came up, and nobody moved. It was a packed house! Nobody moved. Nobody got out of their chairs. Either they all really wanted to hear the Q & A, or they were waiting for the next film to start. I was completely nervous as I walked up to answer questions. It felt great though, as I got up there and people hooted and hollered. After what all we'd been through to make the film, an entire packed audience of 400 people were waiting to hear me speak. Now that's the coolest screening I can think of. The audiences in Austin were so damned nice, I'm trying to get Palm to release the film there first when they start platforming it out.

What was your worst festival experience?

On the flipside, probably the worst festival/screening experience I've had was actually when we screened the film at the AFM for press and buyers. It was a nine o'clock screening. In the morning! Who screens a film at nine o'clock in the morning? Sleepy people, that's who.

It got to about half way through the film, and I noticed the guy in the seat in front of me was snoring. He was snoring pretty loud too. I kicked his chair ever so gently to wake him up. He was still sound asleep, so I leaned forward and nudged the back of his chair, none too gently. He stirred a little but he was still asleep. Finally, I just reached out and pushed his arm, which he was leaning on. His head flopped down and he woke up. I'll be damned if I'm gonna let anybody sleep during my Russian Army scene, it's one of my favorites!

Well, now we just have to wait and see who shows up in theaters when the film comes out. We're gonna have to start the whole hype thing going again, but it's gonna be big, I can feel it in my bones. We're already doing long term press interviews. I'm lucky, because I've had so much fun making *Six String Samurai*, I don't ever completely burn out talking about it. I'm confident that Palm will help give the film the breathing time it's gonna need to find an audience.

How do you keep your sanity as an indie filmmaker?
The worst, and the best thing about filmmaking, is that you never know what's going to happen next.

Lance Mungia maintains a web site for his film at: www.sixstringsamurai.com.

JOAL RYAN, Filmmaker

For each success story of filmmakers like Kevin Smith, Richard Linklater and Robert Rodriguez, there are hundreds, perhaps thousands of failures. Unfortunately, while the press heaps attention on the chosen ones, the losers,

Joal Ryan at her one and only screening of her movie, Former Child Star.

the filmmakers who didn't quite make it, are left with nothing but hard lessons—learned most often in the form of a mountain of credit card debt, an unsold film, and worse, an unfulfilled dream. Regrettably, these lessons are rarely passed on to those who could really use the information—first-time filmmakers ready to make their movie and enter the festival meat grinder. One such tale of woe is that of Joal Ryan.

Joal Ryan is a journalist-turned-filmmaker. Her debut indie feature, *Former Child Star,* failed to get into Sundance, or Slamdance or Slumdance or Slamdunk, failed to get much good press, failed to launch her film career or get her the elusive three-picture deal; the movie itself failed to sell.

Showing tremendous vulnerability, Ryan documents every single mistake she made along the way. She details, with refreshing honesty and a rare flair for the truth, the trials and tribulations of making her first indie feature.

Thankfully, there is a bright side to the story: *Former Child Star* will be released on video from a small distributor and will most likely make its money back. Sometimes, even failure has a happy ending.

How did you begin the process of making your film?

I put an ad in *Drama-Logue,* the Los Angeles casting magazine. *Former Child Star* was, more or less, official. I was going to make a movie—a real one, with film and everything.

I was 28. A journalist. A film buff with no "official" film background. A magazine subscriber with one too many clipped-out
articles about Kevin Smith. Inspired by the do-your-own-movie movement, I'd shot a 67-minute flick on Hi-8 video the year before called
How to Make a Generation X Movie. And that project was how I came
to be making a real movie, with film and everything.

Some quick back story on *How to Make a Generation X Movie*—
the video thing. I wrote, I directed, I cast my friends. Amateur hour?
Maybe. But we approached it professionally. A month of rehearsals. I
even scribbled out a couple of storyboards before I (a) got bored and
(b) realized I had little talent for storyboards.

In the end, Filmmakers United, a screening series in Los Angeles,
invited us to show the flick in Hollywood. A very nice gesture that
turned out pretty badly. The screening was a disaster. The audience
just kind of looked at it—as opposed to, you know, laughing. (It was
a comedy. It was supposed to be, at least.)

And then there was the review. The bad one. The very best the
old *L.A. Village View* could say was that it was "coherent." That was it.
"Coherent."

How did you handle the bad press?

That word—"coherent"—became my albatross. I could do better than
"coherent," couldn't I? Why, sure I could! I could make a GREAT "coherent" movie. Write a better script. Extend my casting net. Get more
input. Shoot on film. And, yes, spend more money.

So, that was how I got to *Former Child Star*.

The story for that thing was something I'd kicked around for a
while: What would happen if someone you grew up watching on TV
suddenly burst into your life—became a living, breathing character
in your own personal drama? Sounds kind of deep. And it probably
could have been. Except when I was writing, I was studying Woody
Allen's *Bananas*. I thought my video movie had been too slow, too
boring. I wanted peppy, fast, funny. So, I dissected *Bananas* scene by
scene and wrote a farce. Except I didn't write farcical characters. Or
farcical situations. (This, I would learn later. About two years later,
while squirming in my seat and watching the final product with a
silent, mummified audience.)

So, fine, we had a script. The actors—a strong bunch, I still think—
came mostly through *Drama-Logue* (and our subsequent auditions).
The locations? My apartment and a bunch of other friends' apart-

ments. (Yes, terribly imaginative. And, as it turned out, terribly uncinematic.) The camera? Hired a camera guy who owned his own CP-16. (Thought about renting a camera and trying to shoot the thing myself, but insurance costs made that idea impossible.) The sound? Hired a sound guy who owned his own Nagra. If it sounds like I hired a lot of people, I did. Too many. There were four paid crew members, in all, I think. Ultra-cheapo, to be sure. But still too much.

Former Child Star taught me the great lesson of self-financed independent filmmaking: DON'T.

Rant all you want about what a great learning experience making an ultra-indie movie is. Sooner rather than later, that deluded line leaves you with a wallet-full of maxed-out credit cards. The artistic reality of moviemaking is that if your idea, script, cast and commitment is strong enough, you'll find funding. Maybe not as much as you want, but you'll find something. The economic reality of moviemaking is that it's an expensive hobby. And a hobby is exactly what it remains until you get someone to offer you so much as a nickel for the reels.

This was your first mistake?

Moviemaking is not novel writing. You can tap away in your attic for a year on the "Next Great Event in Fiction," produce an unreadable mass of pages and not endanger your future ability to, say, buy a can of tuna fish.

But moviemaking? The second you start rolling, is the second you start losing money. The only way to stay ahead of the game is to *spend as little as possible.*

Before hindsight set in, I was seduced. I was convinced I could shoot a feature-length 16mm movie in color, with sound, for about $5,000-7,000. (I'd spent $5,000 on the video project. Also way too much but I considered it to be an "acceptable" loss.)

I probably could have pulled it off, if I'd slowed down and *done my homework.* Ingratiated myself to techies. (I didn't know any.) Enrolled in a class on how to operate a camera. Enrolled in a class on how to edit the old-fashioned way—by hand, with film. And, hey, genius, how about this one? Decided to shoot in *black and white.*

Where did you end up getting the money?

I talked up my movie idea to my father and—bingo!—that's where our money came from. He enthusiastically bankrolled *Former Child Star.*

Bad, *bad* idea.

Not on his part. (Hey, he's my father; he thinks he's investing in genius.) On my part.

Beg, borrow, steal, but do not—DO NOT—let your parents subsidize your artistic whims. It'll save you the trouble of developing a taste for Pepto-Bismol and a springing a guilty head of gray hair.

Anyway, I told my father we could shoot and do a video edit for about $10,000. He ended up being in for $19,000. Not counting the $3,000-plus I spent on processing, food and assorted sundries. That's $22,000-plus on a film—without even getting to the print stage. What can I say? Shameful. Embarrassing. Stupid.

Surely an ultra low budget film will have flaws an audience will look past?
The thing you learn quick enough—even on the festival circuit—is that a $22,000 movie gets no extra credit for being a $22,000 movie. Maybe it did once, but certainly not today. You compete against the big boys and the semi-big boys. If you're not good enough, you're not good enough and your film ain't going nowhere—and you, loser, are out $22,000.

Did you apply to Sundance?
Okay, so I'm either a defeatist or a realist, but I knew *Former Child Star* wasn't getting into Sundance. Not a chance. Three reasons:

(1) In the mistaken belief that the Independent Feature Film Market (IFFM) was the place to take a brand-spanking new movie, we screened at the event in September 1996. (To give you an idea about how naïve I was—I remember nervously awaiting word on whether we'd been "accepted" to the IFFM. And then to compound naïveté with stupidity, I remember thinking that we'd "achieved" something by being "accepted." Then I got to New York and realized that quality control amounted to conferring with the bank to see if the check cleared. The IFFM is a must-*see* for an aspiring indie filmmaker; it's not necessarily a must-*screen*.)

Anyway, back to our IFFM screening. People from Sundance attended. From Slamdance, too. And the Chicago Underground. And probably a half-dozen other festivals. Nobody from these outfits contacted me after the screening. In this case, silence meant a big, fat, loud "NO."

(2) I didn't do my homework. Again. Going into the IFFM, I did little to aid my cause. Sure, I hyped our screening time to as many studio and festival types as I could. But a press release and a phone call is not enough. I showed up in New York with a fresh-from-the-lab print. Nobody *really* knew me. Nobody knew my film. Nobody cared. Sure, it would have helped if the fresh-from-the-lab print featured something akin to "Citizen Kane: 1996," but it also would have helped if I'd worked the festival circuit like Sarah Jacobson, whom I met at IFFM that year.

Jacobson had made a short, *I Was a Teen-age Serial Killer,* in the early 1990s. She screened it everywhere, she pushed it relentlessly. She made people care about her passion for film. When she showed up at IFFM with her first feature, *Mary Jane's Not A Virgin Anymore,* she was ready to make people care about that project, too. And they did. A couple months later, Sarah got accepted into Sundance. That was no luck. That was hard work.

(3) My film wasn't very good. Just another waste of celluloid and money in the post-*Clerks* world of wannabe filmmakers. At least that was my review.

So why did you bother applying to Sundance?

Again, three reasons:

(1) Like I said before, filmmaking is expensive. You've got to do everything you can to protect and preserve your investment, including lying. ("It's a comedy. Really funny!") The results can be embarrassing when someone actually screens the thing and tells you, "It's a mess. Really sucky!," but consider that part of your penance.

(2) Art is subjective. Who knows? Maybe the Sundance guy will actually like the thing. It's not your job to tell him he won't like it. (See the bit about lying in the item above.)

(3) Like the lottery, you can't win if you don't play. Sundance is the mother of all film festivals—you MUST apply. Especially if your father, who paid for the movie, tells you to.

So, anyway, in the fall of 1996, I did what 800 other filmmakers did and mailed off our movie, our press kit and a fifty dollar check. (Why Sundance needs fifty dollars to reject a film its advance team already essentially rejected at the IFFM, I don't know. "To make money," would be my first guess.)

What other festivals did you apply to?

That fall and subsequent winter I also applied to: Toronto, South By Southwest, Film Fest New Haven, San Francisco, New York Underground, Los Angeles Indie, Portland, Taos Talking Picture, New York's Gen Art, Hudson Valley, Laguna Beach and Florida.

Most required entry fees—from twenty five to forty dollars, usually. All of which I wrote. Stupidly so.

Not having yet learned my lesson from IFFM, I failed to realize that unless a festival scout contacts you first, the chance of your unsolicited tape working its way out of the slush pile and into the acceptance pile, is minimal. That's not an indictment of festivals; that's reality.

How do you get a festival's attention?

Think about how the screenplay business works. Do you send your hot, new script directly to Warner Bros? Or do you send it first to an agent, who, if he likes, can get the ear of Warner Bros. on your behalf? You send it to an agent, of course. He's your "in." That's what you're looking for at film festivals.

Before you get to the check-writing, application stage, what you want to do is get your movie before the eyes of festival types. Maybe you do it at IFFM. Maybe you do it at a local fest that takes all comers. Maybe you do it at a private screening on your Moviola. Whatever. Just get them to watch. If they like, they'll let you know. They won't tell you you're a lock. But they'll suggest you apply. That's something; that's one person on your side. You might even get your entry-fee waived.

What festivals accepted your film?

Of all the festivals I listed above, only Los Angeles Indie contacted me first. The program director called. Somebody had listed *Former Child Star* on a list of should-sees. I didn't get in, but at least I knew I had a chance. (I also ended up getting invited—and accepted—to the USA Film Festival in Dallas and the Chattanooga Film Festival in, yes, Chattanooga.)

Anyway, the rejection from Sundance came via the post office. Sundance was classy enough to send a "Dear Filmmaker" letter. It arrived a couple days after the lineup was released in the trades, but still...the other festivals I entered didn't bother to call, write or e-mail. About the best their organizations did was send a sales brochure hyping their events, i.e., the slates of movies that got picked instead of mine. (Not that it's a bad idea to go to a festival where you're just an observer. In fact, it's a great idea. I need to do it more—to see what my peers are up to, to gauge the market, and above all, to learn— maybe even steal a couple tricks.)

How did you handle all the rejections?

Since Sundance never, even seemed as real as a pipe dream, I wasn't exactly crushed when the rejection letter arrived. It was more like, "Next." I didn't wait for Sundance. I didn't expect Sundance. I didn't get Sundance. Fine. Next. Time to move on.

Actually, I'd begun to move on even before that. In early November 1996, I sent a video copy of *Former Child Star* to this little thing in Cleveland that promised to show *anything*. No fee, no standards, no problem. The Off-Hollywood Flick Fest. My kind of crowd.

Was I worried about blowing my Sundance virginity by hosting my world premiere in Cleveland—two months *before* Park City? No. Remember: (a) there wasn't a chance I was getting in; and, (b) if by divine act of God, or mislabeling, I *did* get in—what was Robert Redford going to do? Shoot me? Yell at me? *"You screened at the Off-Hollywood Flick Fest?!?! Infidel!!"* The way I figured, Sundance wouldn't boot me from its shindig. Maybe it would move me out of the competition wing, but it probably would still screen me. And that's all you want. To play Park City in January...needless to say, it was a potential problem that I spent a nanosecond worrying about.

Where did you go at this point?

After Cleveland, after the no-go with Sundance, I pursued the one solid lead I got out of the IFFM: the USA Film Fest. The program director, Alonso Duralde, saw *Former Child Star* in New York and suggested I submit. The festival didn't actually solicit features—its entry form is for short subjects—but Duralde was willing to consider *Former Child Star*. Sounded good to me. I submitted, he considered; a couple months later, he said okay. We were going to our first "real" film festival.

How did you build hype for your film?

It was early 1997. Pauly Shore was in a new sitcom and the reviews weren't great. But instead of cracking a joke, turning the page and looking for somebody else to make fun of (like usual), I stopped and considered the case of Pauly Shore.

The guy's never been a critical darling or a mass-audience favorite. And yet...he keeps working. The world tells him he's not funny; he says he is—and keeps working. He does what he does, figuring somebody out there will, and does, like his work.

An empowering notion.

If Pauly Shore got rejected by Sundance, I thought, would he fold and file *Bio-Dome* away on a shelf? Ha! My man Pauly would keep sellin' it. Keep sellin' himself. And why not? No one has the right to tell you you're lousy. Except yourself.

So, with my new Power of Positive Pauly Shore Thinking in place, I decided to hype the one sure-fire angle of *Former Child Star*—the former child star angle.

If you grew up watching TV, you care about former child stars. You can't help but wonder what happened to Willis on *Diff'rent Strokes* or Natalie on *The Facts of Life*. These actors are our virtual peers. We wonder about their post-TV lives, like we wonder about the post-high school lives of old classmates.

That was my audience. That was my cause.

This was my platform: Former Child Star-Palooza. An e-zine. An e-mail newsletter designed to shamelessly hype the movie. And designed to provide real information on real former child stars—career updates, tabloid news, first-person sightings.

In February 1997, I sent out my first issue. I compiled a list of 75 e-mail addresses—mostly film companies, friends and film festivals. By the second issue, readership doubled. (It's now steadied at about 2,000 a month.)

The e-zine helped you get mainstream press?

In a short time, I was being interviewed by the *Boston Phoenix*. Getting invites to film festivals (Wine Country, Northampton, Cinequest and Las Vegas, none of which I ended up getting got into—but, hey, at least they were waiving the entrance fees now).

By summer, the e-zine and subsequent web site had been blurbed in *Newsweek, Wired* and *Entertainment Weekly*. The e-zine took on a life of its own. It immediately found greater acclaim and acceptance than the film. In turn, it kept the film alive. It gave the film mystery. ("So, what's this *Former Child Star* we keep reading about?") It gave the film relevancy.

It didn't help the film get any press at our big-time film festival screening, but nothing's perfect.

How did you handle that first festival screening?

When we got into the USA Film Festival, some extra hype—beyond the e-zine—was required. Unfortunately, all I had was me. I know you're supposed to call in favors to get stuff like this done right, but I was lousy at asking for freebies. Really, you should be required to take a personality test before making an indie film. (Flunking out in the chutzpah department would have saved me thousands of dollars.)

So, anyway, I sat down, typed up a press release, attached it to our press kit and mailed the whole batch off to Dallas media, newspapers, weeklies, even a couple radio and TV stations. I followed up with regular faxes and phone calls. Even got a couple people on the phone. All very nice. All very noncommittal. No one asked for a screener. (Bad sign.) And, in the end, no one reviewed or mentioned *Former Child Star.* I mean NO ONE. A couple months after the festival (we were there in April 1997), the program director sent me a round-up of clippings on the festival. Maybe 20-30 articles. Went through every single one. Not one word—bad or good—about *Former Child Star* in any of them. A complete swing and miss.

That said, the experience in Dallas was the highlight (so far) of the *Former Child Star* grind. The festival paid for my airline ticket (cool!), paid for my hotel room (double cool!) and inexplicably treated me like a real filmmaker. I got invited to a reception honoring me…and Liza Minnelli. (I showed; she didn't.) I even got asked to sign an autograph.

Nothing like a little adulation to keep you going. And that's all I was looking for, really. Again, I had no illusions about the USA Fest. It's not Sundance, Slamdance or South by Southwest. Agents and studio execs don't roam the theaters with cell phones and checkbooks. It's a local festival hosted and enjoyed by the locals. The focus in the press is not "$20,000 movies by out-of-town nobodies," but rather Hollywood movies (*Volcano, Traveller*) by Hollywood types. It's Dallas' chance to rub elbows with Tommy Lee Jones, Bill Paxton and Molly Ringwald. (A few of the names there that year.)

Dallas didn't make me a media darling, but it gave me something more important: The belief that there's an audience for every movie.

Somewhere, somebody is testifying to what a fabulous character drama *Lost in Space* is. And, yes, somewhere, somebody is attesting to what a brilliant comedy *Former Child Star* is. I don't necessarily want to meet these somebodies, but it is nice to know they exist.

Dallas was where I learned this. As much as I paced and ducked out of the theater in anticipation of the "bad" parts, the movie did okay. Aesthetically, the print never looked or sounded better. (Much better than the tin-eared closet we screened in at the IFFM.) And artistically, the film was genuinely liked. They laughed, applauded, stayed for the Q&A.

How did the Q&A go?

The Q&A was a breeze. In my case, again, the stakes were low. I didn't have Mike Ovitz to win over. I merely had to be nice to an auditorium of nice people who liked my movie.

I told the requisite "funny-things-that-happened-while-we-made-the-movie stories" (#1: How we caused a police incident during the filming of a robbery scene because—rim shot, please!—bystanders thought a real hold-up was in progress; #2: How I unsuccessfully sought out real former child stars to appear in cameos; #3: How I successfully recruited real former child star Rodney Allen Rippy, who starred in TV commercials for Jack in the Box in the 1970s, to do a cameo.)

I stammered when a person asked the inevitable "So, how much did it cost?" (FYI: No one is shy about pumping you for info on that one, so don't get offended.) Anyway, I mumbled an answer—afraid if anybody heard me correctly, they'd charge right back: "You spent how much?!?...and it looks like THAT!?!"

> ". . . then I thanked people profusely for not throwing stuff. At me. Or the screen. All in all, a pretty good night. To date, it's the best festival night I've had. Also, the only one."

And then I thanked people profusely for not throwing stuff. At me. Or the screen. All in all, a pretty good night. To date, it's the best festival night I've had. Also, the only one.

We've had theatrical screenings in New York, Las Vegas, San Francisco and Los Angeles (as the midnight show for a couple weekends at a local theater), but as far as festivals go, Dallas was the ballgame to date.

Sure, there were Cleveland and Chattanooga, but they didn't pay for my trip and I couldn't afford to go on my own. (Also, I lacked that chutzpah thing necessary to finagle myself free airfare, á la a scene from a Jennifer Aniston film.)

The organizers of those two fests weren't mad about my planned absences; they said they weren't anyway. I can't say for sure now. They never took any of my follow-up phone calls.

What did you feel you've learned from the experience?

Look, I was nobody—NOBODY—and people at film festivals and studios still took the time to watch my flick, to take my calls. Did everybody like what they saw? No. But I learned the access IS there. Film people want to see good films. They want to hear good stories. You got that, you're in.

Naïve? I don't care. That's my one plucky attitudinal vice and me and Pauly Shore are sticking to it.

You can subscribe to Joal Ryan's *Former Child Star-Palooza*, which is a free e-mail newsletter, by sending an e-mail to: houseofscooter@dcdu.com.

JOAL RYAN'S ADVICE ON HOW TO WIN THE FILM FESTIVAL GAME (OR AT LEAST NOT BE REDUCED TO TEARS WHILE PLAYING):

1. Attend a film festival. (Preferably the one you'd really like to get into. And, yes, that means planning a year in advance—at least. Don't sweat the lag time. Trust me. I've tried the slap-dash method; I don't recommend it.)
2. Don't submit blind. (Until you know at least somebody at a festival is pulling for you, it's pointless. Take the time to do the proper leg work. Unofficially show your film to as many people as you can. Solicit advice. Make contacts. If all goes well, you'll save yourself a bundle on entry fees.)
3. Keep moving. (Satchel Paige's baseball wisdom works for movies, too. Don't wait for word from Sundance or Slamdance. Keep working other festivals. Keep writing scripts. Keep moving.)
4. If you get in, take your mother with you. (I took mine to Dallas. Parents make a great conversation piece at the nightly cocktail parties.)
5. Make a really, really good movie. (Go figure. Quality has a way of cutting down on the number of scams you need to run to get people to notice your movie.)
   The funny thing with Former Child Star is even though I didn't enjoy, or deserve, one of those Sundance Success Stories, the experience left me hopeful, not despairing.

THE DECISION MAKERS

PETER BRODERICK,
Acquisitions Executive

Peter Broderick

Peter Broderick is President of Next Wave Films, which provides finishing funds to exceptional ultra-low budget, English-language feature films from around the world. Broderick has played a key role in the growth of the ultra-low budget feature movement. He has organized presentations and spoken on ultra-low budget production at workshops, conferences, and panels across the country and overseas.

Broderick is also Vice President of the Independent Feature Project/West (IFP/West), and has been an active board member of both IFP/West and *Filmmaker* magazine for a number of years. He is also chair of the selection committee for the Someone To Watch Award honoring exceptionally talented new independent filmmakers.

Broderick previously worked with Terrence Malick on *Days of Heaven* and ran Malick's production company, Hickory Street. He has also been a consultant to the Sundance Film Festival, PBS, and the Rockefeller Foundation. An expert on new media, he is author of the report *Independents in Cyberspace*. He has written for *The New York Times, The Times of London, The Economist,* and *The Los Angeles Times*. A graduate of Brown University, Cambridge University, and Yale Law School, he practiced law in Washington, DC.

Does every film seeking distribution have to go to a film festival?
Certain types of films are better suited to being launched at festivals than others. A well made genre film that doesn't break any rules or try anything notably different may have a better chance of finding distribution at a screening arranged for distributors than at a festival. Films that take risks in form or content may be well received at certain festivals. Good reviews, strong audience response and awards can provide a comfort zone for distributors considering films that are

unique. The excitement that *Clerks* generated at its Sundance screenings helped convince Miramax to take a chance on a film that wasn't like anything that had come before.

Is a festival strategy recommended?

Determining the right festival strategy for a film and then implementing it requires a substantial amount of time and effort. Some valuable information can be found in print and online, but every filmmaker should also talk with other filmmakers who have recently been on the festival circuit. They will have opinions about which festivals are most helpful and the best ways to approach them. Filmmakers need to learn how playing certain festivals may enhance or limit their chances of being accepted by others. Then filmmakers should develop a Plan A and a Plan B—possible sequences for showing their films at domestic and foreign festivals.

What does Next Wave provide for filmmakers besides completion funding?

Next Wave Films helps develop a festival strategy for each film we provide finishing funds for, and then will work closely with the filmmakers to implement that strategy. We were created to help exceptionally talented filmmakers launch their careers. We are looking for outstanding features that demonstrate such talent and are unique—the same kinds of films that festivals are seeking. Our first film, *Blood, Gut, Bullets & Octane,* premiered at Sundance and was then shown at the Berlin and Edinburgh Film Festivals.

> "Determining the right festival strategy for a film and then implementing it requires a substantial amount of time and effort. Some valuable information can be found in print and online, but every filmmaker should also talk with other filmmakers who have recently been on the festival circuit."

What is the best criteria for evaluating which festivals to launch a film?

When evaluating which festivals would be best to launch a film, it is important to evaluate the extent of distributor and press coverage. Sundance and Toronto have maximum attendance by both. The level of coverage at other festivals varies, but is often similar to what it was the previous year. Over time festival fortunes can rise and fall so it is a good idea to tap into the expertise of festival regulars.

How do you seek out good films?

We regularly attend festivals around the world to spread the word about Next Wave, meet filmmakers, and learn about ultra low budget films in production.

The skyrocketing number of independent films produced each year has made things harder for everyone. Festival programmers, distributors, and critics are feeling overwhelmed by the volume of films. The odds of getting into one of the major festivals are getting steadily longer. The percentage of films finding theatrical distribution is also declining. Consequently the importance of festivals is growing. Many filmmakers feel that their chances of finding distribution depend upon getting into festivals, as do their chances of finding financing for their next features. Unfortunately, there is a growing number of good films made by talented new filmmakers that aren't being selected for the limited number of major festival slots.

STEPHEN GATES, Agent

It is said that agents have to understand every facet of the entertainment business. Stephen Gates' extensive background in both production and creative elements of film, make him an excellent resource on the business of entertainment.

Gates began his education with a B.A. in Economics and Film/Video Studies from the University of Michigan, Ann Arbor, and finished with an M.F.A. in Directing and Production from the Tisch School at NYU. While completing his Masters Degree, he worked as a union assistant cameraman on commercials, videos, and feature films. After finishing his award-winning senior thesis film *Reasonable Doubt*, he did like many in Hollywood and began interning.

Stephen started as a script reader at both Arnold Kopelson Productions and Brillstein-Grey Entertainment. In a short period of time he jumped to creative affairs executive at Sneak Preview Productions, overseeing project progress and packaging and sales of rights. The packaging of projects appealed to him and he went on to work at ICM.

After getting a taste of the agency business, he joined Susan Smith and Associates as a motion picture literary agent. In September 1997, Gates joined the motion picture literary department at Writers & Artists Agency, and continues to apply his knowledge to the benefit of his clients and the industry itself. In his work at Writers & Artists, Gates specializes in representing independent writers and directors.

Why does a filmmaker need an agent?

The most important reason a filmmaker needs an agent is for protection. We are there to protect the interests of our clients from those individuals looking to take advantage of them. Primarily, this is important during the deal making process. You would not believe how many people I've spoken with who have been screwed over by people while making what they thought was a fair deal. Agents are also important in procuring work for clients as well as helping to guide their careers. We are a pipeline to the industry. Every piece of information goes through an agency pipeline.

What sort of questions should a filmmaker ask when hiring a agent?

People should always work with an agent or agency they feel comfortable with. What kind of clients does that agent represent? How does that agent cover the studios and producers with regards to open writing assignments and open directing assignments? Does the agent only represent writers or also directors and filmmakers? Do they have connections with acquisition companies and finance companies? This last question is a little tricky because most literary agents won't have those connections; some do, and that may be important to the person looking for an agent. What agents do is not brain surgery—the most important thing is whether or not that agent is going to work for you. You could be at the most high profile agency in the world, but if your agent isn't servicing you, it's meaningless.

How does one go about getting the attention of an agent?

The best way to get the attention of an agent is through a referral from a reputable source. Referrals from other clients, creative executives, producers, producer's assistants, lawyers, managers, etc. Query letters are not always the best way. Most agents don't have the time to read them. An individual attempting to get to an agent should never sell short trying to make a relationship with the agent's assistant. Assistants are the most important individual to the agent. They usually weed through query letters to find the things *they* find interesting. They also will do the bulk of the script submission reading. This is also true for assistants in every aspect of this business—they control who gets to their bosses—never treat them disrespectfully.

What does a filmmaker give up to an agent in terms of fees?

An agent's fees are fixed at ten percent of what the filmmaker makes in any given deal. This is regulated by the guilds and we are licensed.

What red flags do you look for in any deal?

The red flags I look for in most deals are the reversion and turn around clauses for written material. This pertains to the original writer or filmmaker regaining the rights to their material if it is not made within a certain time period. With young filmmakers I'm always leery about getting them involved in a deal where there is no upfront money to be made. This could be for either additional writing steps or option money. For directors, I try to stay away from the optional pictures that studios try to stick on to the end of deals. Many times I can't eliminate them altogether, but I try to limit the quantity.

What was the best deal you were involved with?

The best deal I've ever been involved with was for a small character-driven screenplay. The writing was incredible but we were unsure of its studio commercial appeal. I sent it out to several producers, all of whom wanted to take it to several buyers. It languished for a bit, then the writer became very hot after procuring two high profile writing assignments. All of a sudden everyone wanted this small, well-written project. We wound up getting a great deal for the script by a major producer with a studio deal who will make the movie within a year. It just proved to me again, how great writing will always win out...

How does an agent participate in creating heat for a client?

Creating heat for a client or a project is a bizarre process. People in Hollywood are easily swayed by word of mouth and perception. I personally believe that the heat I create for a person or a project should be backed up by the material. My passion for a filmmaker or a piece of material along with my reputation are the most important elements in creating heat. Whom the word is spread to is also very important. One should try to create heat and word of mouth at the highest levels. We become cheerleaders for our clients. But, as I stated earlier, the material or the individual I bring to a producer or studio executive better be able to deliver or my ability to create heat for future projects is compromised. I *can't* cry wolf.

> "What agents do is not brain surgery—the most important thing is whether or not that agent is going to work for you."

PATRICK LYNN, Producer's Rep

A graduate of Cal State University, Long Beach, Patrick Lynn began his career in the independent arena in 1990 at the Samuel Goldwyn Company, learning the inner workings of production on such films as *The Playboys, Much Ado About Nothing* and *The Madness of King George.* Lynn was a part of Goldwyn's acquisition team on the marketing of such films as *Big Night, Hard Eight* and *Angels & Insects.* In 1996 he was named director of acquisitions for the Samuel Goldwyn Company where he bought the controversial film *Kissed* at the 1996 Toronto Film Festival and *I Love You, Don't Touch Me* at the 1997 Sundance Film Festival. Lynn left the Samuel Goldwyn Company in August '97, to act as producer's rep and producer for Joe Carnahan's *Blood, Guts, Bullets & Octane (BGB&O)* which gained a tremendous following after only one screening at the 1997 IFFM in New York.

What does a producer's rep do?

A producer's rep is your link to the world of acquisitions and distribution. Reps are the ones who will be there to ask the right questions when a distributor is waving a theatrical release in front of you. Their job is to ask the right questions and get you the best deal possible.

Why does a filmmaker need a producer's rep?

You need a producer's rep to insure you're getting a good deal first and foremost, by getting the right people to see your movie. The people who will potentially be BUYING your movie. Many times you get only one shot at a distributor whether it's at a film festival or a private screening. Once they've seen your film, they've seen it. Many acquisitions people see more movies in a week than most people see in a year.

A producer's rep will get paid a percentage of the deal. Maybe even more so if the producer plays more of a role in the production of the film. Normally it's ten percent of the sale of the film. If you sell your movie for $1 million (and wouldn't we all love to do that?) your rep gets $100,000, plus expenses. But it depends on the deal and the rep. And I should point out that very few independent movies sell for that much. You always hear these stories out of Sundance about such-and-such selling for a gazillion dollars. That is the exception, not the rule. Many films sell for far less, so don't look at it like your rep is making out like a bandit. If you get a sale—a theatrical sale—you're one among few.

What do filmmakers need to know when it comes to a producer's rep?

Before they choose a producer's rep, all filmmakers should know what the rep's track record is. Have they done this before? What did this person do before becoming a producer's rep? Have they sold any films at all and were those people happy with the job they did? Do they know acquisitions and distribution people? Can you talk to the rep's former clients? What filmmakers also need to know is that their labor of love may not garner a huge deal. Then again, it may, but that depends on the film.

Can filmmakers rep themselves?

I don't recommend this. Of course I don't because right now I'm a rep. Anyone certainly can rep themselves, but ask yourself why would you try to do this alone? Is it because you have no more funds left, even for Top Ramen? Or is it because you know your film will sell? I can tell you that you need a producer's rep to get you the best deal possible. If you have experience selling a movie, then okay. That's different. If you don't, you may be saying, "you shoulda" when you have scheduled a private screening and no buyers show up. Once your film has screened, opinions on your movie—either good or bad—will start making the rounds and you might not want that.

If you are going to rep your film by yourself, don't. I don't recommend this unless you are an experienced producer and have done it before. I see too many films go by the wayside that might have gotten distribution if they were handled differently.

A good producer's rep will know who the buyers are and who to go to. They will know them by name. They will be able to call them up and say "see this movie." A producer's rep will be out in the Hollywood arena giving your film good word of mouth. They will be stumping for your film with the people who buy movies.

What was the best deal you were involved with and why?

The best deal I was involved in was *BGB&O*. Best in the terms that here was a tiny film that spoke volumes. It was more than just the film; it was a new filmmaker, Joe Carnahan. It was basically a bunch of unknown guys who really did it right, and for the minuscule price of $7,300. For what was basically the sales tax on a big budget movie craft service, this guy made a movie that was different, it was new. I knew it would sell.

Specifically, how did this deal evolve?

This all started for me on May 20, 1997. I was still working at the Samuel Goldwyn Company as director of acquisitions and had just gotten back from Cannes. I was on America Online one night in the Hollywood Café Chat Room when I get a message from a guy (Joe Carnahan) looking for Patrick Lynn. He said we met very briefly at the Independent Feature Film Market (IFFM) in 1996 with his friend Leon Corcos who was screening a film. He said he had just completed his film and would I look at it? I said, "Sure, send it to me." At the time I was getting anywhere from five to six tapes a day, but I said I would look at it right away. I get the tape and pop it in my VCR. People are coming and going out of my office and I started watching this film and was amazed. I stop the tape, close my door and start it again. Watching it I keep thinking, "Wow, this is different." I called Joe and ask him, "How many people have you shown this to?" He says three and I tell him to stop there, don't send any more tapes out. I like this film. I like it a lot. It's a small film but one that warrants looking at. I screen it at Goldwyn and get as many people to watch it as I can. I told Joe that I would do anything he needed to get this film sold.

We talked about the IFFM and Sundance, but we were too late for the IFFM where I felt it would play extremely well. The IFP (Independent Feature Project) was going to be having a party for the films screening in September so I call Michelle Byrd, Sharon Sklar and Milton Tabbot from the IFP East, tell them about it and bring a tape to the party. I tell them this is the kind of film that needs to screen in the IFFM. I beg them to watch it. They do and love it. So now we're going to the IFFM.

Then Sundance announces there will be an early submission. Joe fires off a tape to Geoff Gilmore and I send a letter to John Cooper giving my two cents worth. Then, Goldwyn shuts its doors. I'm out of a job and one week from going to the Toronto Film Festival. I call Joe, give him my dire news and he responds with, "Good, you now have more time to rep my film." I commit. Joe has been talking to Neil

Friedman at William Morris, I talk to Hans Schiff (also at William Morris) and we decide to rep it together. I call the Toronto Film Festival, tell them what's going on and ask if they'll hold my pass. They do and help me out immensely at the festival. From there I go to New York and hook up with Joe and Dan Leis and the

> "You always hear these stories out of Sundance on so-and-so sold for a gazillion dollars. That is the exception, not the rule. Many films sell for far less, so don't look at it like your rep is making out like a bandit. If you get a sale—a theatrical sale—you're one among few."

BGB&O crew. We have one screening on Tuesday at 4:15 p.m. A bunch of people are going off to the Gotham awards but we hang onto a good number of them. After the screening, Joe, Dan and the crew are inundated with well wishers. That night, we go out and get drunk. The next night we go to the Sundance party where the buzz on the screening was incredible. Peter Broderick from Next Wave Films and Jonathan Sehring from IFC/Bravo want a meeting with us. Amy Taubin from the Village Voice interviews us the next morning for her IFFM piece (calling the film, "Better than the Usual Suspects"). They all LOVE the film. And now it begins.

So, how did you get the film into Sundance?

I had introduced Joe to Geoff Gilmore, John Cooper and Rebecca Yeldham from Sundance outside the Angelika when we were in New York. It was a very brief meeting but one that gave us a lot of confidence. Geoff liked the film and liked what Joe and the guys were doing at the IFFM. The way they were selling themselves and the movie in a guerrilla style marketing campaign. Back in Los Angeles we had all agreed that Sundance was a priority. But we were very hands off with them. We didn't constantly bug them about the film getting in. We knew they liked it so we let the film speak for itself. In the meantime, we needed to get a publicity person. Since Nancy Willen at Dennis Davidson Associates (DDA) had been on the film (and sent it to Neil) early on, we liked her. She understood the film. We had a conference call with Nancy and Mark Urman (then head of DDA) and he tells us that not only did he love the film, so did his son. We wanted DDA to do our publicity. Two days later we found out that Mark was leaving DDA and going to be President of CFP (later to be renamed Lion's Gate). Nancy assured us that even with Mark leaving, they still all supported the film. She and Melinda Hovee (the other publicist at DDA) wanted us. All the better now that Mark was in acquisitions. He could buy our film and in my mind, CFP was the place for the best possible theatrical release for this film. They had already proven themselves with smaller films like *Angel Baby, The Pillow Book* and *The Day Trippers.* So, to make a long story short, we go to Sundance, with our parkas and hats on and we have a blast. We are all staying together in one condo. We see Mark at Sundance; he still loves the movie and has Tom Ortenberg (VP Distribution) see the film as well. Mark loved the movie; Tom loved the movie—I knew these guys were going to buy the movie. One week after Sundance, we're talking numbers with them. We like them, they like us. We do the deal!

What did you do to get acquisition executives into your screenings?

Since I came from an acquisitions background, many of these folks are my friends. I know what they go through on a daily basis and I know what it's like for them to prepare for Sundance. I called them, let them know when and where the film was screening, how to get a hold of us, etc. A few weeks before Sundance, we faxed a contact sheet with the same information to all the acquisitions execs. That's all they need. When, where and why. I had been talking up the film since last July so they already had the pertinent facts. When I did acquisitions, I remember getting all sorts of little knickknacks for films screening at Sundance. Pens, press kits, stickers—you name it. Most of that stuff is a waste because all they really need is a simple postcard about the film. Remember this is a marketing tool. They want to see your film, not get a pen.

SECTION 4
FILM FESTIVAL LISTINGS

"Filmmaking is an art, but film festivals are a business."

—Arthur Borman, filmmaker, ...*And God Spoke*

THE TOP TEN FiLM FESTiVALS

This section contains the complete list of over 500 film festivals worldwide. We have identified the most important festivals and included detailed information which will aid you in your decision to visit a festival or enter your film.

The top ten festivals were selected based on a number of factors, one of the most important being that they qualify as "discovery" festivals—wherein new talent emerges to take center stage on the independent film scene. Each of them carry a certain amount of prestige and better opportunities for filmmakers to get publicity in the form of national media attention. In many ways they also act as back-door markets—the films that play at these ten festivals have a greater chance of getting picked up for distribution. Receiving an award from any of them will get the attention of the industry, which can go a long way toward launching a career. And finally, this select group of festivals make great vacations, simply have the best parties and are just damn good places to see new films.

1. Sundance Film Festival

The mother of all independent film festivals, Sundance sets the tone for the industry which is why you will find as many festival directors from other film fests as you will agents and acquisitions executives. Sundance is the place to be in January whether you're a film lover, filmmaker or film student, no festival comes close to matching the experience. There is an air of excitement and electricity about the films one is about to see. Sundance is inspiring. Hearing tale after tale of the struggle of indie film directors at post-screening Q&A sessions only serves to motivate the next generation of filmmakers to pick up a camera.

Sure there's a certain amount of frustration with the insanely cold weather, sold out screenings and packed parties, but like a strained family gathering at Thanksgiving, you know you'll always come back—and love every minute of it.

The Sundance Kid,
Robert Redford.

SUNDANCE FiLM FESTiVAL

P.O. Box 16450
Salt Lake City, UT 84116
California Headquarters:
225 Santa Monica Blvd. 8th Floor
Santa Monica, CA 90401
TEL: (310) 394-4662 (California)
(801) 328-3456 (Utah)
FAX: (310) 394-8353 (California)
(801) 575-5175 (Utah)
E-MAIL: sundance@xmission.com (Utah)
sundance@deltanet.com (California)
WEB SITE: http://www.sundance.org
FESTIVAL DATE: January
ENTRY DEADLINE: October 3 for short subject entries and October 10 for feature entries.
CONTACT: R.J. Millard, Press Coordinator
DIRECTOR: Nicole Guillemet, Managing Director
PROGRAMMER: Geoffrey Gilmore, Programming Director
CATEGORY: Independent, International
PROFILE: Each January in Park City, Utah, the Sundance Institute presents the Sundance Film Festival, an exhibition of work at the forefront of independent cinema. Each year, the programming staff of the Sundance Institute views over 2,500 submissions to select between 100 and 105 feature films, along with 60 shorts, for exhibition to an audience of more than 12,000.

Sundance was founded in 1969 by Robert Redford as a community that would foster the alliance of art and recreation while preserving the integrity of the land. Nestled at the base of 12,000-foot Mount Timpanogos, the Sundance Village offers guests everything from Film Festival screenings to a unique collection of cozy mountain cottages and homes.

In addition, Sundance's award winning dining, unique shopping, historic Owl Bar, ski area and Nordic Center are the perfect escape between films.

The Sundance Institute adopted sponsorship of the United States Film Festival in 1984, creating an internationally recognized showcase for new independent cinema. The highlight of the Festival is the American Independent Dramatic and Documentary Competition, where new Independent American films are given their premieres. Exposure through the competition brings to prominence scores of films that would not ordinarily be seen by distributors and studios. Indeed, many emerging independent filmmakers now look to the Sundance Film Festival as their first opportunity to present their films before an audience. Film goers and the entertainment industry look to the Festival for the discovery of new talent and as a champion of films that challenge and pique audiences and expand the boundaries of the art of film.

TOURIST INFORMATION: Hey, there's always time to ski.

TRAVEL TIPS: The Sundance Film Festival features a thoroughly integrated transit system effectively linking the Festival Transit with Park City Transit. Both systems are complimentary. Festival Transit stops at Festival Headquarters and at all official Festival venues. Express Festival Transit provides quick links with key areas. Maps designating Festival Transit routes and Park City Transit routes will be available in the upcoming Film Guide, at the Festival Headquarters Information Desk, the Main Box Office, each theatre location, and at local hotels.

TRAVEL TO THE FESTIVAL:

Travel Desk: (800) 933-5025 (801) 355-2300

Email: traveldesk1@juno.com

Contact Travel Desk, the official air travel agency of the Sundance Film Festival, for special Festival rates.

Delta Air Lines: (800) 241-6760

Delta Air Lines, Inc., in cooperation with the Sundance Institute and Travel Desk, is offering special discounted rates on flights to Salt Lake City for Festival participants. To take advantage of these special discounted fares, call Travel Desk and refer to Sundance Institute File Number 122060A.

Filmmaker Ben Affleck
(Chasing Amy, Going All the Way) *stays cool in Park City at the Sundance Film Festival.*

Express Shuttle: (800) 397-0773; (801) 596-1600; Fax: (801) 531-7882

Express Shuttle (formerly Rocky Mountain Super Express) provides round-trip shuttle service between the Salt Lake International Airport and the Festival in Park City. Service is also available between Park City and Opening Night events in Salt Lake City by reservation only. Vans depart the airport approximately every 30 minutes. To make a reservation, please have a major credit card and flight information ready when you call.

LODGING AT THE FESTIVAL:

• Festival Headquarters and Hospitality Suite

Shadow Ridge Resort Hotel and Conference Center: (435) 645-7509 or (801) 328-3456, 8AM—8PM daily

• The Yarrow Resort Hotel & Conference Center: (800) 927-7694 or (435) 649-7000

The Yarrow Resort Hotel and Conference Center is proud to be the Official Press Headquarters for the 1999 Sundance Film Festival. As a major Festival venue, the Yarrow Hotel features public and press screenings, with additional public screenings held at the Holiday Village Cinemas, located directly behind the Hotel. The Yarrow Hotel is conveniently located in the heart of Park City and is on the free Park City and Festival Transit routes for easy access to other Festival venues and Historic Main Street. As a full-service hotel, The Yarrow Hotel features and onsite restaurant and bar, outdoor year-round heated pool and hot tube and fitness facility. In addition, guests of the Hotel will enjoy a refrigerator, coffee maker, full-size ironing board, wall hair dryer, voice mail and data port telephones in every room!

• David Holland's Resort Lodging & Conference Services: (800) SKI-2002 or (435) 655-3315

David Holland's Resort Lodging offers a wide range of rental properties throughout Park City in locations convenient to Festival events and great skiing. If your needs include a condominium, an elegant hotel, an apartment or private home, call on us. For group sales, contact Shawn Lym at 435-649-0800.

• Gables Hotel: (800) 443-1045 or (435) 655-3315

• Park Station Condominium Hotel: (800) 367-1056 or (435) 649-7717

• The Lodge at Resort Center: (800) 824-5331 or (435) 649-0800

• Shadow Ridge Resort Hotel & Conference Center: (800) 451-3031 or (435) 649-4300

• Deer Valley Lodging: (800) 453-3833 or (435) 649-4040 or Fax (435) 645-8419

Deer Valley Lodging offers distinctive accommodations throughout Deer Valley and Park City. Relax in the luxury of unique one to four bedroom condominiums featuring spacious living areas, daily housekeeping and private spa options. New this year are The Lodges at Deer Valley offering hotel rooms, one bedroom suites and assorted condominiums. Call for Festival rates.

• The Lodging Company—The Inn at Prospector Square and The New Claim Condo Suites: (800) 453-3812 or (435) 649-7100; Fax (435) 649-8377

Films shown daily in our Prospector Square Theatre, full service athletic club and spa (available at a discounted fee), outdoor 20 person jacuzzi, and Grub Steak restaurant.

• Park City Resort Lodging: (800) 545-7669 or (435) 649-8200; Fax (435) 645-8419

Park City Resort Lodging features superior to deluxe accommodations throughout Park City. Select from conveniently located Main Street properties to delightful units near the Park City Mountain Resort. All properties feature comfortable living areas and easy access to the free citywide shuttle. Call for assistance with Festival lodging.

• Radisson Inn Park City: (800) 333-3333 or (435) 649-5000

The award-winning Radisson Inn is minutes away from Park City's Historic Main Street and located on the free shuttle. Enjoy Radigan's restaurant and Cooter's Private Club. Relax in our indoor/outdoor heated swimming pool, hydro spas and dry sauna.

• Sundance: (800) 892-1600 or (801) 225-4107; Fax (801) 226-1937

GETTING INTO SUNDANCE

Indie filmmaker Joe Carnahan, writer/director of *Blood, Guts, Bullets & Octane* talks from the trenches:

Anyone who believes that merely dropping a VHS cassette and a check in the mail will ensure the democratic process for themselves and their film where Sundance is concerned is completely delusional.

It is a lobbying job like no other. You are responsible for creating and generating the heat around your film to make the Geoff Gilmores and John Coopers stand up and take note. We were very fortunate in that we had an "ace in the hole" in Patrick Lynn, our producer's rep. Patrick was a very well-liked guy who had come out of acquisitions at Goldwyn and knew the people at Sundance in Santa Monica. He lobbied long and hard for us and basically heard very early on, at the Toronto Film Festival, that things looked good for *Blood, Guts, Bullets & Octane* in Sundance. I had an agent in the esteemed Neil Friedman at William Morris and the PR firm of Dennis Davidson & Associates who, with Nancy Willen's and Mark Urman's enthusiasm, had agreed to rep the film gratis.

It was important for me that I send out VHS tapes of the film. Nobody is going to come to your screening if they don't know you or you don't have some form of reference. It's important to get the tapes to people who can help. One of the majors sources of assistance was the very man authoring this book, Chris Gore, who initially put the call into DDA and got them excited. Everything was a springboard from there.

The way that our film got into Sundance was word of mouth. No other place on the planet serves as a better sounding board for this than the IFFM (Independent Feature Film Market) held annually in New York every September. The IFFM is a gathering of indie hopefuls, shamelessly hawking their wares on the mean streets of New York. There are anywhere from 100 to 200 shorts and features and every major distribution company is there: Miramax, Sony, October, Lion's Gate, Fox Searchlight, everybody.

This is THE BEST way to get your film seen by the big players. It is also a way to market yourself and your film. I had six other guys travelling with me who had worked on the film in various capacities. Each one of us was outfitted with matching shirts and hats that we wore to the market EVERY DAY! We may have been viewed as obnoxious, gratuitous self-promoters, BUT IT WORKED! We were getting noticed in a big way, enough for Amy Taubin of the *Village Voice* to review the film and raving about it, going as far as to say it was "better than *The Usual Suspects*." At the Sundance party two nights later, we were the talk of the room and had a virtual who's who of indie film tracking us down, from Jon Sloss to Bob Hawk, it was quite a night... and it was all keyed by the market and by dogged promotion on our part.

2. Toronto International Film Festival

Toronto, Canada is host to one of the most respected festivals in the industry. There are so many films and programs at Toronto that it is impossible to experience everything, which means that one may create a festival of their own by choosing from a vast range of Canadian films, retrospectives from overseas, debuts of Hollywood fare and independent film premieres. Toronto breaks new talent and has premiered the first films of people like indie fave Tom DiCillo and wise-ass documentarian Michael Moore.

One of the best organized festivals in the world, the amazing staff works diligently with filmmakers to help promote their films to the more than 1,000 members of the press that attend. Toronto is also a key festival for acquisitions executives looking for hot new films. The parties are a blast and the city of Toronto itself provides incredible opportunities for fun.

TORONTO INTERNATIONAL FILM FESTIVAL

2 Carlton Street, Suite 1600
Toronto, Ontario M5B 1J3 USA
TEL: (416) 967-7371
FAX: (416) 967-9477
E-MAIL: tiffg@torfilmfest.ca
WEB SITE: www.bell.ca/filmfest
FESTIVAL DATE: September
ENTRY DEADLINE: April (Canadian Shorts). May (Canada). June (International Features).
YEAR FESTIVAL BEGAN: 1976

CONTACT: Sarah Brooks, Manager, Programme Administration
DIRECTOR: Piers Handling
MANAGING DIRECTOR: Michèle Maheux
PROGRAMMERS: Kay Armatage, Noah Cowan, Liz Czach, Helen du Toit, Dimitri Eipides, Colin Geddes, June Givanni, Steve Gravestock, Piers Handling, Michèle Maheux, David Overbey, Ramiro Puerta
OTHER STAFF: Director of Administration, Peter Roberts; Communications Director, Nuria Bronfman; Director of Development, Ana White; Director of Finance, Penny Weeks; Director of Public Affairs, Allison Bain; Film Reference Library Director, Sylvia Frank; Film Circuit Director, Cam Haynes
CATEGORY: International
PROFILE: To actively cultivate excellence and involvement in film as art and industry. The Toronto International Film Festival Group operates the Toronto International Film Festival; Cinematheque Ontario (a year-round screening programme, specializing in Canadian and international cinema, featuring both classic and contemporary films); The Film Reference Library; SPROCKETS Toronto International Film Festival for Children; and The Film Circuit (coordinates screenings for Canadian and international films for volunteer film groups in over 30 centres throughout Ontario).

The Toronto International Film Festival is a 10-day event held every September featuring nearly 300 films from over 50 countries. The Festival hosts over 700 accredited international media, in excess of 900 invited guests including directors, producers and actors, and more than 2500 industry participants. The Toronto International Film Festival is one of the biggest in North America, is considered a *must attend* by industry professionals, and is ranked among the top four film festivals in the world.
SEMINARS: The Rogers Industry Centre is *the place to do business.* The Centre provides a Canadian perspective on the international business of film and television. In 1997, it included: the Ultra Indie Experience, a series of daily up-close and personal discussions with five of the hottest new directors and their production teams; the Screenplay Café, where industry players peruse scripts from festival films; Micro-Meetings, sessions featuring key industry executives in informal one-hour meetings; Symposium, includes keynote addresses, main sessions, various workshops and panels; and, the Sales Office, representing films programmed in the current Festival, attracts the elite of the international film buying and selling community and has helped nurture the reputation of many young filmmakers.

PANELS: See above

FAMOUS SPEAKERS: 1997 speakers included: Tom Schulman, Mike Newell, Sydney Levine, James Schamus, Roger Ebert, Michael Moore, Errol Morris, Chris Hegedus, David Thompson, Simon Perry

AWARDS: Yes

COMPETITIONS: No

MAJOR AWARDS: The Toronto International Film Festival does not have a market, nor is it competitive but it does have the following awards:

Metro Media Award: *Boogie Nights* (d. Paul Thomas Anderson), *L.A. Confidential* (d. Curtis Hanson)

International Critics Award for film from Festival's Discovery Programme: *Under the Skin* (d. Carine Adler)

People's Choice Award: *The Hanging Garden* (d. Thom Fitzgerald)

1997 Canadian Awards:

CITYTV Award for Best Canadian First Feature (cash prize of $15,000): *Cube* (d. Vincenzo Natali)

Toronto-City Award for Best Canadian Feature Film (cash prize of $25,000): *The Hanging Garden* (d. Thom Fitzgerald) and *The Sweet Hereafter* (d. Atom Egoyan)

NFB-John Spotton Award for Best Canadian Short Film (cash $2500 + $2500 benefits to be applied to costs of a future production): *Cotton Candy* (d. Roshell Bissett)

LAST WINNING FILMS: See Major Awards.

APPLICATION FEE: No entry fee.

ODDS OF ACCEPTANCE: -281 films from 58 countries; 233 features, 49 shorts; 1163 International Submissions; 47 first features; 130 international features making their world or North American premieres

3. Telluride Film Festival

Telluride is the best vacation festival on the planet, period. Sundance may be the place where the industry does business, but in Telluride you'll make lifelong friends. It is the place where film lovers gather to enjoy movies, plain and simple. Set in a former mining town in the Rocky Mountains at a breathtaking (literally) 9,000 foot elevation, the September event in Telluride, Colorado, transforms the whole tiny city into a celebration of cinema. (The city itself is very small and everything is in convenient walking distance—no need to rent a car.) The charming venues remind one of the movie theaters of yesteryear—without the modern, annoying and cumbersome sound systems of theaters today that'll leave your ears ringing.

There's just something special about being at Telluride that one can't describe. Conversation in film lines revolves around the "art" and appreciation of movies rather than "money," current box office or the latest "deal," which is incredibly refreshing. The festival is also short, a four-day event that seems to end too soon, leaving one wanting more.

TELLURiDE FiLM FESTiVAL

"The best film festival in the world."
—*Jennifer Jason Leigh*

"The emphasis here is entirely on the movies. There are no pretenses and it's so refreshing."
—*Laura Dern*

National Film Preserve Ltd.
P. O. Box B1156
Hanover, NH 03755
TEL: (603) 643-1255
FAX: (603) 643-5938
E-MAIL: Tellufilm@aol.com
WEB SITE: http://www.telluridemm.com/trideinfo/filmfest/
FESTIVAL DATE: September
ENTRY DEADLINE: August 1st
YEAR FESTIVAL BEGAN: 1974
DIRECTOR: Stella Pence, General Manager
CATEGORY: Independent, Student
PROFILE: For over twenty-five years, the Telluride

Film Festival has brought the world's best films to the remote mountain town of Telluride, Colorado every Labor Day weekend. Though carefully guarding its line-up until hours before the first program, film lovers can count on a program rich with premieres, revivals, and cinematic tributes. Named the "cozy, one-big-happy-family of film festivals" by the *Los Angeles Times,* organizers work hard to keep the event unique and intimate, while striving to keep its programming and guests accessible. It is not about selling movies or counting big movie stars on the street, it is simply about enjoying good films. The Telluride Film Festival remains one of the premiere cinematic events in the world.

Telluride is well known as one of the major showcases for new and independent film from around the world. Some of the Festival's World Premieres have included Robert Rodriguez' *El Mariachi,* Michael Moore's *Roger and Me,* Neil Jordan's *The Crying Game,* Louis Malle's *Vanya on 42nd Street,* Ken Burns' *The Civil War,* Billy Bob Thornton's *Sling Blade,* and Kasi Lemmon's *Eve's Bayou.*

FAMOUS SPEAKERS: Telluride has orchestrated tributes to the following: Shirley MacLaine, Mike Leigh, Alain Cavalier, John Schlesinger, Zhang Yimou, Judy Davis, Ken Burns, Harriet Andersson, Ken Loach, John Alton, Jennifer Jason Leigh, Elmer Bernstein, Cy Endfield, Harvey Keitel, Jodie Foster, Sven Nykvist, Clint Eastwood, Gerard Depardieu, John Berry and many more.

AWARDS: No

COMPETITIONS: No

APPLICATION TIPS: Entry in the Telluride Film Festival is open to professional and non-professional filmmakers working in all aesthetic disciplines: documentary, narrative, animation, experimental, etc. Features and shorts of all styles and lengths are eligible for consideration provided that they are new works and will remain unseen by the public until the current Labor Day weekend.

Selected short films will play either with a feature or as part of three specially selected programs of "Filmmakers of Tomorrow," "Great Expectations," and "Celluloid Resumes," featuring works by emerging artists.

For students, the most important qualities we seek are: passion for film, an ability to interact with other students and Symposium guests, and a willingness to follow a rigorous, albeit free-form program of screenings and discussions. With only 50 slots available, each student's full commitment to the program is critical.

APPLICATION FEE: Students $25; $35 for films under 20 minutes; $55 for films 20-40 minutes; $75 for films over 40 minutes.

ODDS OF ACCEPTANCE: Over 400 films entered.

TRAVEL TIPS: The festival takes place in Telluride, Colorado which is at a 9,000 foot elevation. (Keep in mind that pilots in the Air Force are given oxygen at 10,000 foot elevations.) Steer clear from alcoholic beverages as their effect in the mountain air is greatly enhanced. Give yourself at least a day to get used to the thin air.

TELLURIDE FILM FESTIVAL TIPS

Independent filmmaker *(Free Enterprise)* and Telluride veteran Mark Altman explains why he loves Telluride:

It's not a bunch of slimy industry-ites with cell phones glued to their ears. The festival attracts real film fans and care about cinema—eclectic people from all around the world. The serene setting helps bring down the decibel level which makes the whole festival a laid back affair with some of the best cinema around.

The Telluride Film Festival is one of the most remarkable experiences any film fan can have. To give up on the hurlyburly of everyday life and immerse oneself in four days of marathon filmgoing each year under the starlit skies of Telluride is an experience I treasure. Exchanging cell phones for hiking boots, even the most jaded industry veterans (myself included) cannot help but be mellowed by the bucolic and serene setting in which the best cinema the world has to offer is unspooled each year.

Every Labor Day weekend, it is a true delight to meet new friends and engage old ones from festival's years past while comparing notes and furiously arguing over the year's fare. There's always some new surprise or special delight to be gleaned. I'll never forget my first year, giddy with anticipation and overwhelmed with excitement, I was disappointed to see that my first adventure at the Sheridan Opera House would be the Nature's Filmmakers tribute. "Nature's Filmmakers?!?" I exclaimed. I didn't want to see that! For me, a dyed in the wool New York transplant to L.A. who shares with Woody being two with nature, the thought of spending two hours with

"Nature's Filmmakers" seemed like sheer torture, but when I emerged from the Opera House I learned the true joy of Telluride: discovering the unexpected. I was enthralled and fascinated by the program and quickly captivated by the spirit of Telluride. By the end of my first year, I couldn't wait to come back. And as I learned in the coming years, the best was yet to come.

The small, intimate and obscure showcases are the ones that are the most unforgettable. Whether it be the tributes to filmmakers like the late John Alton, the litany of silent films played out to the backdrop of the Alloy Orchestra, Vincent Sherman's reaction to the adoring crowd after watching *The Hard Way,* the incredible Lumiere tribute, sharing in the rare treat of the sole unspooling of Kubrick's *Fear & Desire* in the Nugget, discovering *The Crying Game, El Mariachi* or *Once Were Warriors* months before anyone had heard of these films or sitting in the rain-soaked mud watching all three hours of *Apocalypse Now* as well as *Hearts of Darkness.* Watching Abel Ferrara defend *Bad Lieutenant* to an indignant moviegoer who cried out, "Never in Telluride, Never in Telluride."

There are also those unique Telluride memories of bemoaning the end of the Strand Theater only to be even more awestruck by the opening of the Max, a reminiscence that no one but a Telluride veteran could appreciate. Of course, for all the impressively erudite, high-brow fare that Telluride has offered in the last 25 years, the moment that I will never forget is sitting with my head back on the grass, bundled up in a warm winter parka, watching *The Magnificent Seven* on the towering Ralph Lauren outdoor screen with the San Jacinto mountains as a real-life backdrop to the on-screen western action listening to the strains of Elmer Bernstein's bombastically brilliant score.

Final word of advice: Take the charter flight. You always meet interesting people on the plane and the one hour drive from Montrose.

4. Cannes Film Festival

Cannes is home to the most prestigious film festival in the world. (And when in France remember, Cannes is pronounced CAN as in "a trash can", not KHAN from "Star Trek: The Wrath of Khan".) Held in the sprawling city on the French Riviera, the May event known as the Festival International du Film du Cannes (Cannes Film Festival) attracts the top players in the industry world wide from studio executives to moguls, to the biggest celebrities, to press to filmmakers right down to the struggling indies.

There are five sections of the festival you should know: Compètition (Competitive Section), Un Certain Regard (Showcase Section), La Semaine de la Critique (Critic's Week), La Quinzaine des Rèalisateurs (Director's Fortnight), and The Marchè (the Market).

While many film festivals shy away from their obvious market appeal, Cannes embraces this business reality by offering filmmakers a chance to sell their movies to overseases buyers. Any film is welcome to be a part of the market (for a price) which makes the whole event feel more democratic.

Learn a little French, save up some cash (*everything* is expensive) and realize that no amount of preparation is sufficient for the largest and most prestigious film festival in the world. (But seeing topless women on the beach in thong bikinis doesn't require that much preparation, trust me.)

Trey Parker and Matt Stone are naked from the waist down on the beaches of Cannes. No one is shocked.

CANNES FILM FESTIVAL

99 Boulevard Malesherbes
75008 Paris, France
TEL: (33-1) 45-61-6600
FAX: (33-1) 45-61-9760
E-MAIL: festival@festival-cannes.fr
WEB SITE: http://www.festival-cannes.fr/
FESTIVAL DATE: May
ENTRY DEADLINE: March
CONTACT: Gilles Jacob, Pierre Viot
CATEGORY: Independent, International, Markets
AWARDS: Yes
COMPETITIONS: Yes
MAJOR AWARDS: -Palme d'Or; Grand Prix; Best Actress/Actor; Best Director; Best Screenplay; Special Jury Prize; Technical Grand Prix; Camera d'Or
ODDS OF ACCEPTANCE: Over 200 films entered.
SPECIAL NOTES: Press or industry accreditation is available through an organization called Unifrance and entitles you to attend screenings in the official program as well as access the Palais du Festivals and many of the various festival pavillions. Usually you need to obtain the application forms from your home country film office, such as the Australian Film Commission or the French Film Office (USA—Unifrance Film USA, 745 Fifth Ave, New York NY 10151.) Accreditation is free.

Market accreditation entitles you access to the market screenings that take place across the city in addition to the official program. Sometimes holders of market accreditation are given priority when waiting for tickets to official screenings as well. Market registration costs around 4100 French francs (about $700 U.S.); however, this entitles three people to attend from the registered company. Additional people can be registered with a sliding fee for those over the first three.

The selection process for films that screen at Cannes is very different than most festivals. Each country provides a slate of films that it thinks are worthy of entry (this is usually administered by each country's national film commission or equivalent organization). The main criteria for selection in any of the sections is that the film must not have been released theatrically outside its country of origin. Once each country has presented its group of films, the Festival chooses those which will be honored with official selection. You cannot submit a film directly to the festival. However, the market is open to all who wish to pay for the privilege.

5. Los Angeles Independent Film Festival (LAiFF)

This relatively new festival has fast become THE discovery festival on the West Coast. Nothing comes close when it comes to acquisition deals. LAIFF is comprised almost exclusively of American independent films making their debut, the films are screened in cozy settings like the Directors Guild which also makes a great post-screening party palace. (Other screenings take place at Paramount Studios and Raleigh Studios.) In addition, there are great seminars in association with the Writer's Guild and Director's Guild, as well as informative panels on independent filmmaking and financing. Every year the event grows and additions of series like

"Actors Direct" have included films by Sandra Bullock and Rob Lowe. Celebs and indie filmmakers alike hob-nob at what is fast becoming a festival that is the toast of LA.

LOS ANGELES INDEPENDENT FiLM FESTiVAL (LAiFF)

5455 Wilshire Blvd. #1500
Los Angeles, CA 90036
TEL: (323) 937-9155
FAX: (323) 937-7770
E-MAIL: LAIFF@aol.com or info@laiff.com
WEB SITE: http://www.laiff.com/
FESTIVAL DATE: April
ENTRY DEADLINE: January
YEAR FESTIVAL BEGAN: 1993
DIRECTOR: Robert Faust
CATEGORY: Independent
PROFILE: Mission statement: The Los Angeles Independent Film Festival welcomes to L.A. the finest independent films from across the United States. This annual festival continues its efforts towards uniting the independent filmmaking community, bringing together a unique group of non profit organizations to support each other and filmmakers across the country. LAIFF showcases and celebrates the diversity of American independent film, giving film-goers a place to discover and support emerging talent.

The Los Angeles Independent Film Festival (LAIFF) is the only festival in L.A. designed specifically to promote American independent film. It has the honor of being the only festival to combine the efforts of twelve leading non-profit film organizations in order to ensure comprehensive curating. LAIFF provides the Los Angeles filmmaking community and film-goers with the opportunity to see films that have yet to be distributed. The attention filmmakers have received over the last five years as a result of the festival has garnered them meetings, press, representation and a good number of distribution deals.

"The LAIFF is becoming the next breakout festival for independent films in North America... Clearly Sundance and Toronto are the premiere festivals, but LAIFF will take its place as the third stop on the tour," stated producer's rep Jonathan Dana.

SEMINARS: In addition to new films, LAIFF continues its tradition of offering festival-goers a series of diverse, highly informative, (and soldout) seminars.
AWARDS: Yes
COMPETITIONS: Yes

MAJOR AWARDS: -Audience Award; Best Feature-length Film; Best Writer; Best Director; Best Short Film
VALUE OF AWARDS: Awards include cash, various products and services. The feature award comes with a service package totaling more than $14,000, including donations from Eastman Kodak, CFI and REI Media.
FILMS SCREENED: 25 features and 55-60 shorts
ODDS OF ACCEPTANCE: 1300 entered
ATTENDANCE: 12,000

TRAVEL TIP

"Travel light. You will pick up a bunch of crap at the festival—T-shirts, caps, etc... Take advantage of the free food at parties whenever you can. And get lots of sleep— snooze during bad films so you can be fresh and alert for the parties!"
—Gabe Wardell, projectionist for the Slamdance Film Festival

6. New York Film Festival

Location, location, location are the three reasons that the New York Film Festival earns its place as one of the top festivals. Being located in the heart of the world's media elite gives the event an edge when it comes to press coverage. The relatively small program of two dozen or so films that screen means that acceptance into the festival is like winning a prize, something that New York does not do. There is no competition at the festival, something they have been criticized for in the past. As one of the longest running festivals in the United States, as an attention-getter, this fest is the apple of many a moviegoer's eye.

Recognized as a major New York event, the festival has introduced the American public to critically-acclaimed films, many of which have become contemporary classics. Among the outstanding films that have been shown are: Francois Truffaut's *Day For Night* (1973); Marcel Ophuls' *The Sorrow And The Pity* (1970) and *Hotel Terminus: The Life And Times Of Klaus Barbie* (1988); Bernardo Bertolucci's *Last Tango In Paris* (1972); Wim Wenders' *The American Friend* (1977); Akira Kurosawa's *Ran* (1985); Pedro Almodovar's *Women On The Verge Of A Nervous Breakdown* (1988); Barbara's Kopple's *American Dream* (1990); Gus Van Sant's *My Own Private Idaho* (1991); Neil Jordan's *The Crying Game* (1992); Robert Altman's *Short Cuts* (1993); Jane Campion's *The Piano* (1993); Quentin Tarantino's *Pulp Fiction* (1994); Terry Zwigoff's *Crumb* (1994); Wong Kar-wai's *Chungking Express* (1994); Rob Epstein and Jeffrey Friedman's *The Celluloid Closet* (1995); Lars von Trier's *Breaking The Waves* (1996); and Mike Leigh's *Secrets And Lies* (1996)

Films for the New York Film Festival are selected by a five-member committee of film experts.

NEW YORK FiLM FESTiVAL
Film Society of Lincoln Center
70 Lincoln Center Plaza
New York, NY 10023
Tel: (212) 875-5610
Fax: (212) 875-5636
E-mail: sbensman@filmlinc.com
Web Site: http://www.filmlinc.com/index2.html
Festival Date: October
Entry Deadline: Varying July dates for films less than 20 minutes and for films over 20 minutes
Contact: Richard Pena
Category: International
Profile: The New York Film Festival ushers autumn in with the newest and most significant works by directors—established icons and new discoveries alike—from all over the world. This enormously popular event stirs the hearts and minds of audiences and stimulates critical debate on the season's best movie-making.

Over the years, the New York Film Festival has proudly premiered films by Martin Scorsese, Jean-Luc Godard, François Truffaut, Akira Kurosawa, Jane Campion, Louis Malle, Jonathan Demme, James Ivory, Robert Altman, Barbara Kopple and Quentin Tarantino, among others.

The New York Film Festival prefers to screen a small number of films despite its large nature. It has previously showcased a number of popular films such as *Pulp Fiction* (1994), *Secrets & Lies* (1996) and *The People Vs. Larry Flynt* (1996).

Co-sponsored with the Museum of Modern Art, New Directors/New Films has earned an international reputation as the foremost forum for film art that breaks or re-makes the cinematic mold. As a festival dedicated to discovering emerging and overlooked artists, newcomers on the verge of mainstream success and distinguished veterans whose work deserves wider public attention, New Directors nurtures directorial talent by creating an invaluable opportunity for that talent to win public support and acceptance.

Since its beginning in 1972, New Directors' audiences have been treated to an early preview of such diverse talents as Wim Wenders, Steven Spielberg, John Sayles, Spike Lee, Sally Potter, Pedro Almodóvar, Chen Kaige, Ken Burns, Peter Greenaway and Whit Stillman.
Awards: Yes
Competitions: Yes
Application Fee: None
Films Screened: Approximately 30
Odds of Acceptance: 1300 entered

GILLY WENDELL

Outside the Treasure Mountain Inn in Park City, Utah, which is the headquarters for Slamdance, are (left to right) Six String Samurai filmmakers Kristian Bernier, Lance Mungia, Jeffrey Falcon and James Frisa.

7. Slamdance International Film Festival

The rebel film festival "by filmmakers for filmmakers" is charming for its garage band-like atmosphere. Screenings take place in January to coincide with Sundance at the Treasure Mountain Inn on Main Street in Park City in a room littered with fold-up chairs and comfy couches. (The timing is by design and attracts acquisitions executives to the top of Main Street to discover new talent.) The filmmaker-friendly atmosphere is apparent as festival founder and host of the event, the Mad-Hatter Dan Mirvish keeps a low-key cool to the screenings. Slamdance screens about a dozen features by first-time directors in an environment devoid of industry snobbery and annoying elitism. The spirit of DIY filmmaking is present in the halls, in the lines and at the parties in an incredibly supportive environment that at times feels more like a college dorm room than a festival.

Recently, Slamdance has become THE festival to watch for the next big thing. Several Slamdance premiere films have graduated to theatrical distribution, making acceptance into the event an award in itself. Keep your eye on them and when you attend, leave the industry bullshit at the door.

In order to be eligible for Slamdance competition, features have to be by first-time directors, shot on a low budget, in need of domestic distribution and be over 40 minutes in length. Each film goes through a rigorous screening process, with a total of about 20 programmers and screeners (mainly assembled from the ranks of unpaid and underemployed Slamdance alumni) taking a look at films, and ultimately determining the selections in a consensus fashion. Unlike other festivals, Slamdance does not offer any early invitations or make any early decisions, but rather waits until all the films are submitted, and then chooses the competition films all at once. Slamdance is not just about showing good films, it's also about showing films by good directors.

While most of the films selected are premieres, there really is not have any firm policy on the matter.

For the competition, they make a conscientious effort to recruit films from throughout the country—outside of the traditional film centers—and they hope their selections reflect that geographic diversity.

If filmmakers have something to say, and they say it well, they should have the chance to say it. At Slamdance, they would like to give them that chance.

The movies choosen are made by exceptional filmmakers who strongly represent the independent spirit upon which Slamdance is founded. It is our goal to provide filmmakers with an outlet for new and innovative work. We support filmmakers who take risks and challenge the audience, whether they be first-timers or more experienced directors. We are committed to presenting films and filmmakers whose unique visions show us their world.

Dramatic Competition: These films represent a broad cross-section of all the films submitted. Some are comedies, some dramatic. Some have seasoned cast members,

JUDGMENT DAY

"The Jury Film is not always the BEST film, nor is it the most popular film (that's what the audience is for). Rather, a jury film is one which deserves a special honor or recognition by the jury. At Slamdance each of the last three years, the Grand Jury Films were *Daytrippers, Bible and Gun Club,* and *Surrender Dorothy.* In each case, the film captured the fancy of the Slamdance jury—each film is the fiercely independent vision of a talented filmmaker. And the films each deserved and earned the recogntion of the jury."

— Gabe Wardell, sometime juror for the Slamdance Film Festival most do not. Some have beneficent funding sources, but more were made with the help of VISA and MasterCard. But what they do have in common—indeed, what most of the submissions shared—was the driving passion of directors who undertook their first feature films with bold, original visions, at a fraction of Hollywood budgets.

Of course, screening these films at Slamdance is far from an end in itself. . . Slamdance features and shorts have gone on to screen at virtually every major international film festival, including Cannes, Berlin and Venice. Many have been acquired for theatrical distribution, or have embarked on successful paths of self-distribution. Some have found their way onto video shelves across America.

Documentaries: These films strike a crucial balance between intriguing subject matter and good filmmaking. Documentaries act as a window to worlds that many times people have never stopped to consider. This makes many stories facinating but when one considers putting these into a festival a new element is added; the fact that not only does the story need to grab the audience but the way it is told must as well. The real trick is that you have to find both, because this is what makes a story stand apart from the rest. Documentary films need the same attention to story if

not more than fiction films do. They must get their point across in a way that enhances the subject and allows the viewer to be engrossed in the world onto which the filmmakers have turned their cameras.

International Section: One of the goals of Slamdance is to showcase new talent to the creative and industry leaders who come to Park City. This mission has always extended beyond U.S. borders to include some of the finest international filmmakers who embrace the Slamdance spirit of independent filmmaking.

SLAMDANCE iNTERNATiONAL FiLM FESTiVAL

"Slamdance has truly come into its own."
—*Lauren Sydney, CNN*

6381 Hollywood Blvd. Suite 520
Los Angeles, CA 90028
TEL: (323) 466 1786
FAX: (323) 466 1784
E-MAIL: slamdance@earthlink.net
WEB SITE: http://www.slamdance.com
FESTIVAL DATE: January
ENTRY DEADLINE: October, Late entries accepted in November. In contrast to Sundance, which recently announced an "early" deadline, Slamdance is offering a "late" deadline of November 11 in addition to its normal deadline of October 14. "We feel it's important to accomodate filmmakers who are on a later schedule than Sundance's but who still want to come to Park City with their films," said Peter Baxter.
YEAR FESTIVAL BEGAN: 1995
CONTACT: Peter Baxter, Dan Mirvish
DIRECTOR: Peter Baxter
CATEGORY: Independent, International
PROFILE: Slamdance's motto is: "By filmmakers for filmmakers." And they live up to it.

Slamdance was conceived at the 1994 Independent Feature Film Market (IFFM) when a small group of maverick filmmakers decided to support one another on a grassroots level. The first test of their idea came after filmmakers Jon

Fitzgerald (*Self-Portrait*), Shane Kuhn (*Redneck*) and Dan Mirvish (*Omaha (The Movie)*) all had their films declined by Sundance.

Not the kind to accept rejection gracefully, they established an alternative to Sundance which they called "Slamdance '95: Anarchy in Utah—The First Annual Guerilla International Film Festival." Word spread to other filmmakers and the media and, following a front page article in *Variety*, the team quickly assembled an impressive roster of over twenty films, including a dozen features, half of which were world premieres. All the films were made by first-time directors, had unknown casts and an aggregate budget of under $1 million.

The premiere Slamdance screenings took place at the University of Utah in Salt Lake City, concurrent with the Sundance Film Festival, in January 1995. By the second night, the festival moved to Park City, with organizers and filmmakers taking turns running the projectors and handing out fliers in a uniquely cooperative effort. The event was a resounding success, with most of the films finding distribution and all being invited on to other film festivals. Each year, Slamdance has expanded considerably, while maintaining its unique voice as a festival organized by filmmakers primarily devoted to first-time directors.

No longer the new kid on the block, Slamdance '98 was the biggest and best yet, retaining the spirit of integrity and vision that has characterized the festival, while adding a number of unique special events and an expanded film competition. The spirit of solidarity was vividly demonstrated by an overworked staff and faithful volunteer force.

AWARDS: Yes

COMPETITIONS: Yes

MAJOR AWARDS: The Sparky and the Audience Award.

VALUE OF AWARDS: Last year, the festival gave away over $35,000 worth of cash and prizes at its awards ceremony.

LAST WINNING FILMS: *Six String Samurai*

PAST JUDGES: Chris Gore, Steve Montal, Gabe Wardell.

APPLICATION TIPS: Slamdance's main feature competition is devoted to first-time directors who have made films on a low budget and do not yet have U.S. distribution. "However, we usually show several films that fall outside of these criteria—including many shorts," says Peter Baxter. "We do not have any strict 'premiere' requirements and we welcome films in any subject matter, length, format (including video), finished or not."

APPLICATION FEE: The Slamdance entry fee ranges from $25-55 depending on length and deadline. A comprehensive Frequently Asked Questions (FAQ) and film application are available at http://www.slamdance.com.

AVERAGE FILMS ENTERED: 1200 films.

FILMS SCREENED: About 14 features, 20 shorts.

ODDS OF ACCEPTANCE: 1200 films apply and only 14 features are shown so your odds of getting into Sundance are actually better than Slamdance.

FILMMAKER PERKS: Free entry to all screenings. Filmmakers lounge provides breakfast and complimentary food and drinks.

ATTENDANCE: 2,000+

TRAVEL TIPS: Slamdance screenings are all held at the Treasure Mountain Inn on Main Street in the heart of Park City, Utah. Show up early and grab a seat on the couch, otherwise you are stuck sitting on card table chairs which kill your butt after about a half an hour. Bring a pillow for your behind just in case.

FOOD, DRINK & SOCIAL HOUR

FREE BREAKFAST! Slamdance Filmmakers Lounge at the Treasure Mountain Inn has free breakfast bagels and pastries that usually stick around til noon or so. There are comfy couches to crash on, and everyone's invited. (By comparison, the new Sundance hospitality suite looks like a junior high school cafeteria.)

BEST RESTAURANT: Main Street Deli. Other than Hardee's, it's the only affordable place in Park City for filmmakers to eat. They also let you put fliers in the windowsill. For expensive food, try Thea's at the Treasure Mountain Inn.

BEST BAR: The Alamo. This is where locals go when they're done throwing snowballs at black-sweater-wearing studio executives. (Once inside, they throw darts at black-sweater-wearing studio executives.)

BEST PARTIES: The parties at Slamdance are all free and generally easy to sneak into.

Show up early and grab a seat on the couch, otherwise you are stuck sitting on card table chairs which kill your butt after about a half an hour. Bring a pillow for your behind just in case. (Slamdance International Film Festival)

8. Seattle International Film Festival (SIFF)

Seattle celebrates its festival as a nearly month-long event, making it the longest in the world. SIFF is also the largest festival in the United States with over 300 screenings of about 180 feature films, many of them American independents. (With so many films screened, statistically speaking, the chances of getting in are much better.) The festival boasts an attendance over 100,000 and many locals plan their vacations around the event. The Filmmaker's Forum features panels and workshops getting the tools of the craft into the hands of tomorrow's indies. Seattle has attracted the world premieres of some of Hollywood's most anticipated films such as *The Empire Strikes Back,* as well as popular indie films like *Kiss of the Spider Woman, Dazed and Confused* and *Trainspotting.*

SEATTLE INTERNATIONAL FILM FESTIVAL (SIFF)

801 East Pine Street
Seattle, Washington 98122
TEL: 206.324.9996
FAX: 206.324.9998
E-MAIL: mail@seattlefilm.com or kathleen@seattlefilm.com
WEB SITE: www.seattlefilm.com
FESTIVAL DATE: May-June
ENTRY DEADLINE: March
CONTACT: Carl Spence
DIRECTOR: Darryl Macdonald
PROGRAMMER: Carl Spence (Programmer/Promotions), Kathleen McInnis (Programmer, Program Guide Editor), Julie Mullaney (Programmer)

OTHER STAFF: Marketing: Nancy Kennedy; Publicist: Marion Seymour; Membership And Development: Warren Etheredge; Filmmakers Forum: Holly Becker; Film Entry Coordinator: Michele Goodson; Festival Coordinator: Jim Gibbs

CATEGORY: Documentary, Gay Lesbian, Independent, International

PROFILE: Recently cited by the *New York Times* as one of the most influential film festivals in the world. SIFF is the largest and most highly attended film festival in the United States, presenting 170 features and 100 shorts from 40 countries around the world to an audience of over 130,000 filmgoers.

Special sections include Contemporary World Cinema, the New Director's Showcase, the Secret Festival, the Films 4 Families, a tribute section, archival presentations, the short film showcase, Best of the Northwest, Midnight Series, an annual foreign film poster auction, and the Filmmakers Forum, an intensive, three-day program of seminars, workships and panel discussions which includes the amazing fly filmmaking: a challenge to three directors to conceive, shoot and edit a film the last six days of the festival to screen on closing day. The filmmakers are given 400 feet of 16mm film, local producers and crews and limited equipement. In the first year, the directors were Eric Schaeffer (*My Life's In Turnaround, If Lucy Fell, Fall*), Jon Ward (*Equal Impact*), Will Geiger (*Ocean Tribe*). 1998's Fly Filmmakers include Miquel Arteta (*Star Maps*) and Tim Blake Nelson (*Eye Of God*).

SIFF has been selected by the independent feature project as one of five North American festivals in which a film's presentation qualifies it for the Independent Spirit Awards, the independent film industry's most prestigious awards. The festival also offers juried awards for Best New Director and Best American Independent Film, in addition to Golden Space Needle Audience Awards for most popular film, best director, best documentary feature, best short film, best actor and best actress. New in 1998, are the reel network short awards for short films.

SEMINARS: The Filmmakers Forum includes master classes, panels, seminars, one-on-one discussion, etc. Also included is the Screenwriters Salon, a one-on-one conversation with various screenwriters as well as the Script Read Through, a special presentation of a selected script cast with professional actors and directed by a film director.

PANELS: See above.

FAMOUS SPEAKERS: Every year there is a new batch. Some from the past: Mel Gibson, Bryan Singer, John Schlesinger, Todd Haynes, Carl Franklin, Tom Dicillo, Gregg Araki, Gus Van Sant, Sean Penn, Robin Wright Penn, Brendon Fraser, James

Legros, Russell Crowe, Jullianne Moore, Salma Hayek, Bart Freaundlich, David Arquette, Wallace Shawn, Stewart Stern, Griffen Dunne, Dan Ireland, Vincent D'Onfrio, etc.

AWARDS: Yes

COMPETITIONS: Yes

MAJOR AWARDS: Golden Space Needle Audience Award; New Directors Showcase (Juried); American Independent Award (Juried); Reel Network Short Award (Juried)

VALUE OF AWARDS: American Indie Award: $100,0000

APPLICATION TIPS: Complete all supporting material and application. Don't call to say you know someone famous who will vouch for your film. Get as clean and strong a preview tape as possible; if it is a rough cut, say so on the tape (that's fine as long as we know); put your name, the title of the film and your phone number on the cassette.

APPLICATION FEE: $25 for 0-30 min.; $35 for 30-60 min.; $50 for 60-whatever minutes.

INSIDER ADVICE: Get your films in early if possible; sound is your best friend for film festivals-make sure it's great; get your production values as high as possible...the competition is tough out there so do what you can to make sure your production values help your film; make sure you have really strong writing (stong script can help overcome almost anything) and let your editor do their job!!!!! Rarely is it a good idea for first time filmmakers to be producer, director, writer, actor and editor all at once.

AVERAGE FILMS ENTERED: Strongly written, vibrantly performed, expertly directed...new voices, new talent, somthing we haven't seen before...

FILMS SCREENED: 180 features, 70 short films.

ODDS OF ACCEPTANCE: A filmmaker's odds of getting in are about 20% (1 out of 5 or 6)

FILMMAKER PERKS: We invite premiere status directors as our guest, and offer them travel and lodging as well. All filmmakes who come have access to contacts; we help facilitate by parties, functions, a hospitality suite, events, etc...

TRAVEL TIPS: Wear layers!

BEST RESTAURANTS: For hip indie filmmakers it's the Alibi Room in the Pike Place Market. Owned by fellow indie filmmakers with high profile Hollywood money as investors (the Donners, Rob Morrow, Peter Horton, Tom Skerritt, etc...)

Closer to the festival theaters is The Capitol Club (great for Middle Eastern influenced food and outstanding bar drinks); The Wild Ginger (Asian and Pacific Rim) for high brow filmmakers on a studio expense account; Palace Kitchen to be seen; Cafe Septieme for European style cafe and food; New American Broadway Grill for good food and great atmosphere...

Also very cool with great food and lots of the "in" crowd to watch: Flying Fish, Queen City Grill, Metropolitan Grill, Sazarac...

BEST BARS: See above, also The Baltic Room, The Pink Door, and Linda's

BEST HANGOUT FOR FILMMAKERS: The Alibi Room, The Speakeasy Cafe

BEST PLACE FOR BREAKFAST: The Green Cat

FESTIVAL TALES: Once the last reel of a film didn't show up and we didn't know it until the film was almost over. One of our programmers got up on stage and gave the audience the option of their money back or they could hear him recite the ending of the film. No one left, and he gave a rousing rendition of the climax and resolution to the movie!

9. South By Southwest Film Festival (SXSW)

Austin is a party town and there is no better party than SXSW. Oh, yeah, they show some cool films too. The fest began as an extension of the SXSW Music and Media Conference and has quickly established itself as a formidable force in the indie film world. This slightly mesquite-flavored independent festival has attracted the likes of Quentin Tarantino, Richard Linklater (who lives in Austin) and Kevin Smith, among others, who attend annually to sit on panels and simply enjoy the fest. Texas filmmakers are given their due with screenings and why not? It's this attention to regional artists that gives out-of-towners a taste of something new to chew on than the usual indie fare. Organizational problems aside (the fest seems to be a victim of its own success), the atmosphere is incredibly laid back which accounts for their tremendous growth. People come back to Austin for this event.

SOUTH BY SOUTHWEST FiLM FESTiVAL (SXSW)

PO Box 4999
Austin, Texas 78765 USA
TEL: (512) 467-7979
FAX: (512) 451-0754
E-MAIL: sxsw@sxsw.com
WEB SITE: http://www.sxsw.com
FESTIVAL DATE: March
ENTRY DEADLINE: Mid-December
YEAR FESTIVAL BEGAN: 1994
CONTACT: Nancy Schafer or Angela Lee
DIRECTOR: Nancy Schafer
OTHER STAFF: Angela Lee, Festival Coordinator, and Suzanne Mauze, Sales & Marketing
CATEGORY: Independent
PROFILE: SXSW Film is a four-day film conference and nine day film festival providing a unique place to listen to and learn from the best voices in all phases of independent filmmaking, as well as showcasing the best new independent films.

Whether you are a novice to the film world or a seasoned veteran, the SXSW Film Conference will enhance your professionalism, further your knowledge of filmmaking technology and processes, while introducing you to the right people. Two days of panels and workshops will feature some of the most knowledgeable speakers in the independent film world.

The SXSW Film Conference expands with four days of panels, workshops, mini-meetings and industry mentoring sessions with professional filmmakers to answer all your questions about every phase of filmmaking from pre-production through signing that distribution deal, or how to get your film seen if you don't. In addition to being instructional, the SXSW Film Conference is a great place to meet your contemporaries working in independent film, and to talk one-on one with some of the greatest filmmakers working today.

Multimedia Festival: The Festival is designed to focus on the creative side of interactive media with plenty of activites and great opporunities to meet the refion's hottest multimedia talent. Registrants can tour Austin's multimedia facilities, attend panel sicussions and in-depth workshops, get expert, one-on-one advice during mentor sessions, check out some of the newest, products and ideas in the trade show, and meet other festival-goers during daily receptions. The conference program features natinally known leaders sharing the latest news in content devel-opment, interface design, audio, video, animation and more for CD-Roms, the internet and intranet. Past Speakers: Todd Rundgren, Bruce Sterling, Mark Dery, and more.

Film Competition: The Film and Video Competition is a vital aspect of SXSW Film. The prelminary judging committee will select the best works submitted and these will be screened as part of the Festival. A new commitee of judges will view all selected works during the Festival and choose winners in various categories.

Festival Categorization: Independent films from America and all over the world. Panels, workshops, mini-meetings, mentor sessions, demo reel sessions.

Past speakers include: Robert Rodriguez, Quentin Tarantino, Kevin Smith, Ruby Lerner, Judith Helfand, Richard Linklater, Steven Soderbergh, Anne Walker-McBay, Caroline Kaplan, Rana Joy Glickman, John Sloss, John Pierson, Emanuel Levy, Susan Bodine.
AWARDS: Yes
COMPETITIONS: Yes
MAJOR AWARDS: Best Narrative Film, Best Documentary Film.
VALUE OF AWARDS: Feature and short film winners receive plaques commemorating the Silver Armadillo Award and feature length film winners receive lab, film stock and other services.
APPLICATION TIPS: Make a good film. And don't submit until you are ready. It doesn't do you any good to submit a cut that is so rough that it does not give you a good shot at getting in. Most festivals are amenable to accepting films for submission after the deadline, you just have to call and ask for an extension.
APPLICATION FEE: $20
INSIDER ADVICE: The wheel that squeaks the loudest does not get the oil. We would suggest not sending photos until your film is accepted into the Festival, it saves you money and photos do not influence our decision. The Festival has become a great place for contact with distributors, press and fellow filmmakers.
ODDS OF ACCEPTANCE: In 1998, 1010 films were submitted and 148 were accepted.
TOURIST INFORMATION: Austin is beautiful in the springtime, and their is much to do, although most fest-goers don't have time to see and do all Austin has to offer.
TRAVEL TIPS: It is hard to get to Austin on a direct flight at least up until the new airport opens in 2000. Also, Austin is a place where it is possible to get around without renting a car, but it makes life a lot easier if you have one.
BEST RESTAURANTS: Fonda San Miguel.
BEST BARS: Dog & Duck Pub
BEST HANGOUT FOR FILMMAKERS: Dog & Duck Pub

BEST PLACE FOR BREAKFAST: Las Manitas

HOTEL INFORMATION: Platinum Pass registrants are encouraged to stay at the Omni Hotel Downtown, La Quinta-Capitol, or HomeGate (formerly InnHome) where SXSW has rooms blocked during the Film and Interactive conferences. If a Platinum Pass registrant would like to request a different hotel, SXSW will check availability of your requested hotel for dates you require and maker your reservation if room and rate are available. Contact the SXSW office for additional Platinum Registrant hotel information.

Hotel reservations for all conferences must be made through the SXSW housing desk. Your must be a conference registrant to reserve a hotel room.

All hotels require a valid credit card to guarantee a one night deposit. No-shows will be charged one night. You will receive hotel confirmations from the Housing Desk and from your hotel with additional rules and penalites. Read them carefully. A limited number of rooms with two double beds are available. To be given priority for these rooms you must list the additional registrants sharing the room. Rates shown are available on a limiteed number of rooms—some hotels will have additional rooms available at higher rates.

DELUXE HOTELS:

-Hyatt Regency (208 Barton Springs)
-Sheraton Austin (5th st. & IH-35)
-Driskill Hotel (604 Brazos St.)
-Omni Austin Downtown (700 San Jacinto)
-Austin Marriott (Capitol (701 E. 11th St.))
-Doubletree Hotel (6505 North IH-35)

ALL-SUITE HOTELS:

-Embassy Suites Downtown (300 S. Congress)
-Doubletree Guest Suites (303 W. 15th)
-Embassy Suites Airport (5901 N. IH-35)

FIRST CLASS HOTELS:

-Radisson–Town Lake (111 E. 1st St.)
-Holiday Inn–Town Lake (20 North IH-35)
-Holiday Inn–South (3401 South IH-35)

MODERATE PRICE HOTELS:

-La Quinta–Capitol (300 E. 11th St.)
-InnHome America (1001 S. IH-35)
-Quality Inn–South (2200 South IH-35)

CAR RENTALS:

Alamo (800) 732-3232
Hertz (800) 654-2240

SXSW IS THE BEST

"The fanboy groupies are everywhere! (Kidding) South by Southwest was cool, *Mary Jane* had amazing screenings there. The people who work at SXSW are really open and friendly and the town of Austin is so relaxed, it's just so much fun. I love it there. SXSW is a much younger film festival than most other ones, so the audiences are hipper than your regular indie film crowd. The panels bring out a lot of great speakers. I always meet so many interesting people or reconnect with ones I've met in the past and I always learn a lot. I went back as a speaker and was able to get some great bookings all around the country. Then there's all the bands playing, which I love. I know a lot of people involved with music so it's always like a big reunion and I get to totally rock out. I like the MultiMedia section too. And there are a lot of cool computer girls who come out to the festival for that, so the whole event brings together all these normally disparate elements of subculture that have really made it possible for *Mary Jane* to succeed on such a DIY level (i.e. computers and punk rock and girl subculture). SXSW has been a really great experience for me as a filmmaker, business-wise and creative-wise— not too many festivals can do both."

— Sarah Jacobson, filmmaker, *Mary Jane's Not A Virgin Anymore*

10. Taos Talking Pictures Festival

The wild card entry in our list of Top Ten Festivals deserves more recognition than it has received previously. The winner of their innovation award received five acres of land in Taos, which qualifies as the most original award from a festival anywhere. (The land is an effort on their part to create a real community of filmmakers by encouraging like-minded indies to move there.) The four-day event screens close to 70 films including features, documentaries and shorts. The festivities includes a program of mainly American independent films with a Southwestern bent. A friendly festival vibe prevails—attending is like visiting an old friend once a year.

TAOS TALKiNG PiCTURES FESTiVAL

"One of the country's leading film festivals"
—*MovieMaker Magazine*

216-M North Pueblo Rd., #216
Taos, New Mexico 87571
TEL: (505) 751-0637
FAX: (505) 751-7385
E-MAIL: ttpix@taosnet.com
WEB SITE: http://www.taosnet.com/ttpix/
FESTIVAL DATE: April
ENTRY DEADLINE: January
YEAR FESTIVAL BEGAN: 1994
CONTACT: Kelly Clement
DIRECTOR: Ellen Osborne
CATEGORY: International
PROFILE: The festival is produced by Taos Talking Pictures, a New Mexico-based non-profit media arts organization founded in 1994 to encourage the thoughtful production and informed consumption of moving images.

In one of the most dramatic landscapes in the world, Taos is a nature-bound community in a high valley at the edge of a great lava plain at the foot of the Sangre de Cristo Mountains. Situated around an ancient Pueblo, it supports three diverse cultures. One can easily glance backwards here at myths and legends of the Indian/Spanish/ American West.

The Taos Talking Picture Festival should be seen as more than just another film festival. It aspires to serve as a rendezvous where people meet to trade ideas and inspiration in an atmosphere conducive to clear, uncluttered thought; a unique context in which to view and discuss the art of film and media in general in this rapidly unfolding Age of Information.

The leadership role of Art, particularly the art of filmmaking, is unparalleled in our society.

Films serve as our mentors, influencing personal and political choices that shape the future. The purpose of the Taos Talking Picture Festival is to present a celebration of film which exemplifies and explores this role, and to encourage the literate production and informed consumption of the powerful arts of film and video.

PANELS: Yes: The Taos Talking Picture Festival is also known for its Media Forum, which brings together media makers and scholars to discuss the impact of film and TV on our culture and society.

AWARDS: Yes

COMPETITIONS: Yes

MAJOR AWARDS: Innovation Award; The Taos Mountain Award recognizes outstanding achievement by a Native American media professional. The Maverick Award is presented to an individual who has retained his or her personal vision while working within the film industry. The Howard Hawks Storyteller Award recognizes a writer/director who tells powerful stories in innovative ways. Cineaste Award: This award is given to a filmmaker whose works help promote cultural understanding. The famed Land Grant Award—five acres of land given to encourage filmmakers to take a fresh approach to storytelling and/or the cinematic media. The Land Grant Award, which has received worldwide attention from filmmakers and the media, is given each year at the Taos Talking Picture Festival to recognize a talented, passionate and innovative filmmaker who uses his or her talents to tell powerful, socially relevant stories. The ultimate goal of the Land Grant Award is the foundation of a community of talented filmmakers in Taos.

VALUE OF AWARDS: Five acres of land on beautiful Taos Cerro Montoso.

LAST WINNING FILMS: Clement Virgo, for *The Planet of Junior Brown;* Chris Eyre, for *Smoke Signals;* and Juliane Glantz, for *Wilbur Falls.*

APPLICATION FEE: $15 (up to 30 minutes) / $25 (30 minutes or over)

FILMS SCREENED: The Festival features a number of special events and screenings, including: Four new family films; a comprehensive survey of public access TV, one of our greatest democratic forums; a special program in which movies and poetry meet; an evening with legendary video artist Sadie Benning, including a screening of her new work *Flat is Beautiful;* a two-part film program entitled *Girl Culture,* featuring videos about growing up female in our culture; two programs featuring the best new works produced by Native filmmakers; a program featuring innovative animation from around the world; the festival's now-famed shorts programs with work from the filmmakers of tomorrow and highlighted by the

The famed Land Grant Award—five acres of land given to encourage filmmakers to take a fresh approach to storytelling and/or the cinematic media. (Taos Talking Pictures Festival)

George Méliès Award presentation;parties, film-maker receptions and more.

TOURIST INFORMATION: Taos is also an international tourist destination, a world-class ski resort and one of America's oldest art colonies. Simplicity and sophistication coexist here.

Taos remains a last outpost. Almost remote. The town is still adobe, the countryside still rural. For hundreds of years it has attracted adventurers and artists. And, today, its distance from the anxious post-Modern World gives Taos a powerful mind-clearing quietness.

Taos is an ideal place to think through and explore the ethical/technological issues of entertainment and communication in the New Media Age.

See Taos Virtual Vacation Guide, Taos Ski Valley online and La Plaza de Taos Telecommunity, our nonprofit community network, for more about Taos.

FESTIVAL HOTELS:

-El Pueblo Lodge (800) 433-9612

-Fechin Inn (800) 811-2933

-The Historic Taos Inn (800) 826-7466

-Holiday Inn Don Fernando de Taos (800) 759-2736

-Best Western Kachina Lodge (800) 522-4462

-Quality Inn (800) 845-0648

-Rancho Ramada Inn de Taos (800) 659-8267

-San Geronimo Lodge (800) 894-4119

-Sun God Lodge (800) 821-2437

GROUND TRANSPORTATION:

Enterprise Rent-A-Car (800) 680-3013

Pride of Taos (airport shuttle) (800) 273-8340

DOMESTIC FILM FESTIVALS
(United States and Canada)

ALAMO AMERICAN FILM COMPETITION FOR STUDENTS
Alamo Rent-A-Car
Community Affairs
P. O. Box 22776
Ft. Lauderdale, FL 33335
FAX: (305) 468-2184
ENTRY DEADLINE: April
CONTACT: Linda D'Olympio
CATEGORY: Student

AMERICAN FILM INSTITUTE (AFI)– LOS ANGELES INTERNATIONAL FILM FESTIVAL
American Film Institute
2021 North Western Ave.
Los Angeles, CA 90027
TEL: (213) 856-7707
FAX: (213) 462-4049
E-MAIL: afifest@afionline.org
WEB SITE:
http://www.afionline.org
FESTIVAL DATE: October–November
ENTRY DEADLINE: August
CONTACT: Jon Fitzgerald
DIRECTOR: Ken Wlaschin
CATEGORY: Independent, International
PROFILE: Approximately 40,000 attend.
COMPETITIONS: Yes
APPLICATION FEE: $30
FILMS SCREENED: 60
ODDS OF ACCEPTANCE: 400-700 entered

AMERICAS FILM FESTIVAL
19th & Constitution Ave. NW
Washington, DC 20006
TEL: (202) 458-6379
FAX: (202) 458-3122
FESTIVAL DATE: November
CONTACT: Edward W. Cockrell

ANN ARBOR FILM FESTIVAL
P.O. Box 8232
Ann Arbor, Michigan 48107
TEL: (734) 995 5356
FAX: (734) 995-5396
E-MAIL: vicki@honeyman.org
WEB SITE: http://aafilmfest.org
or http://www.citi.umich.edu/u/honey/aaff
FESTIVAL DATE: March
ENTRY DEADLINE: February
CONTACT: Vicki Honeyman
DIRECTOR: Vicki Honeyman
PROGRAMMER: Vicki Honeyman
CATEGORY: Independent, The festival accepts all genre: experimental, animation, documentary, personal documentary, narrative and encourages the works of mutli-cultural artists. It is all about the films and the filmmakers, providing an excellent screening facility for the works. A filmmaker's reception is held at the end of festweek.
PROFILE: Started in 1963, the Ann Arbor Film Festival has a long-standing tradition of showcasing 16mm independent and experimental film. The festival is open to all films of all genre that demonstrate a high regard for film as an art form. Festival goals are to encourage the work of the independent filmmaker, to promote the concept of film as art, and to present a traveling tour of about 25 films in the Ann Arbor Film Festival Tour, traveling to over 20 locations around the US late March through early August.

The Ann Arbor Film Festival has been known as a festival to enter work into but not as a festival to attend. But those filmmakers and film-goers who do attend from out-of-town usually become die-hard festgoers. The festival is held in a huge renovated 1700-seat movie theater and has a very relaxed atmosphere with comfy seats and good popcorn. The projectionists are perfectionists about sound and image. Filmmakers always remark on how great their films look on the Michigan Theater screen and are impressed with the professionalism of the projection staff.

Performance artists open each night's 7:00 shows. The theater lobby is taken over by local artists who create installation pieces, including film-loop installations.

The festival begins every year on a Tuesday night with an opening night reception that features a Mariachi band and free drinks and hors d'oeuvres.
SEMINARS: The three Awards Jurors, independent & experimental filmmakers/instructors/academics, present programs of

their own work each afternoon during fest week.

COMPETITIONS: Yes

MAJOR AWARDS: Best of Festival Award

VALUE OF AWARDS: $2,000 ($13,000 total in cash awards)

LAST WINNING FILMS: *Hauling Toto Big*

LAST WINNING DIRECTORS: Robert Nelson

PAST JUDGES: 1998: Dominic Angerame, Jan Krawitz, Christopher Sullivan

1997: Jeffrey Scher, Barbara Klutinis, Louise Bourque

1996: Christine Panushka, Robb Moss, Craig Baldwin

1995: Jay Rosenblatt, Emily Breer, Midi Onodera

APPLICATION TIPS: Read the entry materials, enter strong work.

APPLICATION FEE: $32 US / $37 overseas

INSIDER ADVICE: Don't enter until your work it has gone beyond the "amateur" level.

AVERAGE FILMS ENTERED: 16mm films of any length, any genre, optical soundtrack or silent.

ODDS OF ACCEPTANCE: About 350 films entered; about 100 programmed into the festival-week screenings. In 1998, 371 films were entered; 113 were programmed.

FILMMAKER PERKS: We house filmmakers with people in the community. We provide fest-week passes to all screenings. We throw a reception for all attending filmmakers.

TRAVEL TIPS: Call Ann Arbor Visitors Bureau: 800-888-8487 for housing, maps, etc

BEST RESTAURANTS: The Earle, Zanzibar, Kerrytown Bistro, Del Rio

BEST BARS: Del Rio Bar

BEST HANGOUT FOR FILMMAKERS: Angelos, Del Rio, Old Town, coffee shops are all over town.

BEST PLACE FOR BREAKFAST: Angelo's Restaurant is where all the out of town filmmakers go.

> We house filmmakers with people in the community. (Ann Arbor Film Festival)

ANNUAL AMERICAN INDIAN FILM AND VIDEO COMPETITION

2100 NE 52nd St.
Oklahoma City, OK 73111

TEL: (405) 521-2931

FESTIVAL DATE: June

ENTRY DEADLINE: January

CONTACT: Patrick Whelan

CATEGORY: Ethnic Other

ANNUAL BALTIMORE INDEPENDENT FILM AND VIDEO MAKERS' COMPETITION

The Baltimore Film Forum at The Baltimore Museum of Art
10 Art Museum Dr.
Baltimore, MD 21218

TEL: (410) 889-1993

FAX: (410) 889-2657

DIRECTOR: Victoria Westover, Executive Director

CATEGORY: Independent

ANNUAL KIDFILM FESTIVAL

2917 Swiss Ave.
Dallas, TX 75104

TEL: (214) 821-6300

FAX: (214) 821-6364

FESTIVAL DATE: January

CONTACT: Ann Alexander

CATEGORY: Kid

ARIZONA INTERNATIONAL FILM FESTIVAL

P. O. Box 40638
Tucson, AZ 85717

FESTIVAL DATE: April

CONTACT: Arizona Center for the Media Arts

ARIZONA STATE UNIVERSITY SHORT FILM AND VIDEO FESTIVAL

College of Fine Arts
P.O. Box 872102
Tempe, Arizona 85287-2102

TEL: (602) 965-8795 or (602) 865-0497

"We want to keep it very informal, with the feel of a Fourth of July picnic. Arizona's beautiful spring weather is a great asset and believe it enhances the event"
—*John Spiak, Festival Director*

WEB SITE: http://asuam.fa.asu.edu/filmfest/main.htm

FESTIVAL DATE: April

YEAR FESTIVAL BEGAN: 1997

CONTACT: Jennifer Pringle

DIRECTOR: John Spiak / Bob Pece

CATEGORY: Independent, Short, Student, Video

PROFILE: This festival is held outdoors and features a variety of short films and videos. There is no entry fee for the film and video makers, or for the audience members.

MAJOR AWARDS: Student Academy Award Gold Medal

LAST WINNING FILMS: *Walk This Way*

APPLICATION FEE: None

AVERAGE FILMS ENTERED: Films must be less than 10 minutes and in VHS format.

ODDS OF ACCEPTANCE: 25 films chosen out of 210.

ARMCHAIR SHORT FILM FESTIVAL

Paul Goode from Kodak, Public Relations NE, said The Armchair was the most fun, quirky, micro film festival he'd ever been to.

Comedy Central
Attn: Constance Van Flandern
110 Leroy Street, 6th Floor
New York, NY 10019

TEL: (212) 982-3818; (212) 529-3997; (212) 334-2274

E-MAIL: connieVF@aol.com

WEB SITE: www.interactive.net/~chris/armchair-film-festival/

YEAR FESTIVAL BEGAN: 1996

CONTACT: Same as above

DIRECTOR: Constance Van Flandern

PROGRAMMER: Constance Van Flandern, Ben Freedman and Rupert

CATEGORY: Independent, Short, Underground, Weird, Video

PROFILE: The Armchair Film Festival is about getting to see (or screen your) fun quirky (mostly narrative) shorts in a cozy non-threatening, non-pretentious comfortable environment. We wanted to set up a sort of cross between sofa lounge/screening room thing where people could relax and really enjoy themselves with a drink or food instead of being hunched in hard seats. We try to give away film relevent door prizes and fun stuff to create a more communal film environment. This festival is designed to feature shorts and animations of filmmakers who invested in making above average films but have limited places in which to show them off to potential future investors or other curious filmmakers. Screenings take place at City Wine and Cigar, 62 Laight St., Tribeca.

SEMINARS: So far we haven't done this stuff because we just began this new format and are settling in our new location, but we would like to sponsor some readings for shorts in the future, and we have had famous short filmmakers come and speak briefly on their work.

COMPETITIONS: Yes

MAJOR AWARDS: This year, the Grand prize was $500 in Kodak film stock to make another film and the Armchair trophy. Runners up received Arnet sunglasses and subscriptions to *Premiere Magazine.*

VALUE OF AWARDS: $500

LAST WINNING FILMS: *The Waiters*

LAST WINNING DIRECTORS: Ken Webb

PAST JUDGES: It is an audience choice award

APPLICATION TIPS: Keep your short under 20min. if you possibly can. Don't be afraid to edit because you think you need to

stretch it out. Really—the shorter and more concise, with one clear point, the better. Some of our most beloved shorts are merely 3-5 min. Humor, even very dark humor, goes a long way. Levity, even in the most serious narrative subjects, or documentaries, helps the audience relate and drives your point home.

APPLICATION FEE: None. But we do not return the VHS tape.

INSIDER ADVICE: Remember to include all your contact information. Submit everywhere you can. The more places your film is seen the better, obviously. We prefer films with some thoughtful narrative, especially those with humor. We are very interested in animation, documentaries, and even very short experimental stuff if it is compelling and relevent to that week's theme. We accept films that have been shown before, old favorites, and good stuff that been on the shelf for a while. If you're proud of it, even if it's old news, we would like to see it.

FILMS SCREENED: We screen between 3-4 a night.

ODDS OF ACCEPTANCE: We get films from other festivals, submission and word of mouth. Of the submissions we probably get 200 in a year and use about 25-30 of those.

FILMMAKER PERKS: We offer a really great place, in the heart of NY's film district (Tribeca), to screen your film. Filmmakers are encouraged to use our screenings as their own showcase for friends, family and agents. We provide a comfortable, semi party-like atmosphere.

BEST RESTAURANTS: Robert DeNiro's Tribeca Grill is just down the street but my favorite is KIM's Sushi on 10th St.

BEST HANGOUT FOR FILMMAKERS: Joe's Bar on 6th Street, Angelica Film House, The MOMA, The Screening Room Bar, Luna Lounge, Fez.

ASIAN AMERICAN INTERNATIONAL FILM FESTIVAL

32 East Broadway, 4th Floor
New York, NY 10002
TEL: (212) 925-8685
FAX: (212) 925-8157
E-MAIL: tellywong@aol.com
WEB SITE: www.asiancinevision.org
FESTIVAL DATE: July
ENTRY DEADLINE: March
CATEGORY: Ethnic Other
APPLICATION FEE: None

ASPEN FILMFEST

110 E. Hallam, Suite 102
Aspen, CO 81611
TEL: (970) 925-6882
FAX: (970) 925-1967
E-MAIL: geldred@aspenfilm.org
WEB SITE: http://www.aspen.com/filmfest/
FESTIVAL DATE: September-October
ENTRY DEADLINE: July
CONTACT: George Eldred
CATEGORY: Documentary, Independent, International
PROFILE: This is a six day festival which celebrates American independent films, documentaries, and foreign films. Over 6,000 attend.
AWARDS: Yes
COMPETITIONS: Yes
APPLICATION FEE: $20
FILMS SCREENED: 25 screened
ODDS OF ACCEPTANCE: 375 entered

ATHENS INTERNATIONAL FILM AND VIDEO FESTIVAL

Box 388
75 W. Union St., Rm. 407
Columbus, OH 45701
TEL: (740) 593-1330
FESTIVAL DATE: May
ENTRY DEADLINE: January-February
CATEGORY: International

If you're proud of it, even if it's old news, we would like to see it. (Armchair Short Film Festival)

ATLANTA FiLM AND ViDEO FESTiVAL

"Other people within the film industry and the entertainment industry and other important festivals are aware of the Atlanta festival, and it's growing to the extent that filmmakers feel like it's important to come down here and meet the audiences and talk about their films, futher their careers. . . . They feel like this is a good place to do that"
—*Anne Hubbell*

IMAGE Film/Video Center
75 Bennett St. NW, Suite N-1
Atlanta, GA 30309
TEL: (404) 352-4225 or (404) 352-4254 (Festival Hotline)
FAX: (404) 352-0173
E-MAIL: afvf@imagefv.org
WEB SITE: http://www.imagefv.org/afuf
FESTIVAL DATE: June
ENTRY DEADLINE: February
YEAR FESTIVAL BEGAN: 1976
CONTACT: Gabriel Wardell
DIRECTOR: Anne Hubbell
PROGRAMMER: Gabriel Wardell
OTHER STAFF: Genevieve McGillicuddy
CATEGORY: Independent
PROFILE: The Atlanta Film & Video Festival celebrates filmmaking from around the world. The festival focuses on the appreciation of independent, experimental and student films. Since 1976, the festival has introduced audiences to some of the most exciting new film and video work being created. Ranging from the hilarious to the visually arresting, from the provocative and highly controversial to the boldly experimental, the AFVF has become one of the country's premiere showcases for work by independent media artists in the U.S. and abroad.
PANELS: Yes
AWARDS: Yes

It is hot, but it is bound to rain—pack accordingly. (Atlanta Film and Video Festival)

COMPETITIONS: Yes
MAJOR AWARDS: Jury Prize
VALUE OF AWARDS: $500
LAST WINNING FILMS: *Kitchen Party*
LAST WINNING DIRECTORS: Gary Burns
PAST JUDGES: Chris Gore, Adolfas Mekas, Lise Raven, Harry Knowles, Liliana Oliveres (Rosebud), Eugene Haynes (October Films), Marlon T. Riggs, Barbara Hammer, Les Blank.
APPLICATION TIPS: Follow directions. Make short films short (and good). Snappy synopses.
APPLICATION FEE: $65- for early admission
INSIDER ADVICE: Get work in on time. Neat and easy to understand—clearly labeled.
AVERAGE FILMS ENTERED: Funny—wide variety—indie.
FILMS SCREENED: 100-150 screened
ODDS OF ACCEPTANCE: over 600 entered
TRAVEL TIPS: It is hot, but it is bound to rain—pack accordingly.
BEST RESTAURANTS: Pasta Puccinello, Raging Burrito, Heaping Bowl & Brew.
BEST BARS: Righteous Room
BEST HANGOUT FOR FILMMAKERS: Manuel's Tavern
BEST PLACE FOR BREAKFAST: Waffle House, Krispy Kreme, or Majestic Diner.

ATLANTiC FiLM FESTiVAL

1549 Lower Water St.
Halifax, Nova Scotia BJ3 1S2
Canada
TEL: (902) 422-3456
FAX: (902) 422-4006
WEB SITE: www.atlanticfilm.com
FESTIVAL DATE: September
ENTRY DEADLINE: June
CONTACT: Gordon Whitteker
CATEGORY: Independent

AUSTiN FiLM FESTiVAL

1600 Nueces
Austin, TX 78701
TEL: (512) 478-4795 or (800) 310-FEST
FAX: (512) 478-6205
WEB SITE: www.austinfilmfestival.org
FESTIVAL DATE: October
ENTRY DEADLINE: September
YEAR FESTIVAL BEGAN: 1993
DIRECTOR: Marsha Milam
PROGRAMMER: Jason White

Robert Rodriguez, camera in hand, lines up a two-shot of party guy Dennis Hopper and Oliver Stone at the Austin Film Festival.

CATEGORY: Independent

PROFILE: "We are thrilled to host the cast party and to be part of the Austin Film Festival," says Roy Spence, president of GSD&M. "We have a new extension called Idea Entertainment that will help identify and nurture talented Austinites in both the film and music business. We want to help Austin as it becomes more and more active and significant in the film industry."

AUSTIN HEART OF FILM FESTIVAL

"The king of screenwriting fests."

1600 Nueces
Austin, TX 78701
TEL: (800) 310-FEST or (512) 478-4795
FAX: (512) 478-6205
E-MAIL: Austinfilm@aol.com
WEB SITE: http://www.Instar.com/austinfilm/ or http://www.austinfilmfestival.org
FESTIVAL DATE: October
ENTRY DEADLINE: August / May (screenplays)
YEAR FESTIVAL BEGAN: 1994
CONTACT: Barbara Morgan
CATEGORY: Documentary, Independent, narrative films
PROFILE: The focus of the festival is on narrative films. Although documentaries are not accepted within the competitive level, they can be submitted.
AWARDS: Yes
COMPETITIONS: Yes
MAJOR AWARDS: Best Feature Film; Best Short Film; Best Student Short Film
VALUE OF AWARDS: $750 (features) $500 (Shorts and Student Films). Winners also are included in the Festival's "Filmmaker Catalog" which is sent to competition judges, distribution companies, and other industry reps.
PAST JUDGES: Previous judges include representatives from

Tri-Mark, ICM, HBO, the Independent Film Channel, Bravo, Columbia Pictures, Bandeira Entertainment, William Morris Agency, and the Sundance Channel.

APPLICATION FEE: $35

AVERAGE FILMS ENTERED: Films must be submitted on VHS, they must be feature-length narratives (75 minutes or longer) or shorts (30 minutes or less).

FILMS SCREENED: Over 80 films.

FILMMAKER PERKS: Transportation, accommodations and complimentary all-access passes to the Austin Film Festival.

TRAVEL TIPS: There are discounted hotel rates for the festival. The participating hotels are the Driskill, Omni, and Radisson.

AUSTIN'S GAY AND LESBIAN FILM FESTIVAL

AGLIFF
P.O. Box L
Austin, Texas 78713
E-MAIL: AusGLFilm@aol.com
WEB SITE: www.aGLIFF.org
FESTIVAL DATE: August-September
ENTRY DEADLINE: July
CONTACT: Mitch Jones
CATEGORY: Gay Lesbian
FESTIVAL TALE: As a film festival dealing with the Gay/Lesbian topic matter we felt that our advertising campaign for our 10th annual was indeed worthy of a celebration and perhaps a time for us to be a little cocky, having been going strong for a decade. Our hook needed to be humorous and topical, yet assertive enough to stand out in a city that is proud to support a veritable cornucopia of entertainment options on any given weekend. We thought about several slogans or phrases to attach to our billboards and posters and finally decided on the one that would have the biting "edge" to it we were looking for and be inclusive of EVERYONE. Just below our Gay

and Lesbian Film Festival logo was the phrase: "Baptist Fundamentalists Welcome!" To say that it caused a little stir would be an understatement. Our billboard company refused to put up our signage with that slogan. Retailers were ripping down the window posters on display. The local papers ran stories about censorship issues and our attempt at humor and the instigation of more ill will between two groups that couldn't be farther apart on the scale. Everything from t-shirts and posters to billboards and flyers had to be changed at the last minute with more tame slogans like: AGLIFF... "From the Same Folks that Brought You the Village People." However, there is no such thing as bad press—period. The festival wound up being a successful celebration of the decade long showcase of Gay/Lesbian filmmaking folks have come to expect from us and the additional media exposure only solidified our place as one of the premiere Gay/Lesbian film festivals in the southwest.

AUSTIN'S ISRAELI FILM FESTIVAL

The Austin Film Society
3109 North IH 35
Austin, Texas 78722
TEL: (512) 471-1365
CONTACT: Joel Miller
DIRECTOR: Yaron Shemer
OTHER STAFF: Diane Watts
CATEGORY: Ethnic Israeli

BACA FILM AND VIDEO FESTIVAL

BACA/Brooklyn Arts Council
195 Cadman Plaza West
Brooklyn, NY 11201
TEL: (718) 625-0080
FAX: (718) 625-3294
FESTIVAL DATE: March
ENTRY DEADLINE: December
CONTACT: Rob Orlinick, Chuck Reichenthal, Mark Dannat
CATEGORY: Video

BALTIMORE INTERNATIONAL FILM FESTIVAL

The Baltimore Film Forum at
The Baltimore Museum of Art
10 Art Museum Dr.
Baltimore, MD 21218
TEL: (410) 889-1993
FAX: (410) 889-2657
FESTIVAL DATE: April
ENTRY DEADLINE: January
DIRECTOR: Victoria Westover, Executive Director

BANFF FESTIVAL OF MOUNTAIN FILMS

Banff Centre
Box 1020, Stn. 38
Banff, Alberta T0L 0C0
Canada
TEL: (403) 762-6125
FAX: (403) 762-6277
FESTIVAL DATE: November
ENTRY DEADLINE: September
DIRECTOR: Bernadette McDonald
CATEGORY: Independent

BERKSHIRE FILM FESTIVAL

Berkshire Film Society
Great Barrington, MA
TEL: (413) 528-6120
FESTIVAL DATE: October
CONTACT: Robert Roessel

BIG MUDDY FILM FESTIVAL

Dept of Cinema and
Photography
Mailcode 6610
Southern Illinois University
Carbondale, IL 62901-6610
TEL: (618) 453-1482
FAX: (618)453-2264
E-MAIL: bigmuddy@siu.edu
WEB SITE: www.siu.edu/~films
FESTIVAL DATE: February-March
ENTRY DEADLINE: January
YEAR FESTIVAL BEGAN: 1978
CONTACT: Susan Duhig and Mike Covell

DIRECTOR: Susan Duhig and Mike Covell
PROGRAMMER: Susan Duhig and Mike Covell
CATEGORY: Independent
PROFILE: The Big Muddy Film Festival is committed to supporting and generating interest in innovative, independent films and videos, encouraging artists who challenge the traditional boundaries of visual media. We seek to provide an artistic and cultural alternative to mainstream cinema in a region where access to this kind of work is extremely limited. Since 1978, the Big Muddy has annually featured an international film and video competition, presentations by guest film and video makers, community outreach programs, and screenings of quality feature films.
FAMOUS SPEAKERS: Past festival judges/guest artists have included Jim Jarmusch, Haskell Wexler and Reginald Hudlin
COMPETITIONS: Yes
MAJOR AWARDS: Best of the Fest
VALUE OF AWARDS: We give the judging panel $3000 to divide up however they see fit.
LAST WINNING FILMS: *Ground Zero/Sacred Ground* (Karen Aqua); *Taylor's Campaign* (Richard Cohen); *Paranoia* (Robert Edwards); *The Andre Show* (Beverly Peterson); *Roam Sweet Home* (Ellen Spiro); *Anna in the Sky* (Mark Edgington)
LAST WINNING DIRECTORS: In parentheses above
PAST JUDGES: See above under Famous Speakers
APPLICATION FEE: $30-$40, depends on length of film.
AVERAGE FILMS ENTERED: A wide range of quality work—animated, documentary, experimental, narrative, cross-genre, all lengths, 16mm or video (1/2 inch or 3/4 inch)
FILMS SCREENED: all that are accepted
ODDS OF ACCEPTANCE: About 200 entries each year, about 70 accepted.

TRAVEL TIPS: The closest major airport is in St. Louis (2 hours); Amtrak passes through town.
BEST RESTAURANTS: Tokyo Restaurant
BEST BARS: Tres Hombres
BEST HANGOUT FOR FILMMAKERS: Long Branch Coffee House
BEST PLACE FOR BREAKFAST: Melange Cafe

BIRMINGHAM INTERNATIONAL EDUCATIONAL FILM FESTIVAL

P. O. Box 2641
Birmingham, AL 35291-2711
TEL: (205) 250-2711
FAX: (205) 933-9080
FESTIVAL DATE: Awards ceremony in May
ENTRY DEADLINE: January
CONTACT: Victoria Baxter
CATEGORY: Education

BLACK FILMWORKS FESTIVAL OF FILM AND VIDEO

405 Fourteenth St., Suite 515
Oakland, CA 94612
TEL: (510) 465-0804
FAX: (510) 839-9858
WEB SITE: http://www.pagelist.com/bfhfi/
FESTIVAL DATE: September—October
ENTRY DEADLINE: June
CONTACT: Dorothy Karvi
CATEGORY: Ethnic Black
PROFILE: Its focus is to encourage black filmmakers and to explore black culture. Entrants in this festival are to be black directors, producers and film writers. Over 5,000 attend annually.
AWARDS: Yes
COMPETITIONS: Yes
MAJOR AWARDS: There are over 10 categories with 3 prizes awarded in each.
VALUE OF AWARDS: First Place: $1,500; Second Place: $750; Third Place: $500

> We give the judging panel $3000 to divide up however they see fit. (Big Muddy Film Festival)

APPLICATION FEE: $25-32

ODDS OF ACCEPTANCE: 33-50 films entered

BLACK HARVEST INTERNATIONAL FILM FESTIVAL

Film Center at the School of the Art Institute of Chicago

Columbus Drive and Jackson Blvd.

Chicago, IL 60603

TEL: (312) 443-3733

FAX: (312) 332-5859

E-MAIL: bschar@artic.edu

FESTIVAL DATE: July

ENTRY DEADLINE: May

CATEGORY: Student

APPLICATION FEE: None

BLACK MARIA FILM AND VIDEO FESTIVAL

c/o Media Arts

New Jersey City University

203 West Side Avenue

Jersey City, NJ 07305

TEL: (201) 200-2043

FAX: (201) 200-3490

E-MAIL: JColumbus@aol.com

FESTIVAL DATE: January

ENTRY DEADLINE: November

PROFILE: We're the biggest small film/video festival going, we are anti-establishment, we are semi-underground, we are not bogus radical, we show really experimental, explorational, intelligent, and inventive work.

VALUE OF AWARDS: $17,000 in cash prizes

BLACK TALKIES ON PARADE FILM FESTIVAL

3617 Montclair St.

Los Angeles, CA 90018

TEL: (213) 737-3292

FAX: (213) 737-2842

FESTIVAL DATE: March

CONTACT: Dr. Mayme A. Clayton

CATEGORY: Ethnic Black

BLACKLIGHT

1507 E Street, #428

Chicago, IL 60615

TEL: (312) 649-4854

FESTIVAL DATE: July-August

ENTRY DEADLINE: June

CONTACT: Floyd Webb

CATEGORY: Ethnic Black

BLUE SKY INTERNATIONAL FILM FESTIVAL

4185 Paradise Rd. #2009

Las Vegas, NV 89109

TEL: (702) 737-3313

FAX: (702) 737-3313

E-MAIL: bsiff98@aol.com

WEB SITE: http://www. blueskyfilmfestival.com

FESTIVAL DATE: September

ENTRY DEADLINE: August

YEAR FESTIVAL BEGAN: 1998

CONTACT: Gottfried Hill, Frank Montgomery

DIRECTOR: Jeffrey Matthews Hill

CATEGORY: Independent

PROFILE: An artisans forum dedicated to the discovery of new talent within the filmmaking community. We create exposure for all filmmakers, no matter how large or small their audience may be.

AWARDS: Yes

COMPETITIONS: Yes

VALUE OF AWARDS: BSIFF Directors Award: $1000, BSIFF Best Screenplay: $1000, Plus a staged reading by the Blue Sky Players.

APPLICATION FEE: $15-$30

FILMS SCREENED: 100

ODDS OF ACCEPTANCE: 100 films submitted, 100 films screened.

TOURIST INFORMATION: The Las Vegas Strip, Hoover Dam and Freemont Street.

BEST BARS: Sunset Station

BOSTON GAY & LESBIAN FILM & VIDEO FESTIVAL

Museum of Fine Arts

465 Huntington Ave.

Boston, MA 02115

TEL: (617) 267-9300 x454

FESTIVAL DATE: June

ENTRY DEADLINE: March

APPLICATION FEE: None

BOSTON INTERNATIONAL FESTIVAL OF WOMEN'S CINEMA

Running Arts

PO Box 391

Cambridge, MA 02139

TEL: (617) 876-6708

FESTIVAL DATE: April

ENTRY DEADLINE: March

CATEGORY: Retro Women

APPLICATION FEE: None

BRECKENRIDGE FESTIVAL OF FILM

P. O. Box 718

Breckenridge, CO 80424

TEL: (970)453-6200

FAX: (970) 453-2692

E-MAIL: filmfest@ brecknet.com

FESTIVAL DATE: September

ENTRY DEADLINE: June

YEAR FESTIVAL BEGAN: 1981

CONTACT: Tamara K. Johnston/ Julie Bullock

DIRECTOR: Terese Keil

CATEGORY: Independent

PROFILE: This is a four-day program of films, receptions, premieres, tributes, writers' seminars and film education activites providing unique and varied filmfare shown at venues throughout the community. Approximately 50 independent U.S. and international films presented from over 300 entries. Since 1981, Breckenridge Festival of Film has emphasized a relaxed atmosphere in which guests are readily accessible to film-goers. Writers, directors, producers and performing artists attend to discuss their work with audiences in informal sessions following screenings, at seminars, receptions and at the outdoor film forums.

MAJOR AWARDS: Best of the Fest
APPLICATION TIPS: For initial selection, film entries must be in VHS format. Final screening accepted in 35mm, 16mm, 3/4". Scripts should meet US Motion Picture Industry standards and be 90-130 pages.
APPLICATION FEE: $35
ODDS OF ACCEPTANCE: 300 films entered, 50 presented.
FILMMAKER PERKS: Lodging accomodations and discounts on ground transportation provided for filmmakers during the festival.

BUCKS COUNTY FILM FESTIVAL

8 East Court St.
Doylestown, PA 18901
TEL: (215) 348-3566
FESTIVAL DATE: November; January-June (tour)
ENTRY DEADLINE: October
CONTACT: John Toner, c/o Smith & Toner

BUCKS COUNTY INDEPENDENT FILM TOUR

150 South Pine St.
Doylestown, PA 18901
TEL: (215) 348-3566
FAX: (215) 348-3569
FESTIVAL DATE: November-June
ENTRY DEADLINE: September
CONTACT: Bucks County Free Library, Film Department

BWAC FILM & VIDEO FESTIVAL

PO Box 020072
Brooklyn, NY 11202
TEL: (718) 858-4702
FESTIVAL DATE: May
ENTRY DEADLINE: March
APPLICATION FEE: None

CANADIAN INTERNATIONAL ANNUAL FILM FESTIVAL

25 Eugenia St.
Barrie, Ontario L4M 1P6
Canada
TEL: (705) 737-2729
FAX: (705) 726-4655
FESTIVAL DATE: Varies
ENTRY DEADLINE: June
CONTACT: Ben V. W. Andrews

CANYONLANDS FILM & VIDEO FESTIVAL

Country Pumpkin Productions
400 North 500 West, Unit 1-8
Moab, UT 84532
TEL: (435) 259-3330
FESTIVAL DATE: April
ENTRY DEADLINE: March
APPLICATION FEE: $25

CAPITOL AMATEUR VIDEO COMPETITION

Capitol Videomakers Association
5002 N. Englewood Dr.
Capitol Heights, MD 20743
FESTIVAL DATE: January-February
ENTRY DEADLINE: December
DIRECTOR: Chris Leech, President
CATEGORY: Video

CAROLINA FILM AND VIDEO FESTIVAL

Broadcasting/Cinema Dept.
100 Carmichael Bldg.
UNC-Greensboro
Greensboro, NC 27412-5001
TEL: (336) 334-5360
WEB SITE: http://www.uncg.edu/cbt/CFVF.html
FESTIVAL DATE: March-April
ENTRY DEADLINE: February
CONTACT: Sarah Westmoreland
CATEGORY: Independent, Student
PROFILE: This festival screens films by students and independents. Over 600 attend.

AWARDS: Yes
COMPETITIONS: Yes
MAJOR AWARDS: Categories and amount awarded are determined by the festival's jury.
VALUE OF AWARDS: At least $2500 awarded.
APPLICATION FEE: $30 U.S. (Independents) / $20 U.S. (Students)
FILMS SCREENED: 45 screened
ODDS OF ACCEPTANCE: 300 entered

CENTRAL FLORIDA FILM AND VIDEO FESTIVAL

1906 East Robinson St
Orlando , Florida 32803
TEL: (407) 898-7111 or (407) 839-6045
FAX: (407) 898-0504
E-MAIL: jneff@magicnet.net
WEB SITE: http://www.cffvf.org:/
FESTIVAL DATE: September-October
ENTRY DEADLINE: June
CONTACT: Jason Neff
DIRECTOR: Jason Neff
PROGRAMMER: Jason Neff
OTHER STAFF: Amy Wieck, Human Resources; Melodie Malfa, Communications Director; Jennifer Pullinger, Marketing Director; Mendi Cowles, Advertising Director; Jack Marsh, Operations Director; Klaus Heesch, Art Director; Website Director, George Scharfetter, Jr.
CATEGORY: Independent
PROFILE: Florida's oldest film and video festival is produced by Frameworks Alliance, Inc.; an educational, cultural, and artistic organization that seeks to foment the value of literacy, culture, and film as a genuine expression of our spiritual and communal experience. The Central Florida Film and Video Festival was created to showcase the discovery of new and emerging artists from the United States and around the world.
SEMINARS: TBA

PANELS: Media Literacy Forum (1998) with George Gerbner, Michael Parenti and Jerry Mander

FAMOUS SPEAKERS: Russ Meyer, George Gerbner, Michael Parenti, and Jerry Mander.

COMPETITIONS: Yes

MAJOR AWARDS: Hammercam

VALUE OF AWARDS: $100-$1000

LAST WINNING FILMS: Narrative—*First Love Second Planet*—David Munro; Experimental—*The Paraclete*—Velko Milosevich; Documentary—*Wayne Freedman's Notebook*—Aaron Lubarsky; Animation—*How Wings Are Attached to the Backs of Angels*—Craig Welch; Feature—*The Sore Losers*—John Micheal McCarthy; Florida Film and Videos—*God Laughed*—Bob Derosa

PAST JUDGES: Keith Bauer, Producer, Time Warner Communications; Aaron Blaise, Supervising Animator, Walt Disney Feature Animation; Steve Schneider, writer/editor, Orlando Weekly; Swami, 3-D Animator; Margaret Yerian, writer; to name just a few.

APPLICATION TIPS: Production values don't matter as much as making a cohesive, interesting film!

APPLICATION FEE: $35 entry fee ($20 for Florida filmmakers, must include a photocopy of current Florida I.D.), $10 for return of feedback forms, $15 late fee (if submitted after June 1st), $15 for special Commemorative 16th Anniversary CFFVF t-shirt

INSIDER ADVICE: Always include supporting materials such as thorough summary of film, photos/stills, press materials which will help to create more exposure for your film

AVERAGE FILMS ENTERED: Any style, genre, or category is accepted.

FILMS SCREENED: Approximately 650 (and more each year).

ODDS OF ACCEPTANCE: 150 Films are accepted each year

FILMMAKER PERKS: Some of the benefits for entering the Central Florida Film and Video Festival: feedback forms with written responses; over $6,000 in cash and services awarded; films exhibited in four cities (1998): Orlando, Melbourne, Gainesville, Tampa; Any style, genre, or category is acceptable; video format is welcome; Our television show, "Ballyhoo!" reaches 70,000 viewers twice a week; website promotion of film/videos; "Best of the CFFVF" compilation tape; Festival Party's including free admission to mix and mingle with filmmakers and film enthusists.

TRAVEL TIPS: Stay Downtown! (This way you are closer to the events and parties.)

BEST RESTAURANTS: Sapphire Supper Club on Orange Avenue

BEST BARS: Sapphire Supper Club

BEST PLACE FOR BREAKFAST: IHOP in Colonial Dr.

CHARLOTTE FiLM AND ViDEO FESTiVAL

Behind the Scenes *magazine recently called the Charlotte festival, "one of nation's most respected" and a festival that looks for "a unique voice, a truly individual vision, a synergy of a filmmaker's heart, mind and craft." Tina DiFeliciantonio, director of* Girls Like Us, *said, "Thanks for an extraordinary experience." Alan Berliner, director of* Nobody's Business, *said, "This festival has arrived!"*

Mint Museum of Art
2730 Randolph Road
Charlotte, NC 28207
TEL: (704) 337-2019 or (704) 337-2065
FAX: (704) 337-2101
E-MAIL: rkwest@mint.uncc. edu or mintfilm@aol.com

WEB SITE: www.mintmuseum. org/filmpage.htm

FESTIVAL DATE: Early June

ENTRY DEADLINE: February

YEAR FESTIVAL BEGAN: 1989

CONTACT: Robert West or Ashby McDonald

DIRECTOR: Robert West

PROGRAMMER: Robert West

CATEGORY: Independent, Video

PROFILE: The Charlotte Film and Video Festival seeks to foster and encourage the art of independent film and video makers, especially those with a unique point of view. Affirming this commitment, the festival also seeks to increase public awareness and accessibility to this art form.

AWARDS: Yes

COMPETITIONS: Yes

MAJOR AWARDS: Jurors Choice Award, Directors Choice Award

VALUE OF AWARDS: Depends, from $1000 to $200

LAST WINNING FILMS: 1998: *Nobody's Business, The Andre Show, Human Remains, POM, If I Can't Do It, Sacrifice, Baby It's You, A Life Apart, Paradise Falls, Wonderland, High Art, Fallen Angels.* 1997: *Motherhood on Trial, Lost Book Found, A Healthy Baby Girl, Family Name, Six O'Clock News, Girls Like Us, The Riddle, Chronic, Two or Three Things But Nothing For Sure, Passing, The Gate of Heavenly Peace, Hide and Seek, It's Elementary*

PAST JUDGES: Alan Berliner, Tina DiFeliciantonio, Tom Kalin, Nancy Gerstmann, Barbara Hammer, Brian Springer, Vivian Kleiman.

APPLICATION TIPS: Films that are truly independent typically do better than standard documentaries or narratives. Creative and experimental films are encouraged. Films that are art, but not necessarily about art, do well. Don't send toys or T-shirts or props. Past screenings or awards are helpful.

APPLICATION FEE: $30

INSIDER ADVICE: Student category is less competitive than general category. Hollywood wannabes shouldn't enter this festival. Make sure preview tapes are in good shape. No works in progress.

AVERAGE FILMS ENTERED: See winners. Strong documentaries and narratives with an edge.

FILMS SCREENED: All accepted films are screened: 50

ODDS OF ACCEPTANCE: 600 films entered, 50 accepted

FILMMAKER PERKS: All accepted films in the festival receive CASH. Range is from $50 to $1000. When Ross McElwee was in town with *Sherman's March,* the commercial theater we were screening in was having an employee dispute. The projectionist took the print of *Sherman's March* and threw in a creek next door to the theater. Ross had to retrieve the print, dry it off, and re-thread it. In 1997, we screened *It's Elementary.* Two county commissioners came to the screening and alerted the local news. After the screening, the commissioners said the film should never have been screened and was about recruiting homosexuals. (It's about tolerance in public schools for all, including gays and lesbians.) All local news stations led with the story. Later that month the same commissioners voted to eliminate $300,000 of taxpayer funding from the museum.

> Learn to write a good 25 word synopsis of the film that details the protagonist, antagonist and their basic conflict. (Chicago Alt.Film Fest)

CHICAGO ALT.FILM FEST

An event for film-goers whose tastes fit somewhere between the foreign-centered International and the edgy Underground.... Programmed with emerging American directors in mind and indie-loving audiences at heart."

—Erik Piepenberg, MSNBC

3430 N. Lake Shore Drive, Suite 19N
Chicago, Illinois 60657
TEL: (773) 525-4559
FAX: (773) 327-8669
E-MAIL: chialtfilm@aol.com
WEB SITE: http://members.aol.com/ChiAltFilm/Fest
FESTIVAL DATE: June
ENTRY DEADLINE: April
YEAR FESTIVAL BEGAN: 1998
CONTACT: Dennis Neal Vaughn
DIRECTOR: Dennis Neal Vaughn
PROGRAMMER: Dennis Neal Vaughn and Sandra Kay Zielinski
OTHER STAFF: Leticia G. Esquivel, Pamela J. Stephens
CATEGORY: Independent
PROFILE: Chicago's premiere film festival of American Independent filmmakers—quality over quantity.
SEMINARS: Scripts—writing, buying, selling; Working with the Guilds, Film technology
PANELS: Meet the filmmakers series
FAMOUS SPEAKERS: "Goreville, USA" filmmakers
AWARDS: Yes
COMPETITIONS: Yes
MAJOR AWARDS: Founder's Award to most promising filmmaker.
VALUE OF AWARDS: $1000
PAST JUDGES: David Sikich
APPLICATION TIPS: Be professional
APPLICATION FEE: $50
INSIDER ADVICE: Learn to write a good 25 word synopsis of the film that details the protagonist, antagonist and their basic conflict. Get decent press photos.
AVERAGE FILMS ENTERED: narrative features and shorts
FILMS SCREENED: Total 35 features, shorts, and docs
ODDS OF ACCEPTANCE: over 200 submitted—15 accepted (Features)
FILMMAKER PERKS: VIP/Filmmaker networking; Lounge and private dinner party

TOURIST INFORMATION: Wrigley Field, the lake front, State Street, Michigan Avenue, Michael Jordan's restaurant
TRAVEL TIPS: Be prepared for anything—the weather can change in 5 minutes here.
BEST BARS: The Rainbo Club
BEST HANGOUT FOR FILMMAKERS: The Rainbo Club
BEST PLACE FOR BREAKFAST:The Rainbo-Just ask any cab driver

CHICAGO INTERNATIONAL CHILDREN'S FILM FESTIVAL

c/o Facets Multimedia, Inc.
1517 West Fullerton Ave.
Chicago, IL 60614
TEL: (312) 281-9075
FAX: (312) 929-5437
E-MAIL: kidsfest@facets.org
FESTIVAL DATE: October
ENTRY DEADLINE: June
CONTACT: Elizabeth Shepherd
CATEGORY: Children's films.
PROFILE: Largest children's film festival in North America. Approximately 10,000 attend.
AWARDS: yes
COMPETITIONS: yes
APPLICATION FEE: $35 (shorts) $75 (features)

CHICAGO INTERNATIONAL FILM FESTIVAL

32 West Randolph St., Ste. 600
Chicago, IL 60601
TEL: (312) 425-9400
FAX: (312) 425-0944
E-MAIL: filmfest@wwa.com
WEB SITE: http://www.chicago.ddbn.com/filmfest/
FESTIVAL DATE: October
CONTACT: Michael J. Kutza
CATEGORY: International
PROFILE: This festival concentrates on finding new filmmaking talent as well as celebrating various aspects of filmmaking history. Approximately 75,000 attend.

AWARDS: yes

COMPETITIONS: yes

MAJOR AWARDS: Golden Hugo

APPLICATION FEE: $35-$150

ODDS OF ACCEPTANCE: 2,000 films entered

CHICAGO LATINO FILM FESTIVAL

Chicago Latino Cinema

600 S. Michigan Ave.

Chicago, IL 60605

TEL: (312) 431-1330

FAX: (312) 360-0629

FESTIVAL DATE: April-May

ENTRY DEADLINE: February

CONTACT: Pepe Vargas

CATEGORY: Ethnic Other

PROFILE: The Chicago Latino Film Festival explores all genres of filmmaking within Latin America, Spain, Portugal and the United States. Approximately 25,000 people attend annually.

AWARDS: Yes

COMPETITIONS: No

MAJOR AWARDS: Kodak Emerging Filmmaker Award

VALUE OF AWARDS: $3,000 worth of "raw film stock"

APPLICATION FEE: None

ODDS OF ACCEPTANCE: 100 films entered

CHICAGO UNDERGROUND FILM FESTIVAL

2501 N. Lincoln Ave.

Suite 278

Chicago, IL 60614

TEL: (773) 866-8660

FAX: (773) 275-8313

E-MAIL: cuff@ripco.com or programmer@cuff.org

WEB SITE: http://www.deafear.com/cuff/

FESTIVAL DATE: August

ENTRY DEADLINE: May

CONTACT: Bryan Wendorf

DIRECTOR: Jay Bliznick

PROGRAMMER: Bryan Wendorf

OTHER STAFF: Donna Jagela, Wendy Solomon, Sonja Pachmeyer, Chris Tillman, Mike Miller, Michael Kopp

CATEGORY: Independent, Underground, Weird

PROFILE: Our festival is designed to showcase the truly independent filmmaker. We don't promote any sort of political agenda other than the free expression of views outside of the entertainment mainstream . . . we're just about the films. We won't discriminate on content but we are firm about intent. We also don't discriminate between first-time and established filmmakers. If you suspect your film is underground, it probably is.

SEMINARS: Yes

FAMOUS SPEAKERS: John Waters, Beth B, Jack Sargeant

AWARDS: Yes

COMPETITIONS: Yes

MAJOR AWARDS: Golden Sewer Cap

VALUE OF AWARDS: $500

LAST WINNING FILMS: *Half Spirit* (feature), *Meat* (short), *Rainbow Man/John 3:16* (Documentary), *Premenstrual Spotting* (Experimental)

LAST WINNING DIRECTORS: Henri Barges (Feature), Jason Hernandez-Rosenblatt (Short), Sam Green (Documentary), Machiko Saito (Experimental).

PAST JUDGES: Tom Palazzolo, Bryan Wendorf, Jay Bliznick, Donna Jagela, Wendy Solomon, Mike Miller, Jonathan Lavan.

APPLICATION TIPS: Read the mission statement. Think about whether our festival is the right place to showcase your film. Read the guidelines and follow them!

APPLICATION FEE: $25 (60 minutes or less) $35 (over 60 minutes)

INSIDER ADVICE: Can't stress enough that you must feel sure that this is the festival where your film belongs. Each year we screen a lot of good entries that are just not right for us. Do your research—don't enter festivals just because you get an application in the mail. If you're not sure, call the festival and talk to a human. That will save you much money and aggravation!

AVERAGE FILMS ENTERED: Out of the mainstream features, shorts, documentaries, experimental and animation.

ODDS OF ACCEPTANCE: 800 submitted, 100 accepted.

FILMMAKER PERKS: Opening and closing night filmmakers are flown in and lodged at our expense. We always have a special hotel rate for filmmakers at a sponsor hotel. A list of press contacts is available prior to the festival to anyone who asks for one. We always have hosted parties where filmmakers drink for free or WAY cheap. And of course, we host the annual VPL (Visible Panty League) (you figure it out) Bowling Night, during which visiting filmmakers and local CUFFers descend upon an all-night bowling alley and roll them balls 'til the sun comes up! Charles Pinion of San Francisco has won the trophy two years running. . . can ANYONE beat him?

> . . . we host the annual VPL (Visible Panty League) (you figure it out) Bowling Night, during which visiting filmmakers and local CUFFers descend upon an all-night bowling alley and roll them balls 'til the sun comes up! (Chicago Underground Film Festival)

CINEQUEST

The San Jose Film Festival

P. O. Box 720040

San Jose, CA 95172-0040

TEL: (408) 995-5033

FAX: (408) 995-5713

E-MAIL: sjfilmfest@aol.com

WEB SITE: www.cinequest.org

FESTIVAL DATE: October

ENTRY DEADLINE: August

CONTACT: Ken Karn

OTHER STAFF: Mike Rabehl

PROFILE: Sections of the festival include: A Maverick Competition of features, documentaries & shorts, Digital and High-Tech Films, Gay & Lesbian Showcase, Latino Film Celebration, After Hours, and Local Spotlight. Special events, Maverick tributes, seminars, technical presentations, catered celebrations and entertainment

MICHELLE VENDELIN

America's darling John Waters at the Cinequest San Jose Film Festival with Cinequest President and film producer Kathleen Powell.

will add to the fun of this warm and extraordinary festival.

FAMOUS SPEAKERS: Past Maverick tributes and presentations have included Kevin Spacey, Jackie Chan, Jennifer Jason Leigh, Barry Sonnenfeld, John Schlesinger, John Waters, Bryan Singer, Sheila Benson, Grace Zabriskie, Gus Van Sant, Russ Meyer, Robert Wise, Carl Franklin Walter Murch, Walter Hill and Ron Shelton. Some past film highlights: *Trekkies, Anarchy TV, Green Chimneys, Lea, It's Elementary, The Nasty Girl, LadyBird, LadyBird, Public Access, My Own Private Idaho, Antonia's Line, Kolya, Luna e l'altra, The Other Side of Sunday,* and *The Quiet Room.*

ATTENDANCE: Last year, Cinequest had over 30,000 ticket buyers anxious to see the over 100 independent, maverick films in our program, and Cinequest '99 is sure to be another exciting event for filmmakers and film lovers alike.

CINEVEGAS FILM FESTIVAL

PoloTowers
Polo Plaza Suite 204
3743 Las Vegas Blvd. South
Las Vegas, NV 89109
TEL: 702-477-7530
FAX: 702-477-7533
E-MAIL: info@cinevegas.com

WEB SITE: www.cinevegas.com
FESTIVAL DATE: December
ENTRY DEADLINE: October
YEAR FESTIVAL BEGAN: 1998
CONTACT: Joshua Abbey
DIRECTOR: Michele Berk
CATEGORY: Independent
PROFILE: "CineVegas is about more than bringing culture to the desert; it's about redefining Las Vegas for the next century as the most progressive and compelling tourist destination in the world," says CineVegas Vice President and Executive Producer Michele Berk, who is also the reigning Mrs. United States. "CineVegas will bring the world to Las Vegas".

"Just as Las Vegas has brought the four corners of the world to one street with their fabulous, themed casinos, CineVegas will bring the four corners of world filmmaking to the entertainment capital." says Joshua Abbey, the Festival's Executive Director. "The goal of CineVegas is to engage the imagination and participation of the entertainment industry and filmgoing public by producing a festival that captures and emulates the inventiveness that has made Las Vegas the focal point of popular American culture."

FILMS SCREENED: Featured the premiere of the feature-length documentary *Stripped And Teased: Tales Of Las Vegas Women,* directed by award winning documentary film maker Amie Williams.

CITY LORE FESTIVAL OF AMERICAN FILM AND VIDEO

City Lore
72 E. 1st St.
New York, NY 10003
TEL: (212) 529-1955
FAX: (212) 529-5062
FESTIVAL DATE: March
ENTRY DEADLINE: January
CONTACT: Eric John or Benjamin Salazar
CATEGORY: Video

CLEVELAND INTERNATIONAL FILM FESTIVAL

1621 Euclid Ave. #428
Cleveland, Ohio 44115
TEL: (216) 623-0400
FAX: (216) 623-0103
E-MAIL: info@clevelandfilm.org
WEB SITE: www.clevelandfilm.org
FESTIVAL DATE: March
ENTRY DEADLINE: November
CONTACT: Angela Stetzy
DIRECTOR: David W. Wittkowsky
PROGRAMMER: David W. Wittkowsky
OTHER STAFF: Joseph G. Discenza, Development Director. Lauren Smith, Membership Director.
CATEGORY: Documentary, Gay Lesbian, Independent, International
PROFILE: Since its founding in 1977, the Cleveland International Film Festival has been the premiere film event in Ohio. Today, the CIFF presents a full survey of contemporary international filmmaking, with approximately 80 features from 30 countries, and more than 100 short subjects presented in collected programs. Annual attendance for this eleven-day event

tops 32,000. Patrons can vote on all the films they see, and their votes select the winner of the Roxanne T. Mueller Award, the CIFF's people's choice award. Special sections of documentary films, American independent features, family films, new films from Eastern Europe, PanAfrican features, and lesbian and gay films, in addition to the main World Tour section, add interest and diversity to the overall program.

Many filmmakers and special guests attend the CIFF, and participate in FilmForums, panel discussions which give our audience members a chance to discuss in-depth the films they've seen at the Festival. Short films compete for many awards, and approximately $2,500 in cash prizes. Award categories include Best Ohio Short, Best Documentary Short, Best Student Short, and Best Women's Short.

In 1998, the CIFF included the first Midwest Filmmakers Conference, a three-day event for independent filmmakers from throughout the region which featured panels, workshops, equipment demonstrations, networking opportunities, film screenings and social events.

Since many screenings sell out in advance (and most sell out at the door), patrons are advised to purchase tickets in advance. Program guides are available three weeks before the Festival opens. For information, call 216/623-0400.

AWARDS: yes

COMPETITIONS: yes

MAJOR AWARDS: Roxanne T. Mueller Award and Best American Independent Feature

VALUE OF AWARDS: $1000 for Best American Independent Feature

LAST WINNING FILMS: Most recent winner Roxanne T. Mueller Award: *Character*; (Netherlands) Best American independent feature: *The Journey*

LAST WINNING DIRECTORS: Mike van Diem and Harish Saluja

APPLICATION TIPS: Submit on time—don't miss the deadline.

APPLICATION FEE: $35 for shorts (30 mins or under), $25 by early deadline (October) $60 for features over 30 mins), $50 by early deadline (October)

ODDS OF ACCEPTANCE: 450 films submitted (features & shorts) in 1998. Of those 55 films were accepted.

COLUMBIA COLLEGE INTERNATIONAL DOCUMENTARY FESTIVAL

Documentary Center
Columbia College
600 S. Michigan
Chicago, IL 60605
TEL: (312) 663-1600 x306
FESTIVAL DATE: April
ENTRY DEADLINE: March
CATEGORY: Documentary
APPLICATION FEE: None

COLUMBUS INTERNATIONAL FILM AND VIDEO FESTIVAL

"Chris Awards"
Film Council of Greater Columbus
5701 North High St., #204
Worthington, OH 43085
TEL: (614) 841-1666
FESTIVAL DATE: October
ENTRY DEADLINE: July
CONTACT: Joyce Long

D.FILM DIGITAL FILM FESTIVAL

"One of the 25 players bringing Hollywood into the 21st century"
—*WIRED Magazine*

8033 Sunset Blvd., Suite 4056
Hollywood, CA 90046
TEL: (323) 769-5088
E-MAIL: bart@dfilm.com
WEB SITE:
http://www.dfilm.com

FESTIVAL DATE: Touring. DFilm travels to Los Angeles, San Francisco, New York, London, Rio, Boston, Manchester, England.

ENTRY DEADLINE: None. Since the festival is continually being shown in different cities throughout the year, deadlines are ongoing.

YEAR FESTIVAL BEGAN: 1997

DIRECTOR: Bart Cheever

OTHER STAFF: Nikos Constant Claire McNulty, Publicity

PROFILE: Our goal is to showcase the very best work being created within the digital medium. We prefer pieces which are approximately 5 minutes in length or less, or excerpts from longer films. We're looking for work that demonstrates some innovative new use of technology. Although we show abstract work, we especially value pieces which are able to strongly convey ideas or tell stories, pieces which will entertain and inspire our audiences to create films themselves.

Our goal at D.FILM is to not only showcase the best in digital filmmaking through our screenings and website but to also actively inspire our audiences to make film themselves. Do it.

D.FILM is a touring festival. This year we'll be bringing the festival to 19 cities around the world. The core traveling festival will expand from 4 to 9 cities and we're setting up a special tour of college campuses which will be organized by Brett Russell, formerly of Spike and Mike's Festival of Animation/Sick and Twisted and Warren Miller Films, which will bring the festival to an additional 10 cities. Last year, every show in every city was sold out.

APPLICATION FEE: None. Entry fees suck.

> We're looking for work that demonstrates some innovative new use of technology. (D.Film Digital Film Festival)

DALLAS ViDEO FESTiVAL

215 A Henry St.
Dallas, TX 75226
TEL: (214) 651-8888
FAX: (214) 651-8896
FESTIVAL DATE: November
ENTRY DEADLINE: August
CONTACT: Barton Weiss
CATEGORY: Video

DANCES WiTH FiLMS: FESTiVAL OF THE UNKNOWNS

P.O. Box 1766
Beverly Hills, California
90213-1766
TEL: (213) 656-1974
FAX: (213) 656-6471
E-MAIL: DWFilmFest@aol.com
WEB SITE: http://members.aol.
com/DWFilmFest/
FESTIVAL DATE: July
ENTRY DEADLINE: Early June
YEAR FESTIVAL BEGAN: 1998
CONTACT: Michael Trent
DIRECTOR: Michael Trent
PROGRAMMER: Leslee Scallon
OTHER STAFF: Jeannette Christensen
CATEGORY: Independent, Weird
PROFILE: No politics. No stars. No shit. Only films with no "known" directors, actor and producers.
AWARDS: Yes
COMPETITIONS: Yes
MAJOR AWARDS: Best Feature, Best Short
VALUE OF AWARDS: Certificates and GREAT Appreciation.
APPLICATION TIPS: We place EV-ERYONE on a level playing field—no politics—no tips
APPLICATION FEE: Features $50, Shorts $35
INSIDER ADVICE: Give us the best you've got. Most important is story.
AVERAGE FILMS ENTERED: Looking for films that have a real shot at distribution—commercial in vein.
FILMS SCREENED: 12 Features, 12

No politics. No stars. No shit. Only films with no "known" directors, actor and producers. (Dances With Films: Festival of the Unknowns)

Shorts
ODDS OF ACCEPTANCE: 12 Features, 12 Shorts
TOURIST INFORMATION: It's LA—are you kidding?
TRAVEL TIPS: Plan Ahead
BEST RESTAURANTS: By the time you read this—it will have changed!
BEST BARS: See "best restaurant."
BEST HANGOUT FOR FILMMAKERS: You name it
BEST PLACE FOR BREAKFAST: Cafe Latte

DCTV YOUTH VIDEO FESTiVAL

Downtown Community Television Center
87 Lafayette St.
New York, NY 10013
TEL: (212) 941-1298
FAX: (212) 219-1298
FESTIVAL DATE: Dates and deadlines vary
CONTACT: Jocelyn Taylor
CATEGORY: Video

DENVER iNTERNATiONAL FiLM FESTiVAL

999 18th St., #1820
Denver, CO 80202
TEL: (303) 595-3456
FAX: (303) 595-0956
FESTIVAL DATE: October
ENTRY DEADLINE: July
DIRECTOR: Ron Henderson

DETROiT iNTERNATiONAL FiLM FESTiVAL

Detroit Filmmakers Coalition
17360 Lahser Road, Suite 200
Detroit, MI 48219
TEL: (313) 255-0098
FAX: (313) 255-1035
E-MAIL: thedfc@juno.com
WEB SITE: www.detroitfilm.org
FESTIVAL DATE: November
ENTRY DEADLINE: August 31
YEAR FESTIVAL BEGAN: 1991

DIRECTOR: Wayne Indyk
CATEGORY: Animation, Ethnic Black, Independent, Short
PROFILE: The Detroit International Film Festival, a prestigious juried competition for independent filmmakers, celebrates the unique visions of independent filmmakers. The event focuses on films by and for a diverse ethnic community, emphasizing work that presents an unusual vision of the world (real or imagined). The festival welcomes films and videos of any subject, length and style including narrative, documentary, animated, experimental and cross-genre. In its short history, the Detroit International Film Festival, formerly the Metropolitan Film Festival, has established itself among the premiere film events in the Midwest, presenting a unique collection of work from throughout the country and the world.
FAMOUS SPEAKERS: Elmore Leonard
APPLICATION TIPS: Becoming a part of this event is truly an honor. From all entries received, only the best are selected for the competitive festival. These are then evaluated by a jury of industry professionals, as well as audience viewers, and awarded in several categories.
TOURIST INFORMATION: Home of the DIA, the Detroit Institute of the Arts and the Detroit Red Wings, there's loads to do.

DOCFEST—NEW YORK iNTERNATiONAL DOCUMENTARY FESTiVAL

159 Maiden Lane
New York, NY 10038
TEL: (212) 668-11008
FAX: (212) 943-6396
E-MAIL: dockfest@aol.com
FESTIVAL DATE: April
ENTRY DEADLINE: By invitation only
DIRECTOR: Gary Pollard
CATEGORY: Documentary

EAST BAY VIDEO FESTIVAL

2054 University Ave., #203
Berkeley, CA 94704
TEL: (510) 843-3699
FESTIVAL DATE: October
ENTRY DEADLINE: September
CONTACT: East Bay Media Center
CATEGORY: Video

EDMONTON ANNUAL FILM FESTIVAL

Edmonton, Alberta Canada
TEL: (403) 421-4084
FAX: (403) 425-8098
CONTACT: National Screen Institute

EURO UNDERGROUND

They observe, comment and experiment... those who went to Euro Underground did not regret it.

—Gazeta Wyborcza,
Krakow Poland

1658 N. Milwaukee Ave., Suite 142
Chicago, Illinois 60647
TEL: (888) 864-9644
FAX: (773) 292-9205
E-MAIL: info@eurounderground.org
WEB SITE: www.eurounderground.org
FESTIVAL DATE: October and November
ENTRY DEADLINE: July
YEAR FESTIVAL BEGAN: 1996
CONTACT: Mark Siska
DIRECTOR: Mark Siska
PROGRAMMER: Amy Beste
OTHER STAFF: Justyna Mielnikiewicz, Ilko Davidov, Eugene Barksdale, Paul Rimple, Franck Ravel, David Pyle, Victor Radev
CATEGORY: Independent, Underground, Weird, Video
PROFILE: Euro Underground is a cross-cultural film organization produced by The International Film and Performance Society a not-for-profit film organization exhibiting new and emerging work of international filmmakers. Euro Underground has just completed a three city festival tour that included Sofia, Bulgaria; Krakow, Poland and Berlin, Germany. Euro Underground's mission is to exhibit Europeans and Americans as well as filmmakers throughout the world by producing a yearly festivals in selected European cities and then tour films presented in Europe in American by presenting a series of screening in selected American Cities.

Euro Underground's exhibit international work on an international level offering a built in cinema network available globally for filmmakers. The types of work Euro Underground exhibit and concentrate on is independent, experimental and underground.

AWARDS: Yes
COMPETITIONS: Yes
APPLICATION TIPS: Send entries in early
APPLICATION FEE: $25 for short, $35 for feature.
INSIDER ADVICE: Try to put together and present your film the best way you can. With limited budgets, try your best and be resourceful. There are a lot of ways to get things for free. It is highly competitive out there.
AVERAGE FILMS ENTERED: Films that work underneath the mainstream. Noncommercial, Real films.
FILMS SCREENED: 100. But since we are a different festival that presents work throughout the year we screen a lot more. We continually take films and are currently exhibiting somewhere in the world every month. But our Festival exhibited about 100 films in a 5 day period.
ODDS OF ACCEPTANCE: Up to 300 are submited and we accept about 30%

F3 FILM FESTIVAL

"The hippest, coolest, low-fi, bad ass independent blow-out ever!"

2716 Guadalupe
Austin, TX 78705
TEL: (512) 494 9273
FAX: (512) 494 9273
E-MAIL: shorts@fringeware.com
WEB SITE: www.fringeware.com/f3films/
FESTIVAL DATE: Quarterly screenings in March, July, October, January.
ENTRY DEADLINE: Open
YEAR FESTIVAL BEGAN: 1998
DIRECTOR: Vincent O'Brien
CATEGORY: Independent, Underground, Weird, Video
PROFILE: F3 Film Festival is to create a venue for independent film and video makers; especially those who otherwise might be marginalized by mainstream, commercial, and entertainment media interests. F3 Film Festival's mission is to deconstruct the stranglehold that Hollywood aesthetics attempt to maintain over independents, by narrowing the gap on stylistic and economic barriers. F3 Film Festival produces several interactive webcast film forums per year, extending its audience and exposure.
AWARDS: Yes
COMPETITIONS: No
VALUE OF AWARDS: Certificate of Excellence in the Industrial Arts for competency in the practices of independent film and video.
APPLICATION FEE: None
AVERAGE FILMS ENTERED: 600
FILMS SCREENED: 180
ODDS OF ACCEPTANCE: 620 submitted, 180 accepted.
FILMMAKER PERKS: Great exposure in an industrial cinema forum. Average audience size is about 1,500. Excellent place to network for independent filmmakers and producers. Filmmakers work and contact information are kept on file for

F3's mission is to deconstruct the stranglehold that Hollywood aesthetics attempt to maintain over independents, by narrowing the gap on stylistic and economic barriers. (F3 Film Festival) future use in major film tours and national festivals.

TOURIST INFORMATION: Fringe-Ware, Inc., locally owned media collective and independent bookstore located at 2716 Guadalupe. Barton Springs, a year round 72 degrees crystal clear stream. Great for swimming and nude bathing!

TRAVEL TIPS: Austin Motel, 441-1157, 1220 South Congress Ave. Vintage accommodations ala 1930's Hollywood bung-a-low!

BEST RESTAURANTS: The Marimont Cafeteria, absolutely the shit! Authentic 1970's decor, with employees to match! Perfect for the Hollywood jet set! Located at 38th/Guadalupe, Good Eats Cafe, 476-8141, 1530 Barton Springs. Awesome Sunday brunch, with live music by "BIG IRON"-the most awesome country honky tonk band ever!

BEST BARS: LuLu's, The greatest lounge ever made...

FiLM FRONT NATiONAL STUDENT FiLM AND VIDEO FESTiVAL

c/o Film Front
206 Performing Arts Building
University of Utah
Salt Lake City, UT 84112
TEL: (801) 328-2428
FESTIVAL DATE: October
ENTRY DEADLINE: October
CONTACT: Festival Director
CATEGORY: Student, Video

FiLMBUREAU 606**
CiRCUS '99

1932 West Nelson St.
Chicago, Illinois 60657
TEL: 773/477-4978
FAX: 773/477-4189
E-MAIL: fb606@aol.com
WEB SITE:
www.filmbureau606.com
FESTIVAL DATE: March
ENTRY DEADLINE: November
YEAR FESTIVAL BEGAN: 1998

CONTACT: Elizabeth Owen, Director of Operations

OTHER STAFF: Nicole Bernari-Reis, Director of Communications; Rob Rownd, Director of Development

CATEGORY: No categories—we look at everything

PROFILE: : FilmBureau 606** is an organization dedicated to promoting, supporting and connecting film/tv/video and related personnel from Chicago and its outlying areas. The festival is ONLY open to filmmakers from this area.

Circus '99 is the production expo with the "big-top" feel. There is no fee for entry. We screen over 30 shorts, trailers, reels and works-in-progress, do readings by 10-12 of Chicago's top theatre companies of 4-6 scripts by local writers.

AWARDS: No

COMPETITIONS: No

MAJOR AWARDS: No awards, but a big prize giveaway

APPLICATION TIPS: Include an application!!!! And PLEASE put your name, phone # and address on your tapes and scripts!!!

APPLICATION FEE: None

FILMS SCREENED: 25-30

ODDS OF ACCEPTANCE: We received over 75 shorts/trailers, etc. this year and accepted 30. We received over 60 scripts and chose 6 for readings.

TRAVEL TIPS: This is a pretty friendly town, and we're a pretty friendly organization. Call with any questions.

BEST RESTAURANTS: Check out Soul Kitchen in the heart of Bucktown (corner of North/Milwaukee/Damen. Also, for a great Sunday Brunch, go to Riverside Deli (Cortland off of Ashland)

BEST BARS: Subterranean is terrific. So's the Double Door. 56 West Illinois is a bit pricey, but the decor is breathtaking.

BEST PLACE FOR BREAKFAST: See Above.

FLORiDA FiLM FESTiVAL

1300 South Orlando Ave.
Maitland, Florida 32751
TEL: (407) 629-1088
FAX: (407) 629-6870
E-MAIL: filmfest@gate.net
WEB SITE:
http://www.enzian.org
FESTIVAL DATE: June
ENTRY DEADLINE: April
CONTACT: Matthew Curtis
DIRECTOR: Melanie Gasper
PROGRAMMER: Matthew Curtis and Dick Morris
OTHER STAFF: Rich Grula, Director of Media and Marketing
CATEGORY: Independent

PROFILE: The 10-day Florida Film Festival showcases several genres of film including features, documentaries and shorts. Over 25,000 attend. Central Florida's biggest film event, the festival is a 10 day celebration featuring Juried & Audience Awards for American Independent films (including features, documentaries, shorts, narrative, experimental, and animation), foreign films, Midnight movies, seminars, sidebars, a Florida student competition, special events and special guests.

SEMINARS: Topics change every year, usually 5 or 6 scattered throughout the 10 days. Some of last year's subjects included "The Role of Digital Media in Film", "Successful Indie Film Development Strategies", "Shoot Today So It Will Play Tomorrow" (the Cinematographers seminar), and the always popular closing day " Filmmaker Forum".

PANELS: Most of our seminars are panel driven.

FAMOUS SPEAKERS: Haskell Wexler, Oliver Stone, Joel Schumacher, Michael Apted, Brian Dennehy, Bob Hawk, Gale Anne Hurd, Diane Ladd, Rod Steiger, Roger Corman, Dennis Hopper

AWARDS: Yes

COMPETITIONS: Yes

MAJOR AWARDS: Grand Jury Prizes for: Best Narrative Feature , Best Documentary Feature, Best Documentary Short, Best Short Film plus one other award at each jury's discretion, plus Audience Awards for: Best Narrative Feature, Best Documentary, Best Short Film

VALUE OF AWARDS: no $ value but a very nice trophy presented to the winning filmmakers at the Closing Night Awards Gala

LAST WINNING FILMS: *The Headhunter's Sister, 35 miles from normal, Hang Your Dog in the Wind, Before I Sleep, Andre the Giant Has a Posse, Hand on a Hardbody, Blue City, Anna in the Sky, The Journey, Nobody's Business, The Spirit of Christmas, Only Child*

LAST WINNING DIRECTORS: Scott Saunders, Mark Schwahn, Brian Flemming, Kristen Schultz, Helen Stickler, S.R. Bindler, David Birdsell, Mark Edgington, Harish Saluja, Alan Berliner, Trey Parker, Christopher Landon and David Ogden

PAST JUDGES: Peter Broderick, Jason Kliot, Robert Hawk, Bingham Ray, Stuart Strutin, Bruce Sinofsky, Chris Gore, John Pierson, Gale Anne Hurd, Jeff Lipsky, Seymour Cassel, Frederick Marx, Bruce Sinofsky, Paul Cohen, Karol Martesko

APPLICATION TIPS: Do something original, spend more money on your film than your video jacket, send as finished a work as possible up to the entry deadline, EDIT!

APPLICATION FEE: $30 for features (50 minutes or more), $15 for shorts (less than 50 mins.), $15 late fee for entries postmarked after early entry deadline.

INSIDER ADVICE: Comedy is hard; work on your script; get your sound mix as good as possible; be original; longer is not necessarily better; get your film in early and be patient; pick your spots—it's hard to get ex-

cited over a film that has already played at numerous other in-state festivals; if you're not going to have a 16 or 35 print by late May you probably want to look for another festival.

AVERAGE FILMS ENTERED: Well-scripted, well-conceived, original visions competently brought to celluloid life...GOOD ones!

FILMS SCREENED: 40—50 student works are screened during the 10 days of the festival.

ODDS OF ACCEPTANCE: Approximately 150 -200 features, 200—300 shorts, and 75-100 docs are submitted. About 10 narrative features, 10 doc features, and enough shorts to fill 4 live action and 1 animated shorts program (perhaps 30—40) are accepted. Then of course, we also program a dozen or so "Spotlight" films , a national sidebar of five films, half a dozen Midnight movies , and a few tribute films. All-in-all, approximately 90—100 films

FILMMAKER PERKS: Due to the limitations of our sponsorships, we are able to fly in some, but not all, of the narrative and documentary feature directors, and put them up for four days or so. Any filmmaker whose film is in the festival and makes their own way to Orlando we guarantee will be put up for at least two nights, regardless whether their film is a short or feature.

Filmmakers will also make contacts with the Orlando Film Commission, Universal Studios, other local and national industry professionals such as film distributors and entertainment lawyers, and many others that could be helpful in their future cinematic endeavors.

TRAVEL TIPS: IT'S HOT! Pack light clothes, a bathing suit, and one decent outfit for the Closing Night Awards Gala at Universal Studios

BEST RESTAURANTS: Depending on your budget, the following are recommended by members

of the festival staff: Enzo's, Chez Vincent, Cafe Tu Tu Tango, West End Grill, Tacqueria Quetzalcoatl, The Melting Pot, Bubbalou's Bodacious Bar- B-Q

BEST BARS: Sapphire Supper Club, Kit Kat Klub, Go Lounge, Copper Rocket

BEST HANGOUT FOR FILMMAKERS: All of the above plus Harold & Maude's and the Nicole St. Pierre lounge

BEST PLACE FOR BREAKFAST: The Coffee Shoppe on Lee Road, First Watch

FESTIVAL TALE: 1) A couple of years ago a very well known character actor with a history in indie film going back to the 60's was being driven down the main drag in downtown Winter park. As he passes the Victoria's Secret store, this absolutely spectacular woman in a very small dress walks out the front door and he leans out the window of the car yelling, "Hey Babe! Love that Wonderbra!" The woman waves , the actor tells the flabbergasted volunteer driver to pull the car over, and he ends up asking the woman out. She agrees, and he still has a smile on his face to this day. 2) How about having your final closing night program, after 10 days and nearly 100 films, be a subtitled French-Canadian film that unfortunately for your 98% English-speaking-only audience turns out to have no subtitles at all!? Lesson learned—make sure all "subtitled" prints really are subtitled during the inspection process.

> ...spend more money on your film than your video jacket (Florida Film Festival)

FORT LAUDERDALE FiLM FESTiVAL

1402 Las Solas #007
Ft. Lauderdale, FL 23301
TEL: (954) 760-9898
FAX: (954) 760-9099
E-MAIL: brofilm@aol.com
WEB SITE: http://vcn.net//filmfest
http://www.filmmag.com/fliff/
FESTIVAL DATE: November
ENTRY DEADLINE: September

YEAR FESTIVAL BEGAN: 1986

CONTACT: Gregory Von Hausch

OTHER STAFF: Lily Majjul

CATEGORY: International

PROFILE: This festival showcases films of all genres. Over 30,000 attend.

AWARDS: yes

COMPETITIONS: yes

MAJOR AWARDS: Lifetime Achievement Award; National Student Film Competition

VALUE OF AWARDS: $1,000

ODDS OF ACCEPTANCE: over 100 films entered

FOUR*BY*FOUR SUPER 8 FiLMFEST

"There's beer!"

—*Collective Anonymous*

Austin Cinemaker Co-op

Austin, TX

TEL: (512) 236-8877

E-MAIL: cinemaker@501studios.com

WEB SITE: http://www. cinemaker.austin.tx.us

FESTIVAL DATE: Late August

ENTRY DEADLINE: Early August

YEAR FESTIVAL BEGAN: 1998

DIRECTOR: Jeff Britt

OTHER STAFF: Gonzo Gonzalez, Richard McIntosh, Danny Chavez, Barna Kantor

CATEGORY: Independent, Underground

PROFILE: "Shut Up And Shoot Something!!" 4X4 Film Festivals are "indie" festivals, in that many of our entrants often spend their "rent paycheck" to make their films. The Cinemaker Co-op has hosted 7 festivals of locally produced short films since 1996.

APPLICATION TIPS: 1) Shot and submitted on super 8 film, four minutes maximum in length; 2) Edited in camera, utilizing a maximum of 4 splices; 3) Accompanied by an original soundtrack; 4) Submitted with a five second countdown at the beginning of the film (either animate it at the beginning of

Films must be clean. Run your film through a projector a couple of times (and clean it afterwards) to make sure we will not have any projection problems during the screening. (Four*By*Four Super 8 Filmfest)

your film, or take your white leader, and write 18 5's, 18 4's, and so on, with a black sharpie pen, carefully on each frame).

APPLICATION FEE: $5

INSIDER ADVICE: Films must be clean. Run your film through a projector a couple of times (and clean it afterwards) to make sure we will not have any projection problems during the screening.

FILMS SCREENED: 20-30

ODDS OF ACCEPTANCE: Usually all films are accepted.

TOURIST INFORMATION: Filmmaker tourists should be amped to be in the hometown of the SXSW Film Festval, Cinematexas Film Festival, Austin Heart of Film Festival, and the Gay and Lesbian International Film Festival. These are the Austin film festivals who "got bank". Not us.

TRAVEL TIPS: Avoid IH35, it's always a huge mess.

BEST RESTAURANTS: Tamale House on Airport Blvd. (this place has great tacos for SUPER CHEAP!)

BEST BARS: Lovejoy's ($2 house pints all the time, great jukebox).

BEST CAFE: Red River Cafe (right off of Red River between 26th and 32nd streets).

FREAKY FiLM FESTiVAL (FFF)

1209 W. Oregon Street

Urbana, IL 61801

TEL: (217) 344-3296 or (217) 344-1176

E-MAIL: freaky@shout.net

WEB SITE: www.shout.net/ ~freaky

FESTIVAL DATE: November

ENTRY DEADLINE: September

YEAR FESTIVAL BEGAN: 1997

DIRECTOR: Eric Fisher and Grace Giorgio

PROGRAMMER: Eric Fisher and Grace Giorgio

OTHER STAFF: Jason Pankoke, Jen Auler, Brian Robertson

CATEGORY: Independent, Short, Underground, Weird, Video

PROFILE: The Freaky Film Festival (FFF) provides a unique cultural experience to Champaign-Urbana. FFF gathers scores of independent films from across the country and abroad to screen locally. These films, until now, were only accessible to the public via urban film festivals such as San Francisco International Film Festival and New York Underground Film Festival. These quirky, out-of-the-ordinary films (hence freaky) represent different cultures and approaches to life and the art of filmmaking. Films such as these enhance the cultural and artistic diversity of our community.

FAMOUS SPEAKERS: Bruce Campbell, Josh Becker.

AWARDS: Yes

COMPETITIONS: Yes

VALUE OF AWARDS: 100 bones for the best flick!

APPLICATION TIPS: Decent quality tapes, labeled and easy to read, do not dub over old tape, picture and sound should be of comparible quality, one should not outshine the other, no mysogynist, homophobic, racist subject... a funny, quirky, freaky flick that is not too long. Do not leave out synopsis, very annoying.

APPLICATION FEE: $20

FILMS SCREENED: 25

ODDS OF ACCEPTANCE: Last year 40 films were submitted and 25 shown. Odds are in your favor!

FILMMAKER PERKS: We do our best to accomodate visiting filmmakers and can assist with lodging and we do have some great restaurant connections... good food and drink!!!

TRAVEL TIPS: Travel from Chicago by first class train, it is six bucks more than flying but worth it, lots of room, no hassles.

BEST RESTAURANTS: Radio Maria, a sponsor!

BEST BARS: The Canopy Club.

GEN ART FiLM FESTiVAL
GEN ART
145 West 28th St. Suite 11C
New York, New York 10001
TEL: 212-290-0312
FAX: 212-290-0254
E-MAIL: info@genart.org
WEB SITE: www.genart.org
FESTIVAL DATE: Late April—
Early May
ENTRY DEADLINE: December
(early deadline)—February
(late deadline).
CONTACT: Adam Walden (managing director—GEN ART)
DIRECTOR: Deena Juras
PROGRAMMER: Graham Leggat
(dir. of programming)
OTHER STAFF: Producer
(1998)—Jordan Rothstein;
Assoc. Producer (1998)—Lori
Benson; Founders & Executive
Directors: Ian & Stefan Gerard
CATEGORY: Independent
PROFILE: A seven day celebration of American independent
filmmaking. The festival focuses on showcasing emerging
filmmakers, especially first and
second time directors. The
unique format of the festival
presents one feature film per
evening (always a New York
Premiere) preceded by a single
short film and followed by a
large scale after-party. Seven
premieres, seven parties. Tickets to the screenings include
both the film and the party.
SEMINARS: None
PANELS: None
AWARDS: Yes
COMPETITIONS: Yes
MAJOR AWARDS: Only an Audience Award for Best Feature
Film—open to all features
shown
APPLICATION TIPS: Make a great
film.
APPLICATION FEE: Early Deadline: $15 short/$20 feature. Late
Deadline $20 short/$25 feature
AVERAGE FILMS ENTERED: Features, Documentaries and
Shorts
FILMS SCREENED: 7 features, 6
shorts

ODDS OF ACCEPTANCE: We show
7 features, and usually 6 shorts.
We receive about 300 submissions
FILMMAKER PERKS: Full festival
passes which get them into all
screenings and each nights
party. Contacts to important
film industry members
BEST RESTAURANTS: NYC—
tough question.

GLOBAL AFRICA INTERNATIONAL FiLM AND ViDEO FESTiVAL
900 Fallon St., 9th Floor
Oakland, CA 94607
TEL: (510) 464-3253
FAX: (510) 464-3418
FESTIVAL DATE: June
ENTRY DEADLINE: March
CONTACT: Frankie A. Sanders
CATEGORY: Video

GREAT PLAiNS FiLM FESTiVAL
Mary Ricmpa Ross Film
Theater
University of Nebraska-Lincoln
Lincoln, NE 68588-0302
TEL: (402) 472-5353
FAX: (402) 472-2756
FESTIVAL DATE: July
ENTRY DEADLINE: April
DIRECTOR: Dan Ladely
APPLICATION FEE: $15—$25

GREEN BADGE FiLM EVENT
50 E. Palisade Ave., Suite #426
Englewood, NJ 07631
TEL: 201-567-0560
FAX: 201-567-1053
E-MAIL: Michael Champlin,
redb522@IDT.net
WEB SITE:
www.greenbadge.com
FESTIVAL DATE: Fall 1999—
New York City
ENTRY DEADLINE: Fall 1999
YEAR FESTIVAL BEGAN: 1998
CONTACT: Michael Champlin

DIRECTOR: Alex Svezia
PROGRAMMER: Michael
Champlin, William Pennell
PROFILE: The Green Badge Film
Event, devoted to returning
indie film to its roots, offers
new cinema, panel discussions,
receptions and an after party
for all ticket holders.
SEMINARS: No
PANELS: Yes
APPLICATION FEE: free to all filmmakers
ATTENDANCE: 400

HAMPTONS INTERNATIONAL FiLM FESTiVAL
*"There has never been a
better time than now for the
state of New York to celebrate
the accomplishments of
the talented filmmakers
participating in the
Hamptons International Film
Festival. The Empire State
prides itself on its thriving
film industry and relishes the
opportunity to welcome the
International Film Community to one of the world's
leading production regions."*
—George E. Pataki, Governor,
State of New York

3 Newtown Mews
East Hampton, NY 11937
TEL: (516) 324-4600 or
(516) 324-2870
FAX: (516) 324-5116
E-MAIL: filmfest@peconic.net
WEB SITE: http://thehamptons.
com/film/main.html
FESTIVAL DATE: October
ENTRY DEADLINE: August
CONTACT: Denise Kasell
DIRECTOR: Denise Kasell
PROGRAMMER: David Schwartz
OTHER STAFF: Linda Blackaby,
Lynda Hansen, Shawn Caila
Folz
CATEGORY: Independent

PROFILE: The Hamptons International Film Festival was created to provide a forum for filmmakers around the world who express an independent vision at an annual five day event each October.

The Festival has doubled the number of panels and added three celebrity "Spotlight" films. The Festival offers diverse programming with premieres by filmmakers, breakthrough films by new directors, and panel discussions with renowned guests from the industry. A distinctive component of the Festival is its cash grants to students and a generous in-kind award to outstanding filmmakers. Our year round program offerings include educational screenings for local school children and seminars for adults which reflect a breadth of creative and industry related topics.

Most importantly, the Hamptons brings together filmmakers and film lovers to immerse themselves in the world of the movies.

This festival focuses on supporting student and independent filmmaking. Approximately 20,000 attend.

SEMINARS: yes

AWARDS: Yes

COMPETITIONS: No

MAJOR AWARDS: Most Popular Film, Best Director, Best Documentary Feature and Best Short Film.

The Golden Arrow Award—Based on audience balloting, this award is presented to the Most Popular Film, Best Director, Best Documentary Feature and Best Short film in the Festival.

Distinguished Achievement Award to be announced for the opening of the Festival.

Golden Starfish Award—A currated selection of American Independent films will introduce the work of newly emerging filmmakers. A jury of film industry professionals, film-makers and film critics select the winning director of the Festival's Golden Starfish Award from among them and present the recipient with a package of goods and services totaling over $100,000.

Student Scholarship Awards—The Student Scholarship Awards, totaling $25,000 in cash prizes, are presented to 10 outstanding film students whose works will be presented at the Festival. A special prize, sponsored by RKO Pictures, is awarded to the graduate student film selected as being the best example of cinematic storytelling.

Documentary Award—A special jury prize, sponsored by the Eastman Kodak Company, will be awarded to the Best Documentary.

Short Film Award—A special jury prize will be awarded to the best Short Subject in this year's Festival.

APPLICATION FEE: $25 (up to 30 minutes) / $50 (over 30 minutes)

FILMS SCREENED: 40

HAWAII INTERNATIONAL FILM FESTIVAL

1001 Bishop Street, Pacific Tower Suite 745

Honolulu, Hawaii 96813

TEL: 800-752-8193 or (808) 528-FILM

FAX: (808) 528-1410

E-MAIL: hiffinfo@hiff.org

WEB SITE: www.hiff.org

FESTIVAL DATE: November

ENTRY DEADLINE: July

CONTACT: Bruce Fletcher, Film Coordinator

DIRECTOR: Christian Gaines

PROGRAMMER: Christian Gaines, Dwight Damon, Jeannette Paulson, Sid Louie, Bruce Fletcher

OTHER STAFF: Didi Chang. Director Of Development; Chuck Boller, Director Of Adminstration; Lani Miyahara, Hawaii Film Fans Coordinator (Film Society); Donne Dawson, Media Director

CATEGORY: Independent, International, Pacific Rim

PROFILE: The only statewide film festival in the United States, the Hawaii International film festival's perennial mission is to promote cultural understanding between the people of the east and the west through the universally popular medium of film. A comprehensive U.S "festival of record" for films from across Asia, Australia, New Zealand, the U.S. and Canada.

SEMINARS: Programmed on an annual basis.

FAMOUS SPEAKERS: Most figures in Asian industry....Hou Hsiao Hsien, Chen Kaige, ZhangYimou, Juzo Itami, all the Asian scholars, etc. Also in 1997 we had Ang Lee, Dave Foley, John Ritter, Toni Collette, Miranda Otto, John Seale, Roger Ebert, Peter Rainer, Paul Theroux, Jonathan Rhys-Myers, Arthur Dong, Rajit Kapur, Qu Ying, Naomi Nishida, Bill Plympton (we had over 400 delegates in 1997).

AWARDS: Golden Maile Award for the Feature Film That Best Promotes Cultural Understanding; Golden Maile Award for the Doc. Film That Best Promotes Cultural Understanding; Primeco Hawaii Audience Award; Eastman Kodak Award for Excellence in Cinematography (1997: John Seale; 1996: Fred Elmes); Aloha Airlines Hawaii Film And Videomaker Award; Vision In Film Award (1997: Ang Lee)

COMPETITIONS: yes

MAJOR AWARDS: Golden Maile Award

LAST WINNING FILMS: Golden Maile Feature: *12 Storeys* (Singapore); Golden Maile Doc: *Homesick Eyes* (Taiwan); Audience Award: *Deep River* (Japan); Vision In Film Award: Ang Lee; Cinematography Award: John Seale

When in Rome... or Hawaii! Film critic Roger Ebert takes part in a panel discussion at the Hawaii International Film Festival, along with Malti Sahai, Director of Directorate of Film Festivals in India.

PAST JUDGES: Toni Collette, Peter Rainer, Paul Theroux, Malti Sahai, Kim Dong-ho

APPLICATION FEE: $35 (waived for Hawaii filmmakers)

INSIDER ADVICE: Complete the entire call for entries...make sure all technical information is complete.

AVERAGE FILMS ENTERED: Films that relate in some way to a Pacific Rim theme (which includes the U.S., of course).

ODDS OF ACCEPTANCE: Generally, we see about 300—500 entries, and we accept approximately 25-40 entries.

FILMMAKER PERKS: We can always provide accommodation for filmmakers, and we are able to fly in quite a few. And, well, it's Hawaii. Also, if your film is playing on the neighbor islands, you can follow it along to some more rural out of the way places in Maui, on the Big Island, Kauai etc. The big shebang is in Honolulu (cool parties, big crowds and media etc), and the community, mellow part is the neighbor islands.

TRAVEL TIPS: The nicer you are, the better you're treated!

BEST RESTAURANTS: Japanese: Tokkuru-tei; Chinese: Chans; "Pacific Rim': A Pacific Cafe, Sam Choys, etc; Local Grinds: Zippy's

BEST BARS: Havana Cabana; Anna Bananas

BEST HANGOUT FOR FILMMAKERS: Havana Cabana and Centaur Zone Coffee Shop

BEST PLACE FOR BREAKFAST: Eggs 'N' Things and Liliha Bakery.

HEARTLAND FiLM FESTIVAL

613 North East Street
Indianapolis, Indiana 46202
TEL: (317) 464-9405 or (317) 635-4201
E-MAIL: hff@pop.iquest.net
WEB SITE: www.heartlandfilmfest.org
FESTIVAL DATE: Late October or Early November
ENTRY DEADLINE: June or July
CONTACT: Claire C. Wishard, Festival Coordinator
DIRECTOR: Jeffrey L. Sparks, Artistic Director
PROGRAMMER: Claire C. Wishard, Festival Coordinator
OTHER STAFF: Victor H. Ruthig, Executive Director, Cindy Williams, Office Manager
CATEGORY: Animation, Documentary, Short
PROFILE: To recognize and honor filmmakers whose work explores the human journey by artistically expressing hope and respect for the positive values of life.

SEMINARS: yes
PANELS: yes
AWARDS: yes
COMPETITIONS: yes
MAJOR AWARDS: Crystal Heart Award
VALUE OF AWARDS: $100,000 cash
APPLICATION TIPS: Follow our statement of purpose
APPLICATION FEE: Yes-TBD-roughly $35 or $55, depending on film type
AVERAGE FILMS ENTERED: Various
ODDS OF ACCEPTANCE: 225 are submitted roughly, and we accept between 6-10.
FILMMAKER PERKS: Free travel and lodging, as well as Crystal Heart Awards and $100,000 in cash
TRAVEL TIPS: Weather could be 60 or 20. Welcome to Indianapolis!
BEST RESTAURANTS: Palomino, Mikado, Ruth's Chris, St. Elmo's
BEST BARS: Canterbury Bar

HOLLYWOOD FiLM FESTiVAL

433 N. Camden Drive, #600
Beverly Hills, CA 90210
TEL: (310) 288-1882
FAX: (310) 475-0193
E-MAIL: awards@ hollywoodawards.com
WEB SITE: http:// hollywoodfilmfestival.com
FESTIVAL DATE: August
CONTACT: Carlos de Abreu
DIRECTOR: Carlos de Abreu
PROGRAMMER: Janice de Abreu
OTHER STAFF: Press Director; Mike Garfinkel, Box Office; Stacey Herrera, Tributes & retrospectives; Gary Graver, Indie Film Liaison; Joshua Beckett, Jury Selection; Ted Kotcheff and Mark Rydell, Industry Liaison; Laifun Chung, Events & New Media; Hossein Farmani, Advertising & Marketing; Chris Davies, Scheduling & Prints; Brian O' Sullivan, Conference & Scout Liaison;

The nicer you are, the better you're treated! (Hawaii International Film Festival)

Mark Litwak, Administration Manager; John Jacobson, Merchandising; Esther Rydell.

CATEGORY: Independent, International

PROFILE: The Hollywood Film Festival was created to bridge the gap between established Hollywood and emerging independent filmmakers.

SEMINARS: We have four days of intensive seminars. From concept to post-production and distribution.

PANELS: Over 100 established industry professional participate in our panels.

FAMOUS SPEAKERS: Almost all our speakers are famous.

AWARDS: yes

COMPETITIONS: yes

MAJOR AWARDS: Hollywood Discovery Awards; Hollywood Young Filmmakers Award; Hollywood Cyberaward; Moviemaker Breakthrough Award

VALUE OF AWARDS: Packages valued at more than $100,000

LAST WINNING FILMS: *Always Say Goodbye*

LAST WINNING DIRECTORS: Joshua Beckett

PAST JUDGES: Tony Bill, James Coburn, Carlos de Abreu, Robbie Greenberg, Henry Jaglom, Martin Landau, Mark Rydell.

APPLICATION TIPS: The artist quality of the film will be the final factor that will determine if said film will be selected or not.

APPLICATION FEE: $50.00

INSIDER ADVICE: The submission package should be packaged professionally — Clean and making sure that it includes all necessary items as per application form.

AVERAGE FILMS ENTERED: We are open top all genres: Features, Shorts, Documentaries and Animation.

ODDS OF ACCEPTANCE: 400 hundred were submitted, 40 were selected to be finalists. Odds: 10 to 1.

FILMMAKER PERKS: VIP Passes for two. Major industry contacts and press exposure.

TRAVEL TIPS: Make your reservations early so that you can get bargain prices.

BEST RESTAURANTS: Spago in Beverly Hills.

BEST BARS: Sky Bar at the Mondrian Hotel.

BEST PLACE FOR BREAKFAST: Four Seasons and the Peninsula Hotels in Beverly Hills.

HOMETOWN CiNEMA, A MiDWESTERN STUDENT FiLM FESTiVAL

899 S College Mall Rd. #349
Bloomington, IN 47401
TEL: (812) 337-1091
FAX: 812-337-1091
E-MAIL: hometownc@hotmail.com
WEB SITE: www.geocities.com/Hollywood/Academy/8656
FESTIVAL DATE: April
ENTRY DEADLINE: January
YEAR FESTIVAL BEGAN: 1998
DIRECTOR: Shannah Compton
CATEGORY: Student
PROFILE: To bridge the gap between midwestern film students and entertainment industry professionals.
AWARDS: Yes
COMPETITIONS: Yes
VALUE OF AWARDS: $2,500-$5,000
APPLICATION FEE: $25
AVERAGE FILMS ENTERED: 200
FILMS SCREENED: 10
ODDS OF ACCEPTANCE: All films are pre-screened but only 6-10 screened.
FILMMAKER PERKS: Contacts, free lodging, transportaion within city, free food.

HOMETOWN ViDEO FESTiVAL

c/o Central States Region
Allen County Public Library
900 Webster St.
Fort Wayne , IN 46802
TEL: (202) 393-2650
FAX: (202) 393-2653
FESTIVAL DATE: July
ENTRY DEADLINE: January
CONTACT: Steve Fortriede

HONOLULU GAY & LESBiAN FiLM FESTiVAL

1877 Kalakaua Ave.
Honolulu, HI 96815
TEL: (808) 941-0424
FAX: (808) 943-1724
FESTIVAL DATE: June
ENTRY DEADLINE: April
DIRECTOR: Adam Baran
CATEGORY: Gay Lesbian

HOT SPRiNGS DOCUMENTARY FiLM FESTiVAL

P.O. Box 6450
Hot Springs, AZ 71902-6450
TEL: (501)321-4747
FAX: (501)321-0211
E-MAIL: hsdff@docufilminst.org
WEB SITE: www.docufilminst.org
FESTIVAL DATE: October
ENTRY DEADLINE: May
YEAR FESTIVAL BEGAN: 1992
CONTACT: Patricia Dooley
DIRECTOR: Patricia Dooley
PROGRAMMER: Gretchen Miller
OTHER STAFF: Michael Bracy
CATEGORY: Documentary, Independent
SEMINARS: Humanities forums accompanying films
PANELS: Lecture series
FAMOUS SPEAKERS: Eric Barnouw, Vittorio DeSeta, James Earl Jones, James Whitmore, Arthur Hiller, Geraldine Chaplin
AWARDS: No
COMPETITIONS: No
APPLICATION TIPS: Early entry.
APPLICATION FEE: $25.00 US, $35.00 international
INSIDER ADVICE: Send as much information on your film as possible.
AVERAGE FILMS ENTERED: Docs of all types: general interest, humor, art, biography, experimental, children's, etc.
FILMS SCREENED: Each member of our Screening Committee screens each film submitted; a total of 60 films are shown at the festival.

Profile: To bridge the gap between midwestern film students and entertainment industry professionals. (Hometown Cinema, A Midwestern Student Film Festival)

ODDS OF ACCEPTANCE: 250 submitted, 50 accepted.

FILMMAKER PERKS: We offer lodging and contacts.

TOURIST INFORMATION: Gorgeous mountain town with art galleries, museums, hiking trails, natural spring bathhouses, excellent restaurants and friendly people

BEST RESTAURANTS: Belle Arti, Three Monkeys, Brauhaus

BEST BARS: Bronze Gorilla

BEST HANGOUT FOR FILMMAKERS: Arlington Resort Hotel & Spa.

BEST PLACE FOR BREAKFAST: Pancake House

HOUSTON INTERNATIONAL FILM AND VIDEO FESTIVAL— ANNUAL WORLDFEST

Worldfest Houston

P. O. Box 56566

Houston, TX 77256-6566

TEL: (713) 965-9955

FAX: (713) 965-9960

E-MAIL: Worldfest@aol.com

WEB SITE: www.vannevar.com/worldfest

FESTIVAL DATE: November

ENTRY DEADLINE: September

DIRECTOR: J. Hunter Todd

PROFILE: This annual Independent film festival, now held in the High Country of Flagstaff, Arizona (previously in Charleston, SC) offers premieres of independent and international features, shorts, documentaries, and video. Enjoy indie films in the cool, clear evergreen-scented mountain air of Flagstaff, where the air smells like Christmas every morning! "Flag" is located at the foot of the snow-covered San Francisco peaks in the middle of the largest Ponderosa Pine forest in North America. The 10-day event also offers in-depth film & video production seminars, from writing screenplays to Cinematography to directing and producing the independent feature film. Screenings are held in a three-screen Dolby theatre, and a select program of only 35-40 new features and 60 shorts are premiered, with directors in attendance. WorldFest screens only Independent Films, and NO major studio films are accepted. We have more than 5,500 very reasonably priced hotel rooms available there, placing FlagFest in direct competition with Sundance and Telluride. It is one hour from the Grand Canyon! Direct Amtrak service from Chicago & LA! Or drive to Flag on John Steinbeck's "Mother Highway" of Route 66! Series VIP Passes start at just $100, singles start at free, then $4 and $5.50 per film! It is the sister-festival to the Spring WorldFest-Houston.

HUDSON VALLEY FILM FESTIVAL

40 Garden St.

Poughkeepsie, NY 12601

TEL: (914) 473-0318

FAX: (914) 473-0082

E-MAIL: hvfo@vh.net

WEB SITE: www.sandbook.com/hvfo

FESTIVAL DATE: May

ENTRY DEADLINE: March

YEAR FESTIVAL BEGAN: 1995

CONTACT: Shawn Caila Folz

DIRECTOR: Denise Kasell

PROGRAMMER: Shawn Caila Folz

OTHER STAFF: Nancy Cozean, Media Director

CATEGORY: Independent

PROFILE: Focus on and celebrate the screenwriter/we showcase new work from established and emerging writers and filmmakers. Over 7,000 attend.

PANELS: Writers Panel Discussion

FAMOUS SPEAKERS: John Pierson, James Earl Jones, Ron Nyswaner, Adrienne Shelly, Chris Noth, Joanna Kerns, Dan Lauria, Joel Coen

AWARDS: yes

COMPETITIONS: no cash prizes

MAJOR AWARDS: We give a distinguished screenwriters award to one established person each year.

APPLICATION TIPS: Submit new work/scripts in proper format.

APPLICATION FEE: $15-screenplays, $20-shorts, $25-features/documentaries

INSIDER ADVICE: The programmers feel bad when films aren't accepted. Not all festivals accept hundred of entries like Sundance. Keep trying!

AVERAGE FILMS ENTERED: ALL

FILMS SCREENED: All films and scripts entered are read.

ODDS OF ACCEPTANCE: Films: submitted 300, accepted 30. Scripts: submitted 400, accepted 26

FILMMAKER PERKS: Pay for travel & lodging for event they are participating in, as well as additional passes to festival events. We offer exposure via direct mail, other press, including press conference, and there are many contacts to be made at the festival itself.

TOURIST INFORMATION: Mohonk Mountain House and The Shawangunk Range (hiking, biking & world famous rock climbing), Many historic mansions on the Hudson River, quaint historic towns

TRAVEL TIPS: If you can, get a rental car—we have discount rates with Enterprise rent-a-car

BEST RESTAURANTS: Callco Restaurant/Patisserie, Le Petit Bistro

BEST BARS: Stoney Creek

BEST HANGOUT FOR FILMMAKERS: Cafe Pongo, Stoney Creek, La Parmigiana

BEST PLACE FOR BREAKFAST: Blondie's, Schemmy's, Another Roadside Attraction Diner

HUMAN RiGHTS WATCH iNTERNATiONAL FiLM FESTiVAL

"Superb World Cinema"
—Geoff Gilmore,
Sundance Film Festival

350 Fifth Avenue, 34th floor
New York, New York 10118
TEL: (212) 216-1264
FAX: (212) 736-1300
E-MAIL: burresb@hrw.org
WEB SiTE: www.hrw.org/iff
FESTIVAL DATE: June (New York), October (London).
ENTRY DEADLINE: January
YEAR FESTIVAL BEGAN: 1988
CONTACT: Heather Harding
DIRECTOR: Bruni Burres
PROGRAMMER: Bruni Burres
OTHER STAFF: John Anderson, Festival Coordinator
CATEGORY: Independent
PROFILE: The Human Rights Watch International Film Festival was created to advance public education on human rights issues and concerns using the unique medium of film. Each year, the Human Rights Watch International Film Festival exhibits the finest human rights films and videos in commercial and archival theaters and on public and cable television throughout the United States. Highlights of the Festival are now presented in a growing number of cities around the world, a reflection of both the international scope of the Festival and the increasingly global appeal that the project has generated. The Festival celebrates the rights and freedoms we all want and deserve, documents the worst of what we have committed, and commemorates the best of what we work towards as a human race. As filmmaking becomes more accessible around the world, movies with themes of human rights and politics, no longer pigeon-holed, have blossomed into some of the most brilliant examples of world cinema today

SEMINARS: vary with location and festival schedule
PANELS: vary with location and festival schedule
FAMOUS SPEAKERS: The Festival has been chaired by a host of committed members of the film industry. Hosts and Co-Chairs and Opening Night Filmmakers have included: (alphabetical) Sam Cohn, Jonathan Demme, Harrison Ford, Costa Gavras, Anita Hill, Dustin Hoffman, Arthur Miller, Michael Moore, Julia Ormond, Alan Pakula, Rosie Perez, Robert Redford, Tim Robbins, Isabella Rosselini, John Turturro, Susan Sarandon, John Sayles, John Singleton, Trudie Styler, and Uma Thurman.
AWARDS: yes
MAJOR AWARDS: The Nestor Almendros Prize which is a $5,000 award given annually to a courageous newer filmmaker and the Irene Diamond Lifetime Achievement Award presented annually to a filmmaker for his or her lifetime contribution to human rights and film.
VALUE OF AWARDS: Nestor Almendros Prize: $5,000; Irene Diamond Lifetime Achievement Award: title only
LAST WINNING FILMS: Nestor Almendros Prize '98: *An Ordinary President*
LAST WINNING DIRECTORS: Yuri Khashchevatsky from Belarus
PAST JUDGES: Festival Planning Committee
APPLICATION TIPS: In selecting films for the Festival, Human Rights Watch concentrates equally on artistic merit and human rights content. The Festival encourages filmmakers around the world to address human rights subject matter in their work and presents films and videos from both new and established international human rights filmmakers. Each year, the Festival's programming committee screens more than 800 films and videos to create a program that represents a wide number of coun-

tries and issues. Once a film is nominated for a place in the program, staff of the relevant division of Human Rights Watch also view it to confirm its accuracy in the portrayal of human rights concerns.
APPLICATION FEE: None—in lieu of fee, VHS screening tapes are not returned
INSIDER ADVICE: Submit early and fully complete all forms.
AVERAGE FILMS ENTERED: Human Rights related features, documentaries, animated and experimental films and videos.
FILMS SCREENED: 5-30 in the New York Festival; 10 in the London Festival and approximately 12 in the traveling festival in the US. On average 5-8 for language tailored overseas "global showcases."
ODDS OF ACCEPTANCE: 500 submitted, 300 we request. 25-30 are accepted each year.
FILMMAKER PERKS: We try to fly in and put up as many filmmakers as possible depending on grants we receive annually.

HUMBOLDT iNTERNATiONAL FiLM AND ViDEO FESTiVAL

Humboldt State University
Theatre Arts Dept.
Arcata, CA 95521
TEL: (707) 826-4113
FAX: (707) 826-5494
E-MAIL: alter@axe.humboldt.edu
FESTIVAL DATE: March
ENTRY DEADLINE: February
CONTACT: Ann Alter
APPLICATION FEE: $30

iMAGES '95

Northern Visions
401 Richmond St. W., #228
Toronto, Ontario M5V 1X3
Canada
TEL: (416) 971-8405
FAX: (416) 971-8405
FESTIVAL DATE: June
CONTACT: Karen Tisch

INDEPENDENT EXPOSURE

2318 Second Ave., #313-A
Seattle, Washington 98121
TEL: 206-568-6051
E-MAIL: joel@speakeasy.org
WEB SITE: http://www.
speakeasy.org/blackchair
FESTIVAL DATE: Ongoing, once
per month.
ENTRY DEADLINE: Ongoing
CONTACT: Joel S. Bachar
DIRECTOR: Joel S. Bachar
PROGRAMMER: Joel S. Bachar
CATEGORY: Independent, Underground
PROFILE: Seattle video and film
artist, Joel S. Bachar founded
Blackchair Productions in 1992.
Due to the overwhelming lack
of independent-oriented
screening venues, Blackchair
Productions began the "Independent Exposure" program in
1996. This program, held every
month at the Speakeasy Cafe
has gained an enviable reputation in the network of
microcinemas around the
country as well as around the
world. The artists whose works
are shown will be paid an honorarium, a gesture that is practically unheard of in the independent film and video arts. "Independent Exposure" is fast reaching a wider audience by being
hosted at other microcinemas
throughout the U.S. and around
the world. Some of the hosting
venues have been: The Knitting
Factory (New York City);
School of the Art Institute of
Chicago; The Museum of the
Rhode Island School of Design;
The Mansion Theatre (Baltimore, MD); Artist's Television
Access (San Francisco, CA); The
Casting Couch (San Francisco);
Eye for an I Cinema (Boulder,
CO); North Carolina Independent Filmmakers Association;
The Can (Tacoma, WA);
Project304 (Bangkok, Thailand); The Terminal Bar
(Prague, Czech Republic).
AWARDS: No
COMPETITIONS: No

APPLICATION TIPS: Clearly labeled VHS entries and support
materials.
APPLICATION FEE: $5. Returned if
work not accepted and SASE
provided.
INSIDER ADVICE: Label tapes, include a SASE, follow-up with
phone call or email, put address
on press materials and/or cover
letter.
AVERAGE FILMS ENTERED: shorts
FILMS SCREENED: approx 120/
year
ODDS OF ACCEPTANCE: I have a
75% acceptance rate
FILMMAKER PERKS: I get their
works shown at several other
microcinemas around the
country and the world and I get
good press
TRAVEL TIPS: Travel Often
BEST RESTAURANTS: Marco's
Supperclub
BEST BARS: Vito's
BEST HANGOUT FOR FILMMAKERS:
Alibi Room
BEST PLACE FOR BREAKFAST: Pike
Place Market
FESTIVAL TALE: The all erotic
show is the only one to sell out
two shows, standing room only.
Go figure.

INDEPENDENT FEATURE FILM MARKET

104 W. 29th St., 12th Floor
New York, NY 10001
TEL: (212) 465-8200
FAX: (212) 465-8525
FESTIVAL DATE: September
ENTRY DEADLINE: July
DIRECTOR: Catherine Tait, Executive Director
CATEGORY: Markets

INDIANA FILM AND VIDEO FESTIVAL

c/o Indiana Film Society
820 E. 67th Street
Indianapolis, IN 46220
TEL: (317) 322-8494 or
(317) 923-4484
DIRECTOR: Tony Marris & Terry
Black

INSIDE OUT LESBIAN AND GAY FILM FESTIVAL OF TORONTO

410 Richmond St W, Ste 456
Toronto, Ontario M5V 3A8
Canada
TEL: (416) 977-6847
FAX: (416) 977-8025
E-MAIL:
inside@insideout.on.ca
WEB SITE:
www.insideout.on.ca
FESTIVAL DATE: late May
ENTRY DEADLINE: February
CONTACT: Shane Smith
DIRECTOR: Ellen Flanders
PROGRAMMER: Jane Farrow
CATEGORY: Gay Lesbian, Independent
PROFILE: We're eight years old
and growing up fast.... the third
largest queer festival in the
world, we present over 200
works over ten days to 15,000
attendees. The festival is run by
filmmakers these days and we
try hard to be the friendly festival, friendly to the audience
and friendly to filmmakers.
SEMINARS: Yeah sure, we usually
have a few, likewise with panels.
PANELS: See above.
FAMOUS SPEAKERS: We have our
share of galas, visiting dignitaries, glitzy parties and media
hype, but we concentrate on
showing extremely high quality work to the always appreciative audience and treating the
filmmakers well with all-access
passes and fun parties. We're in
it for the films, honest.
AWARDS: Yes
COMPETITIONS: Yes
MAJOR AWARDS: Bulloch Award
is for the Best New Canadian
Work, and the Akau Framing
Award is for Best Canadian Lesbian Short
VALUE OF AWARDS: Bulloch
$2,500, plus a beautiful plaque
Akau Framing award = $500.
LAST WINNING FILMS: *Heaven or
Montreal*
LAST WINNING DIRECTORS: Dennis Day

PAST JUDGES: Lynne Fernie, etc.

APPLICATION TIPS: Send the tape earlier than the deadline

APPLICATION FEE: No...

INSIDER ADVICE: Make sure you include a publicity still and a one-sheet with a quick description and the production details of your work, including time, year, exhibition format, etc.

AVERAGE FILMS ENTERED: No generalizations, we do them all, just make a good film/video and we'll love it.

ODDS OF ACCEPTANCE: Over 500 submitted, plus we go out hunting at other festivals and we pick 200.

FILMMAKER PERKS: We give you an all access pass, parties, billets if you want them and sometimes, if its a feature film, we make travel and accomodation arrangements.

TRAVEL TIPS: Trains are pretty cool and they apparently derail a lot less frequently than Amtrak.

BEST RESTAURANTS: The Hacienda, down and dirty Mexican food, cool music and a great patio. The waiters are sometimes snarky, but that's just because they're all such sensitive artists. Poke a bit harder and you'll find a friend for life.

BEST BARS: College Street has an array of trendy wine-bar conversation type hangouts.

BEST HANGOUT FOR FILMMAKERS: Hmmm, Pleasuredome is the coolest indie film exhibitor collective and they put on screenings about once a month. That's where the real indie action is.

BEST PLACE FOR BREAKFAST: KOS on College St or the Lakeview on Dundas West.

INTERNATIONAL FESTIVAL OF FILMS ON ART

FIFART Festival
640 St. Paul Street West, #406
Montreal, Quebec H3C 1L9
Canada
TEL: (514) 874-1637
FAX: (514) 874-9929

> The Hacienda. . . waiters are sometimes snarky, but that's just because they're all such sensitive artists. Poke a bit harder and you'll find a friend for life. (Inside Out Lesbian and Gay Film Festival of Toronto)

FESTIVAL DATE: March

ENTRY DEADLINE: October for registration and pre-selection

CONTACT: Rene Rozon

INTERNATIONAL WILDLIFE FILM FESTIVAL

802 East Front Street
Missoula, MT 59802
TEL: (406) 728-9380
FAX: (406) 728-2881
E-MAIL: iwff@wildlifefilms.org
WEB SITE: www.wildlifefilme.org

FESTIVAL DATE: April

ENTRY DEADLINE: January

YEAR FESTIVAL BEGAN: 1978

CONTACT: Entries: Jennifer Thomas; Festival Events: Amy Hetzler-Sperry

DIRECTOR: Amy Hetzler-Sperry

PROGRAMMER: Amy Hetzler-Sperry

CATEGORY: Independent

PROFILE: The mission of the International Wildlife Film Festival is to foster knowledge and understanding about wildlife and habitat through excellent and honest wildlife films and other media. Any films or videotapes produced with a central focus on non-domesticated wildlife species either singly or in combination with other species qualifies for the International Wildlife Film Festival. Films involving habitat, conservation, ecology, research management, plants, special art forms, or other people's interaction with wildlife are also eligible, but must relate specifically relate to wildlife.

AWARDS: Best of Festival, 1st, 2nd, 3rd; Best of Craft including Photography, Soundmix, Narration, Script, Editing; Best Special Award including : Educational Value, Scientific Content; Best of (each) Category

COMPETITIONS: Yes

MAJOR AWARDS: Best of Festival (First, Second, Third)

VALUE OF AWARDS: Monetary value is minimal, Status Value is immeasurable

PAST JUDGES: Bienvenido Leon, Assistant Director, Audiovisual Communication, University of Navarra, Spain Vicky Stone, Independent Film Maker,

APPLICATION TIPS: Follow the directions on the entry form

APPLICATION FEE: $25—$200 (depends on category)

INSIDER ADVICE: call us!

AVERAGE FILMS ENTERED: Wildlife, Environmental, Conservation, Human Interaction with Wildlife

FILMS SCREENED: 50

ODDS OF ACCEPTANCE: 210 submitted in 1998, 76 were finalists.

FILMMAKER PERKS: discounted registration

TOURIST INFORMATION: High points: Rocky Mountain Elk Foundation, Carousel downtown, art galleries galore, wilderness areas surrounding.

TRAVEL TIPS: Car not necessary! Missoula is very walkable.

BEST RESTAURANTS: The Bridge Bistro

BEST BARS: Union Club

BEST HANGOUT FOR FILMMAKERS: Union Club

BEST PLACE FOR BREAKFAST: The Shack

ISRAEL FILM FESTIVAL

IsraFest Foundation
6404 Wilshire Blvd.,
Suite 1151
Los Angeles, CA 90048
TEL: (213) 966-4166
FAX: (213) 658-6346
WEB SITE: http://www.bway.net/israel

FESTIVAL DATE: October

CONTACT: Meir Fenigstein

CATEGORY: Ethnic Other

JACKSON HOLE WiLDLiFE FiLM FESTiVAL

125 E. Pearl St.
P. O. Box AD
Jackson, WY 83001
TEL: (307) 733-7016
FAX: (307) 733-7376
FESTIVAL DATE: September
DIRECTOR: Kent Noble, Executive Director

JOHNS HOPKiNS FiLM FESTiVAL

Film Fest c/o Film & Media Studies Program Gilman 146
3400 N. Charles St.
Baltimore, Maryland 21218
TEL: 410-516-5048 or
410-516-4757
FESTIVAL DATE: Spring
ENTRY DEADLINE: Winter
DIRECTOR: Gil Jawetz
PROGRAMMER: Teddy Chao
CATEGORY: Independent
PROFILE: To bring the independent film circuit to Baltimore and to highlight local work.
APPLICATION TIPS: Send in a good film.
APPLICATION FEE: $20 early, $35 late (1998 fest fees)
AVERAGE FILMS ENTERED: All kinds.
FILMS SCREENED: About 55 will screen.
ODDS OF ACCEPTANCE: It's unfair, since we were so small this year, to say, so I'd rather have a n/a, but we had about 100 entries and accepted around 55. Now, like I said, we were very small this year and will probably have a lower acceptance rate next year.
FILMMAKER PERKS: Although we're still starting out, we are trying to offer opporuninties for filmmakers to get large audiences. Baltimore is aching for a large film fest and people are responding wonderfully. Our screening spaces are top of the line and the opportunity for feedback is good.
TRAVEL TIPS: Take 95.

BEST RESTAURANTS: Golly, there are a few. The Helmand (Afghan), Blue Nile (Ethiopian), Holy Frijoles (Mexican), Cafe Hon, Pete's Grill (breakfast), Attman's (Jewish deli), and Sip n Bite (24-hour greasy spoon)
BEST BARS: Club Charles (A John Water-ing hole)
BEST HANGOUT FOR FILMMAKERS: Club Charles (A John Water-ing hole)
BEST PLACE FOR BREAKFAST: Pete's Grill

KUDZU FiLM FESTiVAL

(AKA Athens Film Festival)

"Everything was fantastic. . . there will be a festival in Athens for many years to come."

—Tom Legan,
The Sundance Channel

P.O. Box 1461
Athens, Georgia 30603
TEL: 706.227.6090
FAX: 706.227.1083
E-MAIL: kudzufest@aol.com
WEB SITE: www.geocities.com/hollywood/studio/8728
FESTIVAL DATE: Early to mid October
ENTRY DEADLINE: August
YEAR FESTIVAL BEGAN: 1997 as the Athens Film Festival
CATEGORY: Independent, Open and diverse
PROFILE: The Kudzu Film Festival is hoping to turn a music town with a film festival into a film town with a music scene. The overall idea behind the festival is to provide film based events in a culturally rich city which has lacked an organized film contingent. Athens is a proud community with much to offer, and by providing Athens with a film outlet we hope to inspire artists and business people alike to take a more active role in filmmaking in the South Eastern United States. Plus it's just a really great place to be...

SEMINARS: Independent Filmmaking 101, The Role of the Cinematographer, The Art and Craft of Handmade Cinema, Getting Started in The Film Business in The South, Genealogies & Hieroglyphs with David Gatten
PANELS: Exhibition and the Independent Filmmaker
FAMOUS SPEAKERS: Chris Gore, Marcus Hu (President/Strand Releasing), Jeri Cain Rossi
AWARDS: Yes
COMPETITIONS: Yes
MAJOR AWARDS: The Kudzu
LAST WINNING DIRECTORS: Dan Zukovic, Don Hertzfeldt, Jane Wagner & Tina DiFeliciantonio, Gus Van Sant, Daniel Kuttner Leslie McCleave, Chris Jolly
PAST JUDGES: Chris Gore, Charles Eidsvik, Jeri Cain Rossi, Michael Jones, Mark Raker.
APPLICATION TIPS: Make a good looking film or at least make an interesting film; crappy camera work, lighting and sound can kill a film's chances.
APPLICATION FEE: $40 ($35 students) early deadline; $50 ($40 students) late deadline
INSIDER ADVICE: A nice presentation helps but many slick packages don't deliver. If your film is really good it won't matter how much you spend for press kits.
AVERAGE FILMS ENTERED: Deep and twisted plots, animation, and films with music or southern themes play well here.
FILMS SCREENED: About 25-35 films are screened.
ODDS OF ACCEPTANCE: Between 200-300 films are submitted
FILMMAKER PERKS: Well, we throw some kick-ass parties, you might catch a glimpse of some local celebrities, and you might even get to sleep on the Program Directors couch.
TOURIST INFORMATION: For old Athens historic value "The Double-Barrel Cannon" and "The Tree that owns itself" are oddities. University of Georgia

Our screening spaces are top of the line and the opportunity for feedback is good. (Johns Hopkins Film Festival) campus is beautiful and within a minute or two from anywhere downtown.

TRAVEL TIPS: For those people flying if you don't mind connecting in Charlotte, NC. U.S. Air flies direct from Charlotte to Athens, otherwise you have to fly into Atlanta and take an hour plus shuttle ride or rent a car to get to Athens.

BEST RESTAURANTS: Depends on who's sponsoring us any given year! The Grit is tauted by many as the best but I'd just as soon chill out at The Taco Stand with a cheap burrito and a cold beer.

BEST BARS: The Manhattan if you want to see Athens hipsters or The Globe if you want an upscale environment with an academic appeal. Bars are a dime a dozen here, there's one on every corner.

BEST HANGOUT FOR FILMMAKERS: Jittery Joe's, for some reason film people love sitting around getting wired on coffee and chatting about movies at all hours of the day or night.

BEST PLACE FOR BREAKFAST: The Grill, 1950's style diner located right in the heart of downtown Athens.

L. A. ASiAN PACiFiC FiLM ViDEO FESTiVAL

Visual Communications
263 S. Los Angeles St., Ste. 307
Los Angeles, CA 90012
TEL: (213) 680-4462
FAX: (213) 687-4848
FESTIVAL DATE: May
ENTRY DEADLINE: January
CONTACT: Abraham Ferrer

LAS VEGAS iNTERNATiONAL FiLM FESTiVAL

P.O. Box 18000-185
Las Vegas, NV 89114
TEL: 702-547-0877
FAX: 702-732-8407
E-MAIL: lviff@aol.com
WEB SITE: www.lviff.nu
DIRECTOR: Anthony Allison

LOCAL HEROES iNTERNATiONAL SCREEN FESTiVAL

"I'm sure it must be the only festival in the entire world where they send a driver to pick up the maker of a short film at the airport. That sort of set the tone for the festival. The amount of honour and attention they give short filmmakers is rare and I think important. The other great thing about the festival is that the screenings of the films is sequential—no two films are screening at the same time so that over the course of the festival a kind of collective experience is built up between all the filmmakers."

—Guy Bennett, Vancouver

3rd floor, 10022-103 St.
Edmonton, Alberta T5J 0X2
Canada
TEL: (403) 421-4084 or in Canada: 1-800-480-4084
FAX: (403) 425-8098
E-MAIL: filmhero@nsi-canada.ca
WEB SITE: www.nsi-canada.ca
FESTIVAL DATE: March
ENTRY DEADLINE: Mid-December
YEAR FESTIVAL BEGAN: 1986
CONTACT: Any staff member
DIRECTOR: Cheryl Ashton
PROGRAMMER: Global Heroes Section (International Features): Tony King; Declarations of Independents (Canadian Shorts): Scott Rollans
OTHER STAFF: Jami Drake, Associate Director; Debbie Yee, Drama Prize Coordinator; Ron Schuster, Travel and Accommodation Coordinator; Beth Philp, Hospitality Coordinator
CATEGORY: Independent, International
PROFILE: Local Heroes brings the finest independent films and their creators to Edmonton, to share the spotlight with Canada's most exciting new dramatic filmmakers. For five days filmmakers, industry professionals, and the general public mingle together in the open, friendly atmosphere that has made Local Heroes famous. Launched in 1984, it has become one of Canada's most talked about film events.

SEMINARS: Each morning of Local Heroes begins with a case study of current issues facing independent filmmakers. The case study approach has proven to be an effective and entertaining means to disseminate relevant information. Key industry professionals objectively probe and discuss a specific project to provide in-depth examples of problems and problem solving that individuals can apply to their own projects.

FAMOUS SPEAKERS: Costa-Gavras, Paul Cox, Bruce MacDonald, Werner Herzog, Jiri Menzel, Bruce Beresford, Charles Burnett, Ken Loach

AWARDS: No

COMPETITIONS: No. We are proudly non-competitive.

APPLICATION FEE: For the 1998 festival the early bird fee was $20 and the regular fee was $25.

AVERAGE FILMS ENTERED: We only accept Canadian short films, but we do accept international features. We do not accept documentaries, experimental films or student films.

FILMS SCREENED: 21. We screen the films sequentially so no two films are screened at the same time. This way all the filmmakers get individual attention.

ODDS OF ACCEPTANCE: About 140 submissions are received for the short film section, of which 16 are chosen. For the international section, we usually receive 50 submission, five of which are screened.

FILMMAKER PERKS: We cover half of the travel and accomodation costs for Canadian filmmakers featured in the short film section. We also provide one screening pass to them per film.

We cover the entire cost of travel and lodging for our international guests and they also receive a festival pass.

TOURIST INFORMATION: West Edmonton Mall

TRAVEL TIPS: The Local Heroes festival tries to make travel to Edmonton as convenient as possible so please contact our travel coordinator for help. Transportation to and from the airport is also available free of charge.

BEST RESTAURANTS: There are lots of great restaurants in town. In fact we provide a restaurant guide and the hospitality suite is always a great place to get recommendations from locals.

BEST BARS: The best bars in town are the ones where the Local Heroes parties are held. Each night all of the festival guests are invited to attend the receptions along with the movie-goers.

BEST PLACE FOR BREAKFAST: The best place for breakfast during the festival is at the morning seminars where we serve a continental breakfast to the festival goers and filmmakers.

LONG BEACH INTERNATIONAL GAY AND LESBIAN FILM FESTIVAL

2017 East Fourth Street
Long Beach, CA 90814-1001
TEL: (562) 434-4455
FESTIVAL DATE: June
ENTRY DEADLINE: May
APPLICATION FEE: None

LONG ISLAND FILM FESTIVAL

P.O Box 13243
Hauppauge, New York 11788
TEL: (800) 762-4769 or (516) 853-4800
FAX: (516) 853-4888
E-MAIL: festival@lifilm.org
WEB SITE: http://www.lifilm.org/festival

Actor Steve Buscemi (Reservoir Dogs, Trees Lounge) with John Starace, founder and director of Summer Shorts Short Film Festival, at the Long Island Film Festival.

EILEEN BUCCOLA

FESTIVAL DATE: July-August
ENTRY DEADLINE: May
CONTACT: Christopher Cooke
DIRECTOR: Christopher Cooke
PROGRAMMER: Christopher Cooke
OTHER STAFF: Staller Center for the Arts—Stony Brook
CATEGORY: Independent
PROFILE: The Long Island Film Festival is devoted to the screening and support to independently produced films.
SEMINARS: "Script to Screen" Workshop
PANELS: Filmmaker's Panel
FAMOUS SPEAKERS: Steve Buscemi, Matthew Harrison, Dick Fisher, Rod Steiger, Scott Saunders, Sarah Driver, Bob Gosse, Bill Plympton, Greg Mottola, John Pierson
AWARDS: yes
COMPETITIONS: yes
MAJOR AWARDS: First Feature Award, Humanitarian Award, Comedy Award, Grand Jury Awards, Best Foreign Film, Robert Parrish-Best Director Award, Best Feature (35mm) and (16mm), Best Feature (Video), Best Documentary, Best Short (Video), Best of Festival
PAST JUDGES: Hal Hartley, Jerome Brownstein (producer of all of Hartley's films)

APPLICATION FEE: Up to 15min $25.00; Up to 30min $40.00; Up to 60min $60.00; Over 60min $75.00
AVERAGE FILMS ENTERED: All kinds of films from experimental to full length feature.
FILMS SCREENED: Approximately 40 features and documentaries are screened and about 60 shorts.
ODDS OF ACCEPTANCE: 300 to 400 films a submitted eash year.
FILMMAKER PERKS: Travel and lodging is provided for filmmakers accepted for screenings.
TRAVEL TIPS: Long Island Railroad from N.Y.C. to Stony Brook. By plane into Islip-MacArthur Airport or LaGuardia Airport/
BEST RESTAURANTS: The Park Bench which is near the festival (long walk) and train station. Good festival grub and great bar too.
BEST HANGOUT FOR FILMMAKERS: Hospitality Suite

LOS ANGELES INDEPENDENT FILM FESTIVAL (LAiFF)

See "The Top Ten Film Festivals" on page 156

LOS ANGELES INTERNATIONAL ANIMATION CELEBRATION

Expanded Entertainment
28023 Dorothy Dr.
Agoura Hills, CA 91301
TEL: (310) 991-2884
FAX: (310) 991-3773
FESTIVAL DATE: April
ENTRY DEADLINE: November
CONTACT: Terry Thoren
CATEGORY: Animation

LOS ANGELES INTERNATIONAL SHORT FILM FESTIVAL

1260 N. Alexandria Ave.
Los Angeles, CA 90029
TEL: (213) 427-8016
E-MAIL: info@lashortsfest.com
WEB SITE:
www.lashortsfest.com
FESTIVAL DATE: September
CATEGORY: Short
APPLICATION TIPS: In order to qualify, films must be under 45 minutes in length, completed after January 1, 1996, and shot in 35mm, 16mm or video. Those shorts selected will compete for Best Domestic Film and Best Foreign Film, as well as Certificate Awards in Animation, Comedy, Drama, Documentary and Experimental. All submissions should be on VHS.
ODDS OF ACCEPTANCE: Last year, over 500 films were submitted for consideration and 65 films from eleven countries were chosen and screened.

LOS ANGELES LATINO INTERNATIONAL FILM FESTIVAL

7060 Hollywood Blvd., #225
Hollywood, CA 90028
TEL: 323-469-9066
FAX: 323-469-9067
E-MAIL: anvega@latinofilm.org
WEB SITE: http://
www.latinofilm.org
FESTIVAL DATE: August
ENTRY DEADLINE: June

YEAR FESTIVAL BEGAN: 1996
CONTACT: Alan Noel Vega
DIRECTOR: Edward James Olmos
PROGRAMMER: Marlene Dermer
CATEGORY: Documentary, Ethnic Latino, Independent, Short
PROFILE: Covering all aspects of Latino film, the Latino Film Festival is entering its third sucessful year. Films should relate to Latino culture in some way, via origin, story, cast or crew. The program screened is made up of features, documentaries, shorts and independent films. The festival offers six panels each year, free of charge. Seminars are also offered
SEMINARS: Yes
PANELS: Yes
FAMOUS SPEAKERS: Rita Moreno, Mike Medavoy, Andy Garcia, Jimmy Smits
AWARDS: Yes
MAJOR AWARDS: "The Gabby"— Lifetime Achievement Award; "The Rita"—Best Film
VALUE OF AWARDS: The awards total over $35,000
APPLICATION FEE: none
AVERAGE FILMS ENTERED: 150
FILMS SCREENED: 70
ODDS OF ACCEPTANCE: 150 films submitted, 70 screened
FILMMAKER PERKS: For feature filmmakers: airfare, food, lodging
ATTENDANCE: 16,000

LUCILLE BALL SHORT FESTIVAL OF NEW COMEDY

116 East Third St.
Jamestown, NY 14701
TEL: (716) 664-2465
FAX: (716) 661-3829
FESTIVAL DATE: May
ENTRY DEADLINE: March
CATEGORY: Short, Weird
APPLICATION FEE: $20

MADCAT WOMEN'S INTERNATIONAL FILM FESTIVAL

937 Fell Street
San Francisco, CA 94117
TEL: (415) 436-9523
E-MAIL: alionbear@
earthlink.net
FESTIVAL DATE: Mid-May
ENTRY DEADLINE: February
YEAR FESTIVAL BEGAN: 1996
DIRECTOR: Ariella J. Ben-Dov
CATEGORY: Gay Lesbian, Independent, Women
PANELS: In the past we have had panels on: Cross Cultural Representation in Film, representing female sexuality in film, new visions for women filmmakers, and alternative distribution for independent filmmakers.
FAMOUS SPEAKERS: Barbara Hammer, Lynne Sachs
APPLICATION FEE: Sliding scale $10-30. Give what you can afford!
INSIDER ADVICE: Include a SASE
AVERAGE FILMS ENTERED: All are independent and many are experimental...no straight forward talking head documentaries please. But note we do screen docs—we just stick to the more non-traditional pieces. Films that challenge notions of visual story telling
FILMS SCREENED: In 1997 there were 35 in 1998 there were 55. It all depends on how short the shorts are.
ODDS OF ACCEPTANCE: Approx. 250 are submitted
FILMMAKER PERKS: food and drink at opening night bash. Free goodies from local stores. Free travel? not usually. Lodging? Yes
BEST RESTAURANTS: Burrito's at Cancun on 19th and Mission or fancy food at Firefly on 24th and Douglass
BEST PLACE FOR BREAKFAST: Spaghetti Western on Haight and Steiner, Kate's Kitchen on Haight and Fillmore, Chloe's on Church and Clipper

MAINE STUDENT FILM AND VIDEO FESTIVAL

P.O. Box 4320
Portland, ME 04101
TEL: (207) 773-1130
FESTIVAL DATE: June
ENTRY DEADLINE: May
CATEGORY: Student
APPLICATION FEE: None

MAKING SCENES

Arts Court, 2 Daly Avenue
Ottawa, Ontario K1N 6E2
Canada
TEL: 819 775 5423
FAX: 819 775 5422
E-MAIL: scenes@fox.nstn.ca
WEB SITE: http://fox.nstn.ca/~scenes
FESTIVAL DATE: September
ENTRY DEADLINE: May
CONTACT: Donna Quince
DIRECTOR: Donna Quince
PROGRAMMER: Donna Quince & committee (which varies from year to year)
CATEGORY: Gay Lesbian
SEMINARS: We offer production workshops every year. In 1998 we presented an animation workshop aimed at queers.
AWARDS: yes
COMPETITIONS: yes
MAJOR AWARDS: 1. VIACOM Canada Best Canadian Feature Film Award. 2. The Independent Filmmaker's Coop of Ottawa's Best locally-produced Film Award 3. SAW Video Coop's Best locally-produced Video Award
VALUE OF AWARDS: 1. $1,500 CAN; 2. $ 500 CAN; 3. $ 500 CAN
LAST WINNING DIRECTORS: 2. Nancy Darisse; 3. Tracey Clark & Gina Becker
PAST JUDGES: Audience Choice Awards
APPLICATION TIPS: Plain & simple, the story or concept must be good, but not necessarily the production value. I have seen a lot of well-produced works but the story is

dreaful. On the other hand I have seen some really weak productions with fabulous concepts.
APPLICATION FEE: We don't charge one preferring to present as many works as possible without that kind of hindrance.
INSIDER ADVICE: Hang in there, do not quit with one or two letters of rejection.
AVERAGE FILMS ENTERED: All kinds in the "queer" tradition
FILMS SCREENED: 75
ODDS OF ACCEPTANCE: Ottawa is a growing festival. This year we may have about 150-200 films and videos submitted
FILMMAKER PERKS: Free travel—not usually, but it depends
BEST RESTAURANTS: Corriander Thai on Kent Street

MANDALAY LAS COLINAS FESTIVAL

215 Las Colinas Blvd.
Mandalay Canal, Suite 400
Irving, TX 75039
TEL: (214) 831-1881
FAX: (214) 831-1882
FESTIVAL DATE: April
ENTRY DEADLINE: March

MARGARET MEAD FILM FESTIVAL

American Museum of Natural History
Central Park West at 79th St
New York, NY 10024-5192
TEL: (212) 769-5305
FAX: (212) 769-5329
FESTIVAL DATE: October
ENTRY DEADLINE: January-May previewing of films
CONTACT: Elaine Charnov

MARIN COUNTY NATIONAL FILM AND VIDEO FESTIVAL

Marin County Fairgrounds
San Rafael, CA 94903
TEL: (415) 499-6400
FESTIVAL DATE: September
ENTRY DEADLINE: May

CONTACT: Yolanda Sullivan, Fair Manager
CATEGORY: Independent

MIAMI FILM FESTIVAL

444 Brickell Ave #229
Miami, Florida 33131
TEL: (305) 377-3456
FAX: (305) 577-9768
E-MAIL: mff@gate.net
WEB SITE: www.miamifilmfestival.com
FESTIVAL DATE: January-February
ENTRY DEADLINE: November
YEAR FESTIVAL BEGAN: 1983
CONTACT: Stephanie Martino
DIRECTOR: Nat Chediak
PROGRAMMER: Michelle Massanet
CATEGORY: International
PROFILE: The Miami Film Festival presents films from the United States, Latin America, Asia and Europe. It has also become known for its role of bringing Spanish language films into the United States.
SEMINARS: yes
AWARDS: yes
COMPETITIONS: yes
MAJOR AWARDS: Audience Award
LAST WINNING FILMS: 1st Winning film—1998 *Secretos del Corazon*
APPLICATION FEE: No
ODDS OF ACCEPTANCE: 26-30 films accepted into festival

MILL VALLEY FILM FESTIVAL

38 Miller Avenue, Suite 6
Mill Valley, California 94941
TEL: 415-383-5256
FAX: 415-383-8606
E-MAIL: finc@well.com
WEB SITE: www.finc.org
FESTIVAL DATE: October
ENTRY DEADLINE: May (Early deadline)—June (Final Deadline)
CONTACT: Zoë Elton
DIRECTOR: Mark Fishkin

Hang in there, do not quit with one or two letters of rejection. (Making Scenes)

PROGRAMMER: Zoë Elton

CATEGORY: Independent

PROFILE: MVFF was founded in 1978; it celebrates and promotes film, video and new media as art and education. It's an annual, non-competitive, 11-day festival with more than a hundred programs of independent features, world cinema, documentaries, shorts, family films, video and new media, Seminars and Tributes to luminaries of the film world. The festival is run under the auspices of the Film Institute of Northern California. Over 40,000 attend annually.

SEMINARS: Two weekends of seminars and panels, which cover issues related to independent filmmakers and filmmaking, cutting-edge technology, innovations in video and new media, kids' films.

PANELS: Panelists have included Waldo Salt, John Sayles, Barry Levinson, Saul Zaentz, Maggie Renzi, Allison Anders, Marianne Sägebrecht, James L. Brooks, Sam Shepard, Tod Rundgren; international panelists such as Tsitsi Dangaremba (Zimbabwe), Caroline Link (Germany); and representatives from independent distributors such as Miramax, Fox Searchlight, and October Films.

FAMOUS SPEAKERS: See above.

COMPETITIONS: No. The festival will remain non-competitive.

APPLICATION TIPS: Sappy as it may sound, make the film YOU want to make as best you can. Acceptance to a festival is like auditioning—you may be a great actor, but you may not be right for some particular part. You want the right festival for your film—it's not always a match, so don't be disheartened if your film doesn't get in.

APPLICATION FEE: Yes. Call for entry form for current rates.

INSIDER ADVICE: See application process above! Also, if you have questions about the process, call us

AVERAGE FILMS ENTERED: All kinds, all genres. We have a strong American independent contingent—features, docs, shorts, and try to bring strong selections from around the world.

ODDS OF ACCEPTANCE: 700-800 of all genres & lengths are submitted through Call for Entries. Others are considered on top of this through research. With Call for Entries, we estimate the odds are 8-1.

FILMMAKER PERKS: For feature filmmakers, or for makers whose work is the main hook of a program: 1. Free travel; 2. Free Lodging; 3. Contacts; 4. Publicity; 5. Festival Accreditation; 6. A relaxed and friendly place to meet people, make contacts, schmooze and hang out. For others, 3—6 apply if they attend the festival, plus we usually have deals with hotels and car rentals which are available to them.

TRAVEL TIPS: We're near San Francisco—fly in through SFO, bring your hiking gear if the mountains call you, bring your party gear if the clubs call you, bring a driver if you're going to hit the wineries. People are often unsure where Mill Valley is:

it's fifteen minutes north of San Francisco over the Golden Gate Bridge.

BEST RESTAURANTS: Piatti

BEST BARS: The Sweetwater (and during the festival, there have been shows there with the likes of The Bacon Brothers, Rickie Lee Jones, Elvis Costello, as well as locals like Huey Lewis, members of the Grateful Dead, Hot Tuna).

BEST HANGOUT FOR FILMMAKERS: The OAC (Outdoor Art Club)

BEST PLACE FOR BREAKFAST: Sunnyside Café

MONTREAL INTERNATIONAL FESTIVAL OF NEW CINEMA AND NEW MEDIA

3668 Boulevard Saint-Laurent
Montréal, Québec H2X 2V4
Canada

TEL: (514) 843-4725

FAX: (514) 843-4631

E-MAIL: montrealfest @fcmm.com

WEB SITE: www.fcmm.com

FESTIVAL DATE: October

ENTRY DEADLINE: September

YEAR FESTIVAL BEGAN: 1972

CATEGORY: Digital, Short

PROFILE: The event banks on new approaches and technologies while working as a springboard for artists eager to explore the confines of their art.

AWARDS: Yes

COMPETITIONS: Yes

MONTREAL WORLD FILM FESTIVAL

1432 de Bleury Street
Montreal, Quebec H3A 2J1
Canada

TEL: (514) 848 3883

FAX: (514) 848 3886

E-MAIL: ffm@Interlink.net

WEB SITE: http://www.ffm-montreal.org/

FESTIVAL DATE: August-September

ENTRY DEADLINE: July

WHY VOLUNTEER AT A FILM FESTIVAL?

"Do it because you think it would be fun to be a part of the festival. Don't expect too much in return. You'll see some films, you'll meet some people, but mostly you'll go home without any great stories to tell except how you watched so and so walk by you. If you can't afford to attend a festival, this is one way to get into some films and if you're lucky, get some housing."

— Jeff Winograd, Sundance Film Festival Volunteer

CONTACT: Serge Losique
CATEGORY: International
PROFILE: Approximately 350,000 attend.
AWARDS: yes
COMPETITIONS: yes
MAJOR AWARDS: Grand Prix of Americas
APPLICATION FEE: None
ODDS OF ACCEPTANCE: over 200 films entered

MOUNTAiNFiLM

P.O. Box 1088
308 N Willow Street
Telluride, Colorado 81435
TEL: 970 728 4123
FAX: 970 728 6458
E-MAIL: mountainfilm @infozone.org
WEB SITE: mountainfilm.org
FESTIVAL DATE: May
ENTRY DEADLINE: April
YEAR FESTIVAL BEGAN: 1979
CONTACT: Mountainfilm office at 970 728-4123; Rick or Cameron
DIRECTOR: Rick Silverman
PROGRAMMER: Rick Silverman and Cameron Brooks
OTHER STAFF: Lawrence Van Hoey, technical coordinator; Lance Waring, travel and hospitality, sponsor programs; Lucy Lerner, staff and volunteers; Elisabeth Gick, assistant manager
CATEGORY: America's premier festival of mountain, adventure, cultural and environmental film and video since 1979.
PROFILE: Mountainfilm is an extraordinary celebration of film, wild places, and the people who inhabit, explore, and protect them. Set against the backdrop of the high San Juan Mountains, the Festival is a mix of film and filmmaker, gallery exhibits, speakers, authors, symposiums, picnics, climbing, backcountry skiing, and rich conversation. With an emphasis on cutting-edge programming and personal interaction, the Festival has become a gathering place for directors, producers, buyers, activists, photographers, writers, and those who savor this uniquely informal gathering.
FILMS SCREENED: About 50
ODDS OF ACCEPTANCE: 200 to 250 submitted, about 50 accepted.
TOURIST INFORMATION: Former mining town, turned ski resort, surrounded by 13000 foot peaks, hot springs nearby, biking, hiking, backcountry skiing, wildflowers and wild animals: bring your camera—it's spectacular.
TRAVEL TIPS: Difficult to get to, but always worth the trip.
BEST HANGOUT FOR FILMMAKERS: The Hospitality and Main Street

NANTUCKET FILM FESTIVAL

P.O. Box 688 Prince Street Station
New York, New York 10012
TEL: (212) 642-6339
E-MAIL: ackfest@aol.com
WEB SITE: http://www.nantucketfilmfestival.org/
FESTIVAL DATE: June
ENTRY DEADLINE: April
CONTACT: Jonathan Burkhart
PROFILE: This festival focuses on the art of screenwriting. It remains mostly non-competitive except for the screenplay competition. All film types are accepted. However, VHS and NTSC formats are preferred. All screenplays must be written in English.
PANELS: Yes
AWARDS: Yes
COMPETITIONS: Yes
MAJOR AWARDS: Best Screenplay
PAST JUDGES: A jury awards prizes.
APPLICATION FEE: $20 (shorts) $35 (features) ($5 added for video return)

NASHViLLE iNDEPENDENT FiLM FESTiVAL

402 Sarratt Center, VU
Nashville, Tennessee 37240
TEL: 615-343-3419
FAX: 615-343-9461
E-MAIL: sinking.creek @vanderbilt.edu
WEB SITE: www.nashvillefilmfestival.org
FESTIVAL DATE: June
ENTRY DEADLINE: April
YEAR FESTIVAL BEGAN: 1969
CONTACT: Kelly Brownlee
DIRECTOR: Michael Catalano
PROGRAMMER: Michael Catalano / Kelly Brownlee
OTHER STAFF: Kelly Brownlee, David Buchert, Amy Ashbury, Donna Blake
CATEGORY: Independent, Markets
PROFILE: We are the longest running film festival in the South. This is our 29th year of being dedicated to the development and expansion of independent film and video. We screen experimental, Documentary, Student, Feature, Animated and High Shcool Films. These films cover all subject matter are recieved from all over the world.
SEMINARS: Seminars include: Screenwriting, Film Funding, Documentary Selling, Animation Production and Cutting edge equipment.
PANELS: Understanding the Cable Market, Raising the Money, Gender Issues in Film Making and Legal Issues
FAMOUS SPEAKERS: C.J. Cox, Cynthia Carl, Keith Crawford, Linda Seminski, Michael York, Les Blanc, Margeret Drain, Lilly Thomlin and Joan Tweeksbury.
AWARDS: Yes
COMPETITIONS: Yes
MAJOR AWARDS: Best of Festival
VALUE OF AWARDS: $1,500
LAST WINNING DIRECTORS: Barry J. Hershey
PAST JUDGES: C.J. Cox, Peter Wentworth, Ruby Lerner.

Difficult to get to, but always worth the trip. (Mountainfilm)

APPLICATION TIPS: We judge on all around quality; story, production values and originality. Tell a strong story with good actors and clean prodution

APPLICATION FEE: yes

INSIDER ADVICE: Follow the instructions and submit all materials on time.

AVERAGE FILMS ENTERED: Experimental, Documentary, Student, Feature, Animated and films/videos from High School Filmmakers.

ODDS OF ACCEPTANCE: Between 300 and 600 films are recieved each year. 100 are choosen.

FILMMAKER PERKS: We offer a greatly reduced rate on our all festival pass plus rooms for $25 a night, we also provide transportation from the rooms to the festival site, a hospitality suite the remains open throughout the entire event and a number of dinner events plus contacts with all visiting panelists, judges and speakers.

BEST RESTAURANTS: Sunset Grill

BEST BARS: Bluebird Cafe

BEST HANGOUT FOR FILMMAKERS: Bongo Java Coffeehouse

BEST PLACE FOR BREAKFAST: Fido

NATiONAL EDUCATiONAL FiLM AND ViDEO FESTiVAL (NEFVF)

655 13th St. Suite 100
Oakland, CA 94612
TEL: (510) 465-6885
FAX: (510) 465-2835
WEB SITE: www.nemn.org
FESTIVAL DATE: May
ENTRY DEADLINE: November
CONTACT: Susan Davis Cushing
CATEGORY: Educational / Kids
APPLICATION FEE: varies by category

NATiONAL LATiNO FiLM AND ViDEO FESTiVAL

El Museo del Barrio
1230 5th Ave.
New York, NY 10029
TEL: (212) 831-7272 or
(212) 831-7927
DIRECTOR: Lillian Jimenez
CATEGORY: Ethnic Latino

NEW ANGLE iNTERMEDiA ViDEO FESTiVAL

300 Mercer St., #11N
New York, NY 10003
TEL: (212) 228-8307
FESTIVAL DATE: May
CONTACT: Angle Intermedia
CATEGORY: Video

NEW ENGLAND FiLM AND ViDEO FESTiVAL

Boston Film/Video Foundation
1126 Boylston Street
Boston, MA 02215
TEL: (617) 536-1540
FAX: (617) 536-3576
E-MAIL: nefvfest@aol.com
WEB SITE: http://www.actwin.com/BFVF
FESTIVAL DATE: May
ENTRY DEADLINE: December
CONTACT: Anne-Marie Stein
DIRECTOR: Pam Korza, Coordinator
CATEGORY: Independent
PROFILE: This film festival showcases work from New England residents. Approximately 3,00 attend.
AWARDS: Yes
COMPETITIONS: Yes
MAJOR AWARDS: Fourteen awards given
VALUE OF AWARDS: The awards total over $7,000
APPLICATION FEE: $35 (Independents) and $25 (Students)
FILMS SCREENED: 14 films screened

NEW ORLEANS FiLM AND ViDEO FESTiVAL

P. O. Box 50819
New Orleans, LA 70150-0819
TEL: (504) 523-3818
FESTIVAL DATE: October
CONTACT: Tom Ellis
CATEGORY: Video

NEW YORK EXPO OF SHORT FiLM AND ViDEO

532 La Guardia Pl., Suite 330
New York, NY 10012
TEL: (212) 873-1353
FAX: (212) 724-9172
E-MAIL: rswbc@cunyvm.cuny.edu
FESTIVAL DATE: November
ENTRY DEADLINE: July
CONTACT: Robert Withers
CATEGORY: Short
PROFILE: One of the first festivals to recognize the talents of Spike Lee, George Lucas, and Martha Coolidge. Approximately 1,500 attend.
AWARDS: Yes
COMPETITIONS: Yes
MAJOR AWARDS: Jury Award; Gold, Silver, and Bronze Prizes
VALUE OF AWARDS: Cash and filmstock awards given.
APPLICATION FEE: $35
FILMS SCREENED: 45
ODDS OF ACCEPTANCE: 800 films entered, 45 screened.

NEW YORK FiLM FESTIVAL

See "The Top Ten Film Festivals" on page 156

NEW YORK GAY AND LESBiAN FiLM FESTIVAL

47 Great Jones St., 6th floor
New York, NY 10012
TEL: (212) 254-7228
FAX: (212) 254-8655
E-MAIL: newfest@gramercy.ios.com
WEB SITE: http://www.newfestival.com/

FESTIVAL DATE: June
ENTRY DEADLINE: March
CONTACT: Wellington Love
CATEGORY: Gay Lesbian, Independent
AWARDS: Yes
COMPETITIONS: Yes
MAJOR AWARDS: Best Feature; Best Documentary; Short Film
APPLICATION FEE: $15
FILMS SCREENED: 150
ODDS OF ACCEPTANCE: 400 films entered

NEW YORK INTERNATIONAL DOCUMENTARY FESTIVAL (DOCFEST)

159 Maiden Lane
New York, New York 10038
TEL: 212-943-6333
FAX: 212-943-6396
E-MAIL: docfest@aol.com
WEB SITE: www.docfest.org
FESTIVAL DATE: Held for 5 days at end of May at the Directors Guild of America Theater.
ENTRY DEADLINE: No submission procedure: by invitation only (curated).
YEAR FESTIVAL BEGAN: 1998
CONTACT: Gary Pollard
DIRECTOR: Gary Pollard
PROGRAMMER: David Leitner
OTHER STAFF: Alla Verlotsky, Managing Director; David Leitner, Program Director; Susan Norget, Public Relations & Marketing
CATEGORY: Documentary, Independent
PROFILE: An annual international non-competitive event to celebrate and promote the documentary form. Programs are selected from among the best new and classic documentaries worldwide in every format. Of the hundreds of film festivals worldwide, only a handful are dedicated exclusively to documentaries. docfest—uniquely—is the one festival in the U.S. that embraces the entirety of the documentary spectrum: TV, cable, video and film; from low-budget Hi8 videos to network reportage, from Super 8mm to IMAX.
PANELS: Two weekend panels were presented at 1998's inaugural event: "Documentary Making in the Digital World" and "Half a Century of Documentary Making" featuring Jean Rouch, D.A. Pennebaker and Albert Maysles.
FAMOUS SPEAKERS: D.A. Pennebaker, Morley Safer, Albert Maysles, Melvin Van Peebles, Michael Moore. (Famous attendees this year included Madonna, Mira Sorvino, Ingrid Casares, Harmony Korine, Gina Gershon, Rob Morrow, Nicolas Pileggi and mob lawyer Bruce Cutler.)
AWARDS: Independent Film Channel (IFC) $2000 "Documentary Vision Award" and the Zuma Digital DVD Award ($15,000 worth of services to create a complete DVD—digital versatile disk—of a film)
COMPETITIONS: No
APPLICATION TIPS: Filmmakers are welcome to send tapes of their works but the selection is by invitation only.
APPLICATION FEE: None
AVERAGE FILMS ENTERED: Documentaries of all lengths, formats, themes etc.
FILMS SCREENED: 17 were screened this year in 14 feature-length programs.
ODDS OF ACCEPTANCE: Again, festival is by invitation only and has no formal submission procedure as works are generally selected from what is seen "in the field" (festivals, markets etc.) as it were.
FILMMAKER PERKS: Travel and lodging (the famed Algonquin Hotel). Lots of opportunities to network with other documentarians.

NEW YORK LESBIAN AND GAY EXPERIMENTAL FILM AND VIDEO FESTIVAL (MIX)

c/o Anthology Film Archives
11 John St. Suite 801.
New York, NY 10038
TEL: (212) 571-4242
FAX: (212) 571-5155
E-MAIL: mix@echonyc.com
WEB SITE: http://www. echonyc.com/~mix/
FESTIVAL DATE: November
ENTRY DEADLINE: June
CONTACT: Jonathan Aubrey
CATEGORY: Gay Lesbian, Experimental
PROFILE: It focuses mainly on experimental filmmaking. Approximately 3,000 attend.
AWARDS: No
COMPETITIONS: No
APPLICATION FEE: $10
FILMS SCREENED: 100-150
ODDS OF ACCEPTANCE: 400-500 films entered

NEW YORK NATIONAL HIGH SCHOOL FILM AND VIDEO FESTIVAL

Trinity School
101 W. 91st St.
New York, NY 10024
TEL: (212) 873-1650
FAX: (212) 799-3417
ENTRY DEADLINE: February
CONTACT: John Dooley
CATEGORY: Student

NEW YORK UNDERGROUND FILM FESTIVAL

225 Lafayette St. , Suite 401
New York, NY 10012
TEL: (212) 925-3440
FAX: (212) 925-3430
E-MAIL: festival@nyuff.com
WEB SITE: http:// www.nyuff.com/
FESTIVAL DATE: March
ENTRY DEADLINE: January
CONTACT: Ed Halter

CATEGORY: Independent

PROFILE: This annual festival showcases independent and unique films. It focuses on innovative projects that go beyond mainstream filmmaking. Approximately 10,000 attend annually.

SEMINARS: yes

AWARDS: Yes

COMPETITIONS: Yes

MAJOR AWARDS: Best Feature, Short, Documentary, Animation, Experimental and Festival Choice Award.

APPLICATION FEE: $30-35 U.S.

FILMS SCREENED: 75 screened

ODDS OF ACCEPTANCE: 800 films entered

NEW YORK ViDEO FESTiVAL

70 Lincoln Center Plaza
New York, NY 10023
TEL: (212) 875-5610
FAX: (212) 875-5636
FESTIVAL DATE: July
ENTRY DEADLINE: March
DIRECTOR: Marion Masone
CATEGORY: Video
APPLICATION FEE: None

NiGHT OF THE BLACK iNDEPENDENTS

830 Eastwood Ave., Suite B
Atlanta, GA 30316-2414
TEL: (404) 627-9900
FESTIVAL DATE: May
ENTRY DEADLINE: April
CATEGORY: Ethnic Black

NO DANCE FiLM FESTiVAL

703 Pier Avenue #675
Hermosa Beach, CA 90254
TEL: (310) 939-6269
FAX: (310) 374-0134
E-MAIL: Jboyd1@pacbell.net
WEB SITE: www.6161.com
FESTIVAL DATE: January
ENTRY DEADLINE: November
CONTACT: Beth Stolarczyk
DIRECTOR: James Boyd

PROGRAMMER: Jason McHugh

OTHER STAFF: Robert Stenger, Jeff Hefti, Jill Vermeer, Lisa Davis, Media Relations

CATEGORY: Independent

PROFILE: To provide an outlet for low-budget films to screen during Park City's Sundance and Slamdance festivals. Surviving a frenetic first year, NO DANCE: Year Two screened its ten film competition selections on DVD, a global first for the fledgling technology. "This is desk-top level stuff that is quickly becoming affordable to indie filmmakers," says founder and festival director James Boyd. "The DVD projection quality is far superior to VHS tape, and much cheaper than creating a film print. The film print is dead."

AWARDS: Yes

COMPETITIONS: Yes

MAJOR AWARDS: Audience Award

VALUE OF AWARDS: None

LAST WINNING FILMS: *Flushed*

LAST WINNING DIRECTORS: Carrie Ansell

APPLICATION TIPS: Don't get into Sundance or Slamdance.

APPLICATION FEE: Yes

AVERAGE FILMS ENTERED: Quirky. Good first films. Emphasis on new technologies.

FILMS SCREENED: 8-12

ODDS OF ACCEPTANCE: We receive about 200 films and show about 10-12.

FILMMAKER PERKS: (1) Free Mountain air... (2) Platform to self-promote their film... (3) Good damn time. Yee-Haw!

TRAVEL TIPS: Always come for the opening weekend, and leave the mountain before it gets dull.

BEST RESTAURANTS: Sushi Sei

BEST BARS: Who cares, it's all 3.2 alcohol anyway

BEST HANGOUT FOR FILMMAKERS: Slamdance HQ.

BEST PLACE FOR BREAKFAST: What's breakfast?

FESTIVAL TALE: At a NO DANCE party, a young, talented director from the Sundance festival "hooked" with one of my female NO DANCE volunteers. In MY bed. I had to sleep on the couch, and drive the bastard home the next morning. Anyway, I blew off his screening... We are leaning towards new projection technologies like DVD or internet streaming to provide better projection systems for low budget films.

NORTHWEST FiLM & ViDEO FESTiVAL

1219 SW Park Ave.
Portland, Oregon 97205
TEL: 503/221-1156
FAX: 503/294-0874
E-MAIL: info@nwfilm.org
WEB SITE: www.nwfilm.org
FESTIVAL DATE: November
ENTRY DEADLINE: August
YEAR FESTIVAL BEGAN: 1973
CONTACT: Regional Services Coordinator
DIRECTOR: Regional Services Coordinator, Northwest Film Center
PROGRAMMER: judge chosen each year (1998 = Christine Vachon)
OTHER STAFF: Exhibition Program Assistant
CATEGORY: Independent
PROFILE: A juried survey of new moving image arts by independent Northwest film & videomakers, the Festival draws over 300 entries in all genres each year and is judged by a prominent filmmaker, curator or critic. Now in it's 25th year, the Festival provides a forum where outstanding indpendent work receives public recognition, critical appraisal and an engaged and enthusiastic regional audiences. Generally, 30-45 shorts, features and documentaries are screened during the Festival, then 10-15 shorts are selected for the Best of the Northwest Tour program, which travels the following year throughout the Northwest to media arts centers, museums,

Darryl Hannah and Maxwell Caulfield make the rounds for their film, Real Blonde.

RANDALL MICHELSON

arts councils and universities in places as diverse as Billings, Boise, Hood River, Juneau, Kodiak, Moscow, Missoula, Seattle, Yakima and Vancouver, BC. Entries are accepted in all genres from permanent residents of OR, WA, MT, ID, AK and British Columbia as well as from students attending school in those states.

FAMOUS SPEAKERS: Past guests have included John Pierson, Gus van Sant. There are roundtable forums each year focusing on particular issues in independent filmmaking as well as occasional workshops.

AWARDS: yes

COMPETITIONS: yes

VALUE OF AWARDS: $12,000 in production service awards

PAST JUDGES: Gus van Sant, Dan Ireland, Karen Cooper of Film Forum, B. Ruby Rich, Amy Taubin, Jim Hoberman, John Cooper (Sundance programmer) and Christine Vachon.

APPLICATION FEE: None, but $10 for return shipping costs per entry ($15 for Canadian residents)

INSIDER ADVICE: Make sure your contact information is clearly marked on your preview tape, your supporting materials (synopsis, bio, etc.) are concise and well-written and DON'T FORGET to make black-white stills while in production. None of this has any bearing on whether or not your work will be accepted, but if it is, having these things will help the Festival promote your work more effectively.

AVERAGE FILMS ENTERED: There are no predetermined categories, expectations or assumptions. All independent work is considered regardless of length, genre, format. As the majority of works submitted are shorts, they are usually the focal point of the festival.

ODDS OF ACCEPTANCE: Over 300-350 submitted. All works accepted are screened; generally 25-45. 10-15 shorts are selected for the Best of the Northwest Tour program.

FILMMAKER PERKS: This is regional festival where a strong community of filmmakers can converge to share ideas and

work, participate in a dialogue with colleagues and audiences, and generally be greatly appreciated for their determination, hard work and talent. There are roundtables, guest speakers and workshops in addition to screenings. Sometimes free travel and accomodations are available.

TOURIST INFORMATION: Great outdoors: coast and mountains are each an hour away. Powell's Books, microbreweries.

TRAVEL TIPS: Bring an umbrella.

BEST RESTAURANTS: Zefiro, Dots, Saucebox

BEST BARS: Ringler's Annex or Saucebox

BEST HANGOUT FOR FILMMAKERS: San Francisco

BEST PLACE FOR BREAKFAST: Shaker's Cafe, Laurelthirst

OHIO INDEPENDENT FILM FESTIVAL AND MARKET

2258 West 10th Street #5
Cleveland, Ohio 44113
TEL: (216) 781-1755
E-MAIL: OhioIndieFilmFest
@juno.com
WEB SITE:
www.rinestock.com/flickfest
FESTIVAL DATE: November
ENTRY DEADLINE: September or October
CONTACT: Bernadette Gillota
DIRECTOR: Annetta Marion and Bernadette Gillota
PROGRAMMER: Annetta Marion and Bernadette Gillota
CATEGORY: Independent

> We'll treat you like a queen. Or king. But we don't have enough of a budget to pay for travel expenses yet. Ohio Independent Film Festival and Market)

PROFILE: The Ohio Independent Film Festival (formerly known as The Off-Hollywood Flick Fest) is a professional arts organization which creates, presents, and supports independent media art. The OIFF is much more than a film festival; we provide real support and guidance to independent filmmakers all year around, without charging a membership fee.

Five years ago, the OIFF sprang into action, supported by, led by, and for independent filmmakers; the organization was galvanized by the lack of local support for independent filmmakers. To overcome our frustration with the status quo, we started showing one program of short films and videos over a weekend in a small warehouse in Tremont, Ohio, and were thrilled with the positive response from both filmmakers and film lovers. The OIFF has since moved to Cleveland Public Theatre (CPT) in Cleveland, Ohio and expanded into year-round programming to support independent film makers (a Northeast Ohio first).

FAMOUS SPEAKERS: Special guests at past festivals have included entertainment lawyer Alex Murphy, popular indie producer Peter Wentworth, filmmaker Steve Bognar

AWARDS: Yes
COMPETITIONS: Yes
MAJOR AWARDS: Best of the Fest
VALUE OF AWARDS: Small cash award—exact amount fluctuates with our funding level.
LAST WINNING FILMS: *Mary Lou: Reflections*
LAST WINNING DIRECTORS: Jane Temple, Sara Stashower, Jackie Ponsky
PAST JUDGES: The audience at our festivals (that could be you!)
APPLICATION TIPS: Even though we accept work from around the world, it would be beneficial to play up any Ohio connections you (or anyone involved with the project) might have.
APPLICATION FEE: $15 for a short (under 20 minutes). $20 for a feature.
INSIDER ADVICE: Think about what you can do to help get people to your screening(s).
AVERAGE FILMS ENTERED: High-quality work that is innovative either in terms of production or subject.
FILMS SCREENED: approximately 100
ODDS OF ACCEPTANCE: Over 250 films are submitted for each festival. We are primarily a short film festival so if you submit a short that will definitely help your chance of getting in.
FILMMAKER PERKS: We'll treat you like a queen. Or king. But we don't have enough of a budget to pay for travel expenses yet.
TRAVEL TIPS: Cleveland weather can change very quickly; so be prepared for all kinds of weather!
BEST RESTAURANTS: Luchita's for Mexican food, Tortilla Feliz for Central American cuisine

BEST BARS: The Literary Cafe in Tremont, The Brillo Pad
BEST HANGOUT FOR FILMMAKERS: The festival of course and our parties afterward.
BEST PLACE FOR BREAKFAST: The Inn on Coventry, Grumpy's in Tremont, The Drip Stick Coffee and Tea Station, Red Star Cafe.
FESTIVAL TALE: We were showing a short film by a filmmaker from NYC. He and a big group of friends drove into Cleveland for the festival—they all thought they had died and gone to heaven because they were able to buy beer at the festival for only $2 each!

ONE WORLD FILM FESTIVAL

c/o ARUSHA Centre
233 10th St., NW
Calgary, Alberta T2N 1V5
Canada
TEL: (403) 270-3200
FAX: (403) 270-8832
FESTIVAL DATE: March
ENTRY DEADLINE: January
CONTACT: Andrew Eyck

ONION CITY FILM FESTIVAL

Experimental Film Coalition
1467 S. Michigan Ave., 3rd Fl.
Chicago, IL 60605-2801
TEL: (312) 986-1823
FESTIVAL DATE: May
ENTRY DEADLINE: April
CATEGORY: Weird, Video
APPLICATION FEE: $25

OPEN SCREENS

Gulture Enterprises
PO Box 11935
San Rafael, California 94912
TEL: 415.485.2585
FAX: 415.331.8387
E-MAIL: openscreens
@gulture.com
WEB SITE: http://
www.gulture.com

Festival Date: Quarterly
Entry Deadline: Roughly October, Feburary, May & August
Contact: Frank Colin
Director: Frank Colin
Programmer: Stefan G
Category: Underground
Profile: Open Screens is the San Francisco Bay Area's premiere short film & rebel media showcase of visual entertainment.
Famous Speakers: Artists may speak, if they desire
Awards: No
Competitions: No
Application Tips: Keep it short, under 12 minutes. Excerpts of longer pieces are OK.
Application Fee: None.
Insider Advice: Our audience has eclectic tastes, but quality stories count most.
Average Films Entered: Shorts—Indie, CG, Animation, documentary...anything goes.
Films Screened: 40-50 shown per year...15 or so per show.
Odds of Acceptance: 250+ submitted per year
Filmmaker Perks: Tickets for them & guests
Best Restaurants: It's the Bay Area—something for every taste.
Best Bars: It's the Bay Area—you pick it.

OTTAWA INTERNATIONAL ANIMATION FESTIVAL

2 Daly Avenue, Suite 120
Ottawa, Ontario K1N 6E2
Canada
Tel: (613) 232-8769
Fax: (613) 232-6315
E-mail: oiaf@ottawa.com
Web Site: www.awn.com/ottawa
Festival Date: Fall
Entry Deadline: July
Year Festival Began: 1976
Contact: Suzanne Mullett
Director: Chris Robinson
Programmer: Chris Robinson.

We also contract a variety of animation professionals to programme our retrospectives and tribute programmes.
Other Staff: Director of Development: John Connolly; Workshop Coordinator: Tom McSorley
Category: Animation
Profile: The Ottawa International Animation Festival is North America's only competitive animation festival, and one of the largest animation events in the world. The festival attracts a total audience of more than 25,000. Like the industry itself, the OIAF is getting bigger, yet we remain very much committed to the art and culture of animation; independent animators and small animation studios have always—and will always—represent the heart of the OIAF and its activities. New scholarships, networking and recruiting parties, subsidized sponsorships, cash prizes, and free student workshops are only a few of the ways in which we "give back". More than simply a biennial festival, the OIAF has become a year round resource center for independent animators and the animation community alike.
Seminars: At all Ottawa Festivals, we complement our film programmes with a series of creative and professional development and training workshops, seminars and panels. The center of our creative workshops is Storytelling in Animation. Our other creative mainstay is Meet the Master, in which attendees have a chance to sit down and get intimate and interactive with an acclaimed animator.

The OIAF also features over 25 industrial orientated workshops/panels and seminars. Titles include: The Business of Tv Animation, Animating The Net, Preparing A Portfolio, Mechandising Animation, Alternative Avenues, Budgeting, Financing, and Accounting, International Co-Production and

Co-Financing, Distribution: Selling Your Production, New Tools of The Trade and more.
Panels: See Above
Famous Speakers: All workshops are conducted by some of the leading voices in animation. Past participants include: Linda Simensky, Norman McLaren, Chuck Jones, Terry Thoren, Michael Hirsch, Bill Plympton, Corky Quakenbush, Jerry Beck, Clive Smith, Abbe Terkuhle, JJ Sedelmaier, Raoul Servais, Priit Parn, Derek Lamb, Michael Sporn, Richard Condie, Marv Newland, Nick Park, Peter Lord and many more.
Awards: Yes
Competitions: Yes
Major Awards: Grand Prize
Value of Awards: Priceless. No actual cash prize at this time, but the exposure from the Grand Prize is a great asset.
Last Winning Directors: Igor Kovalyov (USSR) and Tim Johnson (USA) respectively.
Past Judges: Joyce Borenstein, Karen Aqua, Chris Cassidy, Paul Driessen, Marv Newland, Linda Simensky, Igor Kovalyov, Raimund Krumme, Janno Poldma, Candy Kugel, Jayne Pilling, Pierre Hebert, Terry Thoren, Frederic Back, John Canemaker, Erica Russell, Mike Smith, Bruno Edera, Otto Alder and too many others to list here.
Application Tips: Make a good film. Seriously though, the OIAF is not interested in stagnant television animation. Uniqueness and a willing to experiment are important. Innovative stories and techniques are also encouraged.
Application Fee: None.
Insider Advice: Label them correctly and make sure that they are cued to the beginning of the film. Don't get down if your film is not selected. The OIAF receives over 1000 entries and features a strict selection process. In order to ensure that we screen only the best films, our

competition programme features only six screenings. Thus, only about 100/1000 are accepted.

AVERAGE FILMS ENTERED: We have two competitions: independent and commissioned films, so we accept a wide variety of films. The only stipulation is that they are under 30 minutes. But you can generally be certain that, for example, Pinky and the Brain won't be accepted. We are an industrial festival to a degree, but it is important to us that our competition and retrospectives remain devoted to independent animation and quality animation in general.

SHAWN-PAUL GILBERT

FILMS SCREENED: Including retrospectives, well over 300 films.

ODDS OF ACCEPTANCE: 1000 are entered. About 100-120 are accepted.

FILMMAKER PERKS: We offer lodging, festival pass, and a small per diem (for independent filmmakers only). For other attendees, we do our best to find them the best rates on lodging and travel. Ottawa also features a number of social activities including our world famous animator's picnic, Chez-Ani (a gathering place for attendees), and a handful of

sponsor hosted parties. It is THE place to be for anyone and everyone in animation.

Contacts? Every major and minor player in animation comes to the festival. Walt Disney, Warner Bros, Pixar, Dreamworks, Nelvana, Pacific Data Images, Hbo, Fox, Cinar, Klasky-Csupo, MTV, Nickelodeon, Cartoon Network and many more.

TOURIST INFORMATION: Ottawa, Canada's capital city, features a number of tourist sites: National Art Gallery, Museum of Civilization, Parliament Buildings, Byward Market, Rideau Canal (longest skating rink in the world come winter), a

Kevin Spacey offers some industry insights during a festival panel discussion.

number of parks and bike paths for those interested in the natural side.

TRAVEL TIPS: In October, you never know what the weather will be like. Prepare for warm and cold winter. Ottawa is walkable. Don't bother renting a car.

BEST RESTAURANTS: There are a number of restaurants in the Byward Market and along Elgin Street (2-3 minute walk from the festival).

BEST BARS: Depends on the person. If you want to drink and chat, the Black Tomato is easily the best bar. They feature a number of local beers and have

a menu for whiskies. They also feature great food and sell cds!

BEST HANGOUT FOR FILMMAKERS: Our own Chez-Ani is where everyone goes

BEST PLACE FOR BREAKFAST: Boko Bakery in the Byward Market.

OUT AT THE MOViES: SAN ANTONiO'S ANNUAL FESTiVAL OF LESBiAN & GAY FiLM

P.O. Box 15705
San Antonio, Texas 78212
TEL: 210/228-0201 r 210/641.8123 voice mail
FAX: Fax: 210.228.0000
E-MAIL: outfilmtx@aol.com
FESTIVAL DATE: September
CONTACT: Dennis Poplin & Graciela Sanchez
CATEGORY: Gay Lesbian
PROFILE: It is the aim of Out At The Movies to exhibit contemporary Lesbian & Gay film/video, to demonstrate the strength and diversity of Lesbian & Gay culture, to increase discussion of current social issues within Queer communities, and to promote media education.
PANELS: Yes
AWARDS: No
COMPETITIONS: No
APPLICATION FEE: No
ODDS OF ACCEPTANCE: 100 submitted; 25-30 accepted
FILMMAKER PERKS: We offer free travel and lodging.

OUTFEST: LOS ANGELES INTERNATIONAL GAY AND LESBiAN FiLM & VIDEO FESTIVAL

1125 N. McCadden Place, Suite 235
Los Angeles, CA 90038
TEL: (323) 960-9200
FAX: (323) 960-2397
E-MAIL: outfest@outfest.org
WEB SITE: http://www.outfest.org
FESTIVAL DATE: July
ENTRY DEADLINE: April

CONTACT: Morgan Rumpf

DIRECTOR: Morgan Rumpf

CATEGORY: Gay Lesbian

AWARDS: Yes

COMPETITIONS: Yes

MAJOR AWARDS: Three winners for excellence in filmmaking. Six audience awards

VALUE OF AWARDS: Cash awards

PALM SPRINGS INTERNATIONAL FILM FESTIVAL

P. O. Box 2230

Palm Springs, CA 92263-2230

TEL: (760) 322-2930

FAX: (760) 322-4087

E-MAIL: filmfest@ix.netcom.com

WEB SITE: http://www. psfilmfest.org/eighth.htm

FESTIVAL DATE: January

ENTRY DEADLINE: November

CONTACT: Craig Prater

AWARDS: Yes

COMPETITIONS: No

MAJOR AWARDS: Charles A. Crain Desert Palm Achievement Award; International Filmmaker Award; Director's Lifetime Achievement; Frederick Loewe Achievement Award; Outstanding Achievement in Craft Award

APPLICATION FEE: $25 (shorts) $60 (features)

ODDS OF ACCEPTANCE: about 400 films entered

PEACHTREE INTERNATIONAL FILM FESTIVAL

2180 Pleasant Hill Rd #A 5221

Duluth, Georgia 30096

TEL: 770-729-8487

FAX: 770-263-0652

E-MAIL: film@peachtreefilm.org

WEB SITE: www.peachtreefilm.org

FESTIVAL DATE: Late October/ Early November

ENTRY DEADLINE: August

CONTACT: Michelle Forren

DIRECTOR: Michelle Forren

CATEGORY: International

PROFILE: The Peachtree International Film Festival is proud of the fact that we love all kinds of movies—independent and studio films alike. A great studio thriller is just as worthy of fanfare as a labor of love that somebody maxed out their credit cards to make. The bottom line is the story—do we care about the characters, and do we want to spend time with them? This can mean anything from the most outrageous cult film to the most serious documentary. We only show movies we love, because life's too short for anything else.

SEMINARS: Vary

PANELS: Visiting filmmakers are invited to join panel discussions separate from the film screenings.

FAMOUS SPEAKERS: Paul Bartel, Paul Seydor (Peckinpah scholar), Dennis D'Oros and Amy Heller from Milestone Films, Helena Bonham Carter

AWARDS: Yes

COMPETITIONS: Competition is not the main focus of the festival, although we do present Audience Awards.

MAJOR AWARDS: Best Feature

VALUE OF AWARDS: No monetary award

PAST JUDGES: Audience ballot

APPLICATION TIPS: Make a good, interesting movie with clear picture and sound, a solid story, and good acting, and submit it on time. Then don't bug us—we're busy!

APPLICATION FEE: 1997 fee was $15.

AVERAGE FILMS ENTERED: Mostly narratives, mostly contemporary, although we certainly have shown documentaries and "vault" films.

FILMS SCREENED: Approximately 30.

ODDS OF ACCEPTANCE: Many of our films are currently selected by invitation, and we reserve

about 25% of the slots for open entry submissions.

FILMMAKER PERKS: We try to offer coach airfare, 2 nights hotel, and 2 meals, but much of what we're able to offer depends upon the flexibility of the filmmaker and what our sponsors are offering that year.

TRAVEL TIPS: Atlanta is very hard to get around in without a car.

BEST RESTAURANTS: Depends on your definition of best—mine is good, fast, and cheap, and by those standards I go for the fantastic Asian and Mexican restaurants on the Buford Highway strip—Don Taco for Mexican, Pho Hoa for Vietnamese noodles, Little Szechuan for Chinese. Another favorite is R. Thomas and Son Deluxe Grill on Peachtree—fabulous wings, open 24 hours, and interesting menu. If you want tremendously exquisite and expensive, ask somebody else because I don't go there.

BEST BARS: Upscale, Tongue & Groove. Clubby, Leopard Lounge.

BEST HANGOUT FOR FILMMAKERS: Atlanta is of course famous for strip clubs, and the filmmaker's favorite is the Clermont Lounge—Lynchian ambience, and dancers that have seen "Irma Vep". Those less inclined to enjoy nudity with their relaxation have their choice of coffee houses.

BEST PLACE FOR BREAKFAST: R. Thomas & Son Deluxe Grille.

FESTIVAL TALE: The filmmakers defy all our preconceived notions of who's going to be wild and who's low-key. The to-remain-unnamed fellow who stepped off the airplane and asked "so, where do you get cocaine and girls around here" took us by surprise. Most filmmakers, for some reason, have heard of the Varsity, and that's the first thing they ask for; that's more along the lines of what we expect to hear.

> The bottom line is the story—do we care about the characters, and do we want to spend time with them? This can mean anything from the most outrageous cult film to the most serious documentary. We only show movies we love, because life's too short for anything else. (Peachtree International Film Festival)

PHILADELPHIA FESTIVAL OF WORLD CINEMA

House of Philadelphia
3701 Chestnut St.
Philadelphia, PA 19104
TEL: (215) 895-6593 or (800) 969-7392
FAX: (215) 895-6562
E-MAIL: pfwc@libertynet.org
WEB SITE: http://www.libertynet.org:80/~pfwc/
FESTIVAL DATE: April—May
CONTACT: Linda Blackaby
CATEGORY: International
COMPETITIONS: No
APPLICATION FEE: varies
ODDS OF ACCEPTANCE: Over 300 films entered

PHILADELPHIA INTERNATIONAL GAY AND LESBIAN FILM FESTIVAL

1520 Locust Street, Suite 200
Philadelphia, PA 19102
TEL: 215-790-1510 (EXT. 10)
FAX: 215-790-1501
E-MAIL: rmurray@tlavideo.com
WEB SITE: www.tlavideo.com
FESTIVAL DATE: July
ENTRY DEADLINE: April
CONTACT: Richard Wolff
DIRECTOR: Raymond Murray
PROGRAMMER: Features: Raymond Murray; Shorts: Bent Hill & Tiffany Naiman
OTHER STAFF: Festival Guide: Eric Moore; Guest Services: Tiffany Naiman
CATEGORY: Gay Lesbian
PROFILE: The Philadelphia International Gay and Lesbian Film Festival screens over 130 films, making it one of the largest gay and lesbian festivals in the country
PANELS: There are several thematic discussions at various locales in the city during the festival
FAMOUS SPEAKERS: John Waters, Clive Barker

AWARDS: Yes
COMPETITIONS: Yes
MAJOR AWARDS: Audience Award For Best Feature Film & Audience Award For Best Documentary Film
VALUE OF AWARDS: None
PAST JUDGES: Audience ballots
APPLICATION FEE: None
AVERAGE FILMS ENTERED: All types of films that either feature gay and lesbian characters prominently in the film, films directed by or starring out gays and lesbians
ODDS OF ACCEPTANCE: In regards to feature films — I usually see the films in Montreal, Toronto, Berlin or London. I track many others and request screeners from them. Very few feature films are submitted through the application process. In regards to short films and videos—hundreds are submitted for the approximately 80 slots
FILMMAKER PERKS: We offer free travel, a food stipend and lodging for the director or star.
BEST RESTAURANTS: Judy's
BEST BARS: Gay: Woody's; Lesbian: Sisters

PHILAFILM—THE PHILADELPHIA INTERNATIONAL FILM FESTIVAL

IAMPTP
215 S. Broad St.
Philadelphia, PA 19107
TEL: (215) 977-2831
FAX: (215) 546-8055
FESTIVAL DATE: July
ENTRY DEADLINE: April
DIRECTOR: Lawrence L. Smallwood Jr.
CATEGORY: International

PORTLAND INTERNATIONAL FILM FESTIVAL

1219 SW Park Ave.
Portland, Oregon 97205
TEL: (503) 221-1156
FAX: (503) 294-0874
E-MAIL: info@nwfilm.org
WEB SITE: www.nwfilm.org
FESTIVAL DATE: February
ENTRY DEADLINE: November
YEAR FESTIVAL BEGAN: 1976
CONTACT: Bill Foster
DIRECTOR: Bill Foster, Director of the Northwest Film Center
PROGRAMMER: Bill Foster
OTHER STAFF: Jenny Jones
CATEGORY: Independent, International
PROFILE: A rich snapshot of contemporary world cinema.
FAMOUS SPEAKERS: Past guests have included Martin Ritt, Steven Soderbergh, Alfonso Aru, Herzog—to name a few.
AWARDS: Yes
COMPETITIONS: Yes
MAJOR AWARDS: Blockbuster Audience Award, New Director Award, Best Short Film
VALUE OF AWARDS: No monetary value—audience chooses
LAST WINNING FILMS: *The Perfect Circle* (Bosnia); New Director: Ademir Kenovic; Best Short Film: *Canhea.*
APPLICATION FEE: None, but $10 for return shipping costs per entry ($15 for Canadian residents)
INSIDER ADVICE: Make sure your contact information is clearly marked on your preview tape, your supporting materials (synopsis, bio, etc.) are concise and well-written and DON'T FORGET to make black-white stills while in production. None of this has any bearing on whether or not your work will be accepted, but if it is, having these things will help the Festival promote your work more effectively.

AVERAGE FILMS ENTERED: There are no predetermined categories, expectations or assumptions. All independent work is considered regardless of length, genre, format. The Portland International Film Festival is largely invitational.

ODDS OF ACCEPTANCE: Again, the Festival is largely invitational. We received 500 unsolicited films, approximately 20 of those were screened.

FILMMAKER PERKS: Sometimes free travel and accomodations are available.

TOURIST INFORMATION: Great outdoors: coast and mountains are each an hour away. Powell's Books, microbreweries.

TRAVEL TIPS: Bring an umbrella.

BEST RESTAURANTS: Zefiro, Dots, Saucebox

BEST BARS: Ringler's Annex or Saucebox

BEST HANGOUT FOR FILMMAKERS: San Francisco

Best BEST PLACE FOR BREAKFAST: Shaker's Cafe, Laurelthirst

PXL THIS VIDEO

2427 1/2 Glyndon Ave.
Venice, CA 90291
TEL: (310) 306-7330
FESTIVAL DATE: August
ENTRY DEADLINE: August
CONTACT: Gerry Fialka
CATEGORY: Underground, Weird

REEL AFFIRMATIONS FILM FESTIVAL

P.O. Box 73528
Washington, D.C. 20056
TEL: (202) 986-1119
Festival director's line: (202) 328-8653
FAX: (202) 319-1158
Festival director's fax: (202) 328-0786
E-MAIL: oi10@aol.com
WEB SITE: http://members.aol.com/oi10/index.html
FESTIVAL DATE: October
ENTRY DEADLINE: May
CONTACT: Matthew Cibellis

DIRECTOR: Matthew Cibellis
PROGRAMMER: Alexa Maros, Cynthia Casas, Larry Tsai, Jose Gabilondo, Kimberley Rush, Matthew Cibellis
OTHER STAFF: Alexa Maros, President; Mark Betchkal, Development Director; Bill Kirkner, Marketing Director; Rick Rose, Publications Director and Public Relations Chair
CATEGORY: Gay Lesbian, Independent
AWARDS: Yes

COMPETITIONS: Yes We award the Director's awards (a programming team jury award) and Audience awards every year for Best Feature, Best Short, Best Documentary, Best Mini-Documentary, and Best Animated

VALUE OF AWARDS: $1000 Work in Progress Grant for Excellence in Filmmaking

LAST WINNING DIRECTORS: John Greyson, Jeanette Buck

APPLICATION TIPS: Everything depends on technical and editorial quality of film, engrossing subject matter of film, and especially for shorts, the ability to marry the short to other shorts as submitted.

APPLICATION FEE: $10

INSIDER ADVICE: Start here, New York, Los Angeles, San Francisco cannot address your individual needs and give you the kind of attention we can because our SIZE affords us the opportunity to be completely filmmaker-oriented.

ODDS OF ACCEPTANCE: We received over 350 films and showed 118 films. Now, not all of those shown came from submitted films. We did show about 40 films which we hunted down

FILMMAKER PERKS: We provide feature filmmakers and the director's award winners free travel, lodging, etc. As we grow in size, we hope to have the sponsors to provide travel and lodging for all filmmakers. We have two Hospitality Coordinators who will work out the de-

tails of your travel, hotel accomodations and travel to and from venues for you.

TRAVEL TIPS: If you're coming from NYC, take Peter Pan or Trailways—it's less used than Amtrak and never has those irritating, excruciating delays out of Penn Station.

BEST RESTAURANTS: This is Washington. That answer varies with the season. Best Chinese: City Lights of China. Best New American: Nora's or the Old Tabard Inn. Best Lunch: Luna Grill or Teaism. Best Italian: Goldoni's

BEST BARS: Are you gay or are you other? It varies! Probably Cobalt or JRs, for our crowd. Slyde is very popular with the women and that's where the women filmmakers are.

BEST HANGOUT FOR FILMMAKERS: JRs and Slyde

BEST PLACE FOR BREAKFAST: Luna Grill

REJECT FILMFEST

"Deliciously twisted"
—*Philadelphia Inquirer*

1124 Walnut Street, Suite 4
Philadelphia, PA 19107
TEL: (215) 574-0911
FAX: (215) 238-0663
E-MAIL: RejectFest@aol.com
WEB SITE: www.rejectfilmfest.org
FESTIVAL DATE: Mid October
ENTRY DEADLINE: September
YEAR FESTIVAL BEGAN: 1997
CONTACT: Don or Virginia Mason
DIRECTOR: D. Mason Bendewald, Don Argott and Virginia Leahy
CATEGORY: Independent, Weird
PROFILE: "The Reject FilmFest showcases rejected films, not bad ones," said Reject FilmFest Co-Founder and Executive Producer D. Mason Bendewald. "This is the festival for films that push the envelope on various levels, and do not fit into the neat categories that other festivals assign."

Serving as an outlet for innovative filmmaking, the Reject FilmFest serves up the best in what Hollywood is ignoring. It enables independent filmmakers to triumph in the face of rejection and, at the same time, to have their work viewed and evaluated by an audience who appreciates great, and too often overlooked, filmmaking.

While the Reject FilmFest has a definite edge (one of its t-shirt slogans is "FUCK L.A.," after all), its producers understand the contribution they are making to the pool of quality independent film. Since its humble beginnings, film and video artists have come to consider the Reject FilmFest as a unique opportunity to present their work before an audience. The festival is gaining prominence among film lovers and the entertainment industry alike as a source of new talent, and as a champion of films that expand the boundaries of the art of filmmaking.

PANELS: Panels from indie professionals

FAMOUS SPEAKERS: John Waters

AWARDS: Yes

COMPETITIONS: Yes

MAJOR AWARDS: The Rejjy

APPLICATION FEE: $15 to $20

AVERAGE FILMS ENTERED: Films outside the mainstream

FILMS SCREENED: 60

ODDS OF ACCEPTANCE: 300 are submitted / 60 are accepted

TOURIST INFORMATION: The Liberty Bell, Independence Mall, Art Museum

BEST BARS: Moriarity's

BEST HANGOUT FOR FILMMAKERS: Dirty Franks or the Last Drop

BEST PLACE FOR BREAKFAST: Blue in Green

RESFEST DiGiTAL FiLM FESTiVAL

109 Minna Street, Suite 390 San Francisco, CA 94105

TEL: (415) 437-2686

FAX: (415) 437-2687

E-MAIL: resfest@resfest.com

ENTRY DEADLINE: None. Accepts entries year-round.

YEAR FESTIVAL BEGAN: 1997

DIRECTOR: Jonathan Wells

PROFILE: ResFest is a touring festival dedicated to the exhibition and promotion of digital filmmaking. We showcase innovative short films that have been empowered by new digital production tools. Entries can be shot on any acquisition format (film, analog/digital video, CGI etc.), but must make use of computer editing and/or effects software. ResFest only exhibits videotape, with the exception of 35mm features, CD-ROMs and DVDs.

APPLICATION FEE: $15—$20

RHODE iSLAND iNTERNATiONAL FiLM FESTiVAL

P.O. Box 162

Newport , RI 02840-0002

TEL: (401) 847-7590

FAX: (401) 847-7590

E-MAIL: flicksart@aol.com

WEB SITE: http:// www.eatinri.com/flickers

FESTIVAL DATE: August

ENTRY DEADLINE: June

CONTACT: Elaine MacLean—Marketing; Nancy Nicholson—Development

DIRECTOR: George T. Marshall

PROGRAMMER: Louise R. Champigny; Julien Bessette; Michel Coutu

OTHER STAFF: Trudy Rhéaume, Christian de Rezendes, Roger Petit, Francis Lanctot, Thomas

> It enables independent filmmakers to triumph in the face of rejection and, at the same time, to have their work viewed and evaluated by an audience who appreciates great, and too often overlooked, filmmaking. (Reject Filmfest)

10 QUICK STEPS TO CREATiNG YOUR OWN FiLM FESTiVAL

1. Find a niche. Who needs another "independent film festival." My all-time favorite is the "Short Attention Span Film and Video Festival."
2. Create a cool website. This will give you great visibility, help gather film submissions from all over and costs very little.
3. Pick an interesting venue and a date far enough in advance to do all the hard work ahead of you.
4. Search out exceptional films that support the mission of your festival. Film and Art schools are good places to look for interesting work from new filmmakers.
6. Promote, promote, promote! Hit the colleges, cafes and record stores in your area with intriguing flyers.
7. Write a clever press release and unleash it on the local media.
8. Gather your friends and other volunteers (who liked your flyers so much they called you up) and run through the gameplan for the event night.
9. Welcome attendees to your festival either at the door or in a brief introduction.
10. Savor the moment, the actual event is over much too quickly for the amount of time poured into it. The day after the festival go back to step 3 and start again.

— Jonathan Wells, Festival Director, ResFest Digital Film Festival

Carrier, Albert Klyberg, Raymond Bacon, Dennis M. Lyden, George Costa, & Daniel R. Peloquin; Interns: Katie J. Martelly, Cherolyn Denomme

CATEGORY: Independent

PROFILE: The Rhode Island International Film Festival is dedicated to the creation of opportunities for artistic interaction and exchange while bridging the gap between the established entertainment industry and the global creative community. Its goal is to recognize achievement and innovation in a variety of filmmaking and storytelling disciplines while providing an opportunity to secure wider distribution. The Festival's vision is to foster contact among film directors, producers, distributors, backers and the film-going community. Because of its unique geographic location and cultural-heritage linkages, one of the chief aims of the Festival is the encouragement of an artistic exchange between filmmakers from the New England region and the Canadian provinces.

SEMINARS: Yes including screenwriting, Getting your script optioned, Film music, film financing, theme oriented (such as global marketing of films from the Province of Québec.)

PANELS: Yes, composed of filmmakers, scholars, critics and industry professionals

FAMOUS SPEAKERS: Yes, though "famous" is a relative term. Bobby Farrelly, Elaine Lorillard, Cheslaw Kyanka.

AWARDS: Yes

COMPETITIONS: Yes

MAJOR AWARDS: Flickers Best Feature; Flickers Best Short

VALUE OF AWARDS: $500 with $1000 in goods/services

APPLICATION TIPS: Be honest and concise. Share your vision with our judging panel.

APPLICATION FEE: $25 for video or short subjects (under 30 min.); $45 for feature films and feature documentaries

AVERAGE FILMS ENTERED: We have an open call—all genres

FILMS SCREENED: 60 Titles, counting shorts, features and documentaries

ODDS OF ACCEPTANCE: We welcome subtitles since we have a large bi-lingual population. About 25% are subtitled, about 20% are accepted.

FILMMAKER PERKS: This is an evolving situation. As our financial base stabilizes, perks will increase. At this point, we offer meals, limited travel, lots on contacts, a media oportunity, some lodging. Depending on the financial circumstances of the artist involved, we have offered mini-grants to be able to attend. We also have a "Discover Rhode Island" bus from Conway Tours that takes folks to the area beaches, seafood restaurants, and Newport mansions.

TRAVEL TIPS: The Film Festival takes place in the historic Blackstone Valley, the seat of American industrialization. Many of the river towns are being restored and the Blackstone River itself has been cleaned up. This is a great area for backpacking, hikes, kayaking and day trips. Contact the Blackstone Valley Tourism Council, 171 Main Street, Pawtucket, R.I. 02895, (401) 724-2200 for a complete packet of information.

BEST RESTAURANTS: Gian Carlo

BEST BARS: Ciros

BEST HANGOUT FOR FILMMAKERS: Chans Fine Oriental Dining

BEST PLACE FOR BREAKFAST: Heritage Coffee House (real local)

MISCELLANEOUS: Our Festival is very laid back and personal. We have a whole army of volunteers who love to chat, trade stories, talk shop. The folks in Woonsocket are used to taking people at face value and don't get too riled up or excited about celebrities. They'll quickly adopt you as one of the community. They are very proud about what they've accomplished from the ongoing restoration of the Stadium Theatre to the Film Festival itself. Don't be surprised if you get a guided tour of the facility by the former Mayor of the City or shown the projection room by the owner of the local radio station. Woonsocket is a totally cool city with great people.

ROCHESTER INTERNATIONAL INDEPENDENT FILM FESTIVAL

Box 17746
Rochester, NY 14617
TEL: (716) 288-5607
FESTIVAL DATE: May
ENTRY DEADLINE: March
CONTACT: Josephine Perini
CATEGORY: Independent, International

SAGUARO FILM FESTIVAL

5645 N 7th Dr.
Glendale, AZ 85303
TEL: (602) 970-8711
FAX: (602) 423-0696
FESTIVAL DATE: April-May
ENTRY DEADLINE: March
CONTACT: Durrie Parks

SAN DIEGO INTERNATIONAL FILM FESTIVAL

Dept. 0078, UEO, UCSD
9500 Gilman Drive
La Jolla, CA 92093-0078
TEL: (619) 534-0497
FAX: (619) 534-7665
E-MAIL: rbaily@ucsd.edu
WEB SITE: http://ueo.ucsd.edu
FESTIVAL DATE: February to June
ENTRY DEADLINE: November
YEAR FESTIVAL BEGAN: 1984
CONTACT: Ruth Baily, Elaine Lea-Chou
DIRECTOR: Ruth Baily
PROGRAMMER: Ruth Baily, Elaine Lea-Chou, Melinda Go, Alain Cohen

Share your vision with our judging panel. (Rhode Island International Film Festival)

OTHER STAFF: Fred Smith, Judi Griffith, Mike Garcia. Many Volunteers

CATEGORY: Animation, Independent, International, We present premieres of major foreign films, but we are also very interested in independent and foreign films that have not been optioned for American distribution. We have one night dedicated to Short Films and another to Animation.

PROFILE: To bring the best of all forms of contemporary filmmaking to San Diego. Successful realization of a distinctive personal vision is important. SDIFF is a relaxed, friendly festival. Very high standards but no "airs." We are particularly proud of our reputation for presenting on of the best Short Night on the Festival circuit; an Animation Celebration we have been told equals or surpasses Mike and Spike's; and a selection of great international films that are often not optioned by US distributors.

SEMINARS: We are just developing this program. In the past, they have been hit or miss depending on the time a specific guest had available.

PANELS: See Above

FAMOUS SPEAKERS: Michael Apted, Robert Rodriguez, George Hickenlooper, Michael York, Vincent Price, Graham Chapman, Gene Wilder

AWARDS: Yes

COMPETITIONS: Yes

MAJOR AWARDS: Patron's Award for Best Film

Festival Award for Best Film

VALUE OF AWARDS: Crystal Trophies; Best Short film includes a $500 cash prize

LAST WINNING DIRECTORS: Luis Armando Roche (Venezuela); Sergei Bodrov (Russia)

PAST JUDGES: Anonymous (Mix of festival personnel, local critics, film scholars)

APPLICATION TIPS: No tricks. Just send your best work. A balance of substance and style is always good.

> Slickness, pretention, "attitude" don't carry much weight. Sensitivity, substance, wit, humor, knowing that a movie is more than a bunch of images on film helps. (San Diego International Film Festival)

APPLICATION FEE: $30

INSIDER ADVICE: Slickness, pretention, "attitude" don't carry much weight. Sensitivity, substance, wit, humor, knowing that a movie is more than a bunch of images on film helps. Don't imitate other filmmakers.

AVERAGE FILMS ENTERED: Our process is subjective. No check list. A film, regardless of genre, works or doesn't work.

FILMS SCREENED: See above. Number varies year to year.

ODDS OF ACCEPTANCE: About 350 submissions. We accepted about 26 features, 17 Short Films, approx 20 Animated Shorts

FILMMAKER PERKS: Domestic airfare, lodging, meals.

TRAVEL TIPS: Suncreen. The Wild Animal Park is better than the Zoo if you have to choose.

BEST RESTAURANTS: Kemosabe

BEST BARS: Cafe Japengo

BEST HANGOUT FOR FILMMAKERS: Pannikin in La Jolla

BEST PLACE FOR BREAKFAST: Mission Beach Cafe

FESTIVAL TALE: At one screening, a silent Orville Redenbacher (a victim of many strokes apparently) was being steered through the crowd by a nurse as he handed out little white cards that read "I met Orville Redenbacher." A completely surreal evening was had by all.

SAN FRANCISCO BI FILM FESTIVAL

1803 Ninth Ave.
San Francisco, CA 94122
TEL: 415-665-5645
E-MAIL: jtpasty@sirius.com
WEB SITE: www.sirius.com/~jtpasty/bipride
FESTIVAL DATE: July
ENTRY DEADLINE: May
YEAR FESTIVAL BEGAN: 1997
DIRECTOR: Jeff Ross
PROGRAMMER: Jeff Ross
CATEGORY: Gay Lesbian, Independent

PROFILE: To show films and videos that explore the ambiguity of sexual attraction and orientation.

APPLICATION TIPS: Please submit films with Bi themes, not just Gay or Lesbian.

APPLICATION FEE: None

FILMS SCREENED: 12-20

SAN FRANCISCO INDIEFEST

1803 Ninth Ave.
San Francisco, CA 94122
TEL: 415-665-5645
E-MAIL: jtpasty@sirius.com
WEB SITE: www.sirius.com/~jtpasty/indie
FESTIVAL DATE: January
ENTRY DEADLINE: October
YEAR FESTIVAL BEGAN: 1999
DIRECTOR: Jeff Ross
PROGRAMMER: Doug Jones
OTHER STAFF: Becky Mertens, Joanne Parsont, Eric Singer, Jane Pavis
CATEGORY: Independent
PROFILE: To introduce Bay Area audiences to the best in independent film and video.
APPLICATION FEE: None
FILMS SCREENED: 12-20

SAN FRANCISCO INTERNATIONAL ASIAN FILM FESTIVAL

346 Ninth St., 2nd Floor
San Francisco, CA 94103
TEL: (415) 863-0814
FAX: (415) 863-7428
WEB SITE: http://www.dnai.com/~abenamer/naata/~naata.html
FESTIVAL DATE: March
ENTRY DEADLINE: October
CONTACT: Paul Mayeda Berges
CATEGORY: Ethnic Asian, International

SAN FRANCISCO INTERNATIONAL FILM FESTIVAL

San Francisco Film Society
1521 Eddy St.
San Francisco, CA 94115
TEL: (415) 929-5000
FAX: (415) 921-5032
E-MAIL: sfiff@sfiff.org
WEB SITE: http://www.sfiff.org/
FESTIVAL DATE: April
ENTRY DEADLINE: December
CONTACT: Brian Gordon
DIRECTOR: Peter Scarlet, Executive Director
CATEGORY: Independent, International
PROFILE: This festival is sponsored by the San Francisco Film Society. The goal of the festival is to spark appreciation for film and video. Approximately 70,000 attend.
AWARDS: Yes
COMPETITIONS: Yes
MAJOR AWARDS: The Golden Gate Awards. There is also an invitational, non-competitive section.
PAST JUDGES: Jury composed of Bay Area media professionals.
APPLICATION FEE: None
ODDS OF ACCEPTANCE: Over 100 films entered

SAN FRANCISCO JEWISH FILM FESTIVAL

346 Ninth Street
San Francisco, CA 94103
TEL: (415) 621-0556 or (510) 548-0556
FAX: (510) 548-0536
E-MAIL: jewishfilm@aol.com
FESTIVAL DATE: July-August
ENTRY DEADLINE: April
DIRECTOR: Janis Plotkin
CATEGORY: Ethnic Jewish

SAN FRANCISCO LESBIAN AND GAY FILM FESTIVAL

Frameline
346 9th St.
San Francisco, CA 94103
TEL: (415) 703-8650
FAX: (415) 861-1404
E-MAIL: info@frameline.org
WEB SITE: http://www.frameline.org/
FESTIVAL DATE: June
ENTRY DEADLINE: February
CONTACT: Mark Finch
CATEGORY: Gay Lesbian, Independent
PROFILE: This diverse festival celebrates lesbian and gay filmmaking. The last day of the festival is always on San Francisco's annual Gay Pride day. Over 53,000 attend.
AWARDS: No
COMPETITIONS: No
APPLICATION FEE: $10 ($20-35 late)
ODDS OF ACCEPTANCE: 550 received and 200 are chosen to be in the festival

SANTA BARBARA INTERNATIONAL FILM FESTIVAL (SBiFF)

1216 State St. #710
Santa Barbara, CA 93101
TEL: (805) 963-0023
FAX: (805) 962-2524
E-MAIL: sbiff@west.net
WEB SITE: http://west.net/~sbiff/
FESTIVAL DATE: March
ENTRY DEADLINE: December
YEAR FESTIVAL BEGAN: 1986
CONTACT: Diane M. Durst
CATEGORY: Documentary, Independent, International, Short, Video
PROFILE: This festival is an 11 day event which focuses on independent films, videos, shorts and documentaries. 32,000 attend annually.
AWARDS: Yes
COMPETITIONS: Yes

MAJOR AWARDS: Best U.S. Feature; Best Foreign Feature; Best Director; Best Documentary Feature and Short; Best Live Action Short; Award for Artistic Excellence; Best Santa Barbara Filmmaker; Audience Choice Award
APPLICATION FEE: $40 (U.S.) $45 (International)
FILMS SCREENED: 125

SEATTLE INTERNATIONAL FILM FESTIVAL (SIFF)

See "The Top Ten Film Festivals" on page 156

SEATTLE LESBIAN & GAY FILM FESTIVAL

1122 E. Pike St., #1313
Seattle, WA 98122
TEL: (206) 323-4247
FAX: (206) 323-4275
E-MAIL: filmfest@drizzle.com
WEB SITE: www.drizzle.com/~filmfest
FESTIVAL DATE: October
ENTRY DEADLINE: July 1, 1999
YEAR FESTIVAL BEGAN: 1996
DIRECTOR: Justine Barda
PROGRAMMER: Kirsten Shaffer
PROFILE: A week-long international film and video festival
PANELS: Yes
APPLICATION FEE: $10.00
AVERAGE FILMS ENTERED: 150+
FILMS SCREENED: 70
FILMMAKER PERKS: Airfare, accomodations, meals, gratitude
ATTENDANCE: 5,000

SEDONA INTERNATIONAL FILM FESTIVAL

PO Box 2515
Sedona, Arizona 86339
TEL: (520) 282-0747 or 1-800-780-ARTS
FAX: (520) 282-5358
E-MAIL: scp@sedona.net
WEB SITE: www.sedona.net.scp
FESTIVAL DATE: March

ENTRY DEADLINE: January

YEAR FESTIVAL BEGAN: 1995

CONTACT: Nadia Caillou

DIRECTOR: Daniel Schay

PROGRAMMER: Daniel Schay

CATEGORY: Independent, International

PROFILE: The Sedona International Film Festival, a program of Sedona Cultural Park, seeks to celebrate independent filmmaking from around the world, in one of the world's most beautiful settings. It also celebrates Sedona's heritage as a filmmaking location and status as second home to many distinuished industry professionals as it examines, through its Filmmaking Workshop, aspects of the creative processes of cinema.

SEMINARS: The Sedona Filmmaking Workshop.

PANELS: Round-tables on dramatic feature and documentary production.

FAMOUS SPEAKERS: Walter Murch, Thelma Schoonmaker, John Burnett, Richard Harris, Richard Chew.

AWARDS: Yes. Festival Favorite in Dramatic, Documentary, and Short categories.

COMPETITIONS: Yes

MAJOR AWARDS: Festival Favorite

VALUE OF AWARDS: None

LAST WINNING FILMS: *Archibald, The Rainbow Painter* (1998)

LAST WINNING DIRECTORS: Les Landau

APPLICATION TIPS: Submit early

APPLICATION FEE: $50 feature, $40 documentary, $35 shorts.

INSIDER ADVICE: Tell us everything you can—provide the interesting angles for pr.

AVERAGE FILMS ENTERED: We have no particular stylistic/topical bent. We look for quality, variety of expression. It is fair to say we are less interested in the Next Big Thing or the Absolute Cutting Edge for its own sake than we are Good Cinema, whether premiere or not, American or not, Dramatic or Doc.

FILMS SCREENED: 29 in 1997, 39 (including shorts) in 1998.

ODDS OF ACCEPTANCE: Over 300 submitted, approximately 30 accepted. Please note: Number of submissions has doubled each year of our existence!

FILMMAKER PERKS: Stipend towards travel, free lodging in Sedona, one of the world's most beautiful places.

TOURIST INFORMATION: Sedona is a well-established tourist destination, with scenery, shopping, galleries, hiking, mountain biking etc.

TRAVEL TIPS: Fly to Phoenix, rent a car, travel during daylight, because the trip north [2 hours] is a remarkable journey through 2500 feet of altitude and four ecological zones, from desert to mountains.

BEST RESTAURANTS: Too many to choose from. Fancy: Heartline Cafe. Trattoria: Troia's

BEST BARS: Shugrues for quiet drinks. Dylan's for dancing.

BEST HANGOUT FOR FILMMAKERS: Festival Gala Friday night, Director's Party Saturday. Also, see "Bars" above.

BEST PLACE FOR BREAKFAST: Cafe & Salad, Safeway Center. "You need Tabasco with those eggs, hon?"

SHORT ATTENTION SPAN FILM AND VIDEO FESTIVAL (SASFVF)

P. O. Box 460316

San Francisco, CA 94146

TEL: (415) 282-4316; (831) 429-6925; (415) 206-1922

E-MAIL: sasfvf@aol.com

WEB SITE: http://www.sirius.com/~sstark/org/fests/sasfvf.html

FESTIVAL DATE: September

ENTRY DEADLINE: August

CONTACT: Elizabeth Hall / Sarah Anderson

CATEGORY: Animation, Underground, Weird, Video

PROFILE: Over 2,000 attend.

AWARDS: Yes

COMPETITIONS: No

MAJOR AWARDS: Viewers' Choice Awards

VALUE OF AWARDS: Receive subscriptions to MovieMaker Magazine, Film Threat Magazine, video compliation tapes, and a festival t-shirt.

APPLICATION FEE: $5

FILMS SCREENED: 60 screened

ODDS OF ACCEPTANCE: 150 entered

SILVER IMAGES FILM FESTIVAL

Terra Nova Films

9848 South Winchester

Chicago, IL 60643

TEL: (773) 881-6940

FAX: (773) 881-3368

FESTIVAL DATE: April

ENTRY DEADLINE: December

CONTACT: Martha Foster

CATEGORY: Senior Citizen

SINKING CREEK FILM AND VIDEO FESTIVAL

Vanderbilt University

402 Saratt Student Center

Nashville, TN 37240

TEL: (615) 322-4234

FAX: (615) 343-8081

FESTIVAL DATE: November

ENTRY DEADLINE: May

CONTACT: Meryl Truett

APPLICATION FEE: $25—$55

SLAMDANCE INTERNATIONAL FILM FESTIVAL

See "The Top Ten Film Festivals" on page 156

SMALL PICTURES INDEPENDENT FILM FESTIVAL (SPiFF)

P.O. Box 18447

Beverly Hills, CA 90209

TEL: (310) 558-6691

E-MAIL: info@spiffest.com

WEB SITE: www.spiffest.com

FESTIVAL DATE: November

ENTRY DEADLINE: August, late entries by October.

Fly to Phoenix, rent a car, travel during daylight, because the trip north [2 hours] is a remarkable journey through 2500 feet of altitude and four ecological zones, from desert to mountains. (Sedona International Film Festival)

Year Festival Began: 1996

Director: Joy Kennelly

Category: Digital, Independent, Short, Underground, Weird, Video

Profile: Short Pictures International Film Festival (SPIFF) is an international film festival hosted by a comedic Mistress/Master of Ceremonies featuring shorts, animation, documentaries, spec. commercials (all 15 min. or less) showcasing the short film genre and benefitting disadvantaged children around the world. Each year a different charity is selected. Last year's beneficiaries were Irish children's charities recommended by the American Ireland Fund. This year's benefit will support inner city children here in the United States.

The festival was launched in 1996 by Kennelly as an in-house event at Sony Pictures Imageworks. A portion of SPIFF's proceeds each year are earmarked for either domestic or international children's charities.

Panels: In addition to cutting-edge workshops, seminars and lectures, the festival's scheduled events include Digital Underground Inc. (DUI), the Spector Anime Club, the Young It Up program, and a Truman Capote-style Black & White Ball.

Awards: Yes

Past Judges: Actor David O'Hara, WIF Board Member/Director Nancy Malone, Billy Gaff, Ann Monn and Suzy Brown.

Application Fee: $35, $55 for late entries.

Insider Advice: Executive Director, Joy A. Kennelly ran a toy drive for Hungarian Orphan children for 4 years prior to starting SPIFF. It is her desire that this tradition continue with SPIFF and different charities will be selected to benefit each year, one year international, one year domestic.

SOUTH BY SOUTHWEST FiLM FESTiVAL (SXSW)

See "The Top Ten Film Festivals" on page 156

SUNDANCE FiLM FESTiVAL

See "The Top Ten Film Festivals" on page 156

TAOS TALKiNG PiCTURES FESTiVAL

See "The Top Ten Film Festivals" on page 156

TELLURiDE FiLM FESTiVAL

See "The Top Ten Film Festivals" on page 156

Dress warm, Park City gets cold in January.

TEXAS FILM FESTIVAL

MSC Film Society
Memorial Student Center,
Box J-1
College Station, TX 77841
TEL: (409) 845-1515
FAX: (409) 845-5117
E-MAIL: caj2960@unix.
tamu.edu
WEB SITE: http://wwwmsc.
tamu.edu/MSC/FilmSociety/
Festival
FESTIVAL DATE: February
ENTRY DEADLINE: November
YEAR FESTIVAL BEGAN: 1992
CONTACT: Carol Jackson or
Penny Ditton
DIRECTOR: Carol Jackson
PROGRAMMER: Penny Ditton,
Carol Jackson, and Jimmy
Severino

OTHER STAFF: Beverly Anserson,
Jennifer Morgan, David
Lieberman, Andrea Bragdon,
Paul Breaux, Dana Dittlinger,
Steven Livingston, Alan Lobo,
Brent Candler, and Sarah
Forbey
CATEGORY: Independent
PROFILE: To promote film as an
art medium. Our focus is on
education rather than securing
distribution. The mission of the
Texas Film Festival is to cel-
ebrate the vision and enterprise
of America's finest contempo-
rary independent filmmakers.
SEMINARS: Last year we had a
music in video, an ethnicity in
video, and a Tarentino work-
shop.
PANELS: none
FAMOUS SPEAKERS: In previous
years Spike Lee, Oliver Stone,
John Waters, and John Landis
have come to speak at the Texas
Film Festival.
AWARDS: No
COMPETITIONS: No
APPLICATION TIPS: Get your entry in early so a hasty decision
is not made at the last minute.
APPLICATION FEE: $10 longer
than 45 minutes, $5 shorter
than 45 minutes, $15 additional
charge for films postmarked
after deadline.

INSIDER ADVICE: Make something you like and would be
proud of.
AVERAGE FILMS ENTERED: We generally accept films with content,
a uniqueness all their own, and
independent film that don't follow mainstream models.
FILMS SCREENED: All of the films
submitted are screened by the
Director and Vice-Director of
the Festival and around 100 are
screened by officers and general
committee members of the
MSC Film Society.
ODDS OF ACCEPTANCE: 150 films
were submitted last year, features and shorts combined. Of
those films 8 features and 20
shorts were accepted. We show
all the films we accept. This year
we will be accepting additional
films to show in our video
screening room.
FILMMAKER PERKS: We provide
travel, food, and lodging for our
feature filmmakers.

THAW VIDEO, FILM, AND DIGITAL MEDIA FESTIVAL

University of Iowa
Iowa City, IA
E-MAIL: joerhall@aol.com
WEB SITE: http://www.
uiowa.edu/~thaw
CATEGORY: Digital, Student,
Video
PROFILE: The Thaw festival of
independent film, video, and
digital media began in the
spring of 1996 in an effort to
promote emerging, independent productions which challenge the conventional language of their media through
innovation in both form and
content.

Thaw is organized by and for
media artists who understand
artistic exploration is never
bound to a single medium.
From the start, the festival has
recognized the expansion of the
moving image into the digital
realm. Thaw celebrates the
interpermeability of media by
presenting video art, indepen-

dent film, CD-ROMs and web
sites together in the context of
a single festival, revealing the
independent spirit of the moving image.

TORONTO INTERNATIONAL FILM FESTIVAL

See "The Top Ten Film Festivals" on page 156

TWO RIVERS NATIVE FILM AND VIDEO FESTIVAL

The Native Arts Circle
1443 E Franklin Ave., Suite 7D
Minneapolis, MN 55404
TEL: (612) 825-5602
FAX: (612) 870-9327
FESTIVAL DATE: November
ENTRY DEADLINE: October
CONTACT: Juanita Espinosa
CATEGORY: Ethnic Other

U. S. OUTDOOR TRAVEL FILM FESTIVAL

Michigan Outdoor Writers'
Association
c/o AAA Michigan
1 Auto Club Dr.
Dearborn, MI 48126
TEL: (313) 336-1503
FAX: (313) 336-1344
FESTIVAL DATE: December
ENTRY DEADLINE: December
CONTACT: Bill Semion

UFVA STUDENT FILM AND VIDEO FESTIVAL

Dept. of Radio-TV-Film
Temple University
Philadelphia, PA 19122
TEL: (215) 923-3532
FAX: (215) 204-5280
WEB SITE: http://
www.temple.edu/~dkluft
FESTIVAL DATE: August
ENTRY DEADLINE: May
CONTACT: Dave Kluft
CATEGORY: Student

UNiTED STATES SUPER 8 FiLM/ViDEO FESTiVAL

c/o Rutgers Film Co-op/NJ Media Arts Center
131 George St. Rutgers University
New Brunswick, NJ 08901
TEL: 732-932-8482
FAX: 732-932-1935
E-MAIL: NJMAC@aol.com
WEB SITE: www.rci.rutgers.edu/~nigrin
FESTIVAL DATE: February
ENTRY DEADLINE: January
CONTACT: A. G. Nigrin
DIRECTOR: A. G. Nigrin
PROGRAMMER: Programming Jury
OTHER STAFF: Jason Currie, Irene Fizer, Ken Orban
CATEGORY: Genre/8mm film/video
PROFILE: The Festival encourages any genre (animation, documentary, experimental, fiction, personal, etc.), but the work must have predominantly originated on Super 8mm film or 8mm video. All works will be screened by a panel of judges who will award $1200 in cash and prizes. The Festival takes as its mandate the spreading of the 8mm word. Toward that end, the Rutgers Film Co-op/NJMAC has sponsored four touring programs culled from Super 8 Festival prize winners for the past four years.
SEMINARS: Yes
PANELS: Yes
FAMOUS SPEAKERS: Martin Scorsese, Paul Morissey, Jem Cohen, Michel Negroponte, Toni Treadway, etc.
AWARDS: Yes, $1,200 in cash and prizes.
COMPETITIONS: Yes
MAJOR AWARDS: 6 Best of Categories and Audience Choice Prize
VALUE OF AWARDS: Best Animation=$150 of Super 8 film and $50 cash; Best Comedy=$150 of Super 8 film and $50 cash; Best Documentary=$150 of Super 8 film and $50 cash; Best Experimental=Tie=$75 of Super 8 film and $25 cash; Best Narrative=$150 of Super 8 film and $50 cash; Best Special Effects=$150 of Super 8 film; Audience Choice Prize=$50 of Super 8 film
APPLICATION TIPS: Pray
APPLICATION FEE: $35
INSIDER ADVICE: Follow entry proceedures
AVERAGE FILMS ENTERED: All films
FILMS SCREENED: 19
ODDS OF ACCEPTANCE: 160 accepted
FILMMAKER PERKS: Exhibition, reduced rate at beautiful Hyatt Regency Hotel in NB, distribution poss., etc.
TRAVEL TIPS: We are 3 minutes walking distance from Train and Bus Stations, 1/2 hour from Newark airport and 45 min from New York City
BEST RESTAURANTS: Too many... Old Bay (Cajun), Makeeda (Ethiopian), Sapporo (Japanese), Theresa's
BEST BARS: See above
BEST HANGOUT FOR FILMMAKERS: See Above
BEST PLACE FOR BREAKFAST: Bagel Dish cafe, Highland Park, NJ

UNiVERSiTY OF OREGON QUEER FiLM FESTiVAL

EMU Suite 2,
University of Oregon
Eugene, Oregon 97403
TEL: (541) 346-4000
FAX: (541) 346-4400
E-MAIL: qff@darkwing.uoregon.edu
WEB SITE: http://www.darkwing.uoregon.edu/~qff/
FESTIVAL DATE: February
ENTRY DEADLINE: November
CONTACT: Debby Martin, (541) 346-4375
dmartin@oregon.uoregon.edu
CATEGORY: Gay Lesbian
PROFILE: With a combination of feature and short films, the UO Queer Film Festival brings the newest queer film to the Eugene community with a wide open selection process run entirely by student coordinators. Started in 1993, the heart of the festival is the short film competition.
SEMINARS: Occasional presentations by grad students.
FAMOUS SPEAKERS: Diane Bonder, Debra Chasnoff, Catherine Saafield
AWARDS: Yes
COMPETITIONS: Yes
MAJOR AWARDS: Jury's Choice
VALUE OF AWARDS: $600 awarded each year
LAST WINNING FILMS: Beauty Before Age
LAST WINNING DIRECTORS: Johnny Symons
PAST JUDGES: UO students and faculty
APPLICATION TIPS: Queer oriented, 45 minutes or less
APPLICATION FEE: None
INSIDER ADVICE: This is a wide open competition, created to encourage a broad range of short films.
AVERAGE FILMS ENTERED: queer subject matter
ODDS OF ACCEPTANCE: 45-60 films submitted, 10-16 screened

US iNTERNATiONAL FiLM & ViDEO FESTiVAL

United States Festivals Assoc.
841 N. Addison Ave.
Elmhurst, IL 60126-1291
TEL: (630) 834-773
FAX: (630) 834-5565
FESTIVAL DATE: June
ENTRY DEADLINE: March
DIRECTOR: J.W. Anderson
CATEGORY: Video
APPLICATION FEE: $100-$200

USA FiLM FESTiVAL

2917 Swiss Avenue
Dallas, Texas 75204
TEL: (214) 821-6300
FAX: (214) 821-6364
WEB SITE: http://
www.usafilmfestival.com/
FESTIVAL DATE: April
ENTRY DEADLINE: March
CONTACT: Alonso Duralde
DIRECTOR: Ann Alexander
PROFILE: Eight day festival with
over 13,000 attendees.
AWARDS: Yes
COMPETITIONS: Yes
MAJOR AWARDS: National Short
Film and Video Competition
VALUE OF AWARDS: $1,000
(drama, non-fiction, anima-
tion, and experimental catego-
ries); $500 (given to the family,
Texas, and student winners);
$250 (best music video)
APPLICATION FEE: $40
ODDS OF ACCEPTANCE: Over 700
entered

VALLEYFEST FiLM FESTiVAL

PO Box 9312
Knoxville, TN 37940
TEL: (423) 971-1792
FAX: (423) 673-8264 or
(423) 573-9447
E-MAIL: mswolfe@esper.com
or euphoric@esper.com
WEB SITE: http://www.
esper.com/valleyfest
FESTIVAL DATE: March
ENTRY DEADLINE: January
CATEGORY: Animation, Documentary, Independent, Short
PROFILE: Valleyfest is America's
newest independent film festival to be held in Knoxville TN,
every Spring. We are highlight-
ing first time efforts by directors of features. We show features, shorts, documentaries
and animations.

The Valleyfest International
Film Festival was founded by a
small group of aspiring filmmakers who have toiled on
their own independent film
projects and have experienced
the rigamarol involved in
bringing a finished work of art
to public attention. After attending many film festivals and
having the pleasure of showcasing our own films, we have decided to start a festival in order
to help other filmmakers get
over that next great hurdle after completing their first
projects. Valleyfest's primary
goal is to offer first time directors and producers of feature
films an opportunity to share
their work with a large festival
audience.

We at Valleyfest believe that
the efforts of hard-working, independent filmmakers should
be rewarded with the opportunity to share their art. We also
believe that they are not the
only individuals reaping re-
wards from our festival.
Valleyfest will draw attention to
quality artists whose work most
of us would not otherwise see.
We wish to encourage artistic
liberation and innovation in
the community of people who
witness the bravado that often
takes place on the screen of a
film made on the strength of
immagination and courage, not
large budgets.

VANCOUVER iNTERNATiONAL FiLM FESTiVAL

1008 Homer St., Suite 410
Vancouver, BC, V6B 2X1
Canada
TEL: Admin.: 604-685-0260
Box Office (Open 10 days
before the festival begins):
604-685-8297
FAX: 604-688-8221
E-MAIL: viff@viff.org
WEB SITE: http://viff.org
FESTIVAL DATE: September-
October
ENTRY DEADLINE: July
CONTACT: Nick Tattersall, Office
Manager
DIRECTOR: Alan Franey

PROGRAMMER: Alan Franey, Fes-
tival Director; PoChu AuYeung,
Programme Coordinator;
Sandy Gow; Tony Rayns (for
East Asia); Ken Anderlini (for
Canada); Programme Consult-
ants: Jack Vermee, David
Rooney, Angela Pressburger,
Gerald Peary, Kathleen Mullen,
Francoise Maupin, Harlan
Jacobson, Melanie Friesen, Pe-
ter Cully, Christopher Adkins
OTHER STAFF: Director of Com-
munications: Jane MacDonald;
Business Manager: Janine
Fraser; Office Manager: Nick
Tattersall; Trade Forum Pro-
ducer: Melanie Friesen; Trade
Forum Associate Producer:
Fran Bergin
CATEGORY: Documentary, Inde-
pendent, International
PROFILE: The purpose of the
Vancouver International Film
Festival is to encourage understanding of other nations
through the art of cinema, to
foster the art of cinema, to facilitate the meeting in British
Columbia of cinema professionals from around the world,
and to stimulate the motion
picture industry in British Columbia and Canada.
SEMINARS: Each year our festival
hosts The Film and Television
Trade Forum—a four-day
event of seminars and guest
speakers covering the myriad
issues filmmakers face in the
community. Subjects covered
include: distribution, marketing, documentaries, animation,
directing your own script, navigating the financial landscapes,
satire for television, TV series,
co-productions, development,
new media, pitching your ides,
tricks of the trade, keynote lun-
cheon speakers, etc. The Trade
Forum also hosts roundtable
discussions, micro meetings
and a full day devoted to new
filmmakers. All seminars take
place in the Rogers Industry
Centre at The Hotel Vancouver.
FAMOUS SPEAKERS: The Trade Forum hosts about 85 guest speakers during the four day period.

Past guests include: John Badham, Nick Broomfield, Charles Burnett, Al Clark, Peter Dekom, Atom Egoyan, Mike Figgis, Norman Jewison, John McNaughton, Michael Moore, John Pierson, Penelope Spheeris, Midge Sanford, Gus Van Sant, Rosalie Swedlin, Robin Swicord

AWARDS: No

COMPETITIONS: No

MAJOR AWARDS: Air Canada People's Choice Award For Most Popular Film

LAST WINNING DIRECTORS: Caroline Link and William Gazecki

PAST JUDGES: Dragons and Tigers Award Jury, Jury for Telefilm Canada Awards and the Rogers Award, National Film Board Awards Jury

APPLICATION TIPS: Follow the directions on the regulations carefully, don't submit after deadline, fill out the form legibly...make good films.

APPLICATION FEE: None

FILMS SCREENED: Approximately 300 films.

TRAVEL TIPS: Be prepared for plenty of rain, try and get to the North Shore Mountains, Stanley Park is an urban must-see, American money works almost as well here as the third world.

BEST RESTAURANTS: Diva at the Metropolitan Hotel or Lola's

BEST BARS: Babalu's at the Dakota

BEST HANGOUT FOR FILMMAKERS: Gerrards lounge at the Sutton Place Hotel.

BEST PLACE FOR BREAKFAST: The Elbow Room Cafe

VANCOUVER UNDERGROUND FILM FESTIVAL

E-MAIL: panic@istar.ca

WEB SITE: www.blindinglight.com

FESTIVAL DATE: November

ENTRY DEADLINE: October

YEAR FESTIVAL BEGAN: 1998

DIRECTOR: Alex MacKenzie

PROGRAMMER: Alex MacKenzie

CATEGORY: Short, Underground, Weird, Video

PROFILE: Recently voted "Vancouver's Best Alternative Cinema." The Blinding Light!! is proud to be presenting Vancouver's first ever underground film festival. The festival's inaugural year will focus on local works exclusively and include numerous premieres, live audiovisual performances as well as opening and closing parties!

"The response to our call for submissions so far has been excellent" says Blinding Light!! programmer and festival organizer Alex MacKenzie, "there are so many wonderful, strange, and stunning films and videos produced right here in our own backyard that are just crying out to be seen, and we're looking forward to receiving a lot more!!"

The festival features workshops on guerilla filmmaking techniques, Super 8 and 16mm hand processing and more. Opening night will feature a collaboration between the critically acclaimed improvisational music group Talking Pictures and The Blinding Light's own in-house visuals wizards Phosphene. Also confirmed for the event is The Light Fantastic, cartoonist Julian Lawrence's visually arresting live scratch animation project. Expect the best in radical film and video works: hand processed, home-made, strange, experimental and challenging.

VERMONT INTERNATIONAL FILM FESTIVAL: IMAGES AND ISSUES FOR SOCIAL CHANGE

One Main Street, Burlington Burlington, Vermont 05401

TEL: 802-660-2600

FAX: 802-860-9555

E-MAIL: viff@together.net

WEB SITE: www.vtiff.org

FESTIVAL DATE: Late October

ENTRY DEADLINE: July

YEAR FESTIVAL BEGAN: 1985

CONTACT: Jennie Bedusa

DIRECTOR: Kenneth Peck

PROGRAMMER: Barry Snyder

PROFILE: Our mission is to inform and motivate people, through film and video, to work for peace, justice and respect for the natural world. We accept films in three categories for competition: War and Peace, Justice and Human Rights, and The Environment, all films must be made in the year prior to the festival, and by independent filmmakers.

SEMINARS: Filmmakers symposium, selected speakers and discussions to complement some of our non-competition films showcases.

FAMOUS SPEAKERS: Martin Sheen, Robbie Leppzer

AWARDS: Yes. Awards are given or the best of each category, as well as Heart of Festival and People's Choice. Awards are a plaque with the filmmakers name and the title of the film.

COMPETITIONS: Yes

MAJOR AWARDS: Best of the Festival

APPLICATION TIPS: Follow the format given in the all-For-Entry form, include the $65 fee.

APPLICATION FEE: $65

INSIDER ADVICE: Our judges appreciate time and care taken to make the submitted works of outstanding cinematic quality.

ODDS OF ACCEPTANCE: Over 100 films are submitted into our festival, about 25-30 will be shown.

BEST RESTAURANTS: Bourbon Street Grill, Trattoria Delia, Leunig's, Sweet Tomatoes, Parima, Isabel's On the Waterfront, Smokejacks

BEST BARS: Red Square, Nectars, Metronome, Higher Ground, Nickanoose.

BEST HANGOUT FOR FILMMAKERS: Muddy Waters (Coffee House), Stone Soup (Vegetarian Bistro)

BEST PLACE FOR BREAKFAST: Sneakers in Winooski, G's, Oasis Diner, First Waltz Cafe, Leunig's.

VICTORIA INDEPENDENT FILM AND VIDEO FESTIVAL

203-732 Princess Ave.
Victoria, British Columbia,
V8T 1K6 Canada
TEL: (250) 389-1590
FAX: (250) 389-1599
E-MAIL: cinevic@coastnet.com
WEB SITE: www.coastnet.com/
~cinevic/
FESTIVAL DATE: End of February
ENTRY DEADLINE: November
CONTACT: Kathy Kay
DIRECTOR: Kathy Kay
PROGRAMMER: Donovan Aikman
CATEGORY: Independent
PROFILE: 1) To promote independent filmmaking by building an educated audience. 2) To offer opportunities to learn from artists and industry professionals through discussions, master classes and networking.
SEMINARS: Putting your Budget on the Screen, How to be Your Own Agent, and more.
PANELS: DVD, the Reality of the $900 Feature, Writing for the Camera Lens and more.
FAMOUS SPEAKERS: John Waters, Lewis Teague, Francis Damberger, Lynne Stopkewich, Scott Rosenfelt, Mary Gail Artz and Barbara Cohen
AWARDS: Yes
COMPETITIONS: Yes

MAJOR AWARDS: Best of the Festival Feature, Best Documentary, Best Canadian Feature. We also offer awards for Best Short Film, Most Innovative Use of Budget and Best BC Short Film

VALUE OF AWARDS: You receive a stunning hunk of glass with your name on it.

PAST JUDGES: Peter Campbell, Donovan Aikman, Stan Fox, Heather McAndrews, Brian Hendricks, Rick Raxlan

APPLICATION TIPS: Follow your vision, don't compromise but be able to listen to experienced people who tell you to cut your film.

APPLICATION FEE: No entry fee. None, nada, doesn't cost a thing to enter! (well except for postage)

INSIDER ADVICE: Make sure the essentials are in place—good acting, sound and lighting

AVERAGE FILMS ENTERED: We are totally open and look at all genres. We screen short film and video, feature films and documentaries

FILMS SCREENED: 104

ODDS OF ACCEPTANCE: This year we screened just over 350 films and accepted 104—this includes features, documentaries and short films.

FILMMAKER PERKS: For winning filmmakers and those selected by the jury and Festival Director we supply travel and lodging. Networking opportunities abound.

TRAVEL TIPS: Book your flight all the way to Victoria, getting dropped off in Vancouver leaves you with an additional 3 hour journey (though very scenic).

BEST RESTAURANTS: The Water Club or Suze

BEST BARS: Swans or the Ocean Pointe

BEST HANGOUT FOR FILMMAKERS: Suze

BEST PLACE FOR BREAKFAST: Sam s Deli

FESTIVAL TALE: John Waters and I went looking for the house in Victoria that his mother lived

in when she was a girl. John had the wrong address and so we called Mom who wasn't in. We drove around (looking at the bad areas of town) until she returned his call and then went off to find the house. Thank goodness nobody was home!

VIRGINIA FESTIVAL OF AMERICAN FILM

P. O. Box 3697
Charlottesville, VA 22903
TEL: (804) 982-5277 or
(800) UVA-FEST
FAX: (804) 982-5297
WEB SITE: http://poe.acc.
virginia.edu/~ljb3g/film.html
FESTIVAL DATE: October
ENTRY DEADLINE: August
CONTACT: Laura Oaksmith

VIRGINIA FILM FESTIVAL

Department of Drama
Culbreth Road
Charlottesville, Virginia 22903
TEL: 804-982-5277
FAX: 804-924-1447
E-MAIL: filmfest@virginia.edu
WEB SITE: www.virginia.edu/
~vafilm
FESTIVAL DATE: October
ENTRY DEADLINE: July
CONTACT: Richard Herskowitz
DIRECTOR: Richard Herskowitz
PROGRAMMER: Richard Herskowitz
OTHER STAFF: James Scales, Asst. Director
CATEGORY: A retreat for filmmakers, scholars and film lovers emphasizing education and entertainment. The Festival examines American film in the context of the international films it influences and reflects. A different theme is explored every year through a mix of classics, mainstream and indie premieres. This is a Festival especially for people who like to talk about film; in fact, it's probably the only Festival with more speakers than films.

PROFILE: The Virginia Film Festival explores American film and the international cinema it influences and reflects in an annual academic forum that brings together authors, critics, directors, actors, artists, and scholars from across the nation.

FAMOUS SPEAKERS: James Stewart, Robert Mitchum, John Sayles, Fay Wray, Robert Altman, Christine Choy, Su Friedrich, Mark Rappaport, Norman Mailer

AWARDS: None

COMPETITIONS: An independents solicitation selects approximately 10% of films submitted for screening, but no awards are given

APPLICATION TIPS: Cue your tape to the best scene for panel viewing. It helps if the film relates to the Festival's theme that year, but this is not essential.

APPLICATION FEE: $30

INSIDER ADVICE: Make your film brilliant, innovative, and revelatory, so we're sure to accept it.

AVERAGE FILMS ENTERED: All kinds — narrative, experimental, documentary — film, video, CD-ROM

FILMS SCREENED: Approximately 70, including features and shorts.

ODDS OF ACCEPTANCE: 120 submitted, 15 accepted.

FILMMAKER PERKS: Lodging and free access to Festival events and parties, plus contacts with many film industry guests.

TRAVEL TIPS: You can get here by plane or train. We're two hours from D.C. and one hour from Richmond. Charlottesville is spectacular in the fall, and we catch the leaves turning at their peak. Jefferson's Monticello and Rotunda are nearby for visits.

BEST RESTAURANTS: Metropolitain.

BEST BARS: Miller's

BEST HANGOUT FOR FILMMAKERS: The Mudhouse.

BEST PLACE FOR BREAKFAST: The Tavern.

Gregory Peck with Wine Country Film Festival board members Margrit Mondavi and Stephen Ashton.

Cue your tape to the best scene for panel viewing. (Virginia Film Festival)

VISIONS OF THE U. S. VIDEO CONTEST

P. O. Box 200
Los Angeles, CA 90078
TEL: (213) 856-7743
FAX: (213) 462- 4049
FESTIVAL DATE: August
ENTRY DEADLINE: June
CONTACT: Lee Arnone-Briggs
CATEGORY: Independent, Student, Video

WASHINGTON, DC INTERNATIONAL FILM FESTIVAL—FILMFEST DC

P. O. Box 21396
Washington, DC 20009
TEL: (202) 724-5613
FAX: (202) 724-6578
E-MAIL: filmfestdc@aol.com
WEB SITE: www.capaccess.org/filmfestdc
FESTIVAL DATE: April-May
ENTRY DEADLINE: January
DIRECTOR: Tony Gittens
PANELS: Yes
COMPETITIONS: No
APPLICATION FEE: None

WEST VIRGINIA INTERNATIONAL FILM FESTIVAL

P.O. Box 2165
Charleston, WV 25328
TEL: 304-340-3797 or 304-776-5174
E-MAIL: Pjlvswv@aol.com
FESTIVAL DATE: October/April
YEAR FESTIVAL BEGAN: 1985
PROGRAMMER: Pam Haynes
PROFILE: Two festivals each year, in October, a 35mm, noncompetitive, international festival; in Aril a 16mm, primarily documentary student festival, open only to students in West Virginia.
VALUE OF AWARDS: total award value: $2,400

WINE COUNTRY FILM FESTIVAL

12000 Henno Rd., Box 303
Glen Ellen, CA 95442
TEL: (707) 996-2536
FAX: (707) 996-6964
WEB SITE: http://www.winery.com/winery-bin/filmfest
FESTIVAL DATE: July-August
ENTRY DEADLINE: May
DIRECTOR: Stephen Ashton, Creative Director
APPLICATION FEE: $25

WOMEN iN FiLM iNTERNATiONAL FiLM FESTiVAL
6464 Sunset Blvd., Suite 900
Los Angeles, CA 90028
TEL: (213) 463-6040
FAX: (213) 463-0963
FESTIVAL DATE: November
DIRECTOR: Harriet Silverman
CATEGORY: Women

WOMEN MAKE MOViES
P. O. Box 19272
Washington, DC 20036
TEL: (202) 232-2254
FESTIVAL DATE: March
CATEGORY: Women

WORLDFEST CHARLESTON
P. O. Box 838
Charleston, SC 29401
TEL: (713) 965-9955
FAX: (713) 965-9660
WEB SITE: http://www.sims.net/organizations/worldfest/worldfest.html/
FESTIVAL DATE: November
ENTRY DEADLINE: September

WOW CAFE WOMEN'S FiLM AND ViDEO FESTiVAL—WOW (WOMEN ONE WORLD) FESTiVAL
151 1st Ave., Suite W
New York, NY 10003
TEL: (212) 674-4736
FESTIVAL DATE: March-April
CATEGORY: Women

YORKTON SHORT FiLM AND ViDEO FESTiVAL
49 Smith St. East
Yorkton, Saskatchewan S3N 0H4 Canada
TEL: (306) 782-7077
FAX: (306) 782-1550
FESTIVAL DATE: May
ENTRY DEADLINE: July
CATEGORY: Short, Video

REALLY CHEAP TRAVEL TiPS

I sleep on people's floors or couches a lot, so I bring a sleeping bag, a travel alarm clock, ear plugs and an eye cover thing and I take a lot of vitamins. I always carry a hard copy list of everyone I've ever met in the vicinity I'm travelling to and send out postcards in advance. I try to have a back up sleeping arrangement just in case your host gets weird or if you've started to overstay your welcome but still want to stay on good terms. If I'm travelling overseas I try not to drink on the plane, sleep as much as possible and then make myself stay up until it's bedtime in that time zone. Then I take melatonin which helps reset your body clock. Also, keep track of your frequent flier miles.

I try to travel light, but it's hard. I like to bring enough stuff so that I'm able to continue with my daily routine, like bringing clothes I normally wear instead of travel clothes that are efficient but not really comfortable. I bring a few nice things like Peppermint foot lotion or bath oil so if I'm really stressed out from travelling or arranging things I can have a moment to chill out. I drink a ton of bottled water and drink alcohol or ingest drugs only at night and not every single night (at least I try!) because that can make you really sick when you're travelling.

I have a powerbook computer which is wonderful. I can still do business and send email and fax and write and I have my whole phone number database with me, which would be totally huge printed out. I also have a 1-800 pager so people can track me down. I used to try and contact press using other people's phones and it's just impossible to get your messages in time, especially if they have voice mail. In each town, I try and find out who are the cool zinesters, bands, filmmakers or artists and make contact so I have a network of support when I come back for distribution. That's been my favorite part, meeting artists from all over the world and being inspired by them, on all different levels. When you meet people from different places, you have such a wide network to ask advice from and that has been the secret to our success, I think. Being able to ask for help when you don't know what you are doing is key.

—Sarah Jacobson, filmmaker, *Mary Jane's Not A Virgin Anymore*

FOREiGN FiLM FESTiVALS
(Alphabetical by Country)

ARGENTINA
---

iNTERNATiONAL FESTiVAL OF FiLMS MADE BY WOMEN
Lavalle 1578 9o piso "B"
1048 Buenos Aires, Argentina
TEL: 54-1-374-7318
FAX: 54-1-311-3062
CONTACT: Beatriz de Villalba Welsh
CATEGORY: International, Women

AUSTRALIA

ADELAiDE iNTERNATiONAL CHiLDREN'S FiLM AND ViDEO FESTiVAL
South Australian Film & Video Centre,
Lumiere Lane, Westside Commerce Center
113 Tapleys Hill Rd.
Hendon, South Australia 5014 Australia
TEL: 08-348-9355
FAX: 08-345-4222
FESTIVAL DATE: Biennial (even years)
DIRECTOR: Priscilla Thomas, Project Officer; Andrew Zielinski, Director

ANiMANiA: iNTERNATiONAL FESTiVAL OF ANiMATiON AND MULTiMEDiA
Flickerfest
P.O. Box 52
Haymarket NSW 2000, Australia
TEL: 61-2-251-4960
FAX: 61-2-251-4970
FESTIVAL DATE: April
ENTRY DEADLINE: November
CONTACT: Craig B. Kirkwood
CATEGORY: Animation

AUSTRALiAN iNTERNATiONAL OUTDOOR SHORT FiLM FESTiVAL
Flickerfest
P. O. Box 52
Haymarket NSW 2000, Australia
TEL: 61-2-251-4960
FAX: 61-2-251-4970
FESTIVAL DATE: January
ENTRY DEADLINE: October
CATEGORY: International, Short

BRiSBANE iNTERNATiONAL FiLM FESTiVAL
Hoyts Regents Bldg., Level 3
167 Queen St. Mall
Brisbane, Q 4000 Australia
TEL: 61-7-22-00-333
FAX: 61-7-22-00-400
FESTIVAL DATE: August
ENTRY DEADLINE: June
CONTACT: Gary Ellis

MELBOURNE iNTERNATiONAL FiLM AND ViDEO FESTiVAL
P. O. Box 43
St. Kilda, 3182 Victoria, Australia
TEL: 03-534-3964
FAX: 03-534-3467
FESTIVAL DATE: June
ENTRY DEADLINE: June
CONTACT: Harvey Hutchinson

MELBOURNE iNTERNATiONAL FiLM FESTiVAL
P. O. Box 2206
Fitzroy, Vic. 3065 Australia
TEL: (61-3)9417 2011
FAX: (61 3)9417 3804
E-MAIL: miff@netspace.net.au
WEB SITE: http://www.cinemedia.nct/MIFF
FESTIVAL DATE: July-August
ENTRY DEADLINE: March (Short Films)—April (Features)
YEAR FESTIVAL BEGAN: 1952
CONTACT: Sandra Sdraulig & Brett Woodward
DIRECTOR: Sandra Sdraulig
PROGRAMMER: Sandra Sdraulig & Brett Woodward
CATEGORY: International
PROFILE: Established in 1952, the Melbourne International Film Festival is one of the country's oldest running arts events and the oldest and largest established film festival in the Southern Hemisphere. It is a major event on the Australian arts calendar.

Screened in some of Melbourne's most celebrated inner city cinemas and theatres, the Festival comprises an eclectic mix of outstanding film-making from around the world. The Melbourne International Film Festival is a showcase for the latest developments in Australian and International film-making, offering audiences a wide range of features and shorts, documentaries, animation and experimental films. The Festival presents a significant showcase of new Australian cinema and its programme of nearly 200 films is viewed by an enthusiastic and dedicated audience of over 67,000 people.

SEMINARS: yes

FAMOUS SPEAKERS: varies from year to year

AWARDS: yes

COMPETITIONS: yes for short film only

MAJOR AWARDS: Best Short Film—$5000 Australian; Best Documentary Short Film—$2000 Australian; Best Experimental Short Film—$2000 Australian; Best Animated Short Film—$2000 Australian; Best Fiction Short Film—$2000 Australian

VALUE OF AWARDS: Prize money value may vary from year to year.

APPLICATION TIPS: Follow guidelines

APPLICATION FEE: Only for the short film competition—$25 U.S. or $30 Australian

AVERAGE FILMS ENTERED: Feature entries in all categories, documentaries and short film in all categories.

FILMS SCREENED: 116 features were screened in 1998.

ODDS OF ACCEPTANCE: Feature entries are generally by invitation only. The festival receives approximately 600 short film entries each year. Around 100 shorts are included in the program.

FILMMAKER PERKS: Travel & accomodation is only offered to guests invited to the festival.

TOURIST INFORMATION: Melbourne is a very easy going city, with plenty of bars, cafes & restaurants at reasonable prices. People are very friendly.

MOOMBA INTERNATIONAL AMATEUR FILM FESTIVAL

c/o P. O. Box 286
Preston, Victoria 3072
Australia

TEL: 03-470-1816

FESTIVAL DATE: March

ENTRY DEADLINE: February

CONTACT: Dudley Harris

REVELATION INDEPENDENT FILM FESTIVAL

PO Box 135
Sth Fremantle WA, 6162,
Australia

TEL: + 61 8 9336 2482

FAX: + 61 8 9336 2482

E-MAIL: dakota@omen.net.au

WEB SITE: http://www.omen.net.au/~dakota

FESTIVAL DATE: Touring

ENTRY DEADLINE: December

DIRECTOR: Richard Sowada

CATEGORY: Independent

PROFILE: Australia's major alternative touring international film festival, the 2nd REVelation Independent Film Festival is calling for entries for the forthcoming event from Australia and beyond. R.I.F.F. is a strongly curated and contextualised film festival designed to showcase the most progressive in new and archival film works to Australian pop/youth/counter-culture audiences. Now in its second year, R.I.F.F. has featured retrospective works from Beat generation filmmakers, wonderful archival animations as well as new feature, short, documentary and experimental works.

SHORT POPPIES: INTERNATIONAL FESTIVAL OF STUDENT FILM AND VIDEO

Flickerfest
P. O. Box 52
Haymarket NSW 2000,
Australia

TEL: 61-2-251-4960

FAX: 61-2-251-4970

FESTIVAL DATE: July

ENTRY DEADLINE: April

CONTACT: Craig B. Kirkwood

CATEGORY: Student

SYDNEY FILM FESTIVAL

PO Box 950
Glebe NSW 2037
Sydney, Australia

TEL: +61 2 9660 3844

FAX: +61 2 9692 8793

E-MAIL: info@sydfilm-fest.com.au

WEB SITE: www.sydfilm-fest.com.au

FESTIVAL DATE: June

ENTRY DEADLINE: February

YEAR FESTIVAL BEGAN: 1954

CONTACT: Jenny Neighbour

CATEGORY: International, We show a wide range of films from all over the world—features, documentaries, shorts, video work, experimental work, retrospectives—primarily for a film-loving audience, but distributors from throughout Australia also attend to see the latest works and assess public reaction before purchasing titles.

PROFILE: This international festival focuses on new features, shorts, and documentaries. Approximately 140,000 attend.

AWARDS: Yes

COMPETITIONS: Yes, but for Australian short films only.

MAJOR AWARDS: The Dendy Awards for Australian Short Films; The Yoram Gross Animation Award; The EAC Award; and The NSW Film and Television Office Rouben Mamoulian Award.

VALUE OF AWARDS: $7,500 (Australian dollars) in the first; $2,500 each in the remaining three.

APPLICATION TIPS: Send your viewing tape early, make sure you enclose a good press kit and contact details.

APPLICATION FEE: $15 (AUD) if you would like your viewing tape returned, otherwise it's free.

AVERAGE FILMS ENTERED: Anything good.

FILMS SCREENED: Around 200

ODDS OF ACCEPTANCE: Around 1,000 tapes submitted to the office and a further 750 viewed overseas.

TOURIST INFORMATION: Sydney Harbour, Bondi Beach, Blue Mountains...

BEST HANGOUT FOR FILMMAKERS: Victoria Street, Darlinghurst

BEST PLACE FOR BREAKFAST: Victoria Street, Darlinghurst, or Bondi beach

---

AUSTRIA

AMERICAN FILM FESTIVAL

Museumstrausse 31
A-6020 Innsbruck, Austria
TEL: 43-512-580723
FAX: 43-512-581762

AUSTRIAN FILM DAYS

Film Fest Wels
Austrian Film Office
Columbusgasse 2
A-1100 Vienna, Austria
TEL: 604-0126
FAX: 602-0795
FESTIVAL DATE: June
CONTACT: Reinhard Pyrker

FESTIVAL DER FESTIVALS

Schaumburgergasse 18
A-1040 Wien, Austria
TEL: 0222-505-53-37
FAX: 0222-505-53-07

FESTIVAL DATE: February
ENTRY DEADLINE: December
CONTACT: Alexander V. Kammel

FILM + ARC INTERNATIONAL FILM FESTIVAL

International Festival fur Film + Architektur
Armitage
Rechbauerstrasse 38
A-8010 Graz, Austria
TEL: 43-316-84-24-87
FAX: 43-316-82-95-11
FESTIVAL DATE: Biennial; November
ENTRY DEADLINE: July
DIRECTOR: Charlotte Pochhacker

INTERNATIONAL JUVENALE FOR YOUNG FILM AND VIDEO AMATEURS

Bahnhofstrasse 59 III
Kaerten
A-9020 Klagenfurt, Austria
TEL: 0463-319654
FESTIVAL DATE: Biennial, odd years; August
ENTRY DEADLINE: July
DIRECTOR: OSR Dir. Wilhelm Elsner
CATEGORY: International, Student

INTERNATIONALE FILMFESTIVAL DES NICHTPROFESSIONELLEN FILMS

International Festival of Non-Professional Films
Hauptplatz 11
9100 Volkermakt/Kranten
(Buchalm 42 A-P141 Eberndorf), Austria
TEL: 04236-2645
FESTIVAL DATE: August-September
ENTRY DEADLINE: August
CONTACT: Paul Kraiger

VIENNALE—VIENNA INTERNATIONAL FILM FESTIVAL

Stiftgasse 6
A-1070 Vienna, Austria
TEL: + 43 1 526 59 47 or + 43 1 523 41 72
E-MAIL: office@viennale.or.at
WEB SITE: http://www.viennale.or.at
FESTIVAL DATE: October
ENTRY DEADLINE: Mid-August
YEAR FESTIVAL BEGAN: 1960
DIRECTOR: Hans Hurch
PROGRAMMER: Hans Hurch
CATEGORY: International
PROFILE: The Viennale is a "fest of fests," introducing local audiences to major films of annual fest circuit. It is fest "in praise of independent politics & visions," emphasizing films off beaten track.
AWARDS: No
COMPETITIONS: No, But at the Viennale the FIPRESCI-Prize is awarded for the first or second film of a director.
MAJOR AWARDS: FIPRESCI Award
LAST WINNING FILMS: Moebius (Argentina, 1997)
APPLICATION TIPS: Just to make a good film...
APPLICATION FEE: None
INSIDER ADVICE: Send synopsis, cast & credits, VHS Tape (PAL/NTSC)
AVERAGE FILMS ENTERED: features, shorts, documentaries, few videos
FILMS SCREENED: 170 main programme and tributes
ODDS OF ACCEPTANCE: 1000 submitted, 170 selected
FILMMAKER PERKS: If invited hotel accomodation & travel, meetings, Q&As
TOURIST INFORMATION: There are so many famous sights worth seeing in Vienna.., tours and special info provided
BEST RESTAURANTS: see above
BEST HANGOUT FOR FILMMAKERS: Festival tent

Teen projectionist Galen Rosenthal tucked away in the makeshift booth.

PROJECTING AN IMAGE

What can filmmakers do to make a projectionist's job easier when it comes to sending their prints? You have just spent your life savings on your film, and it's about to premiere at a film festival. Bear in mind you are not opening at Grauman's Chinese Theater. Here are some very simple things you can do to ensure the smoothest possible screening:

1. Make sure your film arrives early and that the cans are marked with the title. If the film is in two cans, label them: 1 of 2, 2 of 2.
2. Label the heads and tails of your print clearly. Include details of the gauge and the reel number on every head and tail: "CITIZEN KANE, B&W, sound, R 1 of 6, 1.33:1, Heads."
3. Write any special projection instructions on a separate sheet and attach it to the inside of the film case. Example: "Focus on Academy Leader, as film begins on a soft image." or "There is no sound for the first thirty seconds of movie."
4. Mark all change-overs clearly (or ask the lab to do so.)
5. Deliver your film ready to project. Your entire film should arrive inspected, heads out on reels (not cores), with all leaders double-side spliced.

Remember: Once the film is up on the screen, it is out of your hands. If there are problems with the sound, focus, framing, or change-overs, deal with them gracefully. Speaking ill of the equipment, festival, or projectionist during the obligatory Q&A makes you look petty. And most importantly—don't give the projectionist a hard time. You never know when they may turn out to be a festival judge.

—Gabe Wardell, projectionist, programmer and jury member
for Slamdance and the Atlanta Film & Video Festival

BANGLADESH

DHAKA INTERNATIONAL SHORT FILM FESTIVAL

46 New Elephant Rd.
Dhaka 1205, Bangladesh
TEL: 864682, 500382, 864128
FAX: 880-2-863060
FESTIVAL DATE: January
ENTRY DEADLINE: November for entry forms; December for prints
CONTACT: Festival Office
CATEGORY: Short

BELGIUM

ART MOVIE

Kortrijksesteenweg 1104
B-9051 Ghent, Belgium
TEL: 32-9-221-8946
FAX: 32-9-221-9074
FESTIVAL DATE: April
DIRECTOR: Jacques Dubrulle, General Secretary

BRUSSELS INTERNATIONAL CINEMA FESTIVAL

Chausee de Louvain, 30
B-1210 Brussels, Belgium
TEL: 32-2-227-3980
FAX: 32-2-218-1860
FESTIVAL DATE: January
ENTRY DEADLINE: October
CONTACT: Christian Thomas

FESTIVAL DE FILM SUR L'ART

Liege Art Film Festival
University De Liege
Place Du Vingt-Aout, 32
B 4000 Liege, Belgium
TEL: 32-41-42-00-80
FESTIVAL DATE: March
ENTRY DEADLINE: January
CONTACT: Jean-Michel Sarlet

FESTIVAL INTERNATIONAL DU COURT METRAGE DE MONS

Mons Short Film Festival
106, Rue dese Arbalestriers
7000 Mons, Belgium
TEL: 65-31-81-75
FAX: 65-31-30-27
FESTIVAL DATE: March
ENTRY DEADLINE: February
CONTACT: Alain Cardon

FESTIVAL INTERNATIONAL DU FILM FANTASTIQUE, DE SCIENCE FICTION THRILLER DE BRUXELLES

144 Avenue De La Reine Koninginelaan
Brussels 120, Belgium
TEL: 32-2-201-1713
FAX: 32-2-201-1469
FESTIVAL DATE: March
ENTRY DEADLINE: January
CONTACT: M. G. Delmote
CATEGORY: Retro Science

FESTIVAL INTERNATIONAL DU FILM FRANCOPHONE—NAMUR

175 Rue des Brasseurs
B-5000 Namur, Belgium
TEL: 32-81-24-1236
FAX: 32-81-22-4384
WEB SITE: http://www.ciger.be/namur/evenements/fiff95/index.html
FESTIVAL DATE: September-October
ENTRY DEADLINE: August
CONTACT: Dany Martin

FLANDERS INTERNATIONAL FILM FESTIVAL—GHENT

Kortrijksesteenweg 1104
B-9051 Ghent Belgium
TEL: +32-9-221-8946
FAX: +32-9-221-9074
WEB SITE: http://www.rug.ac.be/filmfestival/Welcome.html
FESTIVAL DATE: October
ENTRY DEADLINE: August
DIRECTOR: Jacque Dubrulle, General Secretary

INTERNATIONAL ANIMATED FILM AND CARTOON FESTIVAL

Folioscope ABSL
Rue de la Rhetorique, 19
B-1060 Brussels, Belgium
TEL: 32-2-534-41-25
FAX: 32-2-534-22-79
FESTIVAL DATE: February
ENTRY DEADLINE: December
CONTACT: Phillippe Moins, Doris Cleven

BRAZIL

BANCO NACIONAL INTERNATIONAL FILM FESTIVAL

Rua Voluntarios de Patria 97
Rio de Janeiro, 22270 RJ
Brazil
TEL: 55-21-286-8505
FAX: 55-21-286-4029
WEB SITE: http://www.ibase.org.br/~estacao/tabu.htm
FESTIVAL DATE: September
CONTACT: Adhemar Oliveira
CATEGORY: International

BRASILIA FILM FESTIVAL

Cultural Foundation of Brasilia
Ave. N2 Norte
Anexo Teatro Nacional Claudio Santoro
70040 Brasilia DF, Brazil
TEL: 55-61-226-3016
FAX: 55-61-224-2738
FESTIVAL DATE: July
CONTACT: Fernando Adolfo

GRAMADO INTERNATIONAL FILM FESTIVAL

Rua dos Andradas 736
3 Andar Centro
90 020 004 Porto Alegre,
Brazil
TEL: 55-54-286-2335
FAX: 55-54-286-2397
FESTIVAL DATE: August
CONTACT: Esdras Rubinn

MIX BRASIL FESTIVAL OF SEXUAL DIVERSITY

Rua Agisse 72 05439-010
Sao Paulo, SP, Brazil
TEL: 55 11 2127390
E-MAIL: mixbrasil@uol.com.br
WEB SITE:
www.mixbrasil.com.br
FESTIVAL DATE: September
ENTRY DEADLINE: Mid-July
DIRECTOR: Andre Fischer
PROGRAMMER: Andre Fischer,
Andre Fonseca
CATEGORY: Gay Lesbian, Independent, Experimental
PROFILE: Present and discuss the different expressions of sexuality. Improve the audio-visual production in Brazil on gay/lesbian issues. The Festival takes place every year since 1993 in Fortaleza (capitol of Ceara state, known in Brazil for its very macho population) at the gardens of the Government Palace(!), on a big screen between mango trees. So the population can watch for free gay, lesbian, SM, etc films/videos, enjoying the fruits that fall during the screenings
SEMINARS: Aids, Independent production, gay literature.
PANELS: With foreigner directors
AWARDS: yes
COMPETITIONS: yes
MAJOR AWARDS: Silver Rabbit
VALUE OF AWARDS: Air tickets
LAST WINNING FILMS: Feature: *Alive and Kicking;* Short: *With The Whole Ocean to Swim* (jury), *The Origin of Babies According to Kiki Cavalcanti* (audience)

LAST WINNING DIRECTORS: Nancy Nackler, Karen Harley, Anna Muylaert
PAST JUDGES: Erika Palomino, Lucas Bambozzi, Marina Person, Christian Petermann and Francisco César Filho
APPLICATION FEE: No
AVERAGE FILMS ENTERED: All kind of films. Experimental, more commercial, video, 16/35.. Specially the good humourous ones.
ODDS OF ACCEPTANCE: In 97 we showed 118 films/videos. 62 were invited, we had 95 submissions and 52 were chosen from those
FILMMAKER PERKS: Free travel (some), lodging, contacts
BEST RESTAURANTS: Spot
BEST BARS: Ritz and Glitter
BEST HANGOUT FOR FILMMAKERS: All major nightclubs, bar and restaurants in Sao Paulo sponsor MiX Brasil Festival. So, there's Festival Parties every night during MiX Brasil. The Festival tours 8-10 cities in Brazil every year. In 97 the 5th MiX Brasil went for the first time to smaller cities, some known for their homophobia, and it did really well. MiX Brasil will have special evenings with Brazilian Gay and Lesbian shorts this year at Mexico, Tokyo, New York, Lisbon and (not confirmed yet) Los Angeles.

SÃO PAULO INTERNATIONAL FILM FESTIVAL

Al. Lorena, 937 #303
São Paulo SP , CEP 01424-001
Brazil
TEL: + (55) (11) 883-5137 or
+ (55) (11) 3064-5819
FAX: + (55) (11) 853-7936
E-MAIL: info@mostra.org
WEB SITE: http://www.
mostra.org
FESTIVAL DATE: October
ENTRY DEADLINE: August
CONTACT: Christian Poccard
DIRECTOR: Leon Cakoff

PROGRAMMER: Renata de Almeida
CATEGORY: International
PROFILE: The Festival is a cultural, non-profit event, held by the Associação Brasileira Mostra Internacional de Cinema and recognized by the International Federation of the Association of Film Producers. The Festival includes two sessions: "International Perspective" and "New Filmmakers Competition." It's a competitive event with features and shorts from around 60 countries emphasizing on independents.
AWARDS: The main award is Bandeira Paulista, created by the artist Tomie Ohtake. There is one award from the jury, one from the audience and one from the critics.
COMPETITIONS: yes
MAJOR AWARDS: Bandeira Paulista
LAST WINNING FILMS: *Attachment*
PAST JUDGES: Abbas Kiarostami, Walter Salles, Maria de Medeiros, Godfrey Reggio, Jos Stelling, Eizo Sugawa, Rubens Edwald Filho, etc.
BEST RESTAURANTS: Restaurante Arábia
BEST HANGOUT FOR FILMMAKERS: Maksoud Plaza Hotel
BEST PLACE FOR BREAKFAST: Maksoud Plaza Hotel

SAO PAULO INTERNATIONAL SHORT FILM FESTIVAL

Rua Simao Alvares 784/2
05417-020 Sao Paulo SP,
Brazil
TEL: 55-11-852-9601
FAX: 55-11-282-9601
E-MAIL: spshort@ibm.net
WEB SITE: http://www.puc-rio.br/mis
FESTIVAL DATE: April
DIRECTOR: Zita Carvalhosa
PROGRAMMER: Francisco Cesar Fihlo
CATEGORY: International, Short

BULGARIA

INTERNATIONAL FESTIVAL OF COMEDY FILMS
House of Humor and Satire
P. O. Box 104
5300 Gabrovo, Bulgaria
TEL: 066-27229 or 066-29300
FAX: 066-26989
FESTIVAL DATE: May
ENTRY DEADLINE: March for entry forms; April for prints.
CONTACT: Tatyana Tsankova

PARTNERSHIP FOR PEACE INTERNATIONAL FILM FESTIVAL
Army Audiovisual Centre
23 Stoletov Blvd.
1233 Sofia, Bulgaria
TEL: 359-2-31-71-55
FAX: 359-2-32-00-18
FESTIVAL DATE: May
ENTRY DEADLINE: March
CONTACT: Antonii Donchev, Rossitta Valkanova

CHILE

FESTIVAL INTERNATIONAL DE CINE DE VINA DEL MAR
Villavicencio 352
Santiago, Chile
TEL: 562-632-6387 or 562-632-2892
FAX: 562-632-6389
FESTIVAL DATE: October
CONTACT: Sergio Trabucco, Jaun J. Ulriksen

CHINA

BEIJING INTERNATIONAL CHILDREN'S FILM FESTIVAL
Juvenile Dept. BTV
No. 2A Zaojunmiao
Haidian District
Beijing, 100086 China

TEL: 861-202-5815 or 861-202-5810
FAX: 861-202-5814
FESTIVAL DATE: May-June
CONTACT: Zhang Pengling
CATEGORY: Kid

BEIJING INTERNATIONAL SCIENTIFIC FILM FESTIVAL
25 Xin Wai St.
Beijing, China
TEL: 201-5533
FESTIVAL DATE: November
ENTRY DEADLINE: August
CONTACT: Ju Jian, Organizational Committee of the ISFF

CHINA INTERNATIONAL SCIENTIFIC FILM FESTIVAL
2567 Xietu Road
Shanghai, China
TEL: 389121
FESTIVAL DATE: October
ENTRY DEADLINE: March for application forms; May for entries
CONTACT: Mr. Xu Zhiyi

CHINA INTERNATIONAL SPORTS FILM FESTIVAL
9 Tiyuguan Road
Beijing, China
FESTIVAL DATE: May-June
CONTACT: Chinese Olympic Committee

SHANGHAI INTERNATIONAL ANIMATION FILM FESTIVAL
618 Wang Hang Du Road
Shanghai 200042, China
TEL: 8621-2524349
FAX: 8621-2523352
FESTIVAL DATE: December
ENTRY DEADLINE: May
CONTACT: Li Gian Guo, Film Festival Organizing Committee
CATEGORY: Animation

COLOMBIA

CARTAGENA INTERNATIONAL FILM FESTIVAL
Baluarte San Francisco Javier
Calle San Juan de Dios,
Apartado Aereo 1834
Cartagena, Colombia
TEL: 575 6642345—6600966
FAX: 575 6600970—6601037
E-MAIL: festicinecartagena@axisgate.com
WEB SITE: http://www.rednet.net.co/festicinecartagena
FESTIVAL DATE: March
ENTRY DEADLINE: January
CONTACT: Gerardo Nieto
DIRECTOR: Victor Nieto
PROGRAMMER: Victor Nieto
OTHER STAFF: Monica Duarte (secretary)
CATEGORY: Independent, International, Children's
SEMINARS: Perspectives of contemporary Spanish Film—Mexican films now—100 Years Without Solitude, the best 100 Latin American Films.
PANELS: Children in front of the screen.
FAMOUS SPEAKERS: Luciano Castillo (Cuba), Nelson Carro (Mexico)
AWARDS: Opera Prima, Photograph, Script, Actor, Actress, Supporting Actor/Actress, Director, Film
COMPETITIONS: Yes
MAJOR AWARDS: India Catalina (Gold)
VALUE OF AWARDS: None
LAST WINNING FILMS: *Bajo Bandera* (Argentina)
LAST WINNING DIRECTORS: Juan Jose Jusid
PAST JUDGES: Eduardo Mignona (Argentina), Jaime Humberto Hermosillo (Mexico), Benigno Iglesias (Cuba), German Santa Maria (Colombia), Peter Besas (U.S.A.)
APPLICATION TIPS: Spanish subtitles
APPLICATION FEE: None

INSIDER ADVICE: make sure copies arrive on time

AVERAGE FILMS ENTERED: Latest Latinamerican and Ibero International

ODDS OF ACCEPTANCE: 100 films submitted. 60-70 are accepted.

FILMMAKER PERKS: Some free travel, lodging, and contacts.

TRAVEL TIPS: Cartagena is a tropical place. Very safe. Built in 1533.

BEST RESTAURANTS: La Vitrola

BEST BARS: Pacos

BEST HANGOUT FOR FILMMAKERS: Cafe Santo Domingo

BEST PLACE FOR BREAKFAST: Cafe De La Plaza

FESTIVAL DE CINE IBEROAMERICANO PARA LARGOMETRAGES DE FICCIÓN

Apartado aereo 46361
Bogota, Colombia
TEL: 672-82-59
FESTIVAL DATE: March
CONTACT: Javier Rey

SANTA FE DE BOGOTA INTERNATIONAL FILM FESTIVAL

Calle 26 No. 4-92
Santa Fe de Bogota, Colombia
TEL: 57-1-282-5196
FAX: 57-1-342-2872
FESTIVAL DATE: September
DIRECTOR: Henry Laguado
CATEGORY: International

CROATIA

WORLD FESTIVAL OF ANIMATED FILMS IN ZAGREB

Kneza Mislava 18
Zagreb, 10 000 Croatia
TEL: +385 1 46 11 808; +385 46 11 709; +385 46 11 589
FAX: + 385 1 46 11 808 or + 385 46 11 807
E-MAIL: kdz@zg.tel.hr
WEB SITE: http://animafest.hr

YEAR FESTIVAL BEGAN: 1972

CONTACT: Sanja Borcic-Toth, Festival Secretary, (Mrs.)

DIRECTOR: Margit Antauer, Organising Director, (Mrs.)

PROGRAMMER: Josko Marusic, Programme Director, (Mr.)

CATEGORY: Animation, International

PROFILE: The Festival is a biennial event held every even year. The primary goal of the festival is the support of innovation in animation. Films must be at least 50 % animated, regardless of the catagory being entered. Films between 30 seconds and 30 minutes are eligible.

SEMINARS: Round-tables, Retrospectives, Exhibitions, etc.

AWARDS: Yes

COMPETITIONS: Yes

MAJOR AWARDS: Grand Prix

VALUE OF AWARDS: 15 000 HKN First Prize in Each of 3 categories, 10 000 HKN; Debut, 15 000 HKN; Best Student Film, 10 000 HKN

APPLICATION FEE: No

ODDS OF ACCEPTANCE: This year we have received 803 and 65 have entered an official competition.

FILMMAKER PERKS: Lodging and meals are provided for the filmmakers.

TOURIST INFORMATION: Zagreb is a historical, middle European town with one million inhabitants. There are a lot of cultural monuments, museums, etc.

CUBA

HAVANA INTERNATIONAL FESTIVAL OF NEW LATIN AMERICAN FILM, TV AND VIDEO

Calle 23
N. 1155 Plaza de le Revolucion
Vedado, Havana, Cuba
TEL: 34400 or 305041
FESTIVAL DATE: December

CZECH REPUBLIC

AGROFILM FESTIVAL

Wenzigova 15
Praha 2, 120 00,
Czech Republic
TEL: 00-42-2-298290
FESTIVAL DATE: August
ENTRY DEADLINE: July
CONTACT: Prof. Ing. Jan Plesnik

BRNO 16 INTERNATIONAL NONCOMMERCIAL FILM AND VIDEO FESTIVAL

Kulturni a informacni centrum mesta Brna
B16, Radnicka 4
658 78 Brno, Czech Republic
TEL: 05-4221-6260
FAX: 05-4221-4625
FESTIVAL DATE: October
ENTRY DEADLINE: August-September
CONTACT: Sarka Tryhukova

KARLOVY VARY INTERNATIONAL FILM FESTIVAL

c/o Film Festival Karlovy Vary Foundation
Panska 1
11000 Prague 1,
Czech Republic
TEL: 420-2-2423-5448
FAX: 420-2-2423-3408
E-MAIL: iffkv@tlp.cz
FESTIVAL DATE: July
ENTRY DEADLINE: April
PROGRAMMER: Eva Zaoralova
CATEGORY: International

DENMARK

COPENHAGEN FILM FESTIVAL

Bulowsvej 50A
DK-1870 Frederiksberg C
Copenhagen, Denmark
TEL: 45-35372507
FAX: 45-31355758
FESTIVAL DATE: October
CONTACT: Jonna Jensen

COPENHAGEN GAY AND LESBIAN FILM FESTIVAL

LBL
National Organization for Gays & Lesbians
Knabrostrade 3
Box 1023 DK 1007
Copenhagen, Denmark
TEL: 45-3313-1948 or 45-3315-2002
FAX: 45-3391-0348 or 45-3332-5077
FESTIVAL DATE: October-November
ENTRY DEADLINE: July
CONTACT: Jill Byrnit, Lasse Soll Soude
CATEGORY: Gay Lesbian

INTERNATIONAL ODENSE FILM FESTIVAL

Vindegade 18
DK-5000 Odense C, Denmark
TEL: 45-66-131372 ext. 4044
FAX: 45-65-914318
FESTIVAL DATE: August
ENTRY DEADLINE: May for materials; July for films
DIRECTOR: Jorgen Roos

DOMINICAN REPUBLIC

INTERNATIONAL WOMEN'S FILM FESTIVAL

Equis-Intec
Ap. Postal 342-9
Zona 2
Santo Domingo,
Dominican Republic
TEL: 809-567-9271 x287
FESTIVAL DATE: Biennial, odd years; March
CATEGORY: International, Women

EGYPT

CAIRO INTERNATIONAL FILM FESTIVAL

17 Kasr El Nil St.
Cairo 202, Egypt
TEL: 20-2-392-3562
FAX: 20-2-393-8979
FESTIVAL DATE: November-December
ENTRY DEADLINE: September for entry materials; October for films.
CONTACT: Saad Eldin Wahba
CATEGORY: International

CAIRO INTERNATIONAL FILM FESTIVAL FOR CHILDREN

17 Kasr El Nil St.
Cairo 202, Egypt
TEL: 20-2-392-3562
FAX: 20-2-393-8979
FESTIVAL DATE: September
ENTRY DEADLINE: August
CONTACT: Saad Eldin Wahba
CATEGORY: International, Kid

ENGLAND

BIRMINGHAM INTERNATIONAL FILM AND TV FESTIVAL

9 Margaret St.
Birmingham, B3 3SB U.K.
TEL: 44-121-212-0777
FAX: 44-121-212-0666
FESTIVAL DATE: November
ENTRY DEADLINE: By invitation
CONTACT: Sarah McKenzie

BRIGHTON FESTIVAL

21-22 Old Steine
Brighton, BN1 1EL England
TEL: 44-273-713-875
FAX: 44-273-622-453
FESTIVAL DATE: May
CONTACT: Jim Hornsby

BRITISH SHORT FILM FESTIVAL

BBC Centre House,
Room A-214
56 Wood Lane
London, W12 7SB England
TEL: 81-7438000
FAX: 81-7408540
FESTIVAL DATE: September
CONTACT: Amanda Casson
CATEGORY: Short

CAMBRIDGE INTERNATIONAL FILM FESTIVAL

"Festivals, if they have any real purpose, should be attempting to broaden our notions of what constitutes interesting cinema.... In recent years, Cambridge has established itself as one of the most audacious and relevant of British events."
—*Geoff Andrew of TIME OUT*

City Screen LTD
86 Dean St.
London, WIV 5AA England
TEL: 0171 734 4342
FAX: 0171 734 4027
E-MAIL: festival@cambarts.co.uk
FESTIVAL DATE: Mid-July
ENTRY DEADLINE: April
YEAR FESTIVAL BEGAN: 1977
CONTACT: Tony Jones
DIRECTOR: Tony Jones
CATEGORY: Independent, International
PROFILE: Over the years the Festival has provided Cambridge film-goers with an opportunity to broaden their horizons and enjoy some of the most exciting and innovative work of contemporary cinema. It has charted the British production, new cinema in Eastern Europe, and the emergence of U.S. independents. It has also given many filmmakers their first, and sometimes only opportunity to screen work in Britain.

PANELS: Critic's debate.

FAMOUS SPEAKERS: Wim Wenders, Krzysztof Kieslowski

AWARDS: No

COMPETITIONS: No

FILMS SCREENED: 40 features and 40 shorts

TOURIST INFORMATION: University Colleges

TRAVEL TIPS: Flight to Stansted. Then rail or bus to Cambridge (50 minutes)

BEST BARS: Bar at Cinema

CHILDREN'S LONDON FILM FESTIVAL

South Bank, Waterloo
London, SE1 8XT England
TEL: 071-815-1322/3
FAX: 071-633-0786
FESTIVAL DATE: January-February
CONTACT: Sheila Whitaker
CATEGORY: Kids

INTERNATIONAL ANIMATION FESTIVAL

79 Wardour St.
London, W1V 3PH England
TEL: 71-580-6202
FAX: 71-287-2112
FESTIVAL DATE: April-May
CATEGORY: Animation, International

INTERNATIONAL ANIMATION FESTIVAL, CARDiFF, WALES

c/o The British Film Institute
21 Stephen St.
London, W1P 1PL England
TEL: 071-255-1444 x142
FAX: 071-255-2315
FESTIVAL DATE: May
ENTRY DEADLINE: June
DIRECTOR: Irene Kotlarz
CATEGORY: Animation, International

INTERNATIONAL DOCUMENTARY FILM FESTIVAL

The Workstation
15 Paternoster Row
Sheffield, S1 2BX England
TEL: 44-742-796511
FAX: 44-742-706522
FESTIVAL DATE: March
CONTACT: Midge Mackenzie
CATEGORY: Documentary

INTERNATIONAL FILM AND VIDEO COMPETITION

IAC Competition
24C West Street
Epsom, Surrey
KT18 7RJ England
TEL: 0372-739672
FESTIVAL DATE: March
ENTRY DEADLINE: January
CONTACT: IAC
CATEGORY: Video

JEWISH FILM FESTIVAL—LONDON

South Bank, Waterloo
London, SE1 8XT England
TEL: 071-815-1322/3
FAX: 071-633-0786
FESTIVAL DATE: October
ENTRY DEADLINE: June
CONTACT: Jane Ivey

KINO AMERICAN UNDERGROUND & STUDENT SHOWCASE FILM FEST

Kinofilm
Kino Screen Ltd
48 Princess Street
Manchester, M1 6HR England
TEL: + 44 161 288 2494 or +44 161 281 1374
FAX: + 44 161 237 3423
E-MAIL: john.kino@good.co.uk
WEB SITE: www.hals.demon.co.uk/kino
FESTIVAL DATE: November
ENTRY DEADLINE: September

CONTACT: as above and Abigail Christenson

DIRECTOR: John S. Wojowski

PROGRAMMER: John S. Wojowski

OTHER STAFF: Terry Ponsillo, IT Coordinator; Vannessa Millward, IT R & D; Miles Prowse, Technical Manager; Abigail Christenson, Festival Cordinator; Emma Crisp, Festival Assistant Administrator

CATEGORY: Independent, Student, Underground

PROFILE: To promote the short film art form in its widest form, to support new and young film makers and to develop new audiences for such work. To compliment other cinematic events in the city and to provide a wider and diverse appreciation of new forms of moving image culture.

AWARDS: Yes

APPLICATION TIPS: Though we accept films up to 30 mins long, best shorts no longer than 15 mins. Keep them short and sweet.

APPLICATION FEE: £2.50 (UK) £.00 (International)

INSIDER ADVICE: Make it good.

AVERAGE FILMS ENTERED: Quirky and unusual, different than the norm.

ODDS OF ACCEPTANCE: 60 entered (50 shown)

FILMMAKER PERKS: We don't have the budget so we can only offer free tickets for screenings and the opportunities to meet others

TOURIST INFORMATION: Manchester's clubs and bars, music venues and arts attractions throught the year.

TRAVEL TIPS: Use the trams or get a taxi, the buses are crap!

BEST HANGOUT FOR FILMMAKERS: Kino and Cornerhouse cinemas. Sandbar, Granbys

BEST PLACE FOR BREAKFAST: Bloom Street Cafe

FESTIVAL TALE: The print dilemma is quite a frequent occurence at festivals. Our worst scenario was on the opening night last year when we didn't have a projector until after the show was due to start—let alone the print!!!

KiNO FESTiVAL OF NEW iRiSH CiNEMA

Kinofilm
Kino Screen Ltd
48 Princess Street
Manchester, M1 6HR England
TEL: + 44 161 288 2494 or
+44 161 281 1374
FAX: + 44 161 237 3423
E-MAIL: john.kino@good.co.uk
WEB SITE:
www.hals.demon.co.uk/kino
FESTIVAL DATE: March
ENTRY DEADLINE: January
CONTACT: as above and Abigail Christenson
DIRECTOR: John S. Wojowski
PROGRAMMER: John S. Wojowski
OTHER STAFF: Terry Ponsillo, IT Coordinator; Vannessa Millward, IT R & D; Miles Prowse, Technical Manager; Abigail Christenson, Festival Cordinator; Emma Crisp, Festival Assistant Administrator
CATEGORY: Ethnic Other, Independent
AWARDS: Yes
COMPETITIONS: Yes
MAJOR AWARDS: Innovation for a new Irish Feature (others are all shorts—categories differ each year)
VALUE OF AWARDS: no cash award at present—trophies only
LAST WINNING DIRECTORS: in above order Feature: Alan Gilsenan; Shorts: Enda Hughes, David Tickner, Joel Simon, Paul Duanne, James Finlan & Mike Casey
PAST JUDGES: local judges
APPLICATION TIPS: Though we accept films up to 30 mins long, best shorts no longer than 15 mins. Keep them short and sweet.
APPLICATION FEE: £2.50 (UK) £.00 (International)
INSIDER ADVICE: Make it good.

ODDS OF ACCEPTANCE: 100 entered (60 shown)
FILMMAKER PERKS: We don't have the budget so we can only offer free tickets for screenings and the opportunities to meet others
TOURIST INFORMATION: Manchester's clubs and bars, music venues and arts attractions throught the year.
TRAVEL TIPS: Use the trams or get a taxi, the buses are crap!
BEST HANGOUT FOR FILMMAKERS: Kino and Cornerhouse cinemas. Sandbar, Granbys
BEST PLACE FOR BREAKFAST: Bloom Street Cafe

KiNOFiLM, MANCHESTER iNTERANTiONAL SHORT FiLM & ViDEO FESTiVAL

Kinofilm
Kino Screen Ltd
48 Princess Street
Manchester, M1 6HR England
TEL: 1 44 161 288 2494 or
+44 161 281 1374
FAX: + 44 161 237 3423
E-MAIL: john.kino@good.co.uk
WEB SITE:
www.hals.demon.co.uk/kino
FESTIVAL DATE: October/November
ENTRY DEADLINE: August
YEAR FESTIVAL BEGAN: 1995
CONTACT: Abigail Christenson
DIRECTOR: John S. Wojowski
PROGRAMMER: John S. Wojowski
OTHER STAFF: Terry Ponsillo, IT Coordinator; Vannessa Millward, IT R & D; Miles Prowse, Technical Manager; Abigail Christenson, Festival Cordinator; Emma Crisp, Festival Assistant Administrator
CATEGORY: Independent, Underground
PROFILE: To promote the short film art form in its widest form, to support new and young film makers and to develop new audiences for such work. To compliment other cinematic events in the city and to provide a

wider and diverse appreciation of new forms of moving image culture.
SEMINARS: depends each year
FAMOUS SPEAKERS: (Mike Kuchar attended in 1995)
AWARDS: Yes
COMPETITIONS: Yes (but only the Irish festival) We would like to offer awards for all but we do not have the budget
MAJOR AWARDS: Innovation for a new Irish Feature (others are all shorts—categories differ each year)
VALUE OF AWARDS: no cash award at present—trophies only
LAST WINNING FILMS: *Irish Festival,* 1998
PAST JUDGES: local judges
APPLICATION TIPS: Though we accept films up to 30 mins long, best shorts no longer than 15 mins. Keep them short and sweet.
APPLICATION FEE: £2.50 (UK) £.00 (International)
INSIDER ADVICE: Make it good.
AVERAGE FILMS ENTERED: Quirky and unusual, different than the norm.
ODDS OF ACCEPTANCE: 700 entries received (300 shown)
FILMMAKER PERKS: We don't have the budget so we can only offer free tickets for screenings and the opportunities to meet others.
TOURIST INFORMATION: Manchester's clubs and bars, music venues and arts attractions throught the year.
TRAVEL TIPS: Use the trams or get a taxi, the buses are crap!
BEST HANGOUT FOR FILMMAKERS: Kino and Cornerhouse cinemas. Sandbar, Granbys
BEST PLACE FOR BREAKFAST: Bloom Street Cafe

LEEDS INTERNATIONAL FILM FESTIVAL

"What a bloody marvelous film festival!"

—Pete Postlethwaite, Oscar winner, In The Name Of The Father

The Town Hall, The Headrow
Leeds LS1 3AD
West Yorkshire, England
TEL: + 44 (0)113 247 8389 or
+ 44 (0)113 247 8308
FAX: + 44 (0) 113 247 8397
E-MAIL: liz.rymer@leeds.gov.uk
WEB SITE: www.leeds.gov.uk/liff

FESTIVAL DATE: October
ENTRY DEADLINE: August
YEAR FESTIVAL BEGAN: 1987
CONTACT: Liz Rymer & Carmel Langstaff
DIRECTOR: Liz Rymer
PROGRAMMER: Liz Rymer
OTHER STAFF: Seasonal—different most years.
CATEGORY: L.I.F.F is an umbrella event for all types of cinema
PROFILE: L.I.F.F is now the third largest event of its kind in the UK. The Festival celebrates the most influential artform of the 20th Century and seeks to promote the moving image as a major contributor to the cultural life of the city, the region, and the nation as a whole.
SEMINARS: Educational workshops, lectures and seminars are held each year; some of these will underpin the retrospective season, others examine aspects of filmmaking and media issues.
FAMOUS SPEAKERS: Speakers range from writers, actors, commissioning editors, legal representatives, European funding experts, sales agents etc.
AWARDS: No
COMPETITIONS: No
APPLICATION TIPS: Our forms are quite straightforward and easy to fill in—be sure to include all information asked for especially the format, failure to do

this can really make selection and programming difficult. Please don't send home videos or films shot on VHS, we can't do anything with them as the screening quality is so poor and they are rarely of any real interest to audiences. If your film is selected and it's coming from abroad, make sure it is labelled correctly as a TEMPORARY IMPORT FOR CULTURAL USE ONLY—If not, we get stung for hundreds of pounds in Customs payments and we can't claim it back.

APPLICATION FEE: £5.00 within the UK, £10.00 outside—to help with admin. costs.
AVERAGE FILMS ENTERED: We (and the audiences) love quirky films, Indies which are well written and produced, often humorous slants on life, love, relationships, that kind of thing. We are a big student city so grunge/slacker films go down well. Also, there is a huge audience for animation of all types.
FILMS SCREENED: 200+ including retrospectives and new UK releases.
ODDS OF ACCEPTANCE: 300+ are submitted and 60+ are accepted.
FILMMAKER PERKS: Usually free travel from anywhere in the world (budget and sponsorship permitting), failing that, we can assist with the cost. Flights can be arranged to allow guests to travel to other parts of the UK, e.g. if they've got business in London. At least one night's accommodation in a good hotel—if you've come a long way, we usually stretch this to two. Some food is provided and there is usually some kind of reception and/or hospitality daily throughout the Film Festival. We try to be very friendly and helpful.

Do remember though that we operate on a very tight budget, we like to invite as many people as possible and this costs money—so help us out if you can by offering to buy the odd

round of drinks—you will be rewarded with our undying admiration.
TOURIST INFORMATION: Tourist Attractions etc. Lots of beautiful countryside not far away. Leeds has fantastic bars, cafes and night life—the best in the country apparently.
TRAVEL TIPS: Fly into Manchester and offer to take the train straight to Leeds from the airport—our drivers would much appreciate it even though we would love to pick you all up in person. Those of you from warmer climes, bring warm clothes—you'll need them.
BEST RESTAURANTS: Too many to name but Soho is pretty good, not too expensive. Cheap and cheerful comes in the form of the fastest (and best) Chinese restaurant in the west.
BEST BARS: Oporto, Liquid, Soho, in The Exchange Quarter, and Mojo's, a blouse/rock 'n' roll kind of joint —all hip and happening.
BEST HANGOUT FOR FILMMAKERS: The Coburg and The Barge—pubs right next to the Film School.
BEST PLACE FOR BREAKFAST: Other than the free one in the Hotel...The Hellenic Cafe, full fried English breakfast at its best (or worst) just the thing after a long night.
FESTIVAL TALE: I remember a story about someone (who shall remain nameless) putting director Terry Gilliam in a Mercedes facing downhill and the chauffeur had forgotten to put the handbrake on. The sight of an award-winning director rolling off, albeit slowly, into oncoming traffic was mortifying, but it probably seemed worse than it was. A brave Festival helper turned hero and snatched the handbrake therefore ensuring Gilliam went on to make *The Fisher King*. I think the lovely man has forgiven us.

LONDON FiLM FESTiVAL

National Film Theatre
South Bank, Waterloo
London, SE1 8XT England
TEL: +44 171 813 1323
FAX: +44 171 633 0786
E-MAIL:
sarah.lutton@bfi.org.uk or
carol.coombes@bfi.org.uk
WEB SITE: http://www.
ibmpcug.co.uk/IFF.html
FESTIVAL DATE: November
ENTRY DEADLINE: August
CONTACT: Sarah Lutton
DIRECTOR: Adrian Wootton
PROGRAMMER: Sandra Hebron
OTHER STAFF: Carol Coombes
(Festival Assistant)
CATEGORY: International
PROFILE: The London Film Festival is an established non-competitive international film festival. It does not have a market or competition. There is no application fee for filmmakers or delegates wishing either to submit work or go to the festival. Over 100,000 attend this 18-day festival.
COMPETITIONS: No
APPLICATION TIPS: Film must have been made in last 2 years, must be a UK premiere.
APPLICATION FEE: None. Feature films get rejected simply because the programmers do not think (a) they are not good enough to be screened, blunt but truthful (b) we have to think who our audience is, would we be able to promote and sell this film to an audience, and (c) it has to fit into our programme of work which we are encouraging and developing for that particular year.

Shorts—we simply get far too many submitted. While acknowledging it is difficult to tell, or get a story across in 10mins, or even 5mins, shorts have to fit into a programme of other short films that have been submitted in a particular year. Last year for example shorts were broken down into the following programmes (a) British animation (b) international animation (c) (broadly) British Shorts (d) (broadly) international shorts.

Those that don't make it: Films about trekking in the Grand Canyon, or documentaries on the great bear etc, will not get selected simply because there have been so many other films made on a similar theme. Believe me, these films come in. Badly made, out of focus, badly edited shorts do not get selected. New filmmakers have to critically judge their own work and think whether it is of a good enough standard to submit, to what is a very competitive festival, see figures quoted earlier.

ODDS OF ACCEPTANCE: we had 2000 tapes submitted last year, out of these 170 features and 70 shorts made up the final programme. The odds of being rejected are therefore really high, this might scare off new filmmakers

TOURIST INFORMATION: London, is a lively and vibrant city and there is really no "best" hang-out as such as there is such a variety of choice. *Time Out Magazine,* a listings guide to London published weekly, probably offers the best guide to restaurants, gigs, breakfast venues, films, exhibitions and so on to the new visitor to the capital.

NORTH DEVON FiLM FESTIVAL

The Plough
Fore Street, Torrington
North Devon, EX38 8HQ
England
TEL: 0805-22552
FAX: 0805-24624
FESTIVAL DATE: June

ONEDOTZERO DiGITAL CREATiViTY FESTiVAL

Shane Walter
14M Abbey Orchard St. Estate
SW1P 2DL
FOR SUBMISSION MATERIAL:
onedotzero, c/o Matt Hanson
312 Lexington Building
Fairfield Road
E32UE
London, England
TEL: +44 468 893 466 or
+44 181 983 0463
FAX: +44 171 256 1122
E-MAIL:
shane@onedotzero.com;
matt@onedotzero.com;
info@onedotzero.com
WEB SITE: http//www.
onedotzero.com
FESTIVAL DATE: late April—
Early May
ENTRY DEADLINE: February
YEAR FESTIVAL BEGAN: 1997
CONTACT: Shane Walter + Matt Hanson
DIRECTOR: Shane Walter + Matt Hanson
PROGRAMMER: Shane Walter + Matt Hanson I consultant programmers
OTHER STAFF: Team of freelancers
CATEGORY: Digital Film + Creativity Festival
PROFILE: onedotzero is a festival which presents bleeding edge moving image work from the worlds of digital film, computer gaming, and new media. It features work from critically acclaimed names and rising stars often through pieces specially made for the festival. onedotzero is also a year-round digital creativity initiative which actively explores the digital aesthetic and new creative paradigms through productions which cut through working disciplines to cross-fertilise the area. The festival entertains, educates, and showcases to a new digitally literate audience a range of cutting edge moving image work. New forms of working with desktop digital tools and methods are

explored. After the ground-breaking inaugural festival last year, onedotzero has gained global recognition for its innovative curatorial approach and programming.

SEMINARS: Yes. Examples include: Non-linear narrative creation by AntiRom, Digital Filmmaking case study by Richard Jobson, Building Gaming Experiences with Sony Net Yaroze workshop

PANELS: Yes. Future of Filmmaking cross-disciplinary panels.

FAMOUS SPEAKERS: Yes. Leading lights of UK digital scene.

AWARDS: No

COMPETITIONS: No

APPLICATION TIPS: Festival premiere or work never before shown in Europe or UK has a better chance of acceptance. Send innovative, digitally manipulated work—well thought out with a polished concept. The quirkier the better. Additional supporting materials with application (whether work in other media or other films, test reels, etc.) may lend itself to our innovative intranet supporting programme, or spark of further ideas for new work inclusion.

APPLICATION FEE: None at present, but postage + packing need to be supplied if material is required to be returned. Details on web site.

INSIDER ADVICE: Send quality VHS or pal copies and supporting material. We are looking for unique styles rather than clumsy trend following pieces.

FILMS SCREENED: 70 [mainly shorts]

ODDS OF ACCEPTANCE: We select from about 500, but in addition to submission we have new work included by invitation and commission

FILMMAKER PERKS: Great contact, exposure for their work to a unique and opinion forming audience, networking opportunities that lead to innovative new projects and collaborations.

> We are looking for unique styles rather than clumsy trend following pieces. (onedotzero Digital Creativity Festival)

BEST RESTAURANTS: Italian Kitchen: 43 new oxford street, tel: 0171 836 1011—great Italian food nice service too. well recommended; Moro: 34-36 Exmouth Market EC1: tel: 0171 833 8336—top place, v. friendly service, full mix of beautiful food with a Spanish/Moroccan type hint.

SHEFFIELD INTERNATIONAL DOCUMENTARY FESTIVAL

The Workstation
15 Paternoster Row
Sheffield, S1 2BX England
TEL: +44 (0)114 276 5141
FAX: +44 (0)114 272 1849
E-MAIL: info@sidf.co.uk
WEB SITE: www.sidf.co.uk
FESTIVAL DATE: October
ENTRY DEADLINE: June
YEAR FESTIVAL BEGAN: 1994
DIRECTOR: Kathy Loizou
PROGRAMMER: Brent Woods
CATEGORY: Documentary
PROFILE: The Sheffield International Documentary Festival is the UK's only festival dedicated to Documentary film and television. The week long event is held annually in October in The Showroom and The Workstation in Sheffield. We show the best of documentary films and videos from around the world to both the general public and industry delegates. In addition, we run a full programme of sessions and debates including the Channel 4 Interview. On the Thursday of the week we hold Newcomers Day for up and coming filmmakers and students.

SEMINARS: Yes

PANELS: Yes

AWARDS: No

COMPETITIONS: No

APPLICATION FEE: No

FILMS SCREENED: approx. 80 films

ODDS OF ACCEPTANCE: 300 are accepted

THE FESTIVAL OF FANTASTIC FILMS

95 Meadowgate Road
Salford, Manchester M68EN
England
TEL: (+44) 161-707-3747
FAX: (+44) 161-792-0991
E-MAIL: hnad@globalnet.co.uk
WEB SITE: http://savvy.com/
~festival
FESTIVAL DATE: September
ENTRY DEADLINE: August
CONTACT: Tony Edwards
DIRECTOR: Gil Lane-Young
PROGRAMMER: Harry Nadler
OTHER STAFF: Marge Edwards, Ina Shorrock, Keith Mather, Mike Hardman, Peter Chandley, Steve Hill, Tony Meadows, Dave Trengove, Lincoln Barrett, George Houston.
CATEGORY: Retro Science, Science Fiction, Fantasy and Horror movie fan convention
PROFILE: A weekend convention celebrating 10 decades of Amazing Movies. The Festival of Fantastic Films is a festival of Film and Television which aims to further the art of Fantasy, Science Fiction and Horror Cinema. This event will be the centre of debate and act as a catalyst for new films and a fond retrospective of past classic motion pictures of the three interconnected genres.
SEMINARS: Science Fiction, Fantasy and Horror movie fan convention
PANELS: Past events have included: Censorship, The Woman's Place in the Horror Film, Distribution of Independent Productions, Script to Screen, Showreels and How to Edit Them
FAMOUS SPEAKERS: Ray Harryhausen, John Landis, Roger Corman, Freddie Francis and Roy Ward Baker
AWARDS: The SOFFIA (The Society of Fantastic Films International Award (presented to Guests of Honour), The Delta Award (presented to Best Amateur Film), Best Independent

Feature Award and Best Independent Short Film Award.

COMPETITIONS: Yes

MAJOR AWARDS: New—to be named for future event.

LAST WINNING DIRECTORS: Julian Richards

PAST JUDGES: John Landis, Norman J. Warren, Jimmy Sangster, Stephen Gallagher, Gil Lane Young, Steve Ellsion, Steve Green.

APPLICATION TIPS: Film must be in the Science Fiction, Fantasy or Horror genres

APPLICATION FEE: Yes—Under $66,000 production/acquisition value $40. Over $66,000 production/acquisition value $150

INSIDER ADVICE: Send us a VHS in first instance with application form.

AVERAGE FILMS ENTERED: SF, Horror, Fantasy

FILMS SCREENED: Over 35 features and up to 30 shorts—depending on length

ODDS OF ACCEPTANCE: We are new—last year 28 films submitted and 22 were accepted.

FILMMAKER PERKS: Free ONE DAY Festival Membership

TRAVEL TIPS: All members given info via newsletters during year. Manchester Airport is only 20 minutes via direct rail to City Centre and our convention hotel.

BEST RESTAURANTS: Manchester has a big range of great restaurants—our Chinatown is the biggest in Europe. Big selection of multi ethnic eateries. Hotel based event—good French restaurant.

BEST BARS: Lowest priced is our special bar in the hotel—Beer at £1 per pint!

BEST HANGOUT FOR FILMMAKERS: Hotel event—fans and filmmakers get together all weekend.

BEST PLACE FOR BREAKFAST: Hotel: Excellent all you can eat included in room rate.

TYNESiDE iNTERNATiONAL FiLM FESTiVAL

10 Pilgrim St.
Newcastle-upon-Tyne, NE1 6QG England
TEL: 44-91-232-8289
FAX: 44-91-221-0535
FESTIVAL DATE: November-December
CONTACT: Roy Bristow
CATEGORY: International

FINLAND

ESPOO CiNÉ iNTERNATiONAL FiLM FESTiVAL

PO. Box 95
Espoo, 02101 Finland
TEL: +358-9-466 599
FAX: +358-9-466 458
E-MAIL: aromaa@helsinki.fi
WEB SITE: http://www.espoo.fi/cine/
FESTIVAL DATE: August
ENTRY DEADLINE: May
YEAR FESTIVAL BEGAN: 1990
CONTACT: Liisa Suominen
DIRECTOR: Timo Kuismin
PROGRAMMER: Mikko Aromaa
OTHER STAFF: Ms. Kaija Suni, member of the board; Mr. Peter Toiviainen, member of the board; Mr. Petteri Paasila, member of the board; Mr. Marko Mastomaki, member of the board

CATEGORY: Independent

PROFILE: Espoo Ciné International Film Festival is mainly recognized as the biggest annual showcase of contemporary European cinema in Finland. We focus on fictional features, and occasionally screen some shorts in between as well. The line is drawn just before the

Bill Pullman and Patricia Arquette team up to promote the release of David Lynch's Lost Highway.

documentary works; that's practically the only genre we do not specialize in. Our target audience is as broad as the Finnish cinema audience overall. Thus, we're not genre-driven in any way, either. And even though European cinema is very strongly associated with the festival, we do screen the best offerings from other continents and countries annually, too. Diversity is also our strength, which helps us to attract 20,000+ people to the beautiful garden city of Tapiola, Espoo, for the six hectic festival days every year.

Despite the glorious surroundings (the Espoo Cultural Center in Tapiola, Espoo) and rather high profile, the overall feeling at the festival is very casual. The partying can get rough at times; it's not unusual to have fabulous time and drink Koskenkorva (the Finnish national spirit) until the early morning hours for several days in a row during the festival.... At least by then you'll notice that the legend of the Finns being stubborn and extremely quiet all the time is pure bullshit.

As for parties, there's the opening party, closing party and some cocktails in between (at least one arranged by the national tv channel MTV3, one by the embassy of one European country that the programme focuses on each year, and one by the Finnish Film Producers, who also give out their annual award for the best Finnish producer of the year at Espoo Ciné). The closing party is definitely the best, so if there's a chance to stay until that, it's very highly recommended.

SEMINARS: Annually on subjects in and around the medium (for instance, in 1995 it was film criticism, in 1996 it was the sound fx in the movies, 1997 it was scriptwriting, 1998 it was CGI)

PANELS: See previous answer

> The partying can get rough at times; it's not unusual to have fabulous time and drink Koskenkorva (the Finnish national spirit) until the early morning hours for several days in a row during the festival... (Espoo Ciné International Film Festival)

FAMOUS SPEAKERS: Simon Beaufoy (writer, *The Full Monty*), Val Kuklowsky & Sandy Gerdler (sound designers, *Independence Day*), Peter Parks (SFX designer on tons of well-known titles), Annie Errigo (British film critic)...

AWARDS: No

COMPETITIONS: No

APPLICATION FEE: None. On short film section the production company is suggested to pay the transportation of the print.

INSIDER ADVICE: Send the VHS (NTSC or PAL) review copies of the entries WELL IN ADVANCE since the festival board (7 members) is occasionally willing to take a look at them thoroughly...

AVERAGE FILMS ENTERED: As we're not really genre- or budget-driven, this one's difficult to answer. We have several sections (for U.S. indies, for European arthouse stuff, for big productions, for sneak previews, for midnight movies...), so there is potential space for almost everyone.

FILMS SCREENED: 60-70

ODDS OF ACCEPTANCE: 100 Films are submitted and 25-30 are accepted.

FILMMAKER PERKS: The festival invites annually up to 5 foreign special guests over, providing them with travel and lodging. Filmmakers who have entries in our programme but do not make it in the "special guests" category get free accommodation from the festival; other arrangements are also possible on a case-to-case basis. There's a chance to meet up with representatives of practically every production and distribution company in Finland, as well as the press, during the festival. Opening night is the best for getting together with local celebrities...

TOURIST INFORMATION: The Suomenlinna Fortress on an island just outside Helsinki (the garden city of Tapiola, Espoo,

is just a 15-minute ride away from the heart of the capital, Helsinki), which is easily (& cheaply) accessible via local ferries. The Hvittrask Mansion is a place definitely worth a visit during the summertime; beautiful architecture in even more beautiful surroundings, very spooky at nights—that's the place we take our special guests to annually for a bath in the original Finnish sauna...

TRAVEL TIPS: There are at least 10 bus lines going directly from the Helsinki city center to Tapiola, Espoo, so it's very easy (and cheap) to get around from the earliest morning hours to past midnight.

BEST RESTAURANTS: Well, people going to Tapiola, Espoo, to see the films tend to go to Helsinki during the night; that's where the best restaurants and bars are, and remember: it's just 15 minutes away.

BEST HANGOUT FOR FILMMAKERS: That would be the Corona Bar in Helsinki

BEST PLACE FOR BREAKFAST: Tapiola Garden

HELSINKI INTERNATIONAL FILM FESTIVAL—LOVE AND ANARCHY

Unioninkatu 10
FIN-00130 Helsinki, Finland
TEL: 358-9-629-528 or 358-9-177-501
FAX: 358-9-631-450
WEB SITE: http://www. kaapeli.fi/~hff/
FESTIVAL DATE: May
CONTACT: Pekka Lanerva

MIDNIGHT SUN FILM FESTIVAL

Malminkatu 36
00100 Helsinki, Finland
TEL: 358-9-685-2242
FAX: 358-9-694-5560
FESTIVAL DATE: June
CONTACT: Peter Von Bagh

TAMPERE FiLM FESTiVAL

Box 305

33101 Tampere, Finland

TEL: 358-31-213-0034 or 358-31-219-6149

FAX: 358-41-20-08-27

FESTIVAL DATE: March

ENTRY DEADLINE: January

CONTACT: Kirsi Kinnunen

TAMPERE iNTERNATiONAL SHORT FiLM FESTiVAL

P.O. Box 305

FIN-33101

Tampere, Finland

TEL: +358-3-213 0034; +358-3-3146 6149; +358-3-223 5188

FAX: +358-3-223 0121

E-MAIL: film.festival@ tt.tampere.fi

WEB SITE: http://www. tampere.fi/festival/film

FESTIVAL DATE: March

ENTRY DEADLINE: January

YEAR FESTIVAL BEGAN: 1970

CONTACT: Ms. Kirsi Kinnunen (Int'l relations): tel. +358-3-213 0034

DIRECTOR: Mr. Pertti Paltila

PROGRAMMER: Mr. Raimo Silius

OTHER STAFF: Co-director: Mr. Juhani Alanen, tel. +358-3-223 5681

CATEGORY: International, Short

PROFILE: Tampere Film Festival wants to improve the position of short film and documentary film in Finland and internationally. Tampere Film Festival is one of the biggest short film festivals in Europe. The International Competition of Tampere is highly esteemed. The special charasteristic of Tampere is the emphasis given to different short film genres: there are category prizes for the best documentary, best fiction and best animation. The International Short Film Market has become a lively forum for distributors and buyers. Particular attention is given to the lat-

est productions from Finland and northern and Eastern Europe.

SEMINARS: Multimedia Seminar and Production seminar for professionals.

AWARDS: Yes

COMPETITIONS: Yes

MAJOR AWARDS: Grand Prix: Festival trophy a kiss & 25,000 FIM for the best film in International Competition

VALUE OF AWARDS: A kiss & 5,000 FIM for the best animation, documentary and fiction film.

APPLICATION FEE: None

INSIDER ADVICE: Send a VHS copy of the film with a FULLY filled entry form and a complete list of dialogue in original language and in one internationally used language and one still photo. Films must be 35 mm or 16 mm prints with optical or magnetic sound and the running time may not exeed 30 minutes.

FILMS SCREENED: 80

ODDS OF ACCEPTANCE: 3,000 films are submitted and only 80 are screened.

FILMMAKER PERKS: We offer free accommodation in Tampere during the festival, no travel expenses.

TOURIST INFORMATION: Beautiful lakes around the city of Tampere. In the beginning of March you can walk on ice and even swim in a frozen lake. Actually the festival is famous for its sauna party for the foreign guests and it's a tradition that every guest swims in a frozen lake, too.

BEST RESTAURANTS: Rostisseria La Perla

BEST BARS: Europa, Club Telakka

TURKU LESBiAN AND GAY FiLM FESTiVAL

P.O. Box 288

Turku, FIN 20101 Finland

TEL: +358-2-2500695

FAX: +358-2-2512905

E-MAIL: tuseta@sci.fi

WEB SITE: www.sci.fi/~tuseta/

FESTIVAL DATE: October

ENTRY DEADLINE: July

PROGRAMMER: Erkki Lietzen, email: lietzen@utu.fi

CATEGORY: Gay Lesbian

PROFILE: The film festival is organized for the 8th time by Turun Seudun SETA ry which is a local organization for sexual minorities. The film festival is not the only thing we do, but a very important one. It is also the only lesbian and gay film festival in Finland. Turun Seudun SETA ry is a member of the National SETA in Finland and also a member of the International Lesbian and Gay Association ILGA. The film festival is arranged on a non-profit making basis. Our main goal is to screen films with lesbian/gay/bisexual/ trans-gendered themes that will not reach the Finnish audience through commercial distribution channels.

AWARDS: None

APPLICATION TIPS: Offer a preview tape in VHS (NTSC or PAL format), the film should be in English/Swedish or have English/Swedish subtitles.

APPLICATION FEE: None

INSIDER ADVICE: Offer a preview tape in VHS (NTSC or PAL) format.

AVERAGE FILMS ENTERED: Long feature films, documentaries and short films

ODDS OF ACCEPTANCE: We get about twenty preview tapes of different short films. Less than five are accepted in the main programme, and about half in an additional free video screening before the main screenings. Mostly we pick the films from international festivals like London Lesbian and Gay film Festival.

Actually the festival is famous for its sauna party for the foreign guests and it's a tradition that every guest swims in a frozen lake, too. (Tampere International Short Film Festival)

FRANCE

AFRICAS CINEMA
3 bis quai Gambetta
49100 Angers, France
TEL: 41-20-08-22
FAX: 41-20-08-27
FESTIVAL DATE: May
CONTACT: Michele Barrault,
Gerard Moreau
CATEGORY: Ethnic Black

ALES CINEMA FESTIVAL—ITINERANCES
Mas-Bringer rue, Stendhal
30100 Ales, France
TEL: 66-30-24-26
FAX: 66-56-87-24
FESTIVAL DATE: March-April
ENTRY DEADLINE: February
CONTACT: Holley Benoit

AMATUER AND NON-PROFESSIONAL FILM AND VIDEO FESTIVAL
Maison des Jeunes et de la
Culture rue Rene Binet
89100 Sens, France
TEL: 86-64-44-42
FESTIVAL DATE: April
ENTRY DEADLINE: February
DIRECTOR: Michelle Moisson
CATEGORY: Student

ANIMATED FILMS ABOUT SCIENCE
Animascience Festival
Mediatheque
Cite des Sciences est de
l'Industrie
30 Avenue Corentin Cariou
75930
Oaris Cedex 19, France
TEL: 40-05-71-29
FAX: 40-05-71-06
FESTIVAL DATE: October-November
CONTACT: Marie-Helene Herr
CATEGORY: Animation

ANNECY INTERNATIONAL ANIMATED FILM FESTIVAL
6 Avenue des Iles, BP399
74013 Annecy Cedex, France
TEL: 33-50-57-41-72
FAX: 33-50-67-81-95
FESTIVAL DATE: Bienniel (odd
years); May-June
ENTRY DEADLINE: January for
forms; February for prints/
tapes
CONTACT: M. Jean-Luc Xiberras
CATEGORY: Animation

ARGELES-SUR-MER CINEMA FORUM
Cinemaginaire
Rue de l'Eglise
66720 Rasigueres, France
TEL: 68-29-13-61
FESTIVAL DATE: May
DIRECTOR: Francois Boutonnet,
President

AROUND THE WORLD FESTIVAL
Autour du Monde
3 Avenue Jean Laigret
41000 Blois, France
TEL: 54-43-64-19
FESTIVAL DATE: November
DIRECTOR: Philippe Boulais,
President

BASTIA FILM FESTIVAL OF MEDITERRANEAN CULTURES
Association du Festival du
Film Mediterranean
Rue Favelelli
Theatre Municipal
20200 Bastia, France
TEL: 95-32-08-32 or
95-32-08-86
FAX: 95-32-57-65
FESTIVAL DATE: October
DIRECTOR: Julia Rioni, General
Secretary
CATEGORY: Ethnic Other

BIENNALE INTERNATIONALE DU FILM D'ARCHITECTURE, D'URBANISME ET D'ENVIRONMENT DE BORDEAUX
FIFARC Festival
17, Quai de la Monnaie
2eme Etage
33800 Bordeaux, France
TEL: 33-56-94-79-05
FAX: 33-56-91-48-04
FESTIVAL DATE: December
ENTRY DEADLINE: June
CONTACT: Nicole Ducourau
CATEGORY: International

BILAN DU FILM ETHNOGRAPHIQUE
Musee de l'Homme
Place du Trocadero
75116 Paris, France
TEL: 47-04-38-20
FAX: 45-53-52-82
FESTIVAL DATE: March
ENTRY DEADLINE: Forms: December; Films: January
CONTACT: Francois Foucault
CATEGORY: International

BLOIS CINEMA FORUM
Association Maison de Begon
Rue Pierre et Marie Curie
41000 Blois, France
TEL: 54-43-35-36
FESTIVAL DATE: January
DIRECTOR: Laurence Gondoin
CATEGORY: International

BONDY CINEMA FESTIVAL
Association Bondy Culture
23 bis rue Roger Salengro
93140 Bondy, France
TEL: 1-48-47-18-27
FESTIVAL DATE: February
DIRECTOR: Guy Allombert

BREST SHORT FILM FESTIVAL

Association Cote Quest
40 bis Rue de la Republique
BP 173
29269 Brest Cedex, France
TEL: 98-44-03-94
FAX: 98-80-25-24
FESTIVAL DATE: November
ENTRY DEADLINE: August
CONTACT: Gilbert Le Traon
CATEGORY: Short

BRITISH CINEMA FESTIVAL

Association Travelling
8 Passage Digard
50100 Cherbourg, France
TEL: 3-93-38-94
FAX: 33-01-20-78
FESTIVAL DATE: November
DIRECTOR: Alain Bunel, President

BRITISH FILM FESTIVAL

8 Passage Digard
F-50100 Cherbourg, France
TEL: 33-2-3393-3894
FAX: 33-2-3301-2078
FESTIVAL DATE: November
ENTRY DEADLINE: October
DIRECTOR: Jean-Charles Saint
PROGRAMMER: Jean-Francois Cornu

CABOURG FESTIVAL OF ROMANTIC FILMS

106 bis Avenue de Villiers
75017 Paris, France
TEL: 33-1-4267-2626
FAX: 33-1-4622-9303
FESTIVAL DATE: June
CONTACT: F. Mahout
CATEGORY: Romantic

CANNES FILM FESTIVAL

See "The Top Ten Film Festivals" on page 156

CARREFOUR INTERNATIONAL DE L'AUDIOVISUEL SCIENTIFIC

Cite des Sciences et de l'Industrie
30 Avenue Corentin-Cariou
75930 Paris Cedex 19, France
TEL: 1-40-05-72-49
FAX: 1-40-05-73-44
FESTIVAL DATE: November
ENTRY DEADLINE: September
CONTACT: Dominique Cartier

CERGY-PONTOISE CINEMA FESTIVAL

Theatre des Arts de Cergy-Pontoise
Centre d'Action Culturelle
Place des Arts
BP 307
95027 Cergy, France
TEL: 30-30-33-33
FESTIVAL DATE: January-February
PROGRAMMER: Helen Icart

CEVENNES FESTIVAL OF INTERNATIONAL VIDEO

L'Ecran cevenol
La Moliere
48400 Verbron, France
TEL: 66-44-02-59
FAX: 66-44-02-59
FESTIVAL DATE: July

CHINESE FILM FESTIVAL

Association Chinois de Montepellier
Hotel de Ville
1 Place Francis Ponge
34059 Montpellier cedex, France
TEL: 67-34-73-78 or 67-34-70-54
FAX: 67-64-15-81
FESTIVAL DATE: February
CONTACT: Genevieve Droz

CINEMA AU FEMININ

Marseilles, France
TEL: 331-4068
FAX: 331-4068-0570
FESTIVAL DATE: September
CONTACT: Charlotte Monginet
CATEGORY: Women

CINEMA DU REEL

BPI Centre Georges Pompidou
19 Rue Beaubourg
75197 Paris Cedex 04, France
TEL: 44-78-45-26 or 44-78-44-21
FAX: 44-78-21-24
FESTIVAL DATE: March
ENTRY DEADLINE: November for foreign entries.
CONTACT: Suzette Glenadel

CINEMAS D'AFRIQUE

African Cinema Festival
Hotel de Ville, 1
Rue Gambetta
86200 Loudon, France
TEL: 49-98-77-79
FAX: 49-98-12-88
FESTIVAL DATE: February
CONTACT: Jean-Claude Rullier
CATEGORY: Ethnic Black

CITIES VIDEO FESTIVAL

Mairie de Poitiers
Hotel de Ville
Place du Marechal Leclerc
86021 Poitiers Cedex, France
TEL: 49-88-82-07
FAX: 49-55-13-48
FESTIVAL DATE: Biennial; June
CONTACT: Dominique Royoux

CLERMONT-FERRAND SHORT FILM FESTIVAL

26 Rue des Jacobins
F-63000 Clermont-Ferrand, France
TEL: 33-4-73-91-65-73
FAX: 33-4-73-92-11-93
FESTIVAL DATE: January-February
ENTRY DEADLINE: October
CATEGORY: Short

CLISSON FILM FESTIVAL

Cinema "Le Connetable"
Festival "Le Connetable"
Rue des Halles
44190 Clisson, France
TEL: 40-54-01-49
FESTIVAL DATE: October-
November
DIRECTOR: Dominique
Boisselier, President

COGNAC INTERNATIONAL FILM FESTIVAL OF THE THRILLER

36 Rue Pierret
92200 Neuilly-sur-Seine,
France
TEL: 33-1-46-40-5500
FAX: 33-1-46-40-5539
FESTIVAL DATE: April
CONTACT: M. Lionel Chouchan

DOUARNENEZ FESTIVAL OF ETHNIC MINORITY CINEMA

Festival de Cinema
Douarnenez
BP 6
29172 Douarnenez, France
TEL: 98-92-09-21
FAX: 98-92-28-10
FESTIVAL DATE: August
DIRECTOR: Patrick Marziale,
President
CATEGORY: Ethnic Other

DUNKIRK CINEMA FORUM

Studio 43/MJC
43 Rue du Docteur Louis
Lemaire
59140 Dunkerque, France
TEL: 28-66-47-89
FAX: 28-65-06-98
FESTIVAL DATE: October
DIRECTOR: Jacques Deniel

ENTREVUES FILM FESTIVAL

Cinemas d'Aujourd'hui
Hotel de Ville
Place d'Armes
90020 Belfort Cedex, France
TEL: 84-54-24-43
FAX: 84-21-71-71
FESTIVAL DATE: November-
December
CONTACT: Mairie de Belfort, Di-
rection des Affaires Culturelles

EUROPEAN FILM FESTIVAL

Cinemauteur
Mairie de Vichy
03200 Vichy, France
TEL: 70-97-75-75
FAX: 70-97-84-44
FESTIVAL DATE: June
DIRECTOR: Nario Robert, Presi-
dent

FESTIVAL DU FILM D'ANIMATION POUR LA JEUNESSE

Maison de Societes
Boulevard Joliot Curie
01000 Bourg-en-Bresse,
France
TEL: 74-23-60-39
FAX: 74-21-16-62 or
75-45-25-18
FESTIVAL DATE: October-
November
ENTRY DEADLINE: August
CONTACT: M. Rene Brendel
CATEGORY: Animation

FESTIVAL FOR NATURE AND ENVIRONMENT FILMS

FRAPNA-Section Isere
M. N. E.
5 Place Bir-Hakeim
38000 Grenoble, France
TEL: 33-76-42-64-08
FAX: 33-76-44-63-36
FESTIVAL DATE: Biennial (even
years); February-March
DIRECTOR: Jean-Michel Blanc

FESTIVAL INTERNATIONAL DU 1ER FILM ET DE LA JEUNESSE

M. J. C. d'Annonay
Avenue Jean Jaures
07100 Annonay, France
TEL: 33-75-33-11-77
FAX: 33-75-67-64-63
FESTIVAL DATE: February
ENTRY DEADLINE: November
DIRECTOR: Jean-Louis Vey,
Directeur Adjoint de la M. J. C.

FESTIVAL INTERNATIONAL DU FILM MEDICAL DE MAURIAC

Mauriac Film Festival
14, Place Georges Pompidou
B. P. 53
15200 Mauriac, France
TEL: 33-71-67-37-37
FAX: 33-71-68-10-00
FESTIVAL DATE: March-April
ENTRY DEADLINE: September
CONTACT: Dr. Michel Chassang

FESTIVAL OF ARTS CINEMA FOR CHILDREN

Groupe TSE
Theatre de la Commune
2 Rue Edouard Poisson
BP 157
93304 Aubervilliers cedex,
France
TEL: 1-48-33-16-16
FAX: 1-48-34-35-55
FESTIVAL DATE: October
CONTACT: Christian Richard
CATEGORY: Kids

FESTIVAL OF DEAUVILLE FOR AMERICAN CINEMA

Le Festival du Cinema Americain in Deauville

Deauville is known for offering "the wildest possible showcase for American cinema, always keeping in mind that is is a reflection of what American Film is— studios, independents, documentaries and shorts."

—Daniel Benzakein

Promo 2000
36 rue Pierret
92200 Neuilly-sur-Seine,
France
TEL: 33-1-46-40-55-00
FAX: 33-1-46-40-55-39
E-MAIL: publics@imaginnet.fl
WEB SITE: http://
www.imaginet.fr/deauvillefest
FESTIVAL DATE: September
CONTACT: M. Lionel Chouchan
DIRECTOR: Daniel Benzakein /
Ruda Dauphin (U.S. director)
CATEGORY: Documentary, Independent, Short
PROFILE: France is seen as a market offering good opportunities for independent films. Deauville especially attracts of hundreds of European journalists, giving a major boost to the European box office performance of American films. Approximately 45,000 attend.
COMPETITIONS: Deauville has been building up a new noncompetitive section called Panorama, focused on 11 independent films.
PAST JUDGES: Jean-Paul Rappeneau, Liam Neeson, Eric Serra
APPLICATION FEE: None
FILMS SCREENED: Opening films: *Saving Private Ryan* directed by Steven Spielberg; *The Truman Show* directed by Peter Weir

FESTIVAL OF INTERNATIONAL FILM FOR YOUTH AND CHILDREN (FiFEJ)

35 rue d'Alsace Courcellor II
95231 Levallois-Perret, France
TEL: 1-47-54-11-00
FAX: 1-47-54-13-42
FESTIVAL DATE: June
CONTACT: Louise Maurin, General Delegate
CATEGORY: Kids

INTERNATIONAL FILM FESTIVAL

99 Boulevard Malesherbes
Paris, 75008 France
TEL: Registration Dept.
(33 1) 45-61-66-00
Press—Registration Dept.
(33 1) 45-61-66-08
FAX: Registration Dept.
(33 1) 45-61-97-60
Press—Registration Dept.
(33 1) 45-61-97-61
FESTIVAL DATE: May

GERMANY

BERLIN INTERNATIONAL FILM FESTIVAL

Budapester Strasse 50
Berlin, D-10787 Germany
TEL: 49-30-25 48 90
FAX: 49-30-25 48 92 49
E-MAIL: info@filmfest-berlin.de
WEB SITE: http://www.filmfest-berlin.de/
FESTIVAL DATE: February
CONTACT: Moritz De Hadeln
CATEGORY: Independent, International
PROFILE: The Berlin International Film Festival is one of the most prestigious festivals in Europe. It features several levels of competition and includes a European film market. Over 50,000 attend annually.
AWARDS: yes
COMPETITIONS: yes

MAJOR AWARDS: Golden Berlin Bear (Best Feature Film); Silver Berlin Bear (Best Director, Actor, and Outstanding Achievement); Alfred Bauer Prize; Blue Angel (Award for a European Film)

BRAUNSCHWEIG

Hochstr 21
Braunschweig, 38102
Germany
TEL: (49)-531-75597
FAX: (49)-531-75523
E-MAIL: filmfest@t-online.de
WEB SITE: http://forum.gaertner.de/filmfest/
FESTIVAL DATE: November
ENTRY DEADLINE: End of August
YEAR FESTIVAL BEGAN: 1986
CONTACT: Martina Fuchs
DIRECTOR: Our chairmen are Stephan Vockrodt, Edgar Merkel and Roland Kirsch
PROGRAMMER: The members of the association "filmfest Braunschweig", which are about 25 members.
OTHER STAFF: Harry Binder (Program Coordination), Martina Fuchs (Public Relations, Press Work, Marketing) Gunther Streifthau (Administration, Financial Dep.)
CATEGORY: Independent
PROFILE: Filmfest Braunschweig has established itself as the audience-oriented film festival, with many guests and opportunities for discussions, on the cultural map of the province of Lower Saxony and beyond. Circa 12,000 cinema-loving members of our audience attend screenings in several film theatres. Highlights include thematic and retrospective programmes, German and International premieres, Children's and Young People's Films. In 1987, filmfest Braunschweig was founded by the organisation of the same name. The structure of the festival has remained true to its founding principles.

SEMINARS: Seldom

PANELS: No jury

COMPETITIONS: Yes, for long films

MAJOR AWARDS: A prize is awarded for the film selected by our audience as their favourite (only for films over 61 min. long).

VALUE OF AWARDS: DM 20.000 (one prize)

APPLICATION TIPS: German premieres of international feature films

APPLICATION FEE: No

INSIDER ADVICE: Send a VHS copy of the film (NTSC is fine) and answer our application form

FILMS SCREENED: About 130 films (60 short films)

FILMMAKER PERKS: We don't have the money to invite all, but if you are invited, we pay for travel and lodging.

TOURIST INFORMATION: Locally, what might a tourist want to visit? The Braunschweig dome, Burg Dankwarderode (residence of Henry "The Lion"), the world famous Bibliotheka Augusta (Lessing Library) in Wolfenbüttel or what about a factory tour at Volkswagen in Wolfsburg?

TRAVEL TIPS: There are two nice national mountain resorts close to Braunschweig: the Harz and the elm, Hannover (expocity in 2000) is 60 kilometers and the former border (GDR) is only 30 kilometers.

BEST RESTAURANTS: Ritter St. Georg (French) or Al Trullo (Italian)

BEST BARS: Fischbach and Latino

BEST HANGOUT FOR FILMMAKERS: Our festival center in the LOT-Theatre

BEST PLACE FOR BREAKFAST: Our festival center

EXGROUND—DAS FILMFEST

Jahnstr. 17
Wiesbaden, D-65185
Germany

TEL: ++49/611/371156

FAX: ++49/611/371157

E-MAIL:
exground@screenlink.de

WEB SITE: www.screenlink.de/exground

FESTIVAL DATE: November

ENTRY DEADLINE: August

CONTACT: Andrea Wink, Thomas Kluth

DIRECTOR: Andrea Wink and Thomas Kluth

PROGRAMMER: Andrea Wink, Marion Klomfass, Ulrike Hampl, Thomas Kluth

OTHER STAFF: Katja Faulhaber (Press-cordinator)

CATEGORY: Independent, Underground, Weird

PROFILE: exground, the filmfest for new, unusual, droll and exciting productions, showcases Independents, Videos, Short films, Underground, Retro-spectives, and everything else that usually gets lost in the mainstream.

SEMINARS: No

PANELS: Yes

FAMOUS SPEAKERS: Jörg Buttgereit

AWARDS: Yes

COMPETITIONS: Yes

MAJOR AWARDS: German Short Film Award

VALUE OF AWARDS: 8,000 German Marks

LAST WINNING FILMS: *Pax de deux*

LAST WINNING DIRECTORS: Matthias Lehmann

PAST JUDGES: Audience-Award

APPLICATION TIPS: The film shouldn't be boring!

APPLICATION FEE: No

AVERAGE FILMS ENTERED: Short Films and Features: Fiction, Documentaries, Animation, Experimental

FILMS SCREENED: around 200 shorts and features

ODDS OF ACCEPTANCE: International: over 150, accepted as many are good

FILMMAKER PERKS: Free travel for Feature filmmakers, and part of the travel fee for short filmmakers. Lodging: Private accomodation and in some cases a hotel. Contacts: German Distribution Companies and German Press

BEST RESTAURANTS: Finale

BEST BARS: Finale, 2SE, Basement

FILMMAKER TRAVEL TIP

Wear big pants. That's my biggest secret! Wear big pants with big pockets so you can carry around hats to give out, pens, fliers, scotch tape, glue, breath mints, business cards, videos of your film, and the occasional twinkie to curb that low energy feeling.

You can wear normal pants when you're rich and famous. When you're young and struggling, wear big pants. You should see my festival pants, the pockets are huge!

You think I'm kidding? I actually met Harvey Weinstein as he was leaving a Sundance party CAA threw. Because I had such big pants, I was able to pull out my flier and business card with the flick of a wrist before he could get by me. He took a look at the flier and said, "Six String Samurai? That's a fuckin' cool title." He never did show up to my screening, but that's Hollywood types for you.

—Lance Mungia, writer/director, *Six String Samurai*

BEST HANGOUT FOR FILMMAKERS: Our cinema foyer

BEST PLACE FOR BREAKFAST: Finale, Chat Dor

FANTASY FiLMFEST— iNTERNATiONAL FiLM FESTIVAL FOR SCiENCE FiCTiON, FiCTiON, HORROR AND THRiLLER

Rosebud Entertainment
Herzog-Wilhelmstr. 27
80331 Munich, Germany
TEL: 49-89-2601-2838
FAX: 49-89-2602-2839
E-MAIL: rosebud-entertainment@t-online.de
WEB SiTE: http://home.t-online.de/home/rosebud_entertainment
CONTACT: Schorsch Muller
DiRECTOR: Rainer Stefan, Schorsch Muller
CATEGORY: Independent
AWARDS: No
COMPETITIONS: No
APPLICATION FEE: None
ODDS OF ACCEPTANCE: 50 films entered
ATTENDANCE: 52,000-60,000

FiLMFEST MUNCHEN

c/o IMF GmbH
Kaiserstrasse 39
Munich, D-80801 Germany
TEL: 49-89 38 19 040
FAX: 49-89 38 19 04 27
FESTIVAL DATE: June-July
ENTRY DEADLiNE: January-April
CONTACT: Eberhard Hauff
CATEGORY: Animation, Documentary, International
PROFILE: Filmfest Munchen includes international films, documentaries and animation.
AWARDS: No
COMPETITIONS: No
APPLICATION FEE: None
ODDS OF ACCEPTANCE: 150 films entered.

FiLMFESTiVAL MAX OPHÜLS PREiS

Mainzerstr. 8
Saarbrücken, 66111 Germany
TEL: 0049 681 39452
FAX: +49 681 905 1943
E-MAIL: Filmhaus@aol.com
WEB SiTE: http://www.saarbruecken.de/filmhaus.htm
FESTiVAL DATE: January
ENTRY DEADLiNE: November
YEAR FESTiVAL BEGAN: 1980
CONTACT: G. Bandel
DiRECTOR: Christel Drawer
PROGRAMMER: E. Blum, P. Thilges, M. Neumann, C. Drawer, A. Knuchel, Th. Altmeyer
OTHER STAFF: M. Künstler etc.
AWARDS: Yes
COMPETITIONS: Yes
MAJOR AWARDS: Max Ophüls Preis
VALUE OF AWARDS: 30.000,- DM
LAST WINNING FILMS: *Mammamia*
LAST WINNING DiRECTORS: Sandra Nettelbeck
PAST JUDGES: Elfi Mikesch, Judith Waldner, Zoran Solomun, Hans König, Rüdiger Vogler
ODDS OF ACCEPTANCE: 200 submitted, 60 accepted.
FiLMMAKER PERKS: Lodging.
BEST HANGOUT FOR FiLMMAKERS: LOLAS Bistro

iNTERNATiONAL FiLMFESTiVAL

Collini-Center, Galerie
D-68161 Mannheim, Germany
TEL: +49-621-10 29 43 or +49-621-15 23 16
FAX: +49-621-29 15 64
E-MAIL: ifmh@mannheim-filmfestival.com
WEB SiTE: www.mannheim-filmfestival.com
FESTiVAL DATE: October
ENTRY DEADLiNE: Mid-July
CONTACT: Christine Schmieder

DiRECTOR: Dr. Michael Koetz
PROGRAMMER: Dr. Michael Koetz
CATEGORY: Independent
PROFiLE: "The time of film festivals that present only good films, and nothing else, is past. The future lies in simultaneously offering a market place for people who trade in film. The survival of indies is directly linked to this . . .Mannheim-Heidelberg is one of the few Fests where you can screen your latest film, find a distributor/buyer for it and find a co-producer for your new project!" — Michael Koetz, Director
SEMiNARS: Together with FIPRESCI (Federation of International Film Critics)
PANELS: Changes annually
COMPETITIONS: Yes
MAJOR AWARDS: International Independent Award of Mannheim Heidelberg
VALUE OF AWARDS: Best Feature: DM 30.000; Best Documentary: DM 10.000; Best Short: DM 5.000; Special Prize In Memoriam Rainer Werner Fassbinder: DM 10.000
APPLICATiON TiPS: Make a good film!
APPLICATION FEE: None
iNSiDER ADViCE: Produce as much promo material you can afford and send it to the festival (e.g. photographs, epks—but mind there is a different TV format in Europe, no NTSC...)
AVERAGE FiLMS ENTERED: Artistically outstanding Indies by unknown directors
FiLMS SCREENED: 75
ODDS OF ACCEPTANCE: More than 1,000—about 25 will be in the International Competition
FiLMMAKER PERKS: Free travel, lodging, contacts and a productive atmosphere
TRAVEL TiPS: Heidelberg Castle, the vineyards of Palatine
BEST RESTAURANTS: Grissini im Mannheim
BEST BARS: Max Bar in Heidelberg

BEST HANGOUT FOR FILMMAKERS: The Festival Lounge, Cafe Odeon in Mannheim

BEST PLACE FOR BREAKFAST: Cafe Journal in Mannheim and Heidelberg

INTERNATIONAL GAY AND LESBIAN FILM FESTIVAL

Rosebud Entertainment
Wittelsbacher Str. 26, 10707 Berlin, Germany
TEL: 49.30.861 4532
FAX: 49.30.861 4539
E-MAIL: rosebud_entertainment@t-online.de
WEB SITE: http://home.t-online.de/home/rosebud_entertainment
FESTIVAL DATE: November/December
ENTRY DEADLINE: August
DIRECTOR: Schorsch Müller, Rainer Stefan, in cooperation with Barbara Wieler and Birgit Scheuch
CATEGORY: Gay Lesbian, International
PROFILE: Non-competitive; largest European genre festival; touring festival; five major German cities, one week each; focus on features, documentaries and shorts of interest to Lesbian, Gay, Bisexual and Transgendered people. The festival tours Munich, Stuttgart, Frankfurt, Cologne, Berlin.
COMPETITIONS: No
APPLICATION FEE: $25

INTERNATIONAL LEIPZIG FESTIVAL FOR DOCUMENTARY AND ANIMATED FILM

Box 940
Leipzig, 04009 Germany
TEL: 49 341 980 39 21 (festival office) or 49 341 980 61 43 (press office)
FAX: 49 341 980 61 41 (festival office) or 49 341 980 61 43 (press office)
E-MAIL: dok-leipzig@t-online.de
WEB SITE: http://www.mdr.de/dokfestival
FESTIVAL DATE: October
ENTRY DEADLINE: September
YEAR FESTIVAL BEGAN: 1955
CONTACT: see above
DIRECTOR: Fred Gehler
PROGRAMMER: selection commitee: Fred Gehler, Tamara Trampe, Dieter Rieken, Klaus Wischnewski, Otto Alder programme organisation: Kerstin Mauersberger (tel/fax: 49 341 980 48 28)
OTHER STAFF: managing director: Dr. Wolfgang Kröplin; spokeswoman/PR dept.: Grit Lemke finances: Hildegard Scheibe; office organisation: Ulrike Schmidt; guest office: Sabine Antoni; filmmaker's assistance: Monica Maurer
CATEGORY: Animation, Documentary
SEMINARS: workshops are included in the festival programme, themes depend on current programming
PANELS: after every section
AWARDS: yes
COMPETITIONS: yes
PAST JUDGES: Documentary: Boudjemaa Kareche (Algerie), Amir Labaki (Brazil), Helke Misselwitz (Germany), Audrius Stonys (Lithunia), Margarethe von Trotta (Germany). Animated film: Boris Pawlow (Russia), Steve Socki (USA), Barry C. Purves (Great Britain)
APPLICATION FEE: None
FILMS SCREENED: In general there are about 300 films screened.
ODDS OF ACCEPTANCE: more than 1.000 accepted: 20 documentaries in competition, 40 animated films in competition, about 100 documentaries and animated films for information programmes
FILMMAKER PERKS: Free travel: In exceptional cases. Lodging: if the film is accepted for competition: 6 nights (whole festival) if the film is accepted for another section: 3 nights.

TOURIST INFORMATION: Historical city centre of Leipzig (old Leipzig fair buildings) nation's battle monument, new Leipzig fair complex.

BEST HANGOUT FOR FILMMAKERS: Festival club at the festival centre

INTERNATIONAL SHORT FILM FESTIVAL OBERHAUSEN

Grillostr. 34
Oberhausen, D-46045 Germany
TEL: +49-208-8252652 or +49-208-8255413
E-MAIL: kurzfilmtage_oberhausen@uni-duisburg.de
WEB SITE: www.shortfilm.de
FESTIVAL DATE: Late April
ENTRY DEADLINE: January
YEAR FESTIVAL BEGAN: 1945
DIRECTOR: Lars Henrik Gass
PROGRAMMER: Hilke Doering, Helmut Krebs
AWARDS: Yes
COMPETITIONS: Yes
MAJOR AWARDS: Großer Preis der Stadt Oberhausen
VALUE OF AWARDS: DM 10000
LAST WINNING FILMS: *Alone. Life wastes Andy Hardy*
LAST WINNING DIRECTORS: Martin Arnold
PAST JUDGES: Peggy Chiao, Marja Pallassalo, Alexander horwath, Nissi Joanny Traoré, Jim Jennings
APPLICATION FEE: No
INSIDER ADVICE: just submit
AVERAGE FILMS ENTERED: films and video of high artistic value
FILMS SCREENED: international competition:65; german competition: 40; Childrens competition: 35
ODDS OF ACCEPTANCE: 3200 submitted, 100 accepted
FILMMAKER PERKS: lodging, food

MAGDEBURG INTERNATIONAL FILM FESTIVAL

Magdeburg Filmburo
Coquistrasse 18a
D-39104 Magdeburg,
Germany
TEL: 49-391-48668
FAX: 49-391-48668
FESTIVAL DATE: September
ENTRY DEADLINE: August
CONTACT: Michael Blume
CATEGORY: International

OKOMEDIA INTERNATIONAL ECOLOGICAL FILM FESTIVAL

Okomedia Institute
Habsburgerstr. 9
D-79104 Freiburg, Germany
TEL: 0761-52024
FAX: 0761-555724
FESTIVAL DATE: November
ENTRY DEADLINE: July for forms;
August for films
CONTACT: Heidi Knott
CATEGORY: International

OLDENBURG INTERNATIONAL FILM FESTIVAL

Bahnhofstr. 15
Oldenburg, 26122 Germany
TEL: +49.441.25659
FAX: +49.441.26155
E-MAIL: ritter@filmfest-oldenburg.de
WEB SITE: www.filmfest-oldenburg.de
FESTIVAL DATE: September
ENTRY DEADLINE: June
CONTACT: Thorsten Ritter
DIRECTOR: Torsten Neumann,
Thorsten Ritter
PROGRAMMER: Torsten
Neumann, Thorsten Ritter
OTHER STAFF: Jan Wittkopp,
Tina Tietjen
CATEGORY: Independent
PROFILE: The Oldenburg International Film Festival is dedicated to showcasing a wide range of versatile and individual filmmaking from all over the world. In a personal atmosphere of communication and exchange, films and guests find themselves presented to a responsive and openminded audience.

Aside from the International Section, the Portrait, dedicated to a female director with a distinctive voice and vision, and the Retrospective, dedicated to a unique and outstanding body of work, the festival focuses on us-american independent filmmaking with the Independent Section at the heart of the festival. Former participants were Larry Fessenden (*Habit*), Daniel J. Harris (*The Bible & Gun Club*), both were nominated for the Independent Spirit Award, John Gallagher (*The Deli, Men Lie*), Peter Koper (producer & author of *Headless Body in Topless Bar*), Maria Maggenti (*Two Girls in Love*), Daisy von Scherler Mayer (*Party Girl*), or Dan Mirvish (*Omaha*). The portraits were dedicated to Nancy Savoca, Katt Shea, and Iciar Bollain, the retrospectives featured Alex Cox, Frank Oz, James B. Harris, and Tim Hunter (all attended the festival).
AWARDS: No
COMPETITIONS: No
APPLICATION TIPS: Please include photos!
APPLICATION FEE: No
AVERAGE FILMS ENTERED: feature, short, documentary
FILMS SCREENED: 50 feature films, 20 short films
ODDS OF ACCEPTANCE: About 500 submissions, 30 entries.
FILMMAKER PERKS: Depending on the section and whether it is a short or feature film. For main sections we offer free travel & free lodging for the director and one/two actors/actresses. Free lodging for the short film section. Contacts for all participants.
BEST RESTAURANTS: Restaurant Tafelfreuden, Restaurant Leon.
BEST BARS: Der Schwan, Schmitz café
BEST HANGOUT FOR FILMMAKERS: Kulturetage
BEST PLACE FOR BREAKFAST: Restaurant Leon, Schmitz café

POTSDAM FILM FESTIVAL

Friedrich-Ebert-Str. 90
14467 Potsdam, Germany
TEL: 49-331-2801271
FAX: 49-331-2801273
FESTIVAL DATE: June
DIRECTOR: Irina Knochenauer

PRIX JEUNESSE INTERNATIONAL

Bayerischer Rundfunk
München, D 80300 Germany
TEL: (+49 89) 5900 2058
FAX: (+49 89) 5900 3053
E-MAIL: info@prixjeunesse.de
or uvz@prixjeunese.de
WEB SITE: http://www.prixjeunesse.de
FESTIVAL DATE: June
YEAR FESTIVAL BEGAN: 1964
CONTACT: US contact David Kleeman, Director of the American Children's Television Center in Chicago dkleeman@mcs.com
DIRECTOR: Ursula von Zallinger
PROGRAMMER: Kirsten Schneid
CATEGORY: The world's premier festival for children's and youth television programmes
SEMINARS: during the off-years, mainly in Third World countries
AWARDS: Yes
COMPETITIONS: Yes
MAJOR AWARDS: Prix Jeunesse
VALUE OF AWARDS: No prize money
PAST JUDGES: All participants vote in the contest: over 300 producers, executives and researchers from more than 50 nations come to Prix Jeunesse. They spend days screening and discussing the nominated programs.

APPLICATION TIPS: Enter a high-quality program (innovative in content or technique) which is geared to children or young people (age categories: up to 7, 7-12, 12-17 split in fiction and non-fiction)

APPLICATION FEE: No

AVERAGE FILMS ENTERED: Innovative kids programs

FILMS SCREENED: 84

ODDS OF ACCEPTANCE: More than 200 are submitted. A nomination commmittee cuts down to approx 80.

FILMMAKER PERKS: No registration fee for programs or participants. Contacts with specialists from around the world—more than 50 countries represented.

TOURIST INFORMATION: Munich is a great city. Opera, concerts, museums but also the famous "beergardens," good restaurants, etc.

BEST RESTAURANTS: 3-star restaurant "Tantris" Johann Fichte Str. 7 (Tel 36 19 59 0) and the newcomer in the city center "Marstall", Maximilianstr. 16 (Tel 29 16 55 11

BEST HANGOUT FOR FILMMAKERS: Park Café, Lenbach, Sausalito, Cafe Puck, etc.

WURZBURG INTERNATIONAL FILM FESTIVAL

Filminitiative Wurzburg
Gosbertsteige 2
D-8700 Wurzburg, Germany
TEL: 49-931-414-098
FAX: 49-931-416-279
FESTIVAL DATE: January
CONTACT: Berthold Kremmler
CATEGORY: International

GREECE

ATHENS INTERNATIONAL FILM FESTIVAL

Eleftherotypia/Daily Paper
8 Kolokotroni St.
10561 Athens, Greece
TEL: 32-42-071 or 32-44-048
FAX: 32-42-418
DIRECTOR: Ninos Feneck Mikelides
CATEGORY: International

INTERNATIONAL THESSALONIKI FILM FESTIVAL

Paparigopoulou 40
11473Athens, Greece
TEL: 30-1-645-3668
FAX: 30-1-644-8143
E-MAIL: info@filmfestival.gr
FESTIVAL DATE: November
ENTRY DEADLINE: October
DIRECTOR: Michel Demopoulos

HONG KONG

HONG KONG INTERNATIONAL FILM FESTIVAL (HKiFF)

Level 7, Administration Bldg.
Hong Kong Cultural Centre
10 Salisbury Road
TsimShaTsui
Kowloon, Hong Kong
TEL: 852-734-2903
FAX: 852-366-5206
WEB SITE: http://imsp007. netvigator.com/hkiff/
FESTIVAL DATE: April
ENTRY DEADLINE: December
CONTACT: Angela Tong
CATEGORY: International
PROFILE: This annual festival is a non-competitive showcase of international films. It is 16 days in length and is held in six theaters. Over 80,000 attend.
AWARDS: No
COMPETITIONS: No
APPLICATION FEE: None
ODDS OF ACCEPTANCE: 200 films entered

INDIA

BOMBAY INTERNATIONAL FILM FESTIVAL FOR DOCUMENTARY, SHORT AND ANIMATION FILMS

Films Division, Ministry of Information & Broadcasting
Film Bhavan
24 Dr. Golparao Deshmukh Marg.
Bombay, 400 026 India
TEL: 91-22-3864633; 3861421; 3861461
FAX: 91-22-3860308
FESTIVAL DATE: Biennial; February
ENTRY DEADLINE: October for entry forms; November for cassettes; December for film prints
DIRECTOR: R. Krishna Mohan
CATEGORY: Animation, Documentary, International, Short

CALCUTTA FILM FESTIVAL ON MOUNTAINS

81/2/3 Biren Roy Rd. West
Calcutta, 700 061 India
TEL: 77-64-52
FAX: 91-33-26-49-22
FESTIVAL DATE: January
ENTRY DEADLINE: December
CONTACT: K. K. Ray

FILMOTSAV DOCUMENTARY FILM FESTIVAL

Federation of Film Societies of India
No. 3, Northend Complex
R K Ashram Marg
New Delhi, 110 001 India
TEL: 32-04-30
FESTIVAL DATE: January
ENTRY DEADLINE: December
CONTACT: Pankaj Butalia

INTERNATIONAL FILM FESTIVAL OF INDIA

Directorate of Film Festivals
Ministry of Information &
Broadcasting
4th Floor
Lok Nayak Bhavan
Khan Market
New Delhi, 110 003 India
TEL: 91-11-461-59-53
FAX: 91-11-462-34-30
FESTIVAL DATE: January
ENTRY DEADLINE: November
CONTACT: Malti Sahai

IRAN

FAJR INTERNATIONAL FILM FESTIVAL

Farhang Cinema
Dr. Shariati Ave.
Gholhak
Tehran 19139, Iran
TEL: 98-21-200-2088
FAX: 98-21-267-082
FESTIVAL DATE: January
ENTRY DEADLINE: January
CONTACT: Jamal Omid

IRELAND

CORK INTERNATIONAL FILM FESTIVAL

Hatfield House
Tobin Street, Cork, Ireland
TEL: 353-21-271711
FAX: 353-21-275945
DIRECTOR: Donald Sheehan,
Program Director

CORK YOUTH INTERNATIONAL FILM, VIDEO AND ARTS FESTIVAL

Festival Office
94 Arderin Way
The Glen, Cork Ireland
TEL: 021-306019
FAX: 021-272839
FESTIVAL DATE: May
ENTRY DEADLINE: April
CONTACT: Helen Prout

DUBLIN FILM FESTIVAL

1 Suffolk St.
Dublin 2, Ireland
TEL: 353-1-679-2937
FAX: 353-1-679-2939
FESTIVAL DATE: March
ENTRY DEADLINE: December
CONTACT: Martin Mahon,
David McLoughlin

INTERNATIONAL CELTIC FILM AND TELEVISION FESTIVAL

Celtic Film & TV Office
BBC Northern Ireland
Ormeau Ave.
Belfast, County Antrim BT2
8HQ Northern Ireland,
Ireland
TEL: 44-232-338569
FAX: 44-232-338572
FESTIVAL DATE: March-April
CONTACT: Suzy O'Hara

JUNIOR DUBLIN FILM FESTIVAL

Irish Film Center
Eustache St.
Dublin 2, Ireland
TEL: 3531-671-4095
FAX: 3531-677-8755
FESTIVAL DATE: November
CONTACT: Alan Robinson

ISRAEL

HAIFA INTERNATIONAL FILM FESTIVAL

142 Hanassi Ave.
Haifa, Israel
TEL: 04-386246
FAX: 04-384327
FESTIVAL DATE: October
ENTRY DEADLINE: July
DIRECTOR: Pnina Blyer

JERUSALEM INTERNATIONAL FILM FESTIVAL

Derech Hebron 11 POB 8561
Jerusalem, 91083 Israel
TEL: 972 2 672 4131 or
972 2 671 5117
FAX: 972 2 673 3076 or
972 2 671 3044
E-MAIL: jer_cine@inter.net.il
WEB SITE: http://www.qrd.tau.
ac.il/israel_update.
html#jerusalem.
FESTIVAL DATE: July
ENTRY DEADLINE: April
YEAR FESTIVAL BEGAN: 1983
DIRECTOR: Lia van Leer
PROGRAMMER: Avinoam
Harpak, Lia van Leer, Gilli
Mendel
CATEGORY: Independent
PROFILE: Over 160 films are
screened in ten days represent-
ing the finest in recent cinema;
documentaries; short films;
avant garde; gay; aniamtion;
retrospectives; classics; Israeli
Cinema; Mediterranean Cin-
ema; Jewish Themes. Prizes are
given for films that focus on
human rights, peace and toler-
ance. Approximately 50,000 at-
tend.
SEMINARS: Yes
PANELS: Yes
FAMOUS SPEAKERS: Yes
AWARDS: Yes
COMPETITIONS: Yes
MAJOR AWARDS: Two categories
for international competition:
Wim van Leer "In Spirit of
Freedom" Award; Mediterra-
nean Cinema "In Pursuit of
Peace & Tolerance" Award
PAST JUDGES: Guglielmo
Biraghi, Clyde Jeavons, etc.
APPLICATION FEE: None
ODDS OF ACCEPTANCE: 165 films
entered. 50 shown.

ITALY

ALPE ADRIA FEST
Via della Pesscheria 4
34121 Trieste, Italy
TEL: 3940-311-153
FAX: 3940-311-993
FESTIVAL DATE: January
DIRECTOR: Anamaria Percavassi

AMBIENTE-INCONTRI FILM FESTIVAL INTERNAZIONALE SU NATURA E AMBIENTE
Segretaria ODESSA-Steps
Cassella Postale 186
33170 Pordenone, Italy
TEL: 39-434-520-404
FAX: 39-434-520-584
FESTIVAL DATE: July
ENTRY DEADLINE: June
DIRECTOR: Andrea Crozzoli

ANTENNA CINEMA FESTIVAL
Palazzo Sarcinelli
Via XX Septembre 132
31015 Conegliano, Italy
TEL: 39-438-411007
FAX: 39-438-32777
CONTACT: Gianfranco Zoppas

ARCIPELAGO SHORT FILM FESTIVAL
c/o Associazione Culturale
3E-medi@
Circonvallazione Clodia 88
(apt. #20)
Rome, 00195 Italy
TEL: +39-6-3751 6571
FAX: +39-6-3751 8672
E-MAIL:
arcipelago@webcom.com
WEB SITE: http://www.
webcom.com/3e_media/
arcipelago or
http://www.mondocorto.org
FESTIVAL DATE: June
ENTRY DEADLINE: April
DIRECTOR: Fabio Bo, Stefano Martina, andMassimo Forleo
CATEGORY: International, Short

PROFILE: Explores new artistic and productive horizons. This festival welcomes works from all countries.

ARMED FORCES AND PEOPLE FILM FESTIVAL
Rassegna Cinematografica
Internazionale
Eserciti E Popoli
Via A. Catalani, 31
00199 Rome, Italy
TEL: 06-86-20-02-75
FAX: 06-86-20-71-77
FESTIVAL DATE: November
ENTRY DEADLINE: September
CONTACT: General Giorgio Zucchetti

ASOLO INTERNATIONAL ANIMATION FESTIVAL
Amministrazione Provinciale
31100 Treviso, Italy
TEL: 0422-548327
FAX: 0422-50086
FESTIVAL DATE: May
CONTACT: Alfio Bastiancich, Vanna Visentin
CATEGORY: Animation, International

BELLARIA INDEPENDENT CINEMA FESTIVAL
Segretaria Organizzativa
Biblioteca Communale
Via Paolo Guide 108
47041 Bellaria (FO), Italy
TEL: 541-347186
FAX: 541-347186
FESTIVAL DATE: June
CONTACT: Anteprima per il Cinema Indipendente Italiano

BERGAMO INTERNATIONAL WEEK OF AUTEUR FILM
Mostra Internationale del
Film d'Autore
Rotonda Dei Mille, 1
24100 Bergamo, Italy
TEL: 035-243-566 or
035-243-162

FAX: 035-240-816
FESTIVAL DATE: March
ENTRY DEADLINE: January
CONTACT: Nino Zuchelli

BIENNALE DE VENEZIA—MOSTRA INTERNATIONAL DEL CINEMA
Venice International Film
Festival
Via Tomacelli, 139
Venice, Italy
TEL: 06-680041
FAX: 06-6878824
CONTACT: G. Biraghi
CATEGORY: International

COM & COM COMEDY AND COMEDIC FILM FESTIVAL
Piazza Einaudi 2
25041 Boario Terme BS, Italy
TEL: 39-364-53-16-09
FAX: 39-364-53-22-80
FESTIVAL DATE: September-October
CONTACT: Aldo Minelli

DYLAN DOG HORROR FESTIVAL
Sergio Bonelli Editore
Via M. Buonarroti 38
20145 Milan, Italy
TEL: 39-2-4800-2877
FAX: 39-2-4819-5682
FESTIVAL DATE: June
ENTRY DEADLINE: April
CONTACT: Stefano Marzorati

EUROPACINEMA FESTIVAL
Via 20 Settembre 3
00187 Rome, Italy
TEL: 39-6-4201-1184 or
39-6-4200-0211
FAX: 39-6-4201-0599
FESTIVAL DATE: November-December
ENTRY DEADLINE: September
DIRECTOR: Monique Veaute

FESTIVAL DEi POPOLi

Borgo Pinti 82R
50121 Firenze, Italy
TEL: 39-55-244-778
FAX: 39-55-241-364
E-MAIL: fespopol@dada.it
FESTIVAL DATE: November
ENTRY DEADLINE: September
DIRECTOR: Mario Simondi

FLORENCE FiLM FESTiVAL

Via S. Zonobi 54r
50129 Firenze, Italy
TEL: 055-298249
FAX: 055-298249
FESTIVAL DATE: December
DIRECTOR: Fabrizio Fiumi

GiFFONi FiLM FESTiVAL

Piazzi Umberto 1
84095 Giffoni Valle Piana
Salerno, Italy
TEL: 39-89-868-544
FAX: 39-89-866-111
FESTIVAL DATE: July
ENTRY DEADLINE: June
CONTACT: Claudio Gubitosi

GIORNATE PROFESSIONALi Di CiNEMA

Taormina, Sicily, Italy
TEL: 39-6-884-731
FAX: 39-6-440-4255
FESTIVAL DATE: June

iNTERNATiONAL CiNEMA AND TELEViSiON MULTiMEDiA MARKET— MiFED

Largo Domodossola 1
1-20145 Milano MI, Italy
TEL: 02-4997-7267 or
02-4801 2912
FAX: 02-4997-7020
FESTIVAL DATE: October
ENTRY DEADLINE: June; October
for registration information
CONTACT: Elena Lloyd, MIFED/
Fiera Milano
CATEGORY: Markets

iNTERNATiONAL FESTiVAL OF DOCUMENTARiES OF THE SEA

Piazza E. Llussu, 4
80820 San Teodoro
(Sardegna), Italy
TEL: 0784-866010
FAX: 0784-866010
FESTIVAL DATE: May
ENTRY DEADLINE: April
CONTACT: Instituto delle Civita
del Mare
CATEGORY: Documentary

iNTERNATiONAL MYSTERY FiLM FESTiVAL

MYSTFEST
Centro Culturale Polivalente
Piazza Della Repubblica, 34
47033 Cattolica (FO), Italy
TEL: 39-541-967802
FAX: 39-541-967803
FESTIVAL DATE: June-July
ENTRY DEADLINE: May
CONTACT: Gian Pietro Brunetta
CATEGORY: International, Weird

MYSTERY AND NOIR FiLM FESTiVAL

44 Via Dei Coronai
00186 Rome, Italy
TEL: 39-6-6833844 or
39-6-6872890
FAX: 39-6-6867902
FESTIVAL DATE: December
DIRECTOR: Giorgio Gosetti
CATEGORY: Mystery

PORDENONE SiLENT FiLM FESTiVAL

Le Giornate del Cinema Muto
c/o La Cineteca del Friuli
Via Osoppo 26
I-33013 Gemona (UD), Italy
TEL: 0432-980458
FAX: 0432-970542
FESTIVAL DATE: October
DIRECTOR: Livio Jacob, Chair
CATEGORY: Retro Silent

RiMiNiCiNEMA iNTERNATiONAL FiLM FESTiVAL

Riminicinema Mostra
Internazionale
Via Gambalunga 2 7
47037 Rimini, Italy
TEL: 0541-26399 or
0541-22627
FAX: 0561-26167 or
0561-24227
FESTIVAL DATE: September
ENTRY DEADLINE: June
CONTACT: Gianfranco Miro Gori
CATEGORY: International

TORiNO FiLM FESTiVAL

Via Monte di Piet‡ 1
Torino, 10121 Italy
TEL: + 39 011 5623309
FAX: + 39 011 5629796
E-MAIL:
info@torinofilmfest.org
WEB SITE: http://www.
torinofilmfesti.org
FESTIVAL DATE: November
ENTRY DEADLINE: August
(Shorts). September (Features)
YEAR FESTIVAL BEGAN: 1982
CONTACT: Alberto Barbera
DIRECTOR: Alberto Barbera
PROGRAMMER: Alberto Barbera,
Stefano Della Casa, Alexander
Horwath, Roberto Turigliatto,
Fabrizio Grosoli
OTHER STAFF: Gianni
Rondolino, president; Angela
Giulia Savoldi, general secre-
tary; Marzia Milanesi, Press
Office; Elisabetta Bassignana,
Guest Service
CATEGORY: International
PROFILE: This well organized
event (formerly know as Festi-
val Internazionale Cinema
Giovani) takes place each au-
tumn and focuses on films
made by new directors. There
is a competitive section for
shorts, features and Italian independents, as well as a section
for retrospective and spotlights.
The festival has been recognized as a top-drawer showcase
for hot new international talent and dubbed second only to

Filmmakers Tim Robbins and Richard Linklater compare notes
as they make the festival rounds.

Venice on the crowded Italian festival circuit.

SEMINARS: No

PANELS: No

FAMOUS SPEAKERS: Rober Kramer, J. Skolimowski, M. Makhmalbaf

AWARDS: Yes

COMPETITIONS: Yes

MAJOR AWARDS: International Feature-Film Competition: Best Film: $16,600; Two Special Jury Prizes: $5,500 each; Holden Prize for the best screenplay: $1,600; Nestl... Award For Film Distribution: For the winning film's distributor: $55,500; For the winning film's director: $11,100; International Short-Film Competition: Best Film: $2,800; Two Special Jury Prizes: $1,100 each; Italian-Space Competition— Fiction section: First Prize: $5,500 in Kodak film and technical services; Second Prize: $1,100. Non-Fiction section: First Prize: $5,500 in Kodak film and technical services; Second Prize: $1,100; Turin-Space Competition: First Prize: $2,800 in technical services offered by the cooperative, ZaBum Uno; Second Prize:

$550; Cipputi Prize: Best Film on the World of Work: $2,800 in collaboration with the CGIL-CISL-UIL labor unions

LAST WINNING FILMS: *I Premi, Del Festival Internazionale Cinema Giovani*

VENICE INTERNATIONAL FILM FESTIVAL

Ca Giustinian

San Marco 1364-A

30124 Venice, Italy

TEL: 39-41-52-18-711

FAX: 39-41-52-27-539

WEB SITE: http://www. worldmedia.fr/cine/venice96/

FESTIVAL DATE: August-September

ENTRY DEADLINE: July

DIRECTOR: Felice Laudadio

CATEGORY: International

PROFILE: The oldest film festival celebrating over 100 years of awarding filmmakers. It is considered one of the best festivals in the world. Approximately 100,000 attend.

MAJOR AWARDS: Golden Lion (Best Picture); Silver Lion; Grand Special Jury Prize;

Golden Lion (Lifetime Achievement); Best actor/actress/supporting actor/supporting actress.

APPLICATION FEE: None

FILMS SCREENED: over 140 films screened

JAPAN

FILM FESTIVAL OF INTERNATIONAL CINEMA STUDENTS (FFiCS)

Secretariat of the FFICS Organizing Committee c/o Tokyu Agency, Inc.

4-8-18 Akasaka

Minato-ku

Tokyo 107, Japan

TEL: 03-3475-3855

FAX: 03-5411-0382

DIRECTOR: Haruki Iwasaki, Secretary General

FUKUOKA ASIAN FILM FESTIVAL

1-8-1 Tenjin, Chuo-ku

Fukuoka 810, Japan

TEL: 81-92-733-5170

FAX: 81-92-733-5595

FESTIVAL DATE: September

CONTACT: Shu Maeda

DIRECTOR: Tadao Sato

HIROSHIMA INTERNATIONAL AMATEUR FILM AND VIDEO FESTIVAL

c/o Chugoku Broadcasting Co.

21-3 Motomachi

Naka-ku

Hiroshima 730, Japan

TEL: 082-222-1133

FAX: 082-222-1319

FESTIVAL DATE: February

CONTACT: Shozo Murata

INTERNATIONAL ANIMATION FESTIVAL— JAPAN, HIROSHIMA

Hiroshima Festival Office
4-17 Kako-machi Naka-ku
Hiroshima 730, Japan
TEL: 81-82-245-0245
FAX: 81-82-245-0246
FESTIVAL DATE: August
ENTRY DEADLINE: March for entry materials; April for prints and tapes
DIRECTOR: Sayoko Kinoshita
CATEGORY: Animation, International

JAPAN INTERNATIONAL FILM & VIDEO FESTIVAL OF ADVENTURE AND SPORTS

Jifas Organizing Committee
Hakuba City office
7025 Hokujo
Hakuba-mura
Kitaazumi-gun
Nagano-ken, Japan
TEL: 81-261-72-5000
FAX: 81-261-72-6311
FESTIVAL DATE: June
ENTRY DEADLINE: February
CONTACT: Takayuki Ogida
CATEGORY: International, Video

TOKYO INTERNATIONAL FANTASTIC FILM FESTIVAL

5H Asano Bldg.
No 3 2-4-19
Ginza, Chou-ku
Tokyo 104, Japan
TEL: 81-33563-6359
FAX: 81-33563-6235
FESTIVAL DATE: September-October
ENTRY DEADLINE: June
CONTACT: Y. Komatsuzawa
CATEGORY: Retro Science

TOKYO INTERNATIONAL FILM FESTIVAL

4F Landic Ginza Bldg. II
1-6-5 Ginza
Chuo-ku
Tokyo 104, Japan
TEL: 81-3-3563-6305
FAX: 81-3-3563-6310
WEB SITE: http://www.tokyo-filmfest.or.jp/index-e.thm
FESTIVAL DATE: September-October
ENTRY DEADLINE: June
CONTACT: Yasuyoshi Tokuma / Toshiyuki Hone
CATEGORY: International
PROFILE: There are two competitions in this international film festival. The Young Cinema Competition and the International Competition.
AWARDS: yes
COMPETITIONS: yes
MAJOR AWARDS: Tokyo Grand Prix; Special Jury Prize; Best Director/Actor/Actress; Best Artistic Contribution; Best Screenplay. Also: Tokyo Gold, Silver and Bronze awards.
VALUE OF AWARDS: 5-20 million Yen
APPLICATION FEE: None
ODDS OF ACCEPTANCE: 105 films entered

TOKYO VIDEO FESTIVAL

Victor Company of Japan, Ltd.
Victor Bldg.
1-7-1 Shinbashi
Minato-ku
Tokyo 105, Japan
TEL: 03-3289-2815
FAX: 03-3289-2819
FESTIVAL DATE: January
ENTRY DEADLINE: September
CONTACT: Minoru Sato
CATEGORY: Video

YAMAGATA INTERNATIONAL DOCUMENTARY FILM FESTIVAL

Kitagawa Bldg. 4fl.,
6-42 Kagurazaka,
Shinjuku-ku
Tokyo, 162-0825 Japan
TEL: 81-3-3266-9704
FAX: 81-3-3266-9700
E-MAIL: yidff@bekkoame.or.jp
WEB SITE: http://www.city.yamagata./yamagata.jp/yidff/en/home.html
FESTIVAL DATE: October
ENTRY DEADLINE: March
YEAR FESTIVAL BEGAN: 1989
CONTACT: Seiko Ono
DIRECTOR: Kazuyuki Yano
PROGRAMMER: Seiko Ono, Asako Fujioka, Hisao Saito
OTHER STAFF: Hiraku Miyazawa, Aaron Gerow, Jennifer Swanton
CATEGORY: Documentary
PROFILE: Located in a verdant, rolling valley far north of Tokyo, Yamagata City is the site for Asia's first international documentary film festival. The first festival (in 1989) was held to commemorate the 100th anniversary of Yamagata City, the sponsor of the festival, and has been presented biennially ever since in Yamagata's best season, October. The atmosphere of the festival is intimate and affords Asian filmmakers a prime opportunity to meet with their Western counterparts in relaxed surroundings. The first and foremost documentary festival in Asia, the week-long YIDFF is a central force in promoting documentary both in Japan and the region, showcasing recent, ground-breaking work in the International Competition and supporting new Asian filmmakers in New Asian Currents. The YIDFF will always provide a fruitful and enjoyable gathering place for both filmmakers from abroad and film-goers in Yamagata City and Japan.

Eligiblility for the International Competition: Films that

have been produced in 16mm or 35mm. Documentaries shot on video have been tranferred to 16mm or 35mm. Films that have not been relaeased publicly in Japan prior to their showing at Yamagata (Japanese films are exempt.) Shorts will not be accepted. (Less than 45 min might be considered as a short.)

New Asian Currents: Content: Centers on the works of up-and coming Asian documentarists. Eligiblility: Open to all styles of documentary on all formats of film and video.

SEMINARS: None

AWARDS: Yes

COMPETITIONS: Yes

MAJOR AWARDS: Prizes for the International Competition: The Grand Prize (The Robert and Frances Flaherty Prize) 3,000,000 yen; The Mayor's Prize 1,000,000 yen; Two Runner-Up Prizes 300,000 yen each; One Special Prize 300,000 yen. Prizes for New Asian Currents: Ogawa Shinsuke Prize 500,000 yen; Two "Awards of Excellence" 300,000 yen each

VALUE OF AWARDS: See Above

PAST JUDGES: International Competition: Shaji N. Karun, Robert Kramer, Ning Ying, Nogami Teruyo; New Asian Currents: Katsuhiko Fukuda, Yu Hui-chen

APPLICATION TIPS: Applications should be legible and easy to read (typewritten, if possible). Information about the film, such as synopses, should also be informative, but succinct (i.e., neither too short nor too long).

APPLICATION FEE: None

INSIDER ADVICE: The YIDFF tends to favor independent, groundbreaking documenaries that, while tackling important topics, are valuable not just for the information they convey, but also for their contribution to cinematic art. Given that only 15 works are accepted out of over 400 entries for the International Competition, films,

to be accepted, simply have to stand out above the crowd through innovation, technical mastery, and skill in presenting their subject.

ODDS OF ACCEPTANCE: 400 entries (average), and about 15 films will be selected for the International Competition.

FILMMAKER PERKS: The festival covers all travel fees and lodging for the official guests.

TOURIST INFORMATION: During the festival, special day trips are organised for filmmakers and guests. Numbers are limited and spaces always fill quickly. There are usually two trips. One group visits Mt. Zao, renowned for its hot springs and great skiing. It must be said those who choose this trip are the more adventurous type as the visit entails a dip in an outdoor communal hot spring with very little regard to modesty. Meanwhile the other group is taking in the beauty of Yamadera, a site made famous by the haiku poet Basho who wrote one of his most famous haikus there. Yamadera is a made up of several temples nestled into a craggy mountainside. To reach the top, one must scale the 1,000 plus stone steps, but the hike, in amongst huge, shady cedars, is well worth it.

Afterwards the two groups meet up by the Mamigasaki riverside for a traditional and seasonal lunch, followed by local entertainment (taiko drums, traditional dance etc) in which guests can participate. There are many other places to see in and around the city, which are within walking distance. Temples, museums, castle ruins....

TRAVEL TIPS: Maps and pamphlets in English are available from the many information outlets during the festival and all guests receive a festival guide which includes application forms for the day trips. October in Yamagata can be a little cool, so a jacket of some sort is a must. For an entirely Japanese

experience , DO immerse yourself in a hot spring (indoor or outdoor). Absolute Heaven—if you can stand the heat.

BEST RESTAURANTS: By far the best value for money is "Capriciosa", an Italian restaurant which is more often than not packed with hungry diners. Good prices and massive portions. Oh, and the food's pretty darn good too. If you're after Japanese food, there are some good soba and ramen places. The ramen restaurant "Sakaya" is pretty good and as such, there is usually a bit of a wait to be seated. There is also an abundance of "izakayas", which are a cross between a bar/restaurant. They offer a mix of Japanese and Western food

BEST BARS: Most of Yamagata's bars seem to be concentrated around the train station area. Best one? "Jiggers Shot Bar" is classy without being pretentious. "Billy's" is closer to the festival sites but is cozy and well-stocked.

BEST HANGOUT FOR FILMMAKERS: "Komian Club"is the official hangout for festival-goers. A pickle shop by day, this charmingly restored traditional warehouse has become a favorite amongst not only the filmmakers and guests but the locals as well. Yamagata also has some great bakeries

---

KOREA

SEOUL QUEER FiLM & ViDEO FESTiVAL

Nakwon-dong 195-1, Midong Bd #301, Chongno-ku
Seoul Korea

TEL: +82-2-766-5626

FAX: +82-2-766-0598

E-MAIL: queer21@interpia.net

FESTIVAL DATE: September

CATEGORY: Gay Lesbian

LATVIA

ARSENAL FiLM FORUM
ICNC Arsenal
Marstalu Iela 14
P. O. Box 626
Riga, LV 1047 Latvia
TEL: 013-2-221620
FAX: 013-2-8820445
FESTIVAL DATE: September
CONTACT: Augustus Sukuts

MEXICO

FESTiVAL
iNTERNACiONAL
CiNEMATOGRAFiCO
DE CANCUN
Calzada de Tlalpan 1838
Col. Country club
CP 04220 DF, Mexico
TEL: 6-89-08-12
FAX: 6 89 09-88
FESTIVAL DATE: November-
December
ENTRY DEADLINE: October
CONTACT: Jean-Pierre Leleu
Garcia

MOROCCO

iNTERNATiONAL
FESTiVAL OF
CASABLANCA
Commune Urbaine Moulay
Youssef
Poste 228
Casablanca, Morocco
TEL: 212-2-22-12-16
FAX: 212-2-29-94-74
FESTIVAL DATE: September
ENTRY DEADLINE: Fifteen days
prior to start of festival.
CONTACT: A. Masbahi

NETHERLANDS

DUTCH FiLM FESTiVAL
Nederlands Film Festival
Hoogt 4-10
3512 GW Utrecht,
Netherlands
TEL: 30-322684
FAX: 30-313200
FESTIVAL DATE: September
ENTRY DEADLINE: July
DIRECTOR: Jacques E. Van
Heyningen

HOLLAND ANiMATiON
FiLM FESTiVAL
Hoogt 4
3512 GW Utrecht,
Netherlands
TEL: 30-312216
FAX: 30-312940
CONTACT: Gerben Schermer
CATEGORY: Animation

iNTERNATiONAL
DOCUMENTARY
FiLM FESTiVAL
AMSTERDAM (iDFA)
Kleine-Garmanplantsoen, 10
1017 RR Amsterdam,
Netherlands
TEL: 20-627-33-29
FAX: 20-638-53-88
FESTIVAL DATE: December
ENTRY DEADLINE: September
DIRECTOR: Ally Derks, General
Director
CATEGORY: Documentary

ROTTERDAM
iNTERNATiONAL
FiLM FESTiVAL
P. O. Box 21696
NL—3001 AR Rotterdam,
Netherlands
TEL: 31-10-411-8080
FAX: 31-10-413-5132
E-MAIL: iffr@luna.nl
WEB SITE: http://
www.iffrotterdam.nl
FESTIVAL DATE: January-
February

ENTRY DEADLINE: December
(October for Cinemart)
CONTACT: Simon Field
DIRECTOR: Emile Fallaux
CATEGORY: International
PROFILE: Highlights of the fes-
tival include connections with
independent distributors, the
Hubert Bals Fund (awarding
$50,000 to 20 films), and
Cinemart (a showcase of vari-
ous film projects).
AWARDS: Yes
COMPETITIONS: Yes
MAJOR AWARDS: Tiger Awards
Competition. Other Awards:
Citrown Audience Award;
Fipresci Award; KNF Prizes
(awarded by film journalists)
VALUE OF AWARDS: $10,000.00
(U.S.)
APPLICATION FEE: None
FILMS SCREENED: 210 screened

NEW ZEALAND

AUCKLAND
iNTERNATiONAL
FiLM FESTiVAL
P.O. Box 9544, Te Aro
Wellington 6035 New Zealand
TEL: 64-4-385 0162
FAX: 64-4-801 7304
E-MAIL: enzedff@actrix.gen.nz
WEB SITE: http://
www.enzedff.co.nz/
FESTIVAL DATE: July
ENTRY DEADLINE: April
YEAR FESTIVAL BEGAN: 1969
CONTACT: Bill Gosden
CATEGORY: International
PROFILE: Over 80,000 attend
AWARDS: No
COMPETITIONS: No
APPLICATION FEE: None
FILMS SCREENED: 120 features
and shorts
ODDS OF ACCEPTANCE: 900 en-
tered

OUT TAKES

REEL QUEER

P O Box 12 201

Wellington, New Zealand

TEL: 64-4-388 5211 (note this is a private number; please check the time difference before calling!)

FAX: 64-4-474 3127

E-MAIL: rking@globe.net.nz

WEB SITE: http://nz.com/NZ/ Queer/ReelQueer/

FESTIVAL DATE: mid-May to early June

ENTRY DEADLINE: end of February

DIRECTOR: There is no director. All staff are voluntary and work as a team.

CATEGORY: Gay Lesbian

PROFILE: Annual New Zealand film festival for the lesbian/gay/bisexual/transgender communities, organised and showing in Wellington, but also touring (in part) to Auckland and Christchurch. Organised by REEL QUEER, a non-profit community organisation.

SEMINARS: No

PANELS: No

FAMOUS SPEAKERS: If we get funding to bring someone out here

AWARDS: No

COMPETITIONS: No

APPLICATION TIPS: Provide a film that we like!

APPLICATION FEE: none

INSIDER ADVICE: Provide us with a VHS of reasonable quality, an application form (requested or downloaded from our website) and preferably a synopsis, as far in advance of the close-off date as possible.

AVERAGE FILMS ENTERED: Features and shorts of all kinds, so long as they are of interest to our queer communities and are of screenable quality. We accept 35mm, 16mm, video—we prefer Betacam SP (PAL only), or S-VHS (PAL or NTSC)

ODDS OF ACCEPTANCE: Approximately 50 are submitted of which a little more than half are accepted.

FILMMAKER PERKS: We are rarely able to offer free airfares unless we get a grant for this. Ditto with accommodation, though we are usually able to find somewhere they can stay privately.

BEST RESTAURANTS: Logan Brown's, Cuba Street

BEST BARS: Ruby Ruby, Edward Street (gay bar)

BEST PLACE FOR BREAKFAST: Lido cafe, corner of Victoria and Wakefield Streets

THE NEW ZEALAND FILM FESTIVAL

PO Box 9544

Te Aro

Wellington, 6035 New Zealand

TEL: +64 4 385 0162

FAX: +64 4 801 7304

E-MAIL: enzedff@actrix.gen.nz

WEB SITE: www.enzedff.co.nz

FESTIVAL DATE: July

ENTRY DEADLINE: April

CONTACT: Bill Gosden

DIRECTOR: Bill Gosden

PROGRAMMER: Bill Gosden

OTHER STAFF: Richard Bealing, Sandra Reid (Assistant Directors)

PROFILE: Screening an invited program of around 100 features and 50 shorts, the Auckland and Wellington Film Festivals provide a non-competitive New Zealand premiere showcase for a striking diversity of film and video styles. An archival component also enjoys considerable prominence. Now into the second decade of programming under the direction of the apparently tireless Bill Gosden, latest editions played to audiences of 80,000 in Auckland and 50,000 in Wellington.

SEMINARS: Seminars are organised and run depending on who the guests are (usually film directors)

APPLICATION TIPS: Application forms can be requested (please provide a mailing address) or

found at the Festival's website: www.enzedff.co.nz

APPLICATION FEE: No

INSIDER ADVICE: There are no restrictions

FILMS SCREENED: The Festival screens up to 120 films ranging from features to shorts.

ODDS OF ACCEPTANCE: The Festival receives around 1000 written requests for submission forms. From this figure, up to 150 entries would receive requests for a VHS copy for viewing, and approximately 10% of these would be selected to screen at the Festival. The Festival is also continually soliciting material viewed at other Festivals, and viewing recommended by other film makers and Festivals.

WELLINGTON FILM FESTIVAL AND AUKLAND INTERNATIONAL FILM FESTIVAL

Box 9544 Te Aro

Wellington 6035, New Zealand

TEL: 385-0162

FAX: 801-7304

FESTIVAL DATE: July

ENTRY DEADLINE: May

CONTACT: Bill Gosden

NORWAY

NORWEGIAN INTERNATIONAL FILM FESTIVAL

P. O. Box 145

N-5501 Haugesund, Norway

TEL: 47-52-73-44-30

FAX: 47-52-73-44-20

FESTIVAL DATE: August

CONTACT: Gunnar Lovvik

CATEGORY: International

NORWEGIAN SHORT FiLM FESTIVAL

Sorengvn.8B
1342 Jar, Norway
TEL: 47-12-20-13
FAX: 47-12-48-65
FESTIVAL DATE: June
ENTRY DEADLINE: March
CONTACT: Ms. Toril Simonsen
CATEGORY: Short

POLAND

FESTiVAL OF SHORT FiLMS—KRAKOW

c/o Apollo Film
ul. Pychowicka 7
30 364 Krakow, Poland
TEL: 48-12-67-23-40 or
48-12-67-13-55
FAX: 48-12-67-15-52
FESTIVAL DATE: May-June
ENTRY DEADLINE: February
CONTACT: Wit Dudek
CATEGORY: Short

INTERNATiONAL FiLM FESTiVAL OF THE ART OF CiNEMATOGRAPHY

Cameraimage Festival
Foundation Tumult
Rynek Nowomiejeski 28
87-100 Torun, Poland
TEL: 48-56-248-79, 100-19,
194-03
FAX: 48-56-275-95
FESTIVAL DATE: November-
December
ENTRY DEADLINE: September
CONTACT: Kazimierz Parucki,
Marek Zydowicz

POLiSH FiLM FESTiVAL

Box 192
22-23 Piwna St.
80831 Gdansk, Poland
TEL: 48-58-315244
FAX: 48-58-313744
FESTIVAL DATE: November
CONTACT: Jerzy Martys

WARSAW FiLM FESTiVAL

P. O. Box 816
00-950 Warsaw 1, Poland
TEL: 48-22-644-1184
FAX: 48-22-635-7591
FESTIVAL DATE: October
ENTRY DEADLINE: June
CONTACT: Stefan Laudyn

PORTUGAL

FANTASPORTO / OPORTO INTERNATiONAL FiLM FESTiVAL

Rua da Constituição 311—
4200 Porto
Portugal
TEL: 351-2-507-38-80
FAX: 351-2-550-82-10
E-MAIL: fantas@caleida.pt
WEB SITE: http://
www.caleida.pt/fantasporto
FESTIVAL DATE: February-
March
ENTRY DEADLINE: December
YEAR FESTIVAL BEGAN: 1981
CONTACT: António Reis
DIRECTOR: Mário Dorminsky
PROGRAMMER: Beatriz Pacheco-
Pereira
OTHER STAFF: Áurea Soares
Ribeiro
PROFILE: The Oporto Interna-
tional Film Festival is held annually in February and is now
in its nineteenth year. The 1st
edition of FANTASPORTO, as
the festival is usually known,
was held in 1981 and was non-
competitive. All the following
editions included competitive
sections. The festival receives
entry forms from all over the
world, mostly from European
countries and the United States.
It runs in 12 theatres (4,000
seats altogether) and shows
over 200 feature films each year.
The press coverage of the Festival is made by all of the important newspaper, radio stations and television networks.
this allows press dossiers of
nearly 2500 clippings each year
which represents an unique
media coverage in Portugal for
similar cultural events
AWARDS: Yes
COMPETITIONS: Yes
MAJOR AWARDS: Fantasporto
Best Film Award
VALUE OF AWARDS: No commercial value. It's a trophy
LAST WINNING FILMS: *Retroactive*
LAST WINNING DIRECTORS: Louis
Morneau
APPLICATION FEE: None

FESTiVAL INTERNACiONAL DE CiNEMA DO ALGARVE

P. O. Box 8091
1801 Lisboa Codex, Portugal
TEL: 351-1-8513615
FAX: 351-1-8521150
FESTIVAL DATE: May
ENTRY DEADLINE: March
DIRECTOR: Carlos Manuel, Gen-
eral Director

INTERNATiONAL ANiMATED FiLM FESTiVAL—CiNANiMA

Rua 62, No. 251
4501 Espinho Codex, Portugal
TEL: 2-721-611
FAX: 2-726-015
FESTIVAL DATE: November
CATEGORY: Animation, Interna-
tional

INTERNATiONAL FESTiVAL OF CiNEMA FOR CHiLDREN AND YOUTH

R. D. Aurora de Macedo, 72
P-2300 Tomar, Portugal
TEL: 049-31-32-47
CONTACT: Manuel Faria
CATEGORY: Kids

INTERNATIONAL VIDEO FESTIVAL OF ALGARVE

Racal Clube
8300 Silves
Algrave, Portugal
TEL: 082-44-25-87
FAX: 082-44-25-30
CONTACT: FIVA
CATEGORY: Video

VIDEOEIRAS FESTIVAL

Gabinete de Relacoes Publicas
Largo de Marques de Pombal
2780 Oeiras, Portugal
TEL: 4411500
FESTIVAL DATE: April
ENTRY DEADLINE: March
CONTACT: City Council of
Oeiras

Don't use a taxi on the way from airport, as well as in the city, unless you speak Russian as a native speaker. (International Documentary, Short and Animated Films Festival)

PUERTO RICO

PUERTO RICO INTERNATIONAL FILM FESTIVAL

70 Mayaguez St., Suite B-1
Hato Rey, 00918 Puerto Rico
TEL: (809) 763-4997
FAX: (809) 753-5367
FESTIVAL DATE: November
CONTACT: Juan Gerard Gonzalez
CATEGORY: International

RUSSIA

INTERFEST MOSCOW FILM FESTIVAL

10, Khokovsky Pereulok
109028 Moscow, Russia
TEL: 7-095-297-7645
FAX: 7-095-227-4600
FESTIVAL DATE: July
ENTRY DEADLINE: March
CONTACT: Yuri Khodjaev

INTERNATIONAL DOCUMENTARY, SHORT AND ANIMATED FILMS FESTIVAL

"Your festival is unique. It is the only festival where not only documentaries, but also short feature and animation films from many countries are shown. This event is an opportunity for the young generation of filmmakers— the future of cinema—to show their debut works."

— Boris Yeltsin, The President of Russian Federation

Kravannaya str., 12
St. Petersburg, 191011 Russia
TEL: +7 (812) 235-2660
(Festival Coordinator, Alexandra Leibovitch),
+7 (812) 230-2200 (General Director, Mikhail Litviakov)
FAX: +7 (812) 235-3995
E-MAIL: centaur@mail.wplus.net
FESTIVAL DATE: Late June— Early July
ENTRY DEADLINE: May
YEAR FESTIVAL BEGAN: 1989
CONTACT: Alexandra (Sasha) Leibovitch
DIRECTOR: Mikhail S. Litviakov, documentary filmmaker
PROGRAMMER: Viktor Semeniuk, documentary filmmaker
OTHER STAFF: Boris Peirik, Financial Director
CATEGORY: Animation, Documentary, International, Short, Artistic and Intellectual
PROFILE: The Festival is a good opportunity for communication and exchanging experience and ideas between filmmakers from different countries, who develop themes of good will, spirituality, justice, morality and peace in their work realizing them by the means of cinema. The Festival aims to encourage the creative search and innovations by young filmmakers.

SEMINARS: They are different every year, so we still don't have any ideas what seminars will proceed this or next year. Every year we have PROKK (Professional Cinematographists' Club), a gathering of film directors, screen-writers and critics, who seek for chatting and discussing their needs and problems.
PANELS: See above
AWARDS: Yes
COMPETITIONS: Yes
MAJOR AWARDS: Grand Prize Golden Centaur for the best Festival film
VALUE OF AWARDS: Golden Centaur: $5,000; Centaur: $2,000 for the best full length documentary film; Centaur: $2,000 for the best short documentary film; Centaur: $2,000 for the best short feature film; Centaur: $2,000 for the best animated film; Five prizes for the best debut films (in Debut Films International Competition): $1,000

International Competition: The Golden Centaur Grand Prix and 5000 USD for the best film; The Centaur Prize and 2000 USD for the best short feature film; The Centaur Prize and 1000 USD to the best animated films; Special Diploma and 1000 USD; Special Prize and 1000 USD; Debut Film International Competition: Festival Diploma and 1000 USD
PAST JUDGES: International Jury: Volker Schlondorff (Chairman), Raoul Servais, Mikhail Kobakhidze, Alain Berliner. International Jury for Debut Competition: Valery Todorowsky, Priit Parn
APPLICATION FEE: None
FILMS SCREENED: Every film accepted for competition or special program is actually screened.
ODDS OF ACCEPTANCE: Last year we received 420 films, this year the number of films is already up to 720. We used to admit about 60 films, this year we plan to admit 110-120 films.

TOURIST INFORMATION: No need to describe all the opportunities for tourist in St. Petersburg, Russia. This town, I believe, is one of the most beautiful European cities, matching Paris, Prague, Bruxelles...

TRAVEL TIPS: Don't use a taxi on the way from airport, as well as in the city, unless you speak Russian as a native speaker. Russian accompanee for safety would be of much help. Never take a lot of money with you, and don't keep your passport in the outer pocket. Don't expect any help from cops, they don't speak English.

BEST RESTAURANTS: Don't know much about restaurants. Perhaps, Brasserie in Europe Hotel.

BEST BARS: Idiot (for Dostoyevsky's romance): come and see the world's best place for intellectuals, artists or journalists hanging out

BEST HANGOUT FOR FILMMAKERS: Manhattan (Kotyol simply)— an art club pretending for independent spirit, founded by several city filmmakers, particularly, Mcskhiev.

BEST PLACE FOR BREAKFAST: If you're bored of McDonalds and other fast food events, you can use Idiot as well. It opens at 11:00 a.m. If it's too late, use different cafes dispersed all over the town.

INTERNATIONAL FESTIVAL OF DOCUMENTARY AND SCIENCE FILMS

Sovinterfest
10 Khokhlovsky Pereulok
109028 Moscow, Russia
TEL: 227-8924
FESTIVAL DATE: January
CONTACT: Yuri Khodjaev
CATEGORY: Documentary

INTERNATIONAL FILM FESTIVAL OF FESTIVALS

10 Kamennoostrovsky Ave.
197101 St. Petersburg Russia
TEL: 812-2385811
FAX: 812-2332174
FESTIVAL DATE: June
ENTRY DEADLINE: May
CONTACT: Alexander Mamontov

ST. PETERSBURG DOCUMENTARY FESTIVAL

Message to Man Nonfiction Film Festival
12 Karavannaya St.
St. Petersburg 191011, Russia
TEL: 7-812-235-2660
FAX: 7-812-235-5318
FESTIVAL DATE: Biennial, even years; February-March
ENTRY DEADLINE: December
CONTACT: Mikhail Litviakov
CATEGORY: Documentary

SCOTLAND

DRAMBUIE EDINBURGH INTERNATIONAL FILM FESTIVAL

Eliff Filmhouse
88 Lothian Rd.
Edinburgh, EH3 9BZ
Scotland
TEL: 44-31-228-4051
FAX: 44-31-229-5501
FESTIVAL DATE: August
ENTRY DEADLINE: May
CONTACT: Penny Thompson

DUNDEE MOUNTAIN FILM FESTIVAL

Tayview
15 Ardestie Place
Monifieth
Dundee, DD5 4PS Scotland
TEL: 0382-533146
FAX: 0382-201767
FESTIVAL DATE: November
ENTRY DEADLINE: August
DIRECTOR: J. W. Burdin, Programme Director

Rene Zwelleger mugs for the camera.

SERBIA

BELGRADE INTERNATIONAL FILM FESTIVAL

Sava Center
Milentija Popovica 9
11070 Belgrad, Serbia
TEL: 39 11-222-4961
FAX: 38-11-222-1156
FESTIVAL DATE: January-February
ENTRY DEADLINE: January
CONTACT: Ms. Nevena Djonlic

SINGAPORE

SINGAPORE INTERNATIONAL FILM FESTIVAL

29A Keong Saik Road
Singapore 089136, Singapore
TEL: 65-738-7567
FAX: 65-738-7579
E-MAIL: filmfest@pacific.net.sg
FESTIVAL DATE: April
ENTRY DEADLINE: January
CONTACT: Phillip Cheah
DIRECTOR: Philip Cheah & Teo Swee
CATEGORY: International

RANDALL MICHELSON

SLOVAK REPUBLIC

ART FiLM FESTiVAL TRENCiANSKE TEPLiCE

Koventna 8
81103 Bratislava, Slovak
Republic
TEL: +421-7-5319481,
5319327, 5319479, 5319480
FAX: +421-7-5319372,
5311679
E-MAIL: festival@artfilm.sk
WEB SITE: http://
www.artfilm.sk
FESTIVAL DATE: June
ENTRY DEADLINE: April

INTERNATiONAL ART FiLM FESTiVAL— TRENCiANSKE TEPLiCE

Art Film Foundation
Brectanova 1
833 14 Bratislava,
Slovak Republic
TEL: 42-7-371-426 or
42-7-371-926
FAX: 42-7-371-426 or
42-7-372-224
FESTIVAL DATE: June
ENTRY DEADLINE: April
CONTACT: Peter Hledik

PRiX DANUBE FESTiVAL

Slovenska Televizia
Mlynska dolina
845 45 Bratislava,
Slovak Republic
TEL: 42-7-727-448
FAX: 42-7-729-440
FESTIVAL DATE: May-June
ENTRY DEADLINE: February
CONTACT: Mikulas Gavala

SOUTH AFRICA

CAPE TOWN iNTERNATiONAL FiLM FESTiVAL

University of Cape Town
Private Bag
Rodenbosch, 7700
South Africa
TEL: 021-23-8257/8
FAX: 021-24-2355
FESTIVAL DATE: April-May
CONTACT: James Polley
CATEGORY: International

DURBAN FiLM FESTiVAL

University of Natal
King George V Avenue
Durban 4001, South Africa
TEL: 27-31-811-3978
FAX: 27-31-261-7107
FESTIVAL DATE: July
CONTACT: Ron Sarkin

DURBAN iNTERNATiONAL FiLM FESTiVAL

Centre for Creative Arts
University of Natal
4041 Durban
Kwazulu-Natal, South Africa
TEL: (+27 31) 260-2594
FAX: (+27 31) 260-3074
E-MAIL: ivanidea@iafrica.com
FESTIVAL DATE: August
ENTRY DEADLINE: June
YEAR FESTIVAL BEGAN: 1978
CONTACT: Gulam Mather
DIRECTOR: Gulam Mather
PROGRAMMER: Gulam Mather
CATEGORY: Independent
PROFILE: South Africa's largest and longest running non-profit film festival out to challenge, provoke, and stimulate.
SEMINARS: We call them workshops and yes we have a few.
PANELS: A small committee is formed each year to discuss the films and give notice to those which stood out by rewarding the director with a really cool trophy.
FAMOUS SPEAKERS: Each year the festival invites famous directors/producers/actors out for the openings.
AWARDS: No
COMPETITIONS: No
APPLICATION TIPS: We're not into technical training videos, so really anything else will stand a chance. Try to make the deadline or send something now for the following year. We only select films not sourced by ourselves if budget allows for it. Remember—It's normally the packaging that helps sell the product, so before you drop your video cassette in the post make sure that you have included information on the film, your contact details, photos and anything else that represents both you and your film. Good luck!
APPLICATION FEE: None—Don't believe in them.
INSIDER ADVICE: We've seen a lot of movies, so we will carefully look at yours and if there is something that we like then we will do our best to make sure that the players in Southern Africa know it. If it's not what we're looking for, don't get upset, maybe there's a good reason why we didn't, and besides there are hundreds of festivals out there that might.
AVERAGE FILMS ENTERED: You name it, we show it.
FILMS SCREENED: 50 to 100—Depends on a number of factors like budget.
ODDS OF ACCEPTANCE: We have in the past accepted half or more. Because our festival is programmed, we are sometimes tight with space.
FILMMAKER PERKS: The only perk we can offer is if you do want to come out with your film, then we will do our best to accomodate you. We'll also show you around, help you make contacts and make you feel really important. In return we ask only for your valuable insight into filmmaking and ask that you share it with others through workshops.

We'll also show you around, help you make contacts and make you feel really important. (Durban International Film Festival)

TOURIST INFORMATION: Some of the world's best game parks (it is Africa after all), stunning beaches and resorts, winefarms (best wines in the world), beautiful cities and people. South Africa is a unique country with a booming film and television industry.

TRAVEL TIPS: It's hot here so leave your woolies at home!

BEST RESTAURANTS: In Durban there is something for everyone. Indian cuisine is popular.

BEST BARS: The Windsor, just because we hang out there.

BEST HANGOUT FOR FILMMAKERS: Try the Windsor. Unfortunately all the filmmakers hang out in Cape Town at Longkloof Studios.

BEST PLACE FOR BREAKFAST: Beachfront—Any hotel with a view of the sea.

FESTIVAL TALE: If you can imagine having to handcrank a projector whose reel motors blow 5 minutes before the screening to a 450+ packed house on one of the hottest days of the year (40+) when the air conditioning packed up that afternoon and you only have one shot at getting the speed of the film just right or burn—and to make things worse, it's a 3 hour Finnish film!!! Then you know what we mean.

JOHANNESBURG FILM FESTIVAL

Festival Films Pty. Ltd.
8th Floor, Hallmark Towers
54 Siemert Road
P. O. Box 16427
Doornfontein 2028
Johannesburg, South Africa
TEL: 27-11-402-5477/8/9
FAX: 27-11-402-6646
CONTACT: Len Davis

SPAIN

BIENAL DE CINE Y VIDEO CIENTIFICO ESPANOL

Independencia No. 10
50004 Zaragova, Spain
TEL: 976-71-81-51
FAX: 976-71-81-53
FESTIVAL DATE: November
CONTACT: Dr. Eugenio Tutor Larrosa

BIENAL NACION CAJALICANTE DE CINE AMATEUR DE LIBRE CREACION

No. 41, 3a Planta
Alicante, Spain
TEL: 5206544 or 5219556
FESTIVAL DATE: March
CONTACT: Rafael Sanchez Olmos, Jefe Dpto. Actividades
CATEGORY: International

CADIZ INTERNATIONAL VIDEO FESTIVAL

Pl. Espana Edf. Roma
11071 Cadiz, Spain
TEL: 56-24-01-03
FAX: 56-22-98-13
FESTIVAL DATE: November
ENTRY DEADLINE: September
CATEGORY: International

CERTAMEN DE CINE AMATEUR

Area de Cine
Delegacion Municipal de Cultura
Juan R. Jimenez, 11
29600 Marbella, Spain
TEL: 5-282-34-85
FAX: 5-282-52-87
FESTIVAL DATE: March
ENTRY DEADLINE: February
CONTACT: Juan Caracuel

CERTAMEN DE CINE Y VIDEO ETNOLOGICO DE LAS COMMUNIDADES AUTONMAS

Apartado do Correso, 159
Huesca 22080, Spain
TEL: 947-227058
FESTIVAL DATE: April
ENTRY DEADLINE: February
CONTACT: Eugenio Monesma Molines

CERTAMEN DE VIDEO ELIES ROGENT REHABILITACIO I RESTAURACIO

Colegio de Aparejadores Y Arquitectos Tecnicos de Barcelona
Carrer Del Bon Pastor, #5
08021 Barcelona, Spain
TEL: 34-3-414-33-11
FAX: 34-3-414-34-34 or 34-3-414-33-68
FESTIVAL DATE: May
ENTRY DEADLINE: September-October for registration; January for entries
CONTACT: Secretaria de la Muestra-concurso Elies Rogetn de Video de Rehabilitacion y Restauracion

CERTAMEN INTERNACIONAL BADALONA

Cineistes Independents de Badalona
Apartat de Correus 286
08911 Badalona BCN, Spain
TEL: 3-464-01-91
FAX: 3-464-04-50
FESTIVAL DATE: October
ENTRY DEADLINE: September
CONTACT: Jordi Pinana, Agusti Argelich

It's hot here so leave your woolies at home! (Durban International Film Festival)

CERTAMEN INTERNACIONAL DE CINE AMATEUR— CIUTAT D'IGUALADA

Apartado 378
08700 Igualada
Barcelona, Spain
TEL: 34-3-804-69-07
FAX: 34-3-804-43-62
FESTIVAL DATE: Biennial;
October
ENTRY DEADLINE: July
CONTACT: Joana Morera

CERTAMEN INTERNACIONAL DE CINE CORTOMETRAJE

c/Salzillo No 7
Murcia 30001, Spain
TEL: 968-217751
FESTIVAL DATE: March
CATEGORY: International

CERTAMEN INTERNACIONAL DE CINE TURISTICO DE MADRID

Avda. Portugal, s/n
28011 Madrid, Spain
TEL: 4701014
CONTACT: IFMA FITUR
"Madrid, Capitol Mundial del
Turismo"
CATEGORY: International

CERTAMEN INTERNACIONAL DE CINE Y VIDEO AGRARIO

Carretera Nacional II
Km. 311
P. O. Box 108
50012 Zaragoza, Spain
TEL: 76-70-11-00
FAX: 76-33-06-49
FESTIVAL DATE: April
ENTRY DEADLINE: February
CONTACT: Mr. Cativiela, Mr.
Llera

CERTAMEN INTERNACIONAL DE CINY Y VIDEO TURISTICO—ORIENTE DE ASTURIAS DE LLANES

c/Nemesio Sobrino
1 Llanes (Principado de
Asturias)
33500 Spain
TEL: 98-5400164
FESTIVAL DATE: July
CONTACT: Jose Luis Salomon
Calvo

CERTAMEN INTERNACIONAL DE VIDEO

c/El Pozo 3
44001 Teruel, Spain
TEL: 974-60-00-12
FESTIVAL DATE: December
ENTRY DEADLINE: October
CONTACT: Cineocho-Optica
Tena

CERTAMEN NACIONAL DE CINE SILENCIOSO

Instituto Nacional de
Seguridad e Higiene en el
Trabajo
c/Torrelaguna, 73
28077 Madrid, Spain
TEL: 91-2465776, 2465674,
2465832
FESTIVAL DATE: October
CONTACT: Jesus Pinedo Peydro

EUROPEAN FESTIVAL OF RURAL AND FISHING CINEMA

c/ Uría, 43, 4º, C
33202 Gijon, Spain
TEL: 9-85-364552
FAX: 9-85-364552
DIRECTOR: Isaac Del Rivero

FESTIVAL DE CINE L'ALFAS DEL PI

Festival de Cine
Casa De Cultura
03580 Alfaz Del Pi
Alicante, Spain
TEL: 96-5889423/4
FAX: 96-5889453
FESTIVAL DATE: July
ENTRY DEADLINE: June
DIRECTOR: Juan Luis Iborra

FESTIVAL INTERNACIONAL DE BARCELONA DE CINE Y VIDEO NO PROFESSIONALES

Spain
TEL: 93-246400 ext. 318
FESTIVAL DATE: November
ENTRY DEADLINE: September
CONTACT: Enrique Lopez
Manzano

FESTIVAL INTERNACIONAL DE CINE DE COMEDIA

Plaza Picasso s/n
Torremolinos, Spain
TEL: 952-380038
FESTIVAL DATE: December
CONTACT: Miguel Excalona
Quesada (Alcalde)

FESTIVAL INTERNACIONAL DE CINE ECOLOGICO Y DE LA NATURALEZA

c/Gran Via, 43 9oF
28013 Madrid, Spain
TEL: 5424253 or 5421005
FAX: 5420701
FESTIVAL DATE: November
CONTACT: Alfonso Eduardo
Perez Orozco

FESTIVAL INTERNACIONAL DE CINE ESPELEOLOGICO DE BARCELONA

Espeleo Club de Gracia
Apartado de Correos 9.126
08080 Barcelona, Spain
TEL: 34-3-4571581
FAX: 34-3-4571581
FESTIVAL DATE: November
ENTRY DEADLINE: October
DIRECTOR: Manel Canameras, President

FESTIVAL INTERNACIONAL DE CINE FANTASTICO

c/Diputacion 279 Bajos.
09007 Barcelona, Spain
TEL: 93-317-35-85
FAX: 93-301-22-47
FESTIVAL DATE: October

FESTIVAL INTERNACIONAL DE CINE REALIZADO POR MUJERES

International Festival of Film Directed by Women
Ateneo Feminista de Madrid
c/Barquillo 44-2o I
28004 Madrid, Spain
TEL: 34-1-308-69-35
FAX: 34-1-319-69-02
FESTIVAL DATE: November
ENTRY DEADLINE: June
CONTACT: Paloma Gonzalez

GRAN PREMIO DE CINE ESPANOL

c/Seminario, 4-3o
07001 Palma de Mallorca, Spain
TEL: 722444 or 702242
FESTIVAL DATE: November
ENTRY DEADLINE: September
CONTACT: Manuel Fernandez Penero

HUESCA FILM FESTIVAL

Avda Parque, 1 piso
Huesca, 22002 Spain
TEL: 34 (9) 74 21 25 82
FAX: 34 (9) 74 21 00 65
E-MAIL: huescafest@tsai.es
WEB SITE: www.huesca-filmfestival.com
FESTIVAL DATE: June
ENTRY DEADLINE: April
YEAR FESTIVAL BEGAN: 1973
CONTACT: José María Escriche Otal
DIRECTOR: José María Escriche Otal
PROGRAMMER: Board of Directors
OTHER STAFF: Domingo Malo, Lázaro Alexis
PROFILE: International Short-Film Contest, and Sample of European and Latin American Cinema (Feature Films).
AWARDS: yes
COMPETITIONS: yes-International short film contest
MAJOR AWARDS: Danzante de Oro
VALUE OF AWARDS: 1.000.000 pesetas // $ 6500 approx // 6000 ecus.
LAST WINNING FILMS: *Quiet Desperation* (U.S.)
LAST WINNING DIRECTORS: David Kost (U.S.)
PAST JUDGES: David Kost, Orlando Mora, Amanda Langlet, Andrzej Fidyk, Luciano Berriatúa, Mercedes Juste Werner, Begoña Gutierrez
FILMS SCREENED: 64 short films are screened
ODDS OF ACCEPTANCE: 1000 submitted, 64 selected
FILMMAKER PERKS: Lodging
TOURIST INFORMATION: Apart from the Pyrennes nearby, in the city of Huesca the main attractions include: the 13th Century Cathedral, The Church of San Pedro el Viejo from the 12th Century, The Church of San Lorenzo from the 17th Century, the Provincial Museum, the University, the Park, the Palace of the Kings of Aragón.

TRAVEL TIPS: Closest airport: Zaragoza. Other airports: Madrid and Barcelona.
BEST RESTAURANTS: El Sotón, Las 3 Torres, Lilla Pastia
BEST BARS: In Huesca there are 370 bars...
BEST HANGOUT FOR FILMMAKERS: Meeting point: The Festival itself
BEST PLACE FOR BREAKFAST: Luces de Bohemia in Las Cuatro Esquinas

INTERNATIONAL FESTIVAL OF DOCUMENTARY AND SHORT FILM OF BILBAO

Colon de Larreategui
37-4th D.
Apdo. 579
48009 Bilbao, Spain
TEL: 34-4-424-8696
FAX: 34-4-424-5624
FESTIVAL DATE: November
ENTRY DEADLINE: September
CONTACT: Luis Iturri
CATEGORY: Documentary, Short

INTERNATIONAL FILM FESTIVAL OF GIJON FOR YOUNG PEOPLE

Paseo Begona 24 Entresvelo
33205 Gijon Asturias, Spain
TEL: 34-85-343-735
FAX: 34-85-354-152
FESTIVAL DATE: July
ENTRY DEADLINE: May
CONTACT: Juan Jose Plans
CATEGORY: Kids

INTERNATIONAL MADRID FESTIVAL FOR THE FANTASTIC AND SCIENCE FICTION FILM

Gran Via 62-8o izda.
Madrid 28013, Spain
TEL: 541-55-45 or 541-37-21
FAX: 542-54-95
CONTACT: Rita Sonvella

INTERNATIONAL VIDEO CONTEST

c. El Pozo No. 3
Teruel 44001, Spain
TEL: 974-600012
FESTIVAL DATE: December
ENTRY DEADLINE: November
CONTACT: Fermin Perez
CATEGORY: International

SAN SEBASTIAN INTERNATIONAL FILM FESTIVAL

Plaza Oquendo S/N
20004 San Sebastian
Spain
TEL: 34 943 481212
FAX: 34 943 481218
E-MAIL: ssiff@mail.ddnet.es
WEB SITE: http://www.ddnet.es/san_sebastian_film_festival/
FESTIVAL DATE: September
ENTRY DEADLINE: July
DIRECTOR: Diego Galan
PROFILE: The second fortnight in September sees San Sebastian turn into the European capital of cinema. Eminent directors, famous actors and actresses, critics, buffs and the general public flock from all over the world to this yearly rendezvous.

Each year, the Official Competitive Section, which is recognised as such by the IFFPA, presents a programme comprising the best in recent world film production. This section is accompanied by Zabaltegi, which, with its general look at what's going on in the film world, has become a popular venue for youngsters who are attracted by its informal atmosphere and wide variety of films.

Since 1986, the Festival has been using the Anoeta Velodrome, described by Oliver Stone as "the best film theatre in the world," to present a series of films on an enormous screen together with state-of-the-art lighting and sound. A wide range of interesting and attractive cycles have been admired on this screen, from 3D works and the first Spanish screening of a spectacular Magnapax film, to European and even world premieres.

More than 3,500 seats await the influx of children and adults who come along to discover the magic of cinema in this gigantic theatre, where the morning sessions for primary and secondary pupils from the different schools in San Sebastian and its surrounding areas are one of the most exciting film-related events experienced by the Velodrome. The kids sit open-mouthed as they watch a specially chosen film dubbed into either Spanish or Basque, depending on their choice of language.

The Festival also puts special emphasis on Basque cinema, to which it dedicates an entire day.

Another aspect well worth the mention is the Festival Market. This business platform for potential film buyers takes the shape of the Sales Office, which offers distributors the unique opportunity to view a collection of more than 500 unreleased productions made over the 12 last months. This system makes it possible for producers to ensure that their products can be viewed by market professionals, and in so doing gives them the chance to meet buyers in a relaxed and informal atmosphere where they can successfully conclude their transactions.

The kids sit open-mouthed as they watch a specially chosen film dubbed into either Spanish or Basque, depending on their choice of language. (San Sebastian International Film Festival)

Stephen Kay, Thomas Jane, Claire Forlani and Gretchen Mol promote their film, The Last Time I Committed Suicide.

CATEGORIES: General subject matter, Full length features, Retrospectives

AWARDS: Yes

COMPETITIONS: Yes

MAJOR AWARDS: Gold Shell for the Best Film presented in competition; Special Jury Prize; Silver Shell for the Best Director; Silver Shell for the Best Actress; Silver Shell for the Best Actor; Jury Prize for the Best Photography; Jury Prize for any other technical or artistic aspect considered appropriate by the Jury.

Another international Jury, mainly consisting of renowned journalists, festival directors or historians, awards the New Directors Prize, comprising 25,000,000 pesetas (approx. US$160,000), to the producer and director of the best first or second film presented by a filmmaker in the Official or Zabaltegi sections. The fact that this prize demands nothing in return makes it the most important of its kind to be awarded at a festival.

The Festival also likes to pay tribute to a great figure of cinema and his or her career through the Donostia Prize, established in 1986.

PAST JUDGES: Zhang Yimou (China), President of the Jury), Anna Bonaiuto (Italy), Alfonso Cuaron (Mèxico), Agustin Diaz Yanes (Spain), Katinka Farago (Sweden), Gaston Kabore (Burkina Faso), Serge Toubiana (France)

APPLICATION FEE: None

SiTGES INTERNATiONAL FESTIVAL OF FANTASY FiLMS

c/ Rosselló, 257, 3r.E
Barcelona, 08008 Spain
TEL: 349 3 415 3938
FAX: 349 3 237 6521
E-MAIL: cinsit@sitgestur.com
WEB SITE: http://www.
sitgestur.com/cinema/
index.htm
FESTIVAL DATE: October

ENTRY DEADLINE: July

YEAR FESTIVAL BEGAN: 1968

CONTACT: Mr. Àlex Gorina

DIRECTOR: Mr. Àlex Gorina

PROGRAMMER: Mr. Àlex Gorina, Mr. Àngel Sala, Mr. Jordi Batlle and Mr. Roc Villas

OTHER STAFF: Financial Manager: Mr. Ramon Buxés; Festival Coordinator: Mr. Jaume Flor; Festival Secretary: Ms. Pepa Cordero; Press Office: Ms. Gemma Beltrán; International Relations: Ms. Isabel de Miguel and Mr. Edgar Garcia

PROFILE: The SITGES Festival Internacional de Cinema de Catalunya is a specialised competitive festival in accordance with F.I.A.P.F. regulations. The Festival has the following sections: Fantàstic, Anima't, Gran Angular, Brigadoon, Retrospectiva, Audiovisual Català, Seven Chances

All those films whose content or subject matter can be considered as "Fantasy" are eligible to enter the Fantàstic section. This is the only official competitive section. An international jury, chosen by the Festival, will make the following awards: Best Film, Best Cinematography, Best Director, Best Original Soundtrack, Best Actor, Best Visual Effects, Best Actress, Best Short Film, Best Screenplay. The decision of the jury is final and all categories will be awarded.

The Gran Angular non-competitive section includes films which are not considered to be fantasy films. The Festival chooses them as a selection of the most recent international productions.

The Retrospectiva section brings back classic titles from the history of cinema. The aim of this section is to make these films known to today's audience.

In the Seven Chances section a selection committee formed by international critics chooses 7 films that have no guarantee of commercial distribution in Spain in spite of their high artistic merit.

The Anima't section offers the most recent and creative productions from the world of international film animation. An international jury made up of specialists in the field of animation will award the Anima't prize to the best animated short. The shorts must not run for longer than 30 minutes.

The Brigadoon section offers an alternative screening on video for all those films that cannot enter the other sections because they do not meet the criteria of the selection committee.

In the Audiovisual Català section, the Festival provides a space for the screening and dissemination of Catalan audiovisual productions from the past year which are new or have not been shown. These include feature films, shorts, television productions, video art, commercials, works from film schools and any other alternative. All works should be presented in their original format.

The inclusion of films in the Fantàstic and Gran Angular sections is restricted to those films produced, at most, 18 months before the start of the Festival. Moreover, the films cannot have been commercially released in Spain or previously screened at another Spanish film festival. The inclusion of films in the Anima't section is restricted to those films produced, at most, 18 months before the start of the Festival. Moreover, they cannot have been commercially released or previously screened at another film festival in Catalonia.

AWARDS: Yes

COMPETITIONS: Yes

MAJOR AWARDS: See festival profile. All the awards have the same importance.

VALUE OF AWARDS: no money

LAST WINNING DIRECTORS: Scott Reynolds for *The Ugly*

APPLICATION FEE: None

FILMS SCREENED: Shorts and feature films, 16 mm, 35 mm, 70 mm and video aproximately 500

ODDS OF ACCEPTANCE: Approx. 100 are accepted

FILMMAKER PERKS: Free travel and free lodging

TOURIST INFORMATION: Visit Barcelona, 45 km from Sitges (little town where the festival take place)

BEST RESTAURANTS: There are lots of them. Please contact the SITGES Tourism Office: Tel. 349 3 894 42 51; Fax 349 3 894 43 05; E-mail: info@ sitgestur.com

---

SWEDEN

GÖTEBORG FILM FESTIVAL
Box 7079
Göteborg, 402 32 Sweden
TEL: +46.31.41 05 46
FAX: +46.31.41 00 63
E-MAIL:
goteborg@filmfestival.org
WEB SITE:
www.goteborg.filmfestival.org
FESTIVAL DATE: Late January-Early February
ENTRY DEADLINE: November
YEAR FESTIVAL BEGAN: 1979
CONTACT: Miss Agneta Green, programme coordinator; Mr Ulf Bjurström, managing director; Mr Magnus Telander, festival producer
DIRECTOR: Mr Gunnar Bergdahl
PROFILE: International festival for new movies from all over the world. Scandinavian meeting point for film industry
SEMINARS: Cinemix is the name of the festival's seminar programme. Every year more than 30 seminars are arranged.
AWARDS: yes
COMPETITIONS: yes
MAJOR AWARDS: The Nordic Film Prize for the best new nordic feature.

VALUE OF AWARDS: 50.000 SEK
LAST WINNING FILMS: *Tic Tac*
LAST WINNING DIRECTORS: Daniel Alfredson
APPLICATION FEE: All films are screened by invitation only
FILMS SCREENED: Last year screened 350 features, shorts and documentaries.

GOTHENBURG FILM FESTIVAL
P. O. Box 7079
S-402 32 Gotenborg, Sweden
TEL: 31-41-05-46
FAX: 31-41-00-63
FESTIVAL DATE: February
ENTRY DEADLINE: December for entry forms, stills, posters
CONTACT: Kristina Borjesson

STOCKHOLM INTERNATIONAL FILM FESTIVAL
P.O Box: 3136
Stockholm, S-103 62 Sweden
TEL: +46-8-677 50 00
FAX: +46-8-20 05 90
E-MAIL: info@cinema.se
WEB SITE:
www.filmfestivalen.se
FESTIVAL DATE: November
ENTRY DEADLINE: September
CONTACT: Jakob Abrahamsson
DIRECTOR: Git Scheynius
PROGRAMMER: Jakob Abrahamsson
OTHER STAFF: Astrid Hallenstvedt
PROFILE: Since its start in 1990, the festival has established itself as one of the leading festival and media events in Northern Europe. Stockholm X, a competitive section for directors who have made their first, second or third features; Open Zone, an outlook on where world cinema stands today; U.S. independents; Twilight Zone, films exploring the subculture of cinema; Northern Lights, a Critic's Week for films from the Nordic and Baltic

Countries; and Made in Sweden 1999, a summary of the Swedish films released this year.

Renowned for its focus in new directors and cutting edge cinema, the festival is also a major Scandinavian media event covered by more than 400 journalists. Quentin Tarantino, Steve Buscemi, Joel and Ethan Coen, Dennis Hopper and Elia Kazan are among the many personalities that have enjoyed the only festival in the world that operates 24 hours per day.

SEMINARS: On scriptwriting, low budget production, etc.
AWARDS: Yes
COMPETITIONS: Yes
MAJOR AWARDS: Bronze Horse
VALUE OF AWARDS: Honours $10,000
LAST WINNING FILMS: *Unmade Beds*
LAST WINNING DIRECTORS: Nicholas Barker
APPLICATION FEE: None
INSIDER ADVICE: Send viewing cassette with something on yourself and your film.
AVERAGE FILMS ENTERED: New and inventive films, preferably 1st, 2nd and 3rd director.
FILMS SCREENED: 150
ODDS OF ACCEPTANCE: About 500 are submitted and 150 screened.
FILMMAKER PERKS: Limited funds—some do get travel/lodgings, all get guides/dinner treats.
BEST RESTAURANTS: Mooncake
BEST BARS: Restaurant W.C, Hotel lobby Anglais
BEST HANGOUT FOR FILMMAKERS: Café Schpkowski
BEST PLACE FOR BREAKFAST: Hannas deli

UPPSALA iNTERNATiONAL SHORT FiLM FESTiVAL

P.O. Box 1746
Uppsala, S-751 47 Sweden
TEL: +46-18-12 00 25
FAX: +46-18-12 13 50
E-MAIL: uppsala@
shortfilmfestival.com
WEB SITE:
www.shortfilmfestival.com
FESTIVAL DATE: October
ENTRY DEADLINE: July
YEAR FESTIVAL BEGAN: 1982
CONTACT: Anders Engström
DIRECTOR: Anders Engström
PROGRAMMER: Anders Engström and Christoffer Olofsson
OTHER STAFF: Åsa Garnert: co-director; Joakim Palestro: Treasurer; Lotti Fred: Children's Film Festival coordinator; Anna Winlund: Guest Coordinator; Lars Lambert: Jury coordinator; Sofia Lindskog: Art Director; Johan Wallen: Ticket sales; Christer Grenabo: Entertainment
CATEGORY: Short
PROFILE: The ambitions of Uppsala International Short Film Festival are: to encourage and support film makers, especially the young and innovating; to reach and activate a broad audience; to co-operate with film schools, film organisations and other film festivals; to create a discussion about films in general and short films in particular; to promote distribution of foreign short films in Sweden and increase the attention of Swedish short films abroad.
SEMINARS: 1-2 seminars on special themes.
FAMOUS SPEAKERS: Mostly well known Swedish directors (1997: Vilgot Sjoman
AWARDS: Yes
COMPETITIONS: Yes
MAJOR AWARDS: Uppsala Film-Jackdaw
VALUE OF AWARDS: only the honour and a statuette
PAST JUDGES: Markus Schaefer,

Director of the KurzFilm-Agentur Hamburg (Germany); Annika Hyllander, TV program buyer ZTV (Sweden); Yvonne Leff, FilmCentrum (Sweden); David Borg (Sweden); Peter Ostlund, Film Director (Sweden)
APPLICATION TIPS: Send us the films early. We get lots of subimissions the last week before deadline, this means that the Selection committee gets an enormous workload during a very short period of time. A film submitted in June might get more attention then a film submitted late July.
APPLICATION FEE: No
INSIDER ADVICE: Short film is a very interesting genre with many possibilities. Be imaginative and experimental. Don't try to make feature wannabies. Cramming too much story into 20 minutes is never good.
AVERAGE FILMS ENTERED: Original, imaginative films. Strong subjects, and well written stories. Films that are made with the short film genre in mind. Films that are just made for "my portfolio" are seldom good or interesting.
FILMS SCREENED: 150-170
ODDS OF ACCEPTANCE: submitted films: about 650-750; accepted films: about 120-140
FILMMAKER PERKS: We apply for special funds to pay the travel costs for about 30 filmmakers, and we offer free bed and breakfast at Friends of the festival. About 50-60 directors visit the festival which is generally very director-oriented. We arrange directors-talks, seminars and special activities.
TOURIST INFORMATION: Uppsala is an old university town. The largest cathedral in Northern Europe. The biggest library (Carolina Rediviva). Uppsala was the capital of Sweden during the Viking era, and in Old Uppsala you can visit the burial sites of the ancient kings.
BEST RESTAURANTS: Italian: Pinos; Vegetarian: Max &

Marie; Fish: Hambergs fisk; Indian: Gandhi; Traditional: Domtrappkällaren; Chinese: China River; Greek: Akropolis; Mexican: Los Mexicanos; Modern: Elaka Måns; Post-modern: Grisen
BEST BARS: Katalin
BEST HANGOUT FOR FILMMAKERS: The Festival Pub.
BEST PLACE FOR BREAKFAST: Tea & Sympathy

SWITZERLAND

CiNEMA TOUT ECRAN/ iNTERNATiONAL FiLM & TELEViSiON CONVENTiON

16 rue General Dufour
CP 5305
CH-1211 Geneva 11, Switzerland
TEL: 41 22/328 85 54
FAX: 41 22/329 68 02
E-MAIL: info@cinema-tout-ecran.ch
WEB SITE: www.cinema-tout-ecran.ch
FESTIVAL DATE: September
ENTRY DEADLINE: July
YEAR FESTIVAL BEGAN: 1995
CONTACT: Leo Kaneman and Stephanie Billeter
DIRECTOR: Leo Kaneman
PROGRAMMER: Leo Kaneman and Stephanie Billeter
OTHER STAFF: Dominique Oestreicher (International Selection Of Short Films Coordinator), Nicole Borgeat (Festival Coordinator), Stephanie Billeter (Press Office)
CATEGORY: artistic, public and professional
PROFILE: This festival presents quality films produced by/for television networks. The aim is to prove that "auteurs" may take advantages of television and that television is capable to produce films with originality
SEMINARS: each year there are 2 or 3 seminars
PANELS: audiovisual subjects

FAMOUS SPEAKERS: directors of TV networks (ARTE; CANAL +...), screenwriters, directors (Patrick Grandperret, Claire Simon)...

AWARDS: yes

COMPETITIONS: yes

MAJOR AWARDS: Grand Prix Cinema Tout Ecran

VALUE OF AWARDS: 10'000 Swiss Francs

LAST WINNING FILMS: *Marius & Jeannette*

LAST WINNING DIRECTORS: Robert Guediguian

PAST JUDGES: '95: Christine Pascal; '96: John Schlesinger; '97: Mario Monicelli

APPLICATION TIPS: Originality and personality (and of course to be produced or co-produced by TV)

APPLICATION FEE: None

INSIDER ADVICE: Trust

AVERAGE FILMS ENTERED: Quality films from 60' to 120'

FILMS SCREENED: 50 shorts, 25 new features, 10 old ones, 8 TV series

ODDS OF ACCEPTANCE: about 200 for 15 in competition

FILMMAKER PERKS: Offer free travel, lodging and contacts

TOURIST INFORMATION: waterfronts and lake, old city

BEST RESTAURANTS: Opera Bouffe, Echalotte, Cafe Des Bains, Patio

BEST BARS: A lot in the old town

FESTIVAL DE GENEVE DES EXPOIRS DU CINEMA EUROPEEN

2 Rue Bovy-Lysberg
Case Postale 418
1211 Geneva, Switzerland
TEL: 41-22-321-5466
FAX: 41-22-321-9862
FESTIVAL DATE: October
ENTRY DEADLINE: June
DIRECTOR: Roland Ray, President

GENEVA FILM FESTIVAL

P. O. Box 5615
1211 Geneva 11, Switzerland
TEL: 41-22-809-9450
FAX: 41-22-809-9444
FESTIVAL DATE: October
ENTRY DEADLINE: October
CONTACT: Roland Ray

INTERNATIONAL ELECTRONIC CINEMA FESTIVAL

P. O. Box 1451
CH-820 Montreux, Switzerland
TEL: 21-963-32-20
FAX: 21-963-88-51
FESTIVAL DATE: April-May
CONTACT: Renee Crawford

INTERNATIONAL FESTIVAL OF COMEDY FILMS OF VEVEY

La Grenette
Grand Place 29
CH-1800 Vevey, Switzerland
TEL: 41-21-92-22-027
FAX: 41-21-92-22-024
FESTIVAL DATE: July
ENTRY DEADLINE: End of June previous year
CONTACT: Yves Moser, Patrick Henry, Bureau du Festival de Film de Comedie

INTERNATIONAL FESTIVAL OF FILMS ON ART "FIFART FESTIVAL"

P. O. Box 2783
CH-1002 Lausanne, Switzerland
TEL: 021-803-4053
FAX: 021-803-4053
FESTIVAL DATE: Biennial, even years, October
ENTRY DEADLINE: May
DIRECTOR: Anca Visdei
CATEGORY: International

LOCARNO INTERNATIONAL FILM FESTIVAL

Via Della Posta 6
CH-6600 Locarno, Switzerland
TEL: 41-91-751-0232
FAX: 41-91-751-7465
FESTIVAL DATE: August
ENTRY DEADLINE: June
CONTACT: Marco Muller
CATEGORY: International

NYON INTERNATIONAL DOCUMENTARY FILM FESTIVAL

P. O. Box 98
CH-1260 Nyon, Switzerland
TEL: 41-22-361-70-71
FAX: 41-22-361-70-71
FESTIVAL DATE: September
DIRECTOR: Gaston Nicole, President
CATEGORY: Documentary, International

VIPER INTERNATIONAL FILM AND VIDEO FESTIVAL

VIPER Lucerne
P. O. Box 4929
CH-6002 Lucerne, Switzerland
TEL: 4141-51-74-07
FAX: 4141-52-80-20
FESTIVAL DATE: October
ENTRY DEADLINE: August
CONTACT: Cristoph Settele
CATEGORY: International

TAIWAN

ASIA-PACIFIC FILM FESTIVAL

8F No. 116 Hang Chung St.
Taipei, Taiwan
TEL: 02-371-5191
FAX: 02-311-0681
FESTIVAL DATE: December
DIRECTOR: Hsu Li-Kung, VP
CATEGORY: Ethnic Other

THAILAND

BANGKOK FiLM FESTiVAL

4 Sukhumvit Soi 43
Bangkok, 10110 Thailand
TEL: +66 2 258 7376
FAX: +66 2 259 2987
E-MAIL:
bbennett@suffolk.lib.ny.us
WEB SITE: http://www.
nationmultimedia.com/
bkkfilm
FESTIVAL DATE: September
ENTRY DEADLINE: July
YEAR FESTIVAL BEGAN: 1998
DIRECTOR: Brian Bennett
CATEGORY: Independent, International
PROFILE: Competitive festival for features, shorts, documentaries, and underground programs. Accepts 35mm, 16mm, and video formats.
AWARDS: Yes
COMPETITIONS: Yes
MAJOR AWARDS: Best Feature, Best Documentary, Audience Award, Best Short, Emerging Filmmaker Award
APPLICATION FEE: None
AVERAGE FILMS ENTERED: All types
FILMMAKER PERKS: We offer travel and lodging for select films. Festival pays for print shipping.

TUNISIA

FESTiVAL iNTERNATiONAL DU FiLM AMATEUR DE KELiBiA

P. O. Box 116
1015 Tunis, Tunisia
TEL: 216-1-280-207
FAX: 216-1-336-207
FESTIVAL DATE: July-August
ENTRY DEADLINE: May for registration; June for films
CONTACT: Taoufik Abid

TURKEY

ANKARA iNTERNATiONAL FiLM FESTiVAL

World Mass Media Research Foundation
Bulten Sokak No.64/2
06700 Kavakladere
Ankara, Turkey
TEL: 90-312-468-7745
FAX: 90-312-467-7830
FESTIVAL DATE: March
ENTRY DEADLINE: December for entry forms; February for prints
DIRECTOR: Ms. Sevna Aygun, General Secretary
CATEGORY: International

iSTANBUL SHORT FiLM AND ViDEO FESTiVAL

Consulat General de France
80090 Istikst Caddem
No. 8 Tukeim, Turkey
TEL: 144-44-95
FAX: 144-48-95
FESTIVAL DATE: March
CONTACT: Consulat General de France

UKRAINE

KYiV iNTERNATiONAL FiLM FESTiVAL, MOLODiST

(Molodist means "youth" in Ukrainian)
Dom Kino, Suite 115,
Saksagansky Street, Number 6
Kyiv, 252033 Ukraine
TEL: 280-44 246 67 98
FAX: 380-44- 227-4557
E-MAIL: molodist@gu.kiev.ua
WEB SITE: http://www.
compxpress.com/~dkmedia/
molodist or http://www.uis.
Kiev.ua/~molodist
FESTIVAL DATE: October
ENTRY DEADLINE: July
YEAR FESTIVAL BEGAN: 1970
CONTACT: Lyudmila Novikova

DIRECTOR: Andrei Khalpakhtchi
PROGRAMMER: Alexander Shpyliuk
OTHER STAFF: Alexis Perchko, (programmer and press attache); Virginie Devesa, project manager
CATEGORY: Independent
COMPETITIONS: Yes, 4 categories
MAJOR AWARDS: the Scynthian Deer statuette
VALUE OF AWARDS: grand prix: USD 10.000; Best debut full length feature : USD 2.500; Best debut short film: USD 2.500; Best debut documentary or animation film: USD 2.500; Best actor/actress: FRF 5.000
LAST WINNING FILMS: *Skud* by Donna Swan, in the category of Student Film, best film among the four categories.
LAST WINNING DIRECTORS: Alain Berliner for *Ma Vie En Rose (My Life in Pink)*
APPLICATION TIPS: Send video for pre-selection on time, dialogues' list for translation, filmography and contacts for good info in the catalogue. Pictures of the film and their portrait (for the catalogue), and some publicity material such as posters and flyers.
APPLICATION FEE: None
INSIDER ADVICE: When their film is selected, they should come to the Festival.
AVERAGE FILMS ENTERED: This is the selection's commitee's decision.... new genre welcome.... any kind of professional films !
FILMS SCREENED: For pre-selection and selection : all of them, the selection commitee goes to other film festivals too and brings back videotapes, contacts or strong desire to show the film....
ODDS OF ACCEPTANCE: About 800 films are submitted with 125 selected for competition.
FILMMAKER PERKS: Everybody gets free housing on a cruise boat moored on the Dniepr river, free breakfast on the boat and free lunch in the main

house of cinematographers where good Ukrainian specialties are served...then, for dinner, every night there is a party and everybody is invited to cocktail parties.....the main perk of Molodist festival is certainly the intimate atmosphere where you can meet anybody you want....

TOURIST INFORMATION: Kyiv is located in Ukraine and therefore is the oldest Rus, the first slavonci state is Ukraine... there are lots of things to visit such as: incredible monasteries, the Laura monasteries (one of the oldest in the ex-USSR), St. Sophia Church (in 1037), the 1900's architecture (the center is beautifully kept and you cannot miss hundreds of cariatydes and atlantes statues everywhere... its Stalinist architecture... its parks, the Dniepr river etc....

TRAVEL TIPS: When flying to Kyiv, you need a visa to get in... make sure you make it in advance, it's way much cheaper. When coming by train, it is a real experience as trains are really slow but full of nice people ready to share a glass of vodka with you.

BEST RESTAURANTS: there are plenty.... it depends on your budget... but for sure you can find wonders and nightmares...

BEST BARS: Eric's (founded by a German dude)

BEST HANGOUT FOR FILMMAKERS: The House of Cinematographers/Dom Kino

Everybody gets free housing on a cruise boat moored on the Dniepr river, free breakfast on the boat and free lunch in the main house of cinematographers. (Kyiv International Film Festival, Molodist)

URURGUAY

INTERNATIONAL FILM FESTIVAL FOR CHILDREN AND YOUNG PEOPLE

Lorenzo Carnelli 1311
11200 Montevideo, Uruguay
TEL: 598-2-408-2460 or 598-2-409-5795
FAX: 598-2-409-4572
E-MAIL: cinemuy@chasque.apc.org
FESTIVAL DATE: July 5-16
ENTRY DEADLINE: May 10
DIRECTOR: Ricardo Casas
CATEGORY: Kids

INTERNATIONAL FILM FESTIVAL OF MONTEVIDEO AND PUNTA DEL ESTE

Lorenzo Carnelli 1311
Casilla de correos 1170
Montevideo, Uruguay
TEL: 598-2-48-24-60
FAX: 598-2-49-45-72
FESTIVAL DATE: April
ENTRY DEADLINE: February
DIRECTOR: Manuel Martinez Carril, Director Cinematica Uruguaya

---

WALES

WELSH INTERNATIONAL FILM FESTIVAL

Ty Meandros, 54A Bute Street
Cardiff, CF1 6AF Wales
TEL: +44 1970 617995
FAX: +44 1970 617942
E-MAIL: wiff@pcw-aber.co.uk
WEB SITE: http://www.aber.ac.uk/~wff995/ or http://www.pcw-aber.co.uk/WIFF/
FESTIVAL DATE: November
ENTRY DEADLINE: September
YEAR FESTIVAL BEGAN: 1989
CONTACT: General enquiries: Grant Vidgen; Press enquiries: Sion Jobbins
DIRECTOR: Grant Vidgen

PROGRAMMER: Panel
OTHER STAFF: Press officer: Sion Jobbins; Sponsorship: Jane Walker; External affairs: Paul Smith
CATEGORY: General, non-competitive
PROFILE: The Welsh International Film Festival seeks to bring the best of world cinema to as wide an audience in Wales as possible and to promote the best of Welsh film to as wide an international audience as possible.
SEMINARS: Programme is always supported by a series of afternoon seminars running throughout the Festival. In addition we organise the Broadcasting Weekend, a three day event for those involved in the Broadcast Industry.
AWARDS: Yes
COMPETITIONS: Yes (Only for short films by a Welsh film maker)
MAJOR AWARDS: D M Davies Award
VALUE OF AWARDS: £30 000 sterling
LAST WINNING FILMS: *Little Sisters*
LAST WINNING DIRECTORS: Andy Goddard
APPLICATION TIPS: Get your submission in early, and relate it to one or more of the programme themes.
APPLICATION FEE: No submission fee, but return of viewing tapes is charged.
INSIDER ADVICE: Do complete your film as indicated in your application form—if you're not sure of the final format when you send in the application tell us—don't guess! Bribery of the selection panel doesn't work, but please include as much useful information as possible with your application—any interesting angles for promoting the film, your availability to attend the festival etc. Follow our advice with regard to shipping—it'll often be more expensive and less secure if you don't!

AVERAGE FILMS ENTERED: Works which fit with our programme themes that are well made and we believe will engage our audience.

FILMS SCREENED: 170

ODDS OF ACCEPTANCE: Submitted: 500. Screened: 170

FILMMAKER PERKS: Limited assistance with travel and lodging is available.

TOURIST INFORMATION: National Museum of Wales, Museum of Welsh Life, Cardiff Castle, Castell Coch

TRAVEL TIPS: Our weather in November can be changeable—come prepared!

BEST RESTAURANTS: Scott's Brasserie

ZIMBABWE

KINE INTERNATIONAL FILM FESTIVAL

Kine Centre
Box 580
Harare, Zimbabwe
TEL: 73-69-66
FAX: 72-45-15
FESTIVAL DATE: June
ENTRY DEADLINE: March
CONTACT: Bruce Waters
CATEGORY: International

APPENDiCES

- Index of Festivals by Name
- Listing of Festivals by Month
- Listing of Festivals by Genre
- Best Bars
- Best Places for Breakfast
- Power Invitation List for Festival Screenings and Parties
- Filmmaker Resources

INDEX OF FESTIVALS BY NAME

A

Adelaide International Children's
Film and Video Festival 233
Africas Cinema 250
Agrofilm Festival 240
Alamo American Film Competition
For Students 177
Ales Cinema Festival—Itinerances 250
Alpe Adria Fest 260
Amatuer and Non-Professional
Film and Video Festival 250
Ambiente-Incontri Film Festival
Internazionale Su Natura E Ambiente .. 260
American Film Festival 235
American Film Institute—Los Angeles
International Film Festival 177
Americas Film Festival 177
Animania: International Festival of
Animation and Multimedia 233
Animated Films About Science 250
Ankara International Film Festival 279
Ann Arbor Film Festival 177
Annecy International Animated
Film Festival 250
Annual American Indian Film and
Video Competition 178
Annual Baltimore Independent Film
and Video Makers' Competition 178
Annual Kidfilm Festival 178
Antenna Cinema Festival 260
Arcipelago Short Film Festival 260
Argeles-Sur-Mer Cinema Forum 250
Arizona International Film Festival 178
Arizona State University Short Film
and Video Festival 178
Armchair Short Film Festival 178
Armed Forces and People Film Festival 260
Around the World Festival 250
Arsenal Film Forum 265
Art Film Festival Trencianske Teplice 270
Art Movie 237
Asia-Pacific Film Festival 278
Asian American International
Film Festival 179
Asolo International Animation Festival 260
Aspen Filmfest 179

Athens International Film and
Video Festival 179
Athens International Film Festival 258
Atlanta Film and Video Festival 180
Atlantic Film Festival 180
Auckland International Film Festival 265
Austin Film Festival 180
Austin Heart of Film Festival 181
Austin's Gay and Lesbian Film Festival 181
Austin's Israeli Film Festival 181
Australian International Outdoor
Short Film Festival 233
Austrian Film Days 235

B

Baca Film and Video Festival 181
Baltimore International Film Festival 182
Banco Nacional International
Film Festival 237
Banff Festival of Mountain Films 182
Bangkok Film Festival 279
Bastia Film Festival of
Mediterranean Cultures 250
Beijing International Children's
Film Festival 239
Beijing International Scientific
Film Festival 239
Belgrade International Film Festival 269
Bellaria Independent Cinema Festival 260
Bergamo International Week of
Auteur Film 260
Berkshire Film Festival 182
Berlin International Film Festival 253
Bienal de Cine y Video
Cientifico Espanol 271
Bienal Nacion Cajalicante de Cine
Amateur de Libre Creacion 271
Biennale de Venezia—Mostra
Internazionale del Cinema 260
Biennale Internationale du Film
D'Architecture, D'Urbanisme Et
D'Environment de Bordeaux 250
Big Muddy Film Festival 182
Bilan du Film Ethnographique 250

Birmingham International Educational
Film Festival 182
Birmingham International Film and
TV Festival 241
Black Filmworks Festival of
Film and Video 182
Black Harvest International Film Festival . 183
Black Maria Film and Video Festival 183
Black Talkies on Parade Film Festival 183
Blacklight 183
Blois Cinema Forum 250
Blue Sky International Film Festival 183
Bombay International Film Festival for
Documentary, Short and Animation
Films 258
Bondy Cinema Festival 250
Boston Gay & Lesbian Film &
Video Festival 183
Boston International Festival of
Women's Cinema 183
Brasilia Film Festival 237
Braunschweig 253
Breckenridge Festival of Film 183
Brest Short Film Festival 251
Brighton Festival 241
Brisbane International Film Festival 233
British Cinema Festival 251
British Film Festival 251
British Short Film Festival 241
Brno 16 International Noncommercial
Film and Video Festival 240
Brussels International Cinema Festival 237
Bucks County Film Festival 184
Bucks County Independent Film Tour 184
BWAC Film & Video Festival 184

C

Cabourg Festival of Romantic Films 251
Cadiz International Video Festival 271
Cairo International Film Festival 241
Cairo International Film Festival
for Children 241
Calcutta Film Festival On Mountains 258
Cambridge International Film Festival 241
Canadian International Annual
Film Festival 184
Cannes Film Festival 164
Canyonlands Film & Video Festival 184
Cape Town International Film Festival 270
Capitol Amateur Video Competition 184
Carolina Film and Video Festival 184
Carrefour International de
L'Audiovisuel Scientific 251
Cartagena International Film Festival 239
Central Florida Film and Video Festival ... 184
Cergy-Pontoise Cinema Festival 251
Certamen de Cine Amateur 271

Certamen de Cine y Video Etnologico
de las Communidades Autonmas 271
Certamen de Video Elies Rogent
Rehabilitacio I Restauracio 271
Certamen Internacional Badalona 271
Certamen Internacional de Cine
Amateur—Ciutat D'igualada 272
Certamen Internacional de Cine
Cortometraje 272
Certamen Internacional de Cine
Turistico de Madrid 272
Certamen Internacional de Cine
y Video Agrario 272
Certamen Internacional de Ciny y
Video Turistico—Oriente de
Asturias de Llanes 272
Certamen Internacional de Video 272
Certamen Nacional de Cine Silencioso 272
Cevennes Festival of International Video .. 251
Charlotte Film and Video Festival 185
Chicago Alt.Film Fest 186
Chicago International Children's
Film Festival 186
Chicago International Film Festival 186
Chicago Latino Film Festival 187
Chicago Underground Film Festival 187
Children's London Film Festival 242
China International Scientific
Film Festival 239
China International Sports Film Festival .. 239
Chinese Film Festival 251
Cinema Au Feminin 251
Cinema du Reel 251
Cinema Tout Ecran/ International
Film & Television Convention 277
Cinemas D'Afrique 251
Cinequest 187
Cinevegas Film Festival 188
Cities Video Festival 251
City Lore Festival of American
Film and Video 188
Clermont-Ferrand Short Film Festival 251
Cleveland International Film Festival 188
Clisson Film Festival 252
Cognac International Film Festival
of the Thriller 252
Columbia College International
Documentary Festival 189
Columbus International Film and
Video Festival 189
Com & Com Comedy and Comedic
Film Festival 260
Copenhagen Film Festival 240
Copenhagen Gay and Lesbian
Film Festival 241
Cork International Film Festival 259
Cork Youth International Film,
Video and Arts Festival 259

D

D.Film Digital Film Festival 189
Dallas Video Festival 190
Dances With Films: Festival of
  the Unknowns 190
DCTV Youth Video Festival 190
Denver International Film Festival 190
Detroit International Film Festival 190
Dhaka International Short Film Festival ... 237
Docfest—New York International
  Documentary Festival 190
Douarnenez Festival of Ethnic
  Minority Cinema 252
Drambuie Edinburgh International
  Film Festival 269
Dublin Film Festival 259
Dundee Mountain Film Festival 269
Dunkirk Cinema Forum 252
Durban Film Festival 270
Durban International Film Festival 270
Dutch Film Festival 265
Dylan Dog Horror Festival 260

E

East Bay Video Festival 191
Edmonton Annual Film Festival 191
Entrevues Film Festival 252
Espoo Ciné International Film Festival 247
Euro Underground 191
Europacinema Festival 260
European Festival of Rural and
  Fishing Cinema 272
European Film Festival 252
Exground—Das Filmfest 254

F

F3 Film Festival 191
Fajr International Film Festival 259
Fantasporto / Oporto International
  Film Festival 267
Fantasy Filmfest—International
  Film Festival for Science Fiction,
  Fiction, Horror and Thriller 255
Festival de Cine Iberoamericano para
  Largometrages de Ficcion 240
Festival de Cine L'Alfas del Pi 272
Festival de Film Sur L'Art 237
Festival de Geneve des Expoirs du
  Cinema Europeen 278
Festival dei Popoli 261
Festival der Festivals 235
Festival du Film D'Animation
  pour la Jeunesse 252
Festival for Nature and
  Environment Films 252

Festival Internacional Cinematografico
  de Cancun 265
Festival Internacional de Barcelona
  de Cine y Video No Professionales 272
Festival Internacional de Cine
  de Comedia 272
Festival Internacional de Cine
  Ecologico y de la Naturaleza 272
Festival Internacional de Cine
  Espeleologico de Barcelona 273
Festival Internacional de Cine Fantastico .. 273
Festival Internacional de Cine
  Realizado por Mujeres 273
Festival Internacional de Cinema
  de Algarve 267
Festival International de Cine
  de Vina del Mar 239
Festival International du 1er
  Film et de la Jeunesse 252
Festival International du Court
  Metrage de Mons 237
Festival International du Film
  Amateur de Kelibia 279
Festival International du Film
  Fantastique, de Science Fiction
  Thriller de Bruxelles 237
Festival International du Film
  Francophone—Namur 237
Festival International du Film
  Medical de Mauriac 252
Festival of Arts Cinema for Children 252
Festival of Deauville for
  American Cinema 253
Festival of International Film for
  Youth and Children 253
Festival of Short Films—Krakow 267
Film + Arc International Film Festival 235
Film Festival of International
  Cinema Students (Ffics) 262
Film Front National Student
  Film and Video Festival 192
Filmbureau 606** Circus '99 192
Filmfest Munchen 255
Filmfestival Max Ophüls Preis 255
Filmotsav Documentary Film Festival 258
Flanders International
  Film Festival—Ghent 237
Florence Film Festival 261
Florida Film Festival 192
Fort Lauderdale Film Festival 193
Four*By*Four Super 8 Filmfest 194
Freaky Film Festival (FFF) 194
Fukuoka Asian Film Festival 262

G

Gen Art Film Festival 195
Geneva Film Festival 278
Giffoni Film Festival 261
Giornate Professionali di Cinema 261
Global Africa International Film
    and Video Festival 195
Göteborg Film Festival 276
Gothenburg Film Festival 276
Gramado International Film Festival 238
Gran Premio de Cine Espanol 273
Great Plains Film Festival 195
Green Badge Film Event 195

H

Haifa International Film Festival 259
Hamptons International Film Festival 195
Havana International Festival of New
    Latin American Film, TV and Video 240
Hawaii International Film Festival 196
Heartland Film Festival 197
Helsinki International Film Festival—
    Love and Anarchy 248
Hiroshima International Amateur
    Film and Video Festival 262
Holland Animation Film Festival 265
Hollywood Film Festival 197
Hometown Cinema, A Midwestern
    Student Film Festival 198
Hometown Video Festival 198
Hong Kong International
    Film Festival (HKIFF) 258
Honolulu Gay & Lesbian Film Festival 198
Hot Springs Documentary Film Festival ... 198
Houston International Film and Video
    Festival—Annual Worldfest 199
Hudson Valley Film Festival 199
Huesca Film Festival 273
Human Rights Watch International
    Film Festival 200
Humboldt International Film and
    Video Festival 200

I

Images '95 200
Independent Exposure 201
Independent Feature Film Market 201
Indiana Film and Video Festival 201
Inside Out Lesbian and Gay
    Film Festival of Toronto 201
Interfest Moscow Film Festival 268
International Animated Film and
    Cartoon Festival 237
International Animated Film Festival—
    Cinanima 267
International Animation Festival 242

International Animation Festival,
    Cardiff, Wales 242
International Animation Festival—
    Japan, Hiroshima 263
International Art Film Festival—
    Trencianske Teplice 270
International Celtic Film and
    Television Festival 259
International Cinema and Television
    Multimedia Market—Mifed 261
International Documentary
    Film Festival 242
International Documentary Film Festival
    Amsterdam (IDFA) 265
International Documentary, Short and
    Animated Films Festival 268
International Electronic Cinema Festival .. 278
International Festival of Casablanca 265
International Festival of Cinema for
    Children and Youth 267
International Festival of Comedy Films 239
International Festival of Comedy
    Films of Vevey 278
International Festival of
    Documentaries of the Sea 261
International Festival of Documentary
    and Science Films 269
International Festival of Documentary
    and Short Film of Bilbao 273
International Festival of Films
    Made by Women 233
International Festival of Films On Art 202
International Festival of Films On Art
    "Fifart Festival" 278
International Film and Video
    Competition 242
International Film Festival 253
International Film Festival for
    Children and Young People 280
International Film Festival of Festivals 269
International Film Festival of Gijon
    for Young People 273
International Film Festival of India 259
International Film Festival of
    Montevideo and Punta del Este 280
International Film Festival of the
    Art of Cinematography 267
International Filmfestival 255
International Gay and Lesbian
    Film Festival 256
International Juvenale for Young
    Film and Video Amateurs 235
International Leipzig Festival for
    Documentary and Animated Film 256
International Madrid Festival for the
    Fantastic and Science Fiction Film 273
International Mystery Film Festival 261
International Odense Film Festival 241
International Short Film Festival
    Oberhausen 256

International Thessaloniki Film Festival ... 258
International Video Contest 274
International Video Festival of Algarve 268
International Wildlife Film Festival 202
International Women's Film Festival 241
Internationale Filmfestival Des
    Nichtprofessionellen Films 235
Israel Film Festival 202
Istanbul Short Film and Video Festival 279

J

Jackson Hole Wildlife Film Festival 203
Japan International Film & Video
    Festival of Adventure and Sports 263
Jerusalem International Film Festival 259
Jewish Film Festival—London 242
Johannesburg Film Festival 271
Johns Hopkins Film Festival 203
Junior Dublin Film Festival 259

K

Karlovy Vary International Film Festival ... 240
Kine International Film Festival 281
Kino American Underground &
    Student Showcase Film Fest 242
Kino Festival of New Irish Cinema 243
Kinofilm, Manchester International
    Short Film & Video Festival 243
Kudzu Film Festival 203
Kyiv International Film Festival,
    Molodist 279

L

L. A. Asian Pacific Film Video Festival 204
Las Vegas International Film Festival 204
Leeds International Film Festival 244
Local Heroes International
    Screen Festival 204
Locarno International Film Festival 278
London Film Festival 245
Long Beach International Gay and
    Lesbian Film Festival 205
Long Island Film Festival 205
Los Angeles Independent
    Film Festival (LAIFF) 165
Los Angeles International Animation
    Celebration 206
Los Angeles International Short
    Film Festival 206
Los Angeles Latino International
    Film Festival 206
Lucille Ball Short Festival of
    New Comedy 206

M

Madcat Women's International
    Film Festival 206
Magdeburg International Film Festival 257
Maine Student Film and Video Festival 207
Making Scenes 207
Mandalay Las Colinas Festival 207
Margaret Mead Film Festival 207
Marin County National Film and
    Video Festival 207
Melbourne International Film and
    Video Festival 233
Melbourne International Film Festival 233
Miami Film Festival 207
Midnight Sun Film Festival 248
Mill Valley Film Festival 207
Mix Brasil Festival of Sexual Diversity 238
Montreal International Festival of
    New Cinema and New Media 208
Montreal World Film Festival 208
Moomba International Amateur
    Film Festival 234
Mountainfilm 209
Mystery and Noir Film Festival 261

N

Nantucket Film Festival 209
Nashville Independent Film Festival 209
National Educational Film and
    Video Festival (NEFVF) 210
National Latino Film and Video Festival ... 210
New Angle Intermedia Video Festival 210
New England Film and Video Festival 210
New Orleans Film and Video Festival 210
New York Expo of Short Film and Video .. 210
New York Film Festival 166
New York Gay and Lesbian Film Festival .. 210
New York International
    Documentary Festival (Docfest) 211
New York Lesbian and Gay Experimental
    Film and Video Festival (Mix) 211
New York National High School Film
    and Video Festival 211
New York Underground Film Festival 211
New York Video Festival 212
Night of the Black Independents 212
No Dance Film Festival 212
North Devon Film Festival 245
Northwest Film & Video Festival 212
Norwegian International Film Festival 266
Norwegian Short Film Festival 267
Nyon International Documentary
    Film Festival 278

O

Ohio Independent Film Festival and
Market 214
Okomedia International Ecological
Film Festival 257
Oldenburg International Film Festival 257
One World Film Festival 214
Onedotzero Digital Creativity Festival 245
Onion City Film Festival 214
Open Screens 214
Ottawa International Animation Festival .. 215
Out At the Movies: San Antonio's Annual
Festival of Lesbian & Gay Film 216
Out Takes 266
Outfest: Los Angeles International Gay
and Lesbian Film & Video Festival 216

P

Palm Springs International Film Festival .. 217
Partnership for Peace International
Film Festival 239
Peachtree International Film Festival 217
Philadelphia Festival of World Cinema 218
Philadelphia International Gay and
Lesbian Film Festival 218
Philafilm—The Philadelphia
International Film Festival 218
Polish Film Festival 267
Pordenone Silent Film Festival 261
Portland International Film Festival 218
Potsdam Film Festival 257
Prix Danube Festival 270
Prix Jeunesse International 257
Puerto Rico International Film Festival 268
Pxl This Video 219

R

Reel Affirmations Film Festival 219
Reject Filmfest 219
Resfest Digital Film Festival 220
Revelation Independent Film Festival 234
Rhode Island International Film Festival .. 220
Riminicinema International
Film Festival 261
Rochester International Independent
Film Festival 221
Rotterdam International Film Festival 265

S

Saguaro Film Festival 221
San Diego International Film Festival 221
San Francisco Bi Film Festival 222
San Francisco Indiefest 222

San Francisco International Asian
Film Festival 222
San Francisco International
Film Festival 223
San Francisco Jewish Film Festival 223
San Francisco Lesbian and Gay
Film Festival 223
San Sebastian International
Film Festival 274
Santa Barbara International
Film Festival (SBIFF) 223
Santa Fe de Bogota International
Film Festival 240
São Paulo International Film Festival 238
Sao Paulo International Short
Film Festival 238
Seattle International Film
Festival (SIFF) 171
Seattle Lesbian & Gay Film Festival 223
Sedona International Film Festival 223
Seoul Queer Film & Video Festival 264
Shanghai International Animation
Film Festival 239
Sheffield International Documentary
Festival 246
Short Attention Span Film and
Video Festival (SASFVF) 224
Short Poppies: International Festival
of Student Film and Video 234
Silver Images Film Festival 224
Singapore International Film Festival 269
Sinking Creek Film and Video Festival 224
Sitges International Festival of
Fantasy Films 275
Slamdance International Film Festival 169
Small Pictures Independent
Film Festival (SPIFF) 224
South By Southwest Film
Festival (SXSW) 174
St. Petersburg Documentary Festival 269
Stockholm International Film Festival 276
Sundance Film Festival 157
Sydney Film Festival 234

T

Tampere Film Festival 249
Tampere International Short
Film Festival 249
Taos Talking Pictures Festival 175
Telluride Film Festival 161
Texas Film Festival 226
Thaw Video, Film, and Digital
Media Festival 226
The Festival of Fantastic Films 246
The New Zealand Film Festival 266
Tokyo International Fantastic
Film Festival 263
Tokyo International Film Festival 263

Tokyo Video Festival 263
Torino Film Festival 261
Toronto International Film Festival 160
Turku Lesbian and Gay Film Festival 249
Two Rivers Native Film and
    Video Festival 226
Tyneside International Film Festival 247

U

U. S. Outdoor Travel Film Festival 226
UFVA Student Film and Video Festival 226
United States Super 8
    Film/Video Festival 227
University of Oregon Queer
    Film Festival 227
Uppsala International Short
    Film Festival 277
US International Film & Video Festival 227
USA Film Festival 228

V

Valleyfest Film Festival 228
Vancouver International Film Festival 228
Vancouver Underground Film Festival 229
Venice International Film Festival 262
Vermont International Film Festival:
    Images and Issues for Social Change 229
Victoria Independent Film and
    Video Festival 230
Videoeiras Festival 268
Viennale—Vienna International
    Film Festival 235
Viper International Film and
    Video Festival 278
Virginia Festival of American Film 230
Virginia Film Festival 230
Visions of the U. S. Video Contest 231

W

Warsaw Film Festival 267
Washington, DC International
    Film Festival—Filmfest Dc 231
Wellington Film Festival and Aukland
    International Film Festival 266
Welsh International Film Festival 280
West Virginia International Film Festival .. 231
Wine Country Film Festival 231
Women In Film International
    Film Festival 232
Women Make Movies 232
World Festival of Animated Films
    in Zagreb 240

Worldfest Charleston 232
WOW Cafe Women's Film and Video
    Festival—WOW (Women One World)
    Festival 232
Wurzburg International Film Festival 258

Y

Yamagata International Documentary
    Film Festival 263
Yorkton Short Film and Video Festival 232

LiSTiNG OF FESTiVALS BY MONTH

January

Alpe Adria Fest
Annual Kidfilm Festival
Australian International Outdoor Short Film
    Festival
Black Maria Film and Video Festival
Blois Cinema Forum
Brussels International Cinema Festival
Calcutta Film Festival on Mountains
Dhaka International Short Film Festival
Fajr International Film Festival
Filmfestival Max Ophüls Preis
Filmotsav Documentary Film Festival
International Festival of Documentary and
    Science Films
International Film Festival of India
No Dance Film Festival
Palm Springs International Film Festival
San Francisco Indiefest
Slamdance International Film Festival
Sundance Film Festival
Tokyo Video Festival
Wurzburg International Film Festival

January-February

Göteborg Film Festival
Belgrade International Film Festival
Capitol Amateur Video Competition
Cergy-Pontoise Cinema Festival
Children's London Film Festival
Clermont-Ferrand Short Film Festival
Miami Film Festival
Rotterdam International Film Festival

February

Berlin International Film Festival
Bombay International Film Festival for
    Documentary, Short and Animation Films
Bondy Cinema Festival
Chinese Film Festival
Cinemas D'Afrique
Festival der Festivals

Festival International du 1er Film et de la
    Jeunesse
Gothenburg Film Festival
Hiroshima International Amateur Film and
    Video Festival
International Animated Film and Cartoon
    Festival
Portland International Film Festival
Texas Film Festival
United States Super 8 Film/Video Festival
University of Oregon Queer Film Festival
Victoria Independent Film and Video Festival

February-March

Big Muddy Film Festival
Fantasporto/Oporto International Film
    Festival
Festival for Nature and Environment Films
St. Petersburg Documentary Festival

February-June

San Diego International Film Festival

March

Ankara International Film Festival
Ann Arbor Film Festival
Baca Film and Video Festival
Bergamo International Week of Auteur Film
Bienal Nacion Cajalicante de Cine Amateur de
    Libre Creacion
Bilan du Film Ethnographique
Black Talkies On Parade Film Festival
Cartagena International Film Festival
Certamen de Cine Amateur
Certamen Internacional de Cine Cortometraje
Cinema du Reel
City Lore Festival of American Film and Video
Cleveland International Film Festival
Dublin Film Festival
Festival de Cine Iberoamericano para
    Largometrages de Ficcion

Festival de Film Sur L'Art
Festival International du Court Metrage de
    Mons
Festival International du Film Fantastique, de
    Science Fiction Thriller de Bruxelles
Filmbureau 606** Circus '99
Humboldt International Film and Video
    Festival
International Documentary Film Festival
International Festival of Films on Art
International Film and Video Competition
International Women's Film Festival
Istanbul Short Film and Video Festival
Local Heroes International Screen Festival
Moomba International Amateur Film Festival
New York Underground Film Festival
One World Film Festival
San Francisco International Asian Film Festival
Santa Barbara International Film Festival
Sedona International Film Festival
South By Southwest Film Festival (SXSW)
Tampere Film Festival
Tampere International Short Film Festival
Valleyfest Film Festival
Women Make Movies
Kino Festival of New Irish Cinema

March-April

Ales Cinema Festival—Itinerances
Carolina Film and Video Festival
Festival International du Film Medical de
    Mauriac
International Celtic Film and Television
    Festival
WOW Cafe Women's Film and Video
    Festival—WOW (Women One World)
    Festival

April

Amatuer and Non-Professional Film and
    Video Festival
Animania: International Festival of Animation
    and Multimedia
Arizona International Film Festival
Arizona State University Short Film and Video
    Festival
Art Movie
Baltimore International Film Festival
Boston International Festival of Women's
    Cinema
Canyonlands Film & Video Festival
Certamen de Cine y Video Etnologico de Las
    Communidades Autonmas
Certamen Internacional de Cine y Video
    Agrario
Cognac International Film Festival of the
    Thriller

Columbia College International Documentary
    Festival
Docfest—New York International Documen-
    tary Festival
Hometown Cinema, A Midwestern Student
    Film Festival
Hong Kong International Film Festival
International Film Festival of Montevideo and
    Punta del Este
International Short Film Festival Oberhausen
International Wildlife Film Festival
Los Angeles Independent Film Festival
Los Angeles International Animation
    Celebration
Mandalay Las Colinas Festival
San Francisco International Film Festival
Sao Paulo Internationional Short Film Festival
Silver Images Film Festival
Singapore International Film Festival
Taos Talking Pictures Festival
Usa Film Festival
Videoeiras Festival

April-May

Cape Town International Film Festival
Chicago Latino Film Festival
Gen Art Film Festival
International Animation Festival
International Electronic Cinema Festival
Onedotzero Digital Creativity Festival
Philadelphia Festival of World Cinema
Saguaro Film Festival
Washington, DC International Film Festival—
    Filmfest DC

May

Africas Cinema
Argeles-Sur-Mer Cinema Forum
Asolo International Animation Festival
Athens International Film and Video Festival
Birmingham International Educational Film
    Festival
Brighton Festival
BWAC Film & Video Festival
Cannes Film Festival
Certamen de Video Elies Rogent Rehabilitacio
    I Restauracio
Cork Youth International Film, Video and Arts
    Festival
Festival Internacional de Cinema de Algarve
Helsinki International Film Festival—Love and
    Anarchy
Hudson Valley Film Festival
Inside Out Lesbian and Gay Film Festival of
    Toronto

International Animation Festival, Cardiff, Wales
International Festival of Comedy Films
International Festival of Documentaries of the Sea
L. A. Asian Pacific Film Video Festival
Lucille Ball Short Festival of New Comedy
Madcat Women's International Film Festival
Mountainfilm
National Educational Film and Video Festival
New Angle Intermedia Video Festival
New England Film and Video Festival
New York International Documentary Festival (Docfest)
Night of the Black Independents
Onion City Film Festival
Partnership for Peace International Film Festival
Rochester International Independent Film Festival
Yorkton Short Film and Video Festival
International Film Festival

International Art Film Festival—Trencianske Teplice
International Film Festival of Festivals
Japan International Film & Video Festival of Adventure and Sports
Kine International Film Festival
Long Beach International Gay and Lesbian Film Festival
Maine Student Film and Video Festival
Melbourne International Film and Video Festival
Midnight Sun Film Festival
Nantucket Film Festival
Nashville Independent Film Festival
New York Gay and Lesbian Film Festival
North Devon Film Festival
Norwegian Short Film Festival
Potsdam Film Festival
San Francisco Lesbian and Gay Film Festival
Sydney Film Festival
US International Film & Video Festival
Prix Jeunesse International

May-June

Annecy International Animated Film Festival
Beijing International Children's Film Festival
China International Sports Film Festival
Festival of Short Films—Krakow
Out Takes
Prix Danube Festival
Seattle International Film Festival

June

Annual American Indian Film and Video Competition
Arcipelago Short Film Festival
Art Film Festival Trencianske Teplice
Atlanta Film and Video Festival
Austrian Film Days
Bellaria Independent Cinema Festival
Boston Gay & Lesbian Film & Video Festival
Cabourg Festival of Romantic Films
Caribbean Film Festival
Charlotte Film and Video Festival
Chicago Alt.Film Fest
Cities Video Festival
Dylan Dog Horror Festival
European Film Festival
Festival of International Film for Youth and Children
Florida Film Festival
Giornate Professionali di Cinema
Global Africa International Film and Video Festival
Honolulu Gay & Lesbian Film Festival
Huesca Film Festival
Images '95

June/October

Human Rights Watch International Film Festival

June-July

Filmfest Munchen
International Documentary, Short and Animated Films Festival
International Mystery Film Festival

July

Ambiente-Incontri Film Festival Internazionale Su Natura E Ambiente
Asian American International Film Festival
Auckland International Film Festival
Black Harvest International Film Festival
Brasilia Film Festival
Cambridge International Film Festival
Certamen Internacional de Ciny y Video Turistico—Oriente de Asturias de Llanes
Cevennes Festival of International Video
Dances With Films: Festival of the Unknowns
Durban Film Festival
Festival de Cine L'Alfas del Pi
Giffoni Film Festival
Great Plains Film Festival
Hometown Video Festival
Interfest Moscow Film Festival
International Festival of Comedy Films of Vevey
International Film Festival for Children and Young People

International Film Festival of Gijon for Young
People
Jerusalem International Film Festival
Karlovy Vary International Film Festival
New York Video Festival
Outfest: Los Angeles International Gay and
Lesbian Film & Video Festival
Philadelphia International Gay and Lesbian
Film Festival
Philafilm—The Philadelphia International
Film Festival
San Francisco Bi Film Festival
Short Poppies: International Festival of
Student Film and Video
The New Zealand Film Festival
Wellington Film Festival and Aukland
International Film Festival

July–August

Blacklight
European Festival of Rural and Fishing
Cinema
Festival International du Film Amateur de
Kelibia
Long Island Film Festival
Melbourne International Film Festival
San Francisco Jewish Film Festival
Wine Country Film Festival

August

Agrofilm Festival
Brisbane International Film Festival
Chicago Underground Film Festival
Douarnenez Festival of Ethnic Minority
Cinema
Drambuie Edinburgh International Film
Festival
Durban International Film Festival
Espoo Ciné International Film Festival
Four*By*Four Super 8 Filmfest
Gramado International Film Festival
Hollywood Film Festival
International Animation Festival—Japan,
Hiroshima
International Juvenale for Young Film and
Video Amateurs
International Odense Film Festival
Locarno International Film Festival
Los Angeles Latino International Film Festival
Norwegian International Film Festival
Pxl This Video
Rhode Island International Film Festival
Ufva Student Film and Video Festival
Viper International Film and Video Festival
Visions of the U. S. Video Contest

August–September

Austin's Gay and Lesbian Film Festival
Internationale Filmfestival des
Nichtprofessionellen Films
Montreal World Film Festival
Venice International Film Festival

September

Cinema Tout Ecran/International Film &
Television Convention
Arsenal Film Forum
Atlantic Film Festival
Banco Nacional International Film Festival
Bangkok Film Festival
Blue Sky International Film Festival
Breckenridge Festival of Film
British Short Film Festival
Cairo International Film Festival for Children
Cinema au Feminin
Dutch Film Festival
Festival of Deauville for American Cinema
Fukuoka Asian Film Festival
Independent Feature Film Market
International Festival of Casablanca
Jackson Hole Wildlife Film Festival
Los Angeles International Short Film Festival
Magdeburg International Film Festival
Making Scenes
Marin County National Film and Video
Festival
Mix Brasil Festival of Sexual Diversity
Nyon International Documentary Film
Festival
Oldenburg International Film Festival
Out at the Movies: San Antonio's Annual
Festival of Lesbian & Gay Film
Riminicinema International Film Festival
San Sebastian International Film   Festival
Santa Fe de Bogota International Film Festival
Seoul Queer Film & Video Festival
Short Attention Span Film and Video Festival
Tacoma Tortured Artists Film Festival
Telluride Film Festival
The Festival of Fantastic Films
Toronto International Film Festival

September–October

Aspen Filmfest
Black Filmworks Festival of Film and Video
Central Florida Film and Video Festival
Com & Com Comedy and Comedic Film
Festival
Festival International du Film Francophone—
Namur
Tokyo International Fantastic Film Festival
Tokyo International Film Festival
Vancouver International Film Festival

October

Austin Film Festival
Austin Heart of Film Festival
Bastia Film Festival of Mediterranean Cultures
Berkshire Film Festival
Brno 16 International Noncommercial Film
   and Video Festival
Certamen Internacional Badalona
Certamen Internacional de Cine Amateur—
   Ciutat D'Igualada
Certamen Nacional de Cine Silencioso
Chicago International Children's Film Festival
Chicago International Film Festival
China International Scientific Film Festival
Cinequest
Columbus International Film and Video
   Festival
Copenhagen Film Festival
Denver International Film Festival
Dunkirk Cinema Forum
East Bay Video Festival
Festival de Geneve Des Expoirs du Cinema
   Europeen
Festival Internacional de Cine Fantastico
Festival International de Cine de Vina del Mar
Festival of Arts Cinema for Children
Film Front National Student Film and Video
   Festival
Flanders International Film Festival   Ghent
Geneva Film Festival
Haifa International Film Festival
Hamptons International Film Festival
Hot Springs Documentary Film Festival
International Cinema and Television
   Multimedia Market—Mifed
International Festival of Films On Art
International Filmfestival
International Leipzig Festival for
   Documentary and Animated Film
Israel Film Festival
Jewish Film Festival—London
Kudzu Film Festival (aka Athens Film Festival)
Kyiv International Film Festival, Molodist
Leeds International Film Festival
Margaret Mead Film Festival
Mill Valley Film Festival
Montreal International Festival of New
   Cinema and New Media
New Orleans Film and Video Festival
New York Film Festival
Pordenone Silent Film Festival
Reel Affirmations Film Festival
Reject Filmfest
São Paulo International Film Festival
Seattle Lesbian & Gay Film Festival
Sheffield International Documentary Festival
Sitges International Festival of Fantasy Films
Turku Lesbian and Gay Film Festival
Uppsala International Short Film Festival

Vermont International Film Festival: Images
   and Issues for Social Change
Viennale—Vienna International Film Festival
Virginia Festival of American Film
Virginia Film Festival
Warsaw Film Festival
Yamagata International Documentary Film
   Festival

October–November

American Film Institute (AFI)—Los Angeles
   International Film Festival
Animated Films About Science
Clisson Film Festival
Copenhagen Gay and Lesbian Film Festival
Euro Underground
Festival du Film D'Animation pour la Jeunesse
Heartland Film Festival
Kinofilm, Manchester Interantional Short Film
   & Video Festival
Peachtree International Film Festival

October–April

West Virginia International Film Festival

November

Americas Film Festival
Armed Forces and People Film Festival
Around the World Festival
Banff Festival of Mountain Films
Beijing International Scientific Film Festival
Bienal de Cine y Video Cientifico Espanol
Birmingham International Film and TV
   Festival
Braunschweig
Brest Short Film Festival
British Cinema Festival
British Film Festival
Cadiz International Video Festival
Carrefour International de L'Audiovisuel
   Scientific
Dallas Video Festival
Detroit International Film Festival
Dundee Mountain Film Festival
Exground—Das Filmfest
Festival dei Popoli
Festival Internacional de Barcelona de Cine y
   Video No Professionales
Festival Internacional de Cine Ecologico y de la
   Naturaleza
Festival Internacional de Cine Espeleologico de
   Barcelona
Festival Internacional de Cine Realizado por
   Mujeres
Film + Arc International Film Festival

Fort Lauderdale Film Festival
Freaky Film Festival (FFF)
Gran Premio de Cine Espanol
Hawaii International Film Festival
Houston International Film and Video
  Festival—Annual Worldfest
International Animated Film Festival—
  Cinanima
International Festival of Documentary and
  Short Film of Bilbao
International Thessaloniki Film Festival
Junior Dublin Film Festival
New York Expo of Short Film and Video
New York Lesbian and Gay Experimental Film
  and Video Festival (Mix)
Northwest Film & Video Festival
Ohio Independent Film Festival and Market
Okomedia International Ecological Film
  Festival
Polish Film Festival
Puerto Rico International Film Festival
Sinking Creek Film and Video Festival
Small Pictures Independent Film Festival
Stockholm International Film Festival
Torino Film Festival
Two Rivers Native Film and Video Festival
Vancouver Underground Film Festival
Welsh International Film Festival
Women In Film International Film Festival
Worldfest Charleston
Kino American Underground & Student
  Showcase Film Fest
London Film Festival

November–December

Cairo International Film Festival
Entrevues Film Festival
Europacinema Festival
Festival Internacional Cinematografico de
  Cancun
International Film Festival of the Art of
  Cinematography
International Gay and Lesbian Film Festival
Tyneside International Film Festival

November–June

Bucks County Independent Film Tour

December

Asia-Pacific Film Festival
Biennale Internationale du Film
  D'Architecture, D'Urbanisme et
  D'Environment de Bordeaux
Certamen Internacional de Video
Cinevegas Film Festival

Festival Internacional de Cine de Comedia
Florence Film Festival
Havana International Festival of New Latin
  American Film, TV and Video
International Documentary Film Festival
  Amsterdam
International Video Contest
Mystery and Noir Film Festival
Shanghai International Animation Film
  Festival
Telluride Indiefest
U. S. Outdoor Travel Film Festival

Spring

Johns Hopkins Film Festival

Fall

Green Badge Film Event
Ottawa International Animation Festival

Monthly

Independent Exposure

Quarterly

F3 Film Festival
Open Screens

Touring

D.Film Digital Film Festival
Revelation Independent Film Festival

LiSTiNG OF FESTiVALS BY GENRE

Note: Genre designations provided by the festivals.

Animation

Animania: International Festival of Animation
and Multimedia
Animated Films About Science
Annecy International Animated Film Festival
Asolo International Animation Festival
Bombay International Film Festival for
Documentary, Short and Animation Films
Detroit International Film Festival
Festival du Film D'Animation pour la Jeunesse
Filmfest Munchen
Heartland Film Festival
Holland Animation Film Festival
International Animated Film Festival—
Cinanima
International Animation Festival
International Animation Festival, Cardiff,
Wales
International Animation Festival—Japan,
Hiroshima
International Documentary, Short and
Animated Films Festival
International Leipzig Festival for
Documentary and Animated Film
Los Angeles International Animation
Celebration
Ottawa International Animation Festival
San Diego International Film Festival
Shanghai International Animation Film
Festival
Short Attention Span Film and Video Festival
Valleyfest Film Festival
World Festival of Animated Films In Zagreb

African-American

Africas Cinema
Black Filmworks Festival of Film and Video
Black Talkies on Parade Film Festival
Blacklight
Cinemas D'Afrique
Detroit International Film Festival
Night of the Black Independents

Documentary

Aspen Filmfest
Austin Heart of Film Festival
Bombay International Film Festival for
Documentary, Short and Animation Films
Cleveland International Film Festival
Columbia College International Documentary
Festival
Docfest—New York International Documen-
tary Festival
Festival of Deauville for American Cinema
Filmfest Munchen
Heartland Film Festival
Hot Springs Documentary Film Festival
International Documentary Film Festival
International Documentary Film Festival
Amsterdam
International Documentary, Short and
Animated Films Festival
International Festival of Documentaries of the
Sea
International Festival of Documentary and
Science Films
International Festival of Documentary and
Short Film of Bilbao
International Leipzig Festival for Documen-
tary and Animated Film
New York International Documentary Festival
Nyon International Documentary Film
Festival
Santa Barbara International Film Festival
Seattle International Film Festival
Sheffield International Documentary Festival
St. Petersburg Documentary Festival
Valleyfest Film Festival
Vancouver International Film Festival
Yamagata International Documentary Film
Festival

Gay and Lesbian

Austin's Gay and Lesbian Film Festival
Cleveland International Film Festival
Copenhagen Gay and Lesbian Film Festival
Honolulu Gay & Lesbian Film Festival
Inside Out Lesbian and Gay Film Festival of
 Toronto
International Gay and Lesbian Film Festival
Madcat Women's International Film Festival
Making Scenes
Mix Brasil Festival of Sexual Diversity
New York Gay and Lesbian Film Festival
New York Lesbian and Gay Experimental Film
 and Video Festival (Mix)
Out At the Movies: San Antonio's Annual
 Festival of Lesbian & Gay Film
Out Takes
Outfest: Los Angeles International Gay and
 Lesbian Film & Video Festival
Philadelphia International Gay and Lesbian
 Film Festival
Reel Affirmations Film Festival
San Francisco Bi Film Festival
San Francisco Lesbian and Gay Film Festival
Seattle International Film Festival
Seoul Queer Film & Video Festival
Turku Lesbian and Gay Film Festival
University of Oregon Queer Film Festival

Independent

American Film Institute (AFI)—Los Angeles
 International Film Festival
Ann Arbor Film Festival
Annual Baltimore Independent Film and
 Video Makers' Competition
Arizona State University Short Film and Video
 Festival
Armchair Short Film Festival
Aspen Filmfest
Atlanta Film and Video Festival
Atlantic Film Festival
Austin Film Festival
Austin Heart of Film Festival
Banff Festival of Mountain Films
Bangkok Film Festival
Berlin International Film Festival
Big Muddy Film Festival
Blue Sky International Film Festival
Braunschweig
Breckenridge Festival of Film
Cambridge International Film Festival
Cannes Film Festival
Carolina Film and Video Festival
Cartagena International Film Festival
Central Florida Film and Video Festival
Charlotte Film and Video Festival
Chicago Alt.Film Fest
Chicago Underground Film Festival

Cinevegas Film Festival
Cleveland International Film Festival
Dances With Films: Festival of the Unknowns
Detroit International Film Festival
Durban International Film Festival
Espoo Ciné International Film Festival
Euro Underground
Exground—Das Filmfest
F3 Film Festival
Fantasy Filmfest—International Film Festival
 for Science Fiction, Fiction, Horror and
 Thriller
Festival of Deauville for American Cinema
Florida Film Festival
Four*By*Four Super 8 Filmfest
Freaky Film Festival (FFF)
Gen Art Film Festival
Hamptons International Film Festival
Hawaii International Film Festival
Hollywood Film Festival
Hot Springs Documentary Film Festival
Hudson Valley Film Festival
Human Rights Watch International Film
 Festival
Independent Exposure
Inside Out Lesbian and Gay Film Festival of
 Toronto
International Filmfestival
International Wildlife Film Festival
Jerusalem International Film Festival
Johns Hopkins Film Festival
Kino American Underground & Student
 Showcase Film Fest
Kino Festival of New Irish Cinema
Kinofilm, Manchester Interantional Short Film
 & Video Festival
Kudzu Film Festival
Kyiv International Film Festival, Molodist
Le Festival du Cinema Americain In Deauville
Local Heroes International Screen Festival
Long Island Film Festival
Los Angeles Independent Film Festival
Madcat Women's International Film Festival
Marin County National Film and Video
 Festival
Mill Valley Film Festival
Mix Brasil Festival of Sexual Diversity
Nashville Independent Film Festival
New England Film and Video Festival
New York Gay and Lesbian Film Festival
New York International Documentary Festival
New York Underground Film Festival
No Dance Film Festival
Northwest Film & Video Festival
Ohio Independent Film Festival and Market
Oldenburg International Film Festival
Portland International Film Festival
Reel Affirmations Film Festival
Reject Filmfest
Revelation Independent Film Festival
Rhode Island International Film Festival

Rochester International Independent Film Festival
San Diego International Film Festival
San Francisco Bi Film Festival
San Francisco Indiefest
San Francisco International Film Festival
San Francisco Lesbian and Gay Film Festival
Santa Barbara International Film Festival
Seattle International Film Festival
Sedona International Film Festival
Slamdance International Film Festival
Small Pictures Independent Film Festival
South By Southwest Film Festival (SXSW)
Sundance Film Festival
Telluride Film Festival
Texas Film Festival
Valleyfest Film Festival
Vancouver International Film Festival
Victoria Independent Film and Video Festival
Visions of the U. S. Video Contest

International

American Film Institute (AFI)—Los Angeles International Film Festival
Ankara International Film Festival
Arcipelago Short Film Festival
Asolo International Animation Festival
Aspen Filmfest
Athens International Film and Video Festival
Athens International Film Festival
Auckland International Film Festival
Australian International Outdoor Short Film Festival
Banco Nacional International Film Festival
Bangkok Film Festival
Berlin International Film Festival
Bienal Nacion Cajalicante de Cine Amateur de Libre Creacion
Biennale de Venezia—Mostra International del Cinema
Biennale Internationale du Film D'Architecture, D'Urbanisme et D'Environment de Bordeaux
Bilan du Film Ethnographique
Blois Cinema Forum
Bombay International Film Festival for Documentary, Short and Animation Films
Cadiz International Video Festival
Cairo International Film Festival
Cairo International Film Festival for Children
Cambridge International Film Festival
Cannes Film Festival
Cape Town International Film Festival
Cartagena International Film Festival
Certamen Internacional de Cine Cortometraje
Certamen Internacional de Cine Turistico de Madrid
Chicago International Film Festival
Cleveland International Film Festival

Fifarc Festival
Filmfest Munchen
Fort Lauderdale Film Festival
Hawaii International Film Festival
Hollywood Film Festival
Hong Kong International Film Festival
International Animated Film Festival—Cinanima
International Animation Festival, Cardiff, Wales
International Animation Festival—Japan, Hiroshima
International Documentary, Short and Animated Films Festival
International Festival of Films Made By Women
International Festival of Films on Art "Fifart Festival"
International Gay and Lesbian Film Festival
International Juvenale for Young Film and Video Amateurs
International Mystery Film Festival
International Video Contest
International Women's Film Festival
Japan International Film & Video Festival of Adventure and Sports
Karlovy Vary International Film Festival
Kine International Film Festival
Local Heroes International Screen Festival
Locarno International Film Festival
London Film Festival
Magdeburg International Film Festival
Melbourne International Film Festival
Miami Film Festival
Montreal World Film Festival
New York Film Festival
Norwegian International Film Festival
Nyon International Documentary Film Festival
Okomedia International Ecological Film Festival
Peachtree International Film Festival
Philadelphia Festival of World Cinema
Philafilm—The Philadelphia International Film Festival
Portland International Film Festival
Puerto Rico International Film Festival
Riminicinema International Film Festival
Rochester International Independent Film Festival
Rotterdam Film Festival
San Diego International Film Festival
San Francisco International Asian Film Festival
San Francisco International Film Festival
Santa Barbara International Film Festival
Santa Fe de Bogota International Film Festival
São Paulo International Film Festival
Sao Paulo International Short Film Festival
Seattle International Film Festival
Sedona International Film Festival
Singapore International Film Festival

Slamdance International Film Festival
Stockholm International Film Festival
Sundance Film Festival
Sydney Film Festival
Tampere International Short Film Festival
Taos Talking Pictures Festival
Tokyo International Film Festival
Torino Film Festival
Toronto International Film Festival
Tyneside International Film Festival
Vancouver International Film Festival
Venice International Film Festival
Viennale—Vienna International Film Festival
Viper International Film and Video Festival
World Festival of Animated Films In Zagreb
Wurzburg International Film Festival

Short

Arcipelago Short Film Festival
Arizona State University Short Film and Video Festival
Armchair Short Film Festival
Australian International Outdoor Short Film Festival
Bombay International Film Festival for Documentary, Short and Animation Films
Brest Short Film Festival
British Short Film Festival
Clermont-Ferrand Short Film Festival
Detroit International Film Festival
Dhaka International Short Film Festival
Festival of Deauville for American Cinema
Festival of Short Films—Krakow
Freaky Film Festival
Heartland Film Festival
International Documentary, Short and Animated Films Festival
International Festival of Documentary and Short Film of Bilbao
Le Festival du Cinema Americain In Deauville
Los Angeles International Short Film Festival
Montreal International Festival of New Cinema and New Media
New York Expo of Short Film and Video
Norwegian Short Film Festival
Santa Barbara International Film Festival
Sao Paulo International Short Film Festival
Small Pictures Independent Film Festival
Tampere International Short Film Festival
Uppsala International Short Film Festival
Valleyfest Film Festival
Vancouver Underground Film Festival
Yorkton Short Film and Video Festival

Student

Alamo American Film Competition for Students
Amatuer and Non-Professional Film and Video Festival
Arizona State University Short Film and Video Festival
Black Harvest International Film Festival
Carolina Film and Video Festival
Film Front National Student Film and Video Festival
Hometown Cinema, A Midwestern Student Film Festival
International Juvenale for Young Film and Video Amateurs
Kino American Underground & Student Showcase Film Fest
Maine Student Film and Video Festival
New York National High School Film and Video Festival
Short Poppies: International Festival of Student Film and Video
Telluride Film Festival
Thaw Video, Film, and Digital Media Festival
UFVA Student Film and Video Festival
Visions of the U. S. Video Contest

Underground

Armchair Short Film Festival
Chicago Underground Film Festival
Euro Underground
Exground—Das Filmfest
F3 Film Festival
Four*By*Four Super 8 Filmfest
Freaky Film Festival (FFF)
Independent Exposure
Kino American Underground & Student Showcase Film Fest
Kinofilm, Manchester Interantional Short Film & Video Festival
Open Screens
Pxl This Video
Short Attention Span Film and Video Festival
Small Pictures Independent Film Festival
Vancouver Underground Film Festival

Video

Arizona State University Short Film and Video
　Festival
Armchair Short Film Festival
Baca Film and Video Festival
Capitol Amateur Video Competition
Charlotte Film and Video Festival
City Lore Festival of American Film and Video
Dallas Video Festival
DCTV Youth Video Festival
East Bay Video Festival
Euro Underground
F3 Film Festival
Film Front National Student Film and Video
　Festival
Freaky Film Festival (FFF)
Global Africa International Film and Video
　Festival
International Film and Video
　Competition
International Video Festival of Algarve
Japan International Film & Video Festival of
　Adventure and Sports
New Angle Intermedia Video Festival
New Orleans Film and Video Festival
New York Video Festival
Onion City Film Festival
Santa Barbara International Film Festival
Short Attention Span Film and Video Festival
Small Pictures Independent Film Festival
Thaw Video, Film, and Digital Media Festival
Tokyo Video Festival
US International Film & Video Festival
Vancouver Underground Film Festival
Visions of the U. S. Video Contest
Yorkton Short Film and Video Festival

Weird

Armchair Short Film Festival
Chicago Underground Film Festival
Dances With Films: Festival of the Unknowns
Euro Underground
Exground—Das Filmfest
F3 Film Festival
Freaky Film Festival (FFF)
International Mystery Film Festival
Onion City Film Festival
Pxl This Video
Reject Filmfest
Short Attention Span Film and Video Festival
Small Pictures Independent Film Festival
Vancouver Underground Film Festival

BEST BARS

Brazil

Sao Paulo, SP
Ritz
Glitter

Canada

Vancouver, British Columbia
Babalu's at the Dakota

Victoria, British Columbia
Swans
Ocean Pointe

Ottawa, Ontario
Black Tomato

Toronto, Ontario
Bars on College Street

Colombia

Cartagena
Pacos

England

West Yorkshire
Oporto
Liquid
Soho
Mojo's

Finland

Tampere
Europa
Club Telakka

Germany

Braunschweig
Fischbach
Latino

Mannheim
Max Bar in Heidelberg

Oldenburg
Der Schwan
Schmitz Café

Wiesbaden
Finale
2SE
Basement

Japan

Tokyo
Jiggers Shot Bar
Billy's

New Zealand

Wellington
Ruby Ruby
Edward Street (gay bar)

Russia

St. Petersburg
Idiot

South Africa

Kwazulu-Natal
The Windsor

Sweden

Stockholm
Restaurant W.C
Hotel Lobby Anglais

Uppsala
Katalin

United States

Hot Springs, Arizona
Bronze Gorilla

Sedona, Arizona
Shugrues
Dylan's

Beverly Hills, California
Sky Bar at the Mondrian Hotel

La Jolla, California
Cafe Japengo

Mill Valley, California
The Sweetwater

Telluride, Colorado
Last Dollar Saloon
Sheridan Bar

Washington D.C.
Cobalt
Jr's
Slyde

Maitland, Florida
Sapphire Supper Club
Kit Kat Klub
Go Lounge
Copper Rocket

Orlando, Florida
Sapphire Supper Club

Atlanta, Georgia
Righteous Room

Athens, Georgia
The Manhattan
The Globe

Duluth, Georgia
Upscale
Tongue & Groove
Clubby
Leopard Lounge

Honolulu, Hawaii
Havana Cabana
Anna Bananas

Urbana, Illinois
The Canopy Club

Carbondale, Illinois
Tres Hombres

Chicago, Illinois
The Rainbo Club
Subterranean
The Double Door
56 West Illinois

Indianapolis, Indiana
Canterbury Bar

Baltimore, Maryland
Club Charles

Ann Arbor, Michigan
Del Rio Bar

Missoula, Montana
Union Club

Poughkeepsie, New York
Stoney Creek

Las Vegas, NV
Sunset Station

Cleveland, Ohio
The Literary Cafe in Tremont
The Brillo Pad

Portland, Oregon
Ringler's Annex
Saucebox

Philadelphia, Pennsylvania
Woody's (gay)
Sisters (lesbian)
Moriarity's

Newport , Rhode Island
Ciros

Nashville, Tennessee
Bluebird Cafe

Austin, Texas
Dog & Duck Pub
Lulu's
Lovejoy's

Burlington, Vermont
Red Square
Nectars
Metronome
Higher Ground
Nickanoose

Charlottesville, Virginia
Miller's

Seattle, Washington
Vito's
The Baltic Room
Linda's
The Pink Door

Tacoma, Washington
Bob's Java Jive

Ukraine

Kyiv
Eric's

BEST PLACES FOR BREAKFAST

Australia

Sydney
Victoria Street
Darlinghurst
Bondi Beach

Brazil

São Paulo
Maksoud Plaza Hotel

Canada

Vancouver, British Columbia
The Elbow Room Cafe

Victoria, British Columbia
Sam's Deli

Ottawa, Ontario
Boko Bakery in the Byward Market

Toronto, Ontario
KOS on College St.
Lakeview on Dundas West

Colombia

Cartagena
Cafe De La Plaza

England

Manchester
Bloom Street Cafe

West Yorkshire
The Hellenic Cafe

Finland

Espoo
Tapiola Garden

Germany

Mannheim/Heidelberg
Cafe Journal

Oldenburg
Restaurant Leon
Schmitz Café

Wiesbaden
Finale
Chat Dor

Russia

St. Petersburg
McDonalds
Idiot

Spain

Huesca
Luces de Bohemia in Las Cuatro Esquinas

Sweden

Stockholm
Hannas Deli

Uppsala
Tea & Sympathy

United States

Hot Springs, Arizona
Pancake House

Sedona, Arizona
Cafe & Salad, Safeway Center

Beverly Hills, California
Cafe Latte, Wilshire/Crescent Heights

La Jolla, California
Mission Beach Cafe

Mill Valley, California
Sunnyside Café

Telluride, Colorado
Sofio's
Excelsior

Washington, D.C.
Luna Grill

Maitland, Florida
The Coffee Shoppe on Lee Road
First Watch

Atlanta, Georgia
Waffle House
Krispy Kreme
Majestic Diner

Athens, Georgia
The Grill

Duluth, Georgia
R. Thomas & Son Deluxe Grille

Honolulu, Hawaii
Eggs 'N' Things
Liliha Bakery

Carbondale, Illinois
Melange Cafe

Chicago, Illinois
The Rainbo

Baltimore, Maryland
Pete's Grill

Ann Arbor, Michigan
Angelo's Restaurant

Missoula, Montana
The Shack

Poughkeepsie, New York
Blondie's
Schemmy's

New Brunswick, New Jersey
Bagel Dish Cafe

Cleveland, Ohio
The Inn on Coventry
Grumpy's in Tremont
The Drip Stick Coffee and Tea Station
Red Star Cafe

Portland, Oregon
Best Shaker's Cafe
Laurelthirst

Philadelphia, Pennsylvania
Blue in Green

Newport, Rhode Island
Best Heritage Coffee House

Nashville, Tennessee
Fido

Austin, Texas
Las Manitas

Burlington, Vermont
Sneakers in Winooski
G's,
Oasis Diner
First Waltz Cafe
Leunig's

Charlottesville, Virginia
The Tavern

Seattle, Washington
Pike Place Market
The Green Cat

Tacoma, Washington
The Sunriser

POWER iNViTATiON LiST FOR
FESTiVAL SCREENiNGS AND PARTiES

Artisan Entertainment
2700 Colorado Ave.
Santa Monica, CA 90404
(310) 449-9200
Jeremy Barber
Bill Block

Cinequanon Pictures Intl.
8057 Beverly Blvd.
Los Angeles CA 90048
(323) 658-6043
Jennifer Peckham
Erik Jensen

Cinetel Films
8255 Sunset Blvd.
Los Angeles, CA 90046
(213) 654-4000
Michael Bremer
Paul Hertzberg

Fine Line Features
116 N. Robertson
Los Angeles, CA 90048
(310) 854-5811
Steve Fiedlander

First Look Pictures/
Overseas Film Group
8800 Sunset Boulevard, Suite 302
Los Angeles CA 90069
(310) 855-1199
(310) 855-0719 fax
Maud Nadler
M.J. Peckos

Fox-Lorber Associates
419 Park Ave. South, 20th Floor
Nerw York, NY 10016
(212) 686-6777
Krysanne Katsoolis

Fox Searchlight
10201 Pico Blvd.
Los Angeles, CA 90035
(310) 369-1000
Lindsay Law

Goldcrest Films International
1240 Olive Dr.
Los Angeles, CA 90069
(213) 650-4551
Dawn Arroya

Samuel Goldwyn Co.
10203 Santa Monica Blvd.
Los Angeles, CA 90067
(310) 552-2255
John Bard Manulis

Good Machine Intl
417 Canal Street, 4th Fl.
New York NY 10003
(212) 343-9230
(212) 343-9645 fax
Mary Jane Skalski
Monica Vespe
Amy Kaufman

HBO
1100 Avenue Of The Americas
New York NY 10036
(212) 512-8000
(212) 512-5055 fax
Colin Callendar

Image Org. / MDP
1925 Century Park East, Suite 1700
Los Angeles, CA 90067
(310) 226-8300
Clark Peterson

J & M Entertainment
1289 Sunset Plaza Dr.
Los Angeles, CA 90069
(310) 652-7733
Karen Roberts

Arthur Kananack & Associates
7 Woodland Way
Weston, CT 06883
(203) 454-3032
Claude Kananack

The Kushner-Locke Co.
11601 Wilshire Blvd., 21st Floor
Los Angeles, CA 90025
(310) 445-1111
Phil Mittleman
Donald Kushner

Lions Gate
561 Broadway, Suite 12 B
New York, NY 10012
(212) 966-4670
Mike Pasternak

Mainline
1801 Ave. of the Stars, Suite 1200
Los Angeles, CA 90067
(310) 286-1001
Joseph Dickstein

Miramax Films
375 Greenwich St.
New York, NY 10013
(212) 941-3800
Harvey Weinstein
Bob Weinstein
Jason Blum

The Movie Group
1900 Avenue of the Stars, Suite 1425
Los Angeles CA 90067
(310) 556-2830
Peter E. Strauss

Mutual Film
650 N. Bronson, Clinton Bldg.
Los Angeles, CA 90004
(323) 871-5690
Mark Lindsay

New Castle Pictures
150 E. Olive Ave., Suite 110
Burbank, CA 91502
(818) 563-13563
Scott A. Paterra

New Line Cinema
116 N. Robertson
Los Angeles, CA 90048
(310) 854-5811
Mark Ordesky

Nu Image
9145 Sunset Blvd., 2nd Floor
Los Angeles, CA 90069
(310) 246-0240
Danny Dimbort

October Films
65 Bleecker St.
New York, NY 10012
(212) 539-4000
(212) 539-4099 fax
Scott Greenstein
Susan Glatzer

Paramount Pictures
5555 Melrose Ave.
Sturges Bldg., Suite 101
Hollywood, CA 90038
(213) 956-5942
John Ferraro

Shooting Gallery
145 Ave. of the Americas, 7th Floor
New York, NY 10013
(212) 243-3042
Larry Meistrich

Shooting Gallery
9350 Wilshire Blvd., Suite #300
Beverly Hills, CA 90212
(310) 273-4141
Steve Bickel

Showtime Networks
10880 Wilshire Blvd., Suite 1600
Los Angeles, CA 90024
(310) 234-5200

Sony Pictures Classics
550 Madison Ave.
New York, NY 10022
(212) 833-8833
Dylan Leiner

Stone Canyon
1800 Ave. of the Stars, Suite 430
Los Angeles, CA 90067
(310) 788-9555
Alain Berger

Summit Entertainment
2308 Broadway
Santa Monica, CA 90404
(310) 315-6000
Heidi Lester

Trident Releasing
8401 Melrose Place, 2nd Fl.
Los Angeles, CA 90069
(323) 655-8818
Barbara Mannion

Trimark
2644 30th Street
Santa Monica, CA 90405
(310) 314-2000
Peter Block
Guy Stodel
Matthew Duda

Troma, Inc.
733 Ninth Avenue
New York NY 10019
(212) 757-4555
(212) 399-9885 fax
Lloyd Kaufman
Patrick Cassidy

Twentieth Century Fox
(310) 369-1000
Tony Safford

Universal Studios
(818) 777-8717
Matt Wall

Warner Bros.
(818) 954-6000
Clifford Werber

Press

Daily Variety
Todd McCarthy
(213) 857-6600
(213) 857-0742 fax

Hollywood Reporter
Duan Byrge
(213) 525-2000
(213) 525-2377 fax

LA Weekly
Manohla Dargis
(213) 465-9909
(213) 465-3220 fax

Los Angeles Times
Kenneth Turan
(213) 237-5000
(213) 237-7630 fax

New Times
Andy Klein
(310) 477-0403
(310) 478-9873 fax

Literary Agents for Writers and Directors

Above the Line Agency
9200 Sunset Blvd., #401
Los Angeles, CA 90069
(310) 859-6115

The Agency
1800 Ave. of the Stars
Los Angeles, CA 90067
(310) 551-3000

APA/Agency for the Performing Arts
9000 Sunset Blvd., #900
Los Angeles, CA 90069
(310) 273-0744

The Artists Agency
10000 Santa Monica Blvd., #305
Los Angeles, CA 90067
(310) 277-7779

Becsey-Wisdom-Kalajian
9229 Sunset Blvd., #710
Los Angeles, CA 90069
(310) 550-0535

Broder-Kurland-Webb-Uffner
9242 Beverly Blvd., #200
Beverly Hills, CA 90210
310-281-3400

Don Buchwald & Associates
10 E 44th St.
New York, NY 10017
(212) 867-1200

Creative Artists Agency
9830 Wilshire Blvd.
Beverly Hills, CA 90212-1825
(310) 288-4545

Duva-Flack Associates, Inc.
200 W. 57th St., #407
New York, NY 10019
(212) 957-9600

Endeavor
9701 Wilshire Blvd., 10th Fl
Beverly Hills, CA 90212
(310) 248-2000

Epstein/Wyckoff & Associates
280 S. Beverly Dr., #400
Beverly Hills, CA 90212
(310) 278-7222

Maggie Field Agency
12725 Ventura Blvd., #D
Studio City, CA 91604
(818) 980-2001

The Gage Group
9255 Sunset Blvd., #515
Los Angeles, CA 90069
(310) 859-8777

The Gersh Agency
232 N. Canon Dr.
Beverly Hills, CA 90210
(310) 274-6611

Innovative Artists
1999 Ave. of the Stars, #2850
Los Angeles, CA 90067
(310) 553-5200

International Creative Mgmt.
8942 Wilshire Blvd.
Beverly Hills, CA 90211
(310) 550-4000

Major Clients Agency
345 Maple Dr., #395
Beverly Hills, CA 90210
(310) 205-5000

Metropolitan Talent Agency
4526 Wilshire Blvd.
Los Angeles, CA 90010
(213) 857-4500

William Morris Agency
151 El Camino Dr.
Beverly Hills, CA 90212
(310) 274-7451

The Daniel Ostroff Agency
9200 Sunset Blvd., #402
Los Angeles, CA 90069
(310) 278-2020

Paradigm
10100 Santa Monica Blvd., 25th floor
Los Angeles, CA 90067
(310) 277-4400

Preferred Artists
16633 Ventura Blvd., #1421
Encino, CA 91436
(818) 990-0305

Jim Preminger Agency
1650 Westwood Blvd., #201
Los Angeles, CA 90024
(310) 475-9491

Shapiro-Lichtman, Inc.
8827 Beverly Blvd., #C
Los Angeles, CA 90048
(310) 859-8877

United Talent Agency
9560 Wilshire Blvd., #500
Beverly Hills, CA 90212
(213) 273-6700

Writers & Artists
924 Westwood Blvd., #900
Los Angeles, CA 90024
(310) 824-6300

FiLMMAKER RESOURCES

Screening Rooms— Los Angeles

Charles Aidikoff Screening Room
150 S. Rodeo Dr., #140
Beverly Hills, CA 90210
(310) 274-0866

The Culver Studios Screening Rooms
9336 W. Washington Blvd
Culver City, CA 90232
(310) 202-3253

Raleigh Studios
650 N. Bronson
Los Angeles, CA 90038
(213) 871-5649

Ocean Ave. Screening Room
1401 Ocean Ave., #301
Santa Monica, CA 90401
(310) 576-1831

Sunset Screening Rooms
2212 W. Magnolia Blvd.
Burbank, CA 91506
(818) 556-5190
www.screeningrooms.com

Sunset Screening Rooms
8730 Sunset Blvd.
W. Hollywood, CA 90069
(310) 652-1933

Screening Rooms— New York

The Screening Room
54 Varick St
New York, NY
(212) 334-2100

The Broadway Screening Room
1619 Broadway
New York, NY
(212) 307-0990

Magno Sound & Video
729 Broadway
New York, NY
(212) 302-2505

Millenium
66 East 4th Street
New York, NY
(212) 673-0090

Tribeca Film Center
375 Greenwich St.
New York, NY
(212) 941-4003

Lab Services/Transfers (Film and Tape)

Ringer Video Services
2408 W. Olive Ave.
Burbank, CA 91506
(818) 954-8621

Big Time Dailies
6464 Sunset Blvd., Suite 1090
Hollywood, CA 90028
(323) 464-0616

Forde Motion Picture Labs
306 Fairview Ave. North
Seattle, WA 98109
(206) 682-2510

Metropolis Film Labs
300 Phillips Park Road
Mamaroneck, NY 10543
(914) 381-0893

DuArt Film and Video
245 West 55th Street
Nerw York, NY 10019
(212) 757-4580

Film Score/ Soundtrack Advice

ASCAP
7920 Sunset Blvd., Suite 300
Los Angeles, CA 90046
(323) 883-1000
Nancy Knutsen

BMI
8730 Sunset Blvd., 3rd Floor
Los Angeles, CA 90069
(310) 659-9109
Doreen Ringer-Ross

Production Software

The Writers' Computer Store
11317 Santa Monica Blvd.
Los Angeles, CA 90025
(800) 272-8927

Film Bookstores

Larry Edmund's Bookstore
6644 Hollywood Blvd.
Hollywood, CA 90028
(213) 463-3273

Samuel French Bookstores
7623 Sunset Blvd,
Los Angeles, CA 90046
(213) 876-0570
(213) 876-6822 fax

Samuel French Bookstores
11963 Ventura Bl.
Studio City, CA
(818) 762-0535

Book Soup
8818 Sunset Blvd.
Los Angeles, CA 90069
(310) 659-3110

Drama Book Shop
723 Seventh Ave.
New York, NY 10019
(212) 944-0595

Cinema Books
4753 Roosevelt Way N.E.
Seattle, WA 98105
(206) 547-7667

Theatre Books
11 St. Thomas Street
Toronto, Ontario, Canada MSS 287
(416) 922-7175

Biz Books
136 E. Cordova St.
Vancouver, BC V6A 1K9
(604) 669-6431

ABOUT THE AUTHOR

Chris Gore has been called everything from "...the Gen-X Leonard Maltin" to the "pit bull of journalism." In 1985, he founded *Film Threat Magazine* (www.filmthreat.com) as a college fanzine in Detroit. As the fanzine evolved into a respected national magazine, Gore relocated to Los Angeles in 1989. The magazine became famous for covering cult films, midnight movies, underground shorts and, before a market even emerged, independent films such as Spike Lee's *She's Gotta Have It,* Jim Jarmusch's *Stranger Than Paradise* and Quentin Tarantino's *Reservoir Dogs.* Gore continued to self-publish until 1991 when *Film Threat* was purchased by Larry Flynt Publications. He remained *Film Threat*'s editor-in-chief, and the magazine became the leading source for information about the growing explosion of independent films. After leaving LFP, Gore reacquired *Film Threat* and formed Gore Group Publications. *Film Threat* and Gore have been featured on television shows such as MTV's *Big Picture,* The Cartoon Network, *American Journal, Premiere Story, Geraldo,* and Bravo's *Split Screen,* among others. Gore was also named one of "L.A.'s 50 Most Interesting People" by *Los Angeles* magazine. He has written and directed three short films. He has also been a judge at the Florida Film Festival, the Athens Film Festival, the Slamdance Film Festival and for the American Film Institute.